Nuclear Weapons and International Security

This volume brings together more than three decades of research and writings by Professor Ramesh Thakur on the challenges posed by nuclear weapons.

Following an introduction to the current nuclear state of play, the book addresses the challenge of nuclear weapons in three parts. Part I describes the scholar–practitioner interface in trying to come to grips with this challenge, the main policy impact on security strategy, and the various future nuclear scenarios. Part II addresses regional nuclear challenges from the South Pacific to East, South and West Asia and thereby highlights serious deficiencies in the normative architecture of the nuclear arms control and disarmament regime. In the third and final part, the chapters discuss regional nuclear-weapon-free zones, NPT anomalies (and their implications for the future of the nuclear arms control regime) and, finally, assess the global governance architecture of nuclear security in light of the three Nuclear Security Summits between 2010 and 2014. The concluding chapter argues for moving towards a world of progressively reduced nuclear weapons in numbers, reduced salience of nuclear weapons in national security doctrines and deployments, and, ultimately, a denuclearized world.

This book will be of much interest to students of nuclear proliferation, global governance, international organizations, diplomacy and security studies.

Ramesh Thakur is Director of the Centre for Nuclear Non-Proliferation and Disarmament in the Crawford School of Public Policy, The Australian National University. A former United Nations Assistant Secretary-General, he is the Editor-in-Chief of *Global Governance* and the author/editor of 50 books and 400 journal articles and book chapters, including, most recently, *The Group of Twenty (G20)* (2013); *Nuclear Weapons: The State of Play* (2013); and *The Oxford Handbook of Modern Diplomacy* (2013).

Routledge Global Security Studies
Series Editors: Aaron Karp and Regina Karp

Global Security Studies emphasizes broad forces reshaping global security and the dilemmas facing decision-makers the world over. The series stresses issues relevant in many countries and regions, accessible to broad professional and academic audiences as well as to students, and enduring through explicit theoretical foundations.

Nuclear Proliferation and International Security
Edited by Morten Bremer Maerli and Sverre Lodgaard

Global Insurgency and the Future of Armed Conflict
Debating fourth-generation warfare
Terry Terriff, Aaron Karp and Regina Karp

Terrorism and Weapons of Mass Destruction
Responding to the challenge
Edited by Ian Bellany

Globalization and WMD Proliferation
Terrorism, transnational networks, and international security
Edited by James A. Russell and Jim J. Wirtz

Power Shifts, Strategy, and War
Declining states and international conflict
Dong Sun Lee

Energy Security and Global Politics
The militarization of resource management
Edited by Daniel Moran and James A. Russell

US Nuclear Weapons Policy after the Cold War
Russians, 'rogues' and domestic division
Nick Ritchie

Security and Post-Conflict Reconstruction
Dealing with fighters in the aftermath of war
Edited Robert Muggah

Network Centric Warfare and Coalition Operations
The new military operating system
Paul T. Mitchell

American Foreign Policy and the Politics of Fear
Threat inflation since 9/11
Edited by A. Trevor Thrall and Jane K. Cramer

Risk, Global Governance and Security
The other war on terror
Yee-Kuang Heng and Kenneth McDonagh

Nuclear Weapons and Cooperative Security in the 21st Century
The new disorder
Stephen J. Cimbala

Political Economy and Grand Strategy
A neoclassical realist view
Mark R. Brawley

Iran and Nuclear Weapons
Protracted conflict and proliferation
Saira Khan

US Strategy in Africa
AFRICOM, terrorism and security challenges
Edited by David J. Francis

Great Powers and Strategic Stability in the 21st Century
Competing visions of world order
Edited by Graeme P. Herd

The Globalisation of NATO
Intervention, security and identity
Veronica M. Kitchen

International Conflict in the Asia-Pacific
Patterns, consequences and management
Jacob Bercovitch and Mikio Oishi

Nuclear Proliferation and International Order
Challenges to the Non-Proliferation Treaty
Edited by Olav Njølstad

Nuclear Disarmament and Non-Proliferation
Towards a nuclear-weapon-free world?
Sverre Lodgaard

Nuclear Energy and Global Governance
Ensuring safety, security and non-proliferation
Trevor Findlay

Unipolarity and World Politics
A theory and its implications
Birthe Hansen

Disarmament Diplomacy and Human Security
Regimes, norms and moral progress in international relations
Denise Garcia

Causes and Consequences of Nuclear Proliferation
Edited by Robert Rauchhaus, Matthew Kroenig and Erik Gartzke

Why Did the United States Invade Iraq?
Edited by Jane K. Cramer and A. Trevor Thrall

Regional Powers and Security Orders
A theoretical framework
Edited by Robert Stewart-Ingersoll and Derrick Frazier

A Perpetual Menace
Nuclear weapons and international order
William Walker

Iran's Nuclear Programme
Strategic implications
Joachim Krause

Arms Control and Missile Proliferation in the Middle East
Edited by Bernd Kubbig

The National Politics of Nuclear Power
Economics, security and governance
Benjamin Sovacool and Scott Valentine

Arms Controls in the 21st Century
Between coercion and cooperation
Edited by Oliver Meier and Christopher Daase

Reconceptualising Deterrence
Nudging toward rationality in Middle Eastern rivalries
Elli Lieberman

Psychology, Strategy and Conflict
Perceptions of insecurity in International Relations
Edited by James W. Davis

Nuclear Terrorism and Global Security
The challenge of phasing out highly enriched uranium
Edited by Alan J. Kuperman

Ballistic Missile Defence and US National Security Policy
Normalisation and acceptance after the Cold War
Andrew Futter

Economic Statecraft and Foreign Policy
Sanctions, incentives and target state calculations
Jean-Marc F. Blanchard and Norrin M. Ripsman

Technology Transfers and Non-Proliferation
Between control and cooperation
Edited by Oliver Meier

Northern Security and Global Politics
Nordic-Baltic strategic influence in a post-unipolar world
Edited by Ann-Sofie Dahl and Pauli Järvenpää

Geopolitics and Security in the Arctic
Regional developments in a global world
Edited by Rolf Tamnes and Kristine Offerdal

Precision Strike Warfare and International Intervention
Strategic, ethico-legal, and decisional implications
Edited by Mike Aaronson, Wali Aslam, Tom Dyson and Regina Rauxloh

Nuclear Proliferation and the Psychology of Political Leadership
Beliefs, motivations and perceptions
K. P. O'Reilly

Nuclear Weapons and International Security
Collected essays
Ramesh Thakur

'Ramesh Thakur is the most comprehensive thinker on nuclear disarmament active today. Nuanced and sensitive to the underlying security dilemmas and political forces, his perspective elevates disarmament beyond familiar clichés, placing it at the core of security policy. His work should be part of any discussion of disarmament imperatives and prospects.'
– *Aaron Karp, Old Dominion University*

'Ramesh Thakur is one of the few internationally renowned authors who has written on nuclear weapon issues in a coherent, consistent and cogent manner so that the most complex issues are presented to both the academic and the general reader objectively and lucidly . . . this is an indispensable volume for students, diplomats and the general reader as a framework of reference on one of most vital issue of our times.'
– *Jayantha Dhanapala, former UN Under-Secretary-General for Disarmament Affairs 1998–2003*

'This essay collection consolidates Ramesh Thakur's reputation as one of the most knowledgeable and eloquent world authorities on nuclear weapons issues, showcasing nearly 30 years of outstanding scholarship and addressing some of the most serious challenges that have confronted the nuclear non-proliferation regime. It will appeal to any reader seeking a lively, balanced and well-informed analysis of the nuclear past, and concerned – as we all must be – for the nuclear future.'
– *Gareth Evans, Convenor, Asia Pacific Leadership Network (APLN) and Co-Chair, International Commission (ICNND) on Nuclear Non-Proliferation and Disarmament*

'From his perch at universities in Australia, Canada and New Zealand, and with the United Nations in Tokyo, Ramesh Thakur has been thinking and writing on nuclear arms control and disarmament for close to three decades. There will be few better guides to the topic, especially as it shapes Asia's geopolitics. His deep learning and key insights are channelled into the commitment to eliminate the scourge of nuclear weapons from the world. Few nuclear-armed countries are spared critical scrutiny. A rare and welcome blend of analysis and advocacy, scholarship and policy, and realism and vision.'
– *Kishore Mahbubani, National University of Singapore, Singapore*

Nuclear Weapons and International Security
Collected essays

Ramesh Thakur

LONDON AND NEW YORK

First published 2015
by Routledge
2 Park Square, Milton Park, Abingdon, Oxon OX14 4RN

and by Routledge
711 Third Avenue, New York, NY 10017

Routledge is an imprint of the Taylor & Francis Group, an informa business

© 2015 Ramesh Thakur

The right of Ramesh Thakur to be identified as author of this work has been asserted by him in accordance with sections 77 and 78 of the Copyright, Designs and Patents Act 1988.

All rights reserved. No part of this book may be reprinted or reproduced or utilised in any form or by any electronic, mechanical, or other means, now known or hereafter invented, including photocopying and recording, or in any information storage or retrieval system, without permission in writing from the publishers.

Trademark notice: Product or corporate names may be trademarks or registered trademarks, and are used only for identification and explanation without intent to infringe.

British Library Cataloguing-in-Publication Data
A catalogue record for this book is available from the British Library

Library of Congress Cataloging-in-Publication Data
A catalog record for this book has been requested.

ISBN: 978-1-138-78755-1 (hbk)
ISBN: 978-1-315-74948-8 (ebk)

Typeset in Baskerville
by Apex CoVantage, LLC

Contents

List of tables	xi
List of abbreviations	xii
Acknowledgements	xvi
Preface – A tale from Hiroshima	xviii
1 Introduction: The challenge of nuclear weapons	1

PART I
The nuclear debate   19

2 Nuclear nonproliferation and disarmament: can the power of ideas tame the power of the state?	21
3 The nuclear debate	36
4 Envisioning nuclear futures	51

PART II
Regional challenges in Asia, the Pacific
and the Middle East   63

5 The last bang before a total ban: French nuclear testing in the Pacific	65
6 The nuclear option in India's security policy	78
7 The South Asian nuclear challenge	93
8 The inconsequential gains and lasting insecurities of India's nuclear weaponization	109

9 Follow the yellowcake road: balancing Australia's security, commercial and bilateral national interests against international anti-nuclear interests   125

10 Capping North Korea's weapons and Iran's capability   141

PART III
The nuclear regime   161

11 Stepping stones to a nuclear-weapon-free world   163

12 NPT regime change: has the good become the enemy of the best?   182

13 The global governance architecture of nuclear security   198

14 The problem of nuclear weapons and what to do about it   216

Index   235

Tables

1.1	The world's nuclear forces, 2010–2014	3
1.2	Number of nuclear warheads in the inventory of the five NWS, 1945–2014	3
11.1	The world's nuclear-weapon-free zones	164
11.2	Dates of NWS ratification of NWFZ treaty protocols	165
12.1	Public opinion on nuclear weapons	194
13.1	Status of CPPNM, CPPNM amendment, and ICSANT (21 July 2014)	205
14.1	Planned nuclear warhead deployments in 2020	228

Abbreviations

ABM	anti-ballistic missile
ACDA	Arms Control and Disarmament Agency (US)
AEC	Atomic Energy Commission
AFCONE	African Commission on Nuclear Energy
ALP	Australian Labor Party
ANU	Australian National University
ANZUS	Australia–New Zealand–United States Security Treaty
ARF	ASEAN Regional Forum
ASEAN	Association of Southeast Asian Nations
ASPI	Australian Strategic Policy Institute
BICC	Bonn International Center for Conversion
BJP	Bharatiya Janata Party
bn	billion
BRICS	Brazil Russia India China South Africa
BWC	Biological Weapons Convention
C3I	command control communications and intelligence
CANDU	Canada Deuterium Uranium
CBM	confidence building measure(s)
CD	Conference on Disarmament
CHOGM	Commonwealth Heads of Government Meeting
CIA	Central Intelligence Agency
CNND	Centre for Nuclear Non-Proliferation and Disarmament
CPPNM	Convention on the Physical Protection of Nuclear Material
CTBT	Comprehensive Nuclear Test Ban Treaty
CTBTO	Preparatory Commission for the CTBT Organization
CWC	Chemical Weapons Convention
DMZ	demilitarized zone
DPRK	Democratic People's Republic of Korea
DRDO	Defence Research and Development Organization
EEZ	exclusive economic zones
EURATOM	European Atomic Energy Community
FMCT	fissile materials cut-off treaty

FMWG	Fissile Materials Working Group
FSM	Federated States of Micronesia
G-7/8	Group of Seven/Eight countries
G-20	Group of Twenty countries
G-77	Group of 77 countries
HEU	highly enriched uranium
IAEA	International Atomic Energy Agency
ICAN	International Campaign to Abolish Nuclear Weapons
ICBM	intercontinental ballistic missile
ICC	International Criminal Court
ICISS	International Commission on Intervention and State Sovereignty
ICJ	International Court of Justice
ICNND	International Commission on Nuclear Non-Proliferation and Disarmament
ICSANT	International Convention for the Suppression of Acts of Nuclear Terrorism
IDSA	Institute for Defence Studies and Analyses
IEA	International Energy Agency
IISS	International Institute for Strategic Studies
IMF	International Monetary Fund
INF	Intermediate Range Nuclear Forces
IPCC	Intergovernmental Panel on Climate Change
IPPAS	International Physical Protection Advisory Service
IPPNW	International Physicians for the Prevention of Nuclear War
ISI	Inter-Services Intelligence (Pakistan)
kg	kilogramme
km	kilometre
kt	kilotonne
MAD	Mutually Assured Destruction
MIRV	Multiple independently targetable re-entry vehicle
mn	million
MTCR	Missile Technology Control Regime
N5	The five NPT-recognized nuclear weapons states
NAM	Non-Aligned Movement
NATO	North Atlantic Treaty Organization
NCA	Nuclear Command Authority
NEANWFZ	Northeast Asian NWFZ
NGO	non-governmental organization
NNSA	National Nuclear Security Administration
non-NPT N3	The three extra-NPT de facto nuclear armed states: India, Pakistan, Israel
NPR	Nuclear Posture Review
NPT	Nuclear Non-Proliferation Treaty

NPT-N5	The five nuclear powers recognized as such by the NPT
NPTREC	NPT Review and Extension Conference
NSG	Nuclear Suppliers Group
NSS	Nuclear Security Summit(s)
NTI	Nuclear Threat Initiative
NUTS	Nuclear Utilization Theories or Nuclear Utilization Target Selection
NWC	nuclear weapons convention
NWFZ	nuclear weapons free zone(s)
NWS	nuclear weapons state(s)
OAS	Organization of American States
OAU	Organization of African Unity
OPANAL	Agency for the Prohibition of Nuclear Weapons in Latin America and the Caribbean
OPCW	Organization for the Prohibition of Chemical Weapons
OPEC	Organization of the Petroleum Exporting Countries
P5	The five permanent members of the UN Security Council
PACDAC	Public Advisory Committee on Disarmament and Arms Control
PAL	Permissive Action Link
PrepCom	Preparatory Committee of the NPT Review Conference
PRIO	Peace Research Institute of Oslo
PSI	Proliferation Security Initiative
SAARC	South Asian Association for Regional Cooperation
SALT	Strategic Arms Limitation Treaty
SANWFZ	South Asian NWFZ
SDIO	Strategic Defense Initiative Organization
SEANWFZ	Southeast Asian NWFZ
SIPRI	Stockholm International Peace Research Institute
SLBM	submarine launched ballistic missile
SPF	South Pacific Forum
SPNFZ	South Pacific Nuclear Free Zone
START	Strategic Arms Reduction Treaty
TMD	theatre missile defence
tn	trillion
UAE	United Arab Emirates
UK	United Kingdom
UN	United Nations
UNCLOS	UN Convention on the Law of the Seas
UNDP	UN Development Programme
UNESCO	UN Educational Scientific and Cultural Organisation
UNFCCC	UN Framework Convention on Climate Change
UNIDIR	UN Institute for Disarmament Research
UNU	United Nations University

US	United States
USAF	US Air Force
USSR	Union of Soviet Socialist Republics (Soviet Union)
WHO	World Health Organization
WINS	World Institute for Nuclear Security
WMD	weapon(s) of mass destruction

Acknowledgements

Many people have been involved in the preparation of this book in various ways who deserve appreciation. First I would like to thank Andrew Humphrys and his team at Routledge. Their help, assistance and encouragement throughout, from conception to completion, was thoroughly professional and it has been a pleasure working with them.

Second, I'd like to thank Srinjoy Bose, my research assistant in the Asia–Pacific College of Diplomacy at The Australian National University (ANU) who diligently followed up various missing bits of information and citation details as required and also read the manuscript multiple times to catch repetitions and duplications as well as errors.

Third, my colleagues in the Centre for Nuclear Non-Proliferation and Disarmament (CNND) at the ANU with whom various conversations on the topics discussed in the book have helped to clarify my understanding and sharpen my thinking.

Fourth, Mr. Shogo Yamahata kindly agreed to let us use the poignant photo of Nagasaki taken by his father Yosuke Yamahata as the cover for this book.

Finally, I am grateful to the following for permission to re-use my earlier articles and book chapters:

> Chapter 2: Ramesh Thakur, 'Nuclear Nonproliferation and Disarmament: Can the Power of Ideas Tame the Power of the State?', *International Studies Review* 13:1 (March 2011): 34–45.
> Chapter 3: Ramesh Thakur, 'The Nuclear Debate', from *In Defence of New Zealand: Foreign Policy Choices in the Nuclear Age* (Boulder, CO: Westview Press, 1986): 7–40.
> Chapter 4: Ramesh Thakur, 'Envisioning Nuclear Futures', *Security Dialogue* 31:1 (March 2000): 25–40.
> Chapter 5: Ramesh Thakur, 'The Last Bang before a Total Ban: French Nuclear Testing in the Pacific', *Pacific Research* (Canberra: Peace Research Centre, Australian National University, Working Paper No 159, 1995).
> Chapter 6: Ramesh Thakur, 'The Nuclear Option in India's Security Policy', *Asia Pacific Review* 5:1 (Spring/Summer 1998): 39–60.

Chapter 7: Ramesh Thakur, 'The South Asian Nuclear Challenge', in John Baylis and Robert O'Neill, eds., *Alternative Nuclear Futures: The Role of Nuclear Weapons in the Post-Cold War World* (Oxford: Oxford University Press, 2000): 101–24.

Chapter 8: Ramesh Thakur, 'The Inconsequential Gains and Lasting Insecurities of India's Nuclear Weaponization', *International Affairs* 90:5 (September 2014): 1101–24.

Chapter 9: Ramesh Thakur, 'Follow the Yellowcake Road: Balancing Australia's Security, Commercial and Bilateral National Interests against International Anti-nuclear Interests', *International Affairs* 89:4 (July 2013): 943–61.

Chapter 10: Ramesh Thakur, 'To Stop Iran Getting the Bomb, Must We Learn to Live with Its Nuclear Capability?' *Strategic Analysis* 36:2 (March 2012): 328–34.

Chapter 11: Ramesh Thakur, 'Stepping Stones to a Nuclear-Weapon-Free World', in Ramesh Thakur, ed., *Nuclear Weapons-Free Zones* (London/New York: Macmillan and St. Martin's Press, 1998): 3–32.

Chapter 12: Ramesh Thakur, 'NPT Regime Change: Has the Good Become the Enemy of the Best?', in Jane Boulden, Ramesh Thakur and Thomas G. Weiss, eds., *The United Nations and Nuclear Orders* (Tokyo: United Nations University Press, 2009): 273–97.

Chapter 13: Ramesh Thakur, 'The Global Governance Architecture of Nuclear Security', *Policy Analysis Brief* (Muscatine, Iowa: Stanley Foundation, March 2013).

Preface

A tale from Hiroshima

The chapters that follow bring together the fruits of thinking and writing about the nuclear threats, in their many dimensions and theatres, for almost three decades. The passion animating the great anti-nuclear movements in the 1980s may have faded and their memories dimmed, but the challenges and threats have mutated, not disappeared. The essays have not been changed from their original published versions, although the style has been rendered uniform and repetitions have been eliminated. They thus stand as a record of analysis and commentary as written at the time and as observed from perches in Asia–Pacific from New Zealand and Australia to Japan, plus Canada. The inspiration behind them might well be the experience of a commemorative ceremony in Hiroshima to honour and atone for the atomic dead.[1]

Hiroshima holds a special affection in my heart. On 6 August 2002, I had the privilege and responsibility of representing UN Secretary-General Kofi Annan at the ceremony commemorating the atomic bombing of Hiroshima in 1945. The commemoration is at once haunting, sombre and soul-cleansing. Some 40,000 people assemble in the sultry heat to recall the searing, dazzling blast that announced the birth of the atomic age with the death of a hundred thousand people at one stroke and the horror-filled stories of the larger number of survivors.

There is a word in Japanese, *hibakusha* ('explosion-affected people'), that describes the survivors of the Hiroshima and Nagasaki atomic bombings. Truly the living envied the dead. There are about a quarter million hibakusha recognized by the Japanese government. On 24 March 2009, the government officially recognized Tsutomu Yamaguchi as a double survivor. In Hiroshima on a business trip on 6 August 1945, he decided to return home to Nagasaki the day before it too was bombed on 9 August. There are times when belief in the Hindu concept of *karma* (loosely translated as destiny) becomes a comforting solace.

The 6 August ceremony is incredibly moving and indelibly poignant. The cenotaph memorializing the bombing is set in a beautiful peace park that was designed shortly after the war by Kenzo Tange, one of Japan's most famous postwar architects. (Coincidentally, he was also the architect for the United Nations University building in Tokyo, where I worked for almost a decade.) The names of the atomic bomb victims are inscribed on the arc-shaped cenotaph which stands atop a reflecting pool. Every year on 6 August, the living gather there to atone for the dead.

The park is framed at one end by the Atomic Bomb dome (A-dome), a structure that survived the blast in skeleton form and today functions as one of the most iconic and recognizable images of the horrors of atomic weapons and a potent rallying point for the anti-nuclear peace movement. It has been inscribed as a World Heritage Site by the United Nations Educational, Scientific and Cultural Organisation (UNESCO). At the other end of the park is the Peace Museum that houses various memorabilia and displays. Again, it is difficult not be shocked into contemplation of human folly and our capacity to inflict pain on one another by many of the images and items, for example spectacles that fused onto facial bones in the intense heat of the radiation.

For world leaders going to certain countries in Europe, it is obligatory to visit sites like Auschwitz and Buchenwald, pay respects to the victims lest we forget, and offer silent prayers for their souls. I am yet to understand what it is about Western culture that holds leaders back from the same gesture to a common human history when they visit Japan. I was told that no serving US president has ever visited Hiroshima or Nagasaki. Would such a visit raise unnecessary controversy by suggesting penance? Is it not possible to recognize and honour a defining event in human history without implying guilt? Will the 'yes, we can' president dare to break the taboo and act on his dream of a world free of nuclear weapons and freed of the nuclear dread?

We tend to remember the consequences of what others do to us, and so grievance festers. We know why we did what we did to others, and so that becomes an understandable action and we are puzzled that the others should still bear a grudge. It is rare to find former enemies join in common atonement of a shared human tragedy. Yet that surely is what Hiroshima symbolizes, and it is in the recognition of our common humanity that we shall find redemption. The citizens of Hiroshima, in rebuilding their city, have consecrated it as a testimonial to social resilience, human solidarity and nuclear abolition.

Then there is the beautiful story of the cranes. Sadako Sasaki, two when she was exposed to the Hiroshima bombing, fell ill in 1954 and was diagnosed to be suffering from leukaemia. Serene in the belief that folding 1,000 paper cranes would fulfil her wish for a normal life, she was still short of the magic number (she had the time but not the paper) when she died on 25 October 1955. Friends completed her task and a thousand cranes were buried with her. As her story spread, a children's peace monument was built in the Peace Park from funds donated from across the country. By now around ten million cranes are offered annually before her monument, where she stands with her arms fully stretched overhead holding up a giant, stylized folded paper crane.

Hiroshima, once again a beautiful, scenic and thriving city, lives by three codes: To forgive and atone, but never to forget; never again; and transformation from a military city to a city of peace. The sacred Buddhist text *The Dhammapada* tells us:

> We are what we think
> All that we are arises with our thoughts
> With our thoughts we make the world.

As we mark the anniversary of the bombing of Hiroshima each year, it is worth joining together in turning our thoughts to the three inspiring principles that symbolize death, destruction and resurrection. What we need is a multi-phased roadmap to abolition that prioritizes concrete immediate steps in the first couple of years like introducing more robust firewalls to separate possession from use of nuclear weapons; further significant cuts in existing nuclear arsenals and a freeze on production of fissile materials in the medium term of up to three years; a verifiable and enforceable new international nuclear weapons convention within a target timeframe of about five years; and their total and verified destruction in ten to twenty years.

By these actions shall we release the souls of the atomic dead, ease the pain of the *hibakusha*, and liberate ourselves from bondage to a weapon that increases not our net security but does diminish our common humanity.

Note

1 The rest of the Preface was published as 'Road map for abolition of nuclear arms needed', *Daily Yomiuri*, 7 August 2009.

1 Introduction

The challenge of nuclear weapons

> 'The threat of global nuclear war has become remote, but the risk of nuclear war has increased. Today's most immediate and extreme danger remains nuclear terrorism. . . .Today's other pressing threat is nuclear proliferation'.
> — *Report on Nuclear Employment Strategy of the United States*, 12 June 2013[1]

> 'We may no longer live in fear of global annihilation, but so long as nuclear weapons exist, we are not truly safe'.
> — US President Barack Obama, Berlin, 19 June 2013[2]

In 1962, with America trapped in an expanding arms race with the Soviet Union, US President John F. Kennedy described the bomb as having turned the world into a prison in which humanity awaits its execution and called for progress on nuclear disarmament.[3] In 2014, there were still more than 16,000 nuclear warheads distributed among nine nuclear-armed states, 94 percent of them in Russian and US arsenals. There are many fewer nuclear weapons today than during the Cold War, and the risk of a deliberate nuclear war being started between the United States and Russia may well be negligible. Yet, paradoxically, the overall risks of nuclear war have grown – as more countries in more unstable regions have acquired these deadly weapons, terrorists continue to seek them, and as command-and-control systems in even the most sophisticated nuclear-armed states remain vulnerable to human error, system malfunction and, increasingly, cyber attack. Even a limited regional nuclear war could have catastrophic global consequences.

While the need for total nuclear disarmament is more urgent than ever, its achievement remains little or no closer, both among the nuclear weapons states (NWS) as defined in the Treaty on the Non-Proliferation of Nuclear Weapons (NPT) – China, France, Russia, the United Kingdom and the United States – and the other four nuclear-armed states outside the NPT: India, Israel, Pakistan and North Korea. There has been dramatic progress in reducing the overall US and Russian nuclear weapons stockpiles and the number of deployed strategic weapons and some progress in improving transparency among some NWS. But there has been only minimal progress in shifting nuclear doctrine and none in taking weapons off high-alert launch status. Issues of ballistic missile defence and conventional arms imbalances continue seriously to inhibit further disarmament movement.[4] Moreover, the cause of nuclear disarmament has gradually lost civil society traction and eased serious political pressure on governments.

The net result is that the nuclear arms control regime centred on the 1968 NPT is under challenge on many fronts. In some quarters of the international community of states and civil society, there is exasperation at the failure of an accelerated timetable of nuclear disarmament by the five NPT-licit NWS (the N5). In western circles, there are worries about some non-nuclear signatories cheating on their NPT obligations, especially North Korea and Iran. The 2008 India–US civil nuclear cooperation deal split analysts on whether it would mark an advance on or a setback to the nonproliferation agenda. Almost everyone remains concerned about the potential of terrorists acquiring and using nuclear weapons and also about the safety and security of Pakistan's nuclear arsenal in the midst of grave political crises and turmoil.[5]

In recent times, on the one hand, there was fresh interest in the longstanding goal of nuclear abolition by a surprising coalition of heavyweights from the US strategic community who have published a series of influential articles in *The Wall Street Journal* (2007–13).[6] As Ivo Daalder and Jan Lodal tell us, 'this vision of a world free of nuclear weapons . . . has been endorsed by no less than two-thirds of all living former secretaries of state, former secretaries of defence, and former national security advisers'.[7] On the other side, a group of former NATO generals issued their own clarion call for a commitment to the first-use of nuclear weapons by the West in order to prevent undesirable actors from acquiring them and threatening their use.[8]

This chapter proceeds as follows. First I will provide a very brief historical sketch of the growing interest in arms control. Then I will describe the current state of the nuclear arsenals and doctrines of the nine nuclear-armed states in alphabetical order. Third, I will briefly discuss the possible renaissance in nuclear power. In the final part, I will outline the agenda for action adopted by the NPT Review Conference in 2010 and recommended by the last authoritative blue ribbon international commission in 2009.

Arms control

Other P5 countries (the UN Security Council's five permanent members who happen to be the five NPT NWS) were quick to join the United States in the exclusive nuclear club (Table 1.1). The global stockpile of nuclear weapons climbed steeply until 1986 but has been falling steadily since then (Table 1.2). Along with an interest in the normative framework for going to war and then regulating the conduct of belligerents engaged in hostilities, analysts and policymakers have long been interested in regulating the tools and weapons of warfare as a means of limiting the death and injury toll of armed conflicts, as well as lessening the temptation to go to war because of the ready availability of an abundant supply of weaponry. As an old saying has it, to him who has a hammer, the world looks like a nail. At the same time, however, states believed that to protect themselves from becoming

Table 1.1 The world's nuclear forces, 2010–2014

	First test	2010	2011	2012	2013	2014 Deployed*	Other	Total
US	1945	9600	8500	8000	7700	1920	5380	7300
Russia	1949	12000	11000	10000	8500	1600	6400	8000
UK	1952	225	225	225	225	160	65	225
France	1960	300	300	300	300	290	10	300
China	1964	240	240	240	250		250	250
Israel	...	80	80	80	80		80	80
India	1974	60–80	80–100	80–100	90–110		90–110	90–110
Pakistan	1998	70–90	90–110	90–110	100–120		100–120	100–120
North Korea	2006						6–8	6–8
Totals		**22,595**	**20,535**	**19,035**	**17,245**	**3,970**	**12,402**	**16,372**

Source: 'Nuclear forces reduced while modernization continue, says SIPRI', SIPRI Press Release, 16 June 2014; http://www.sipri.org/media/pressreleases/2014/nuclear_May_2014.

*'Deployed' means warheads placed on missiles or located on bases with operational forces

Table 1.2 Number of nuclear warheads in the inventory of the five NWS, 1945–2014

Year	US	USSR/Russia	Britain	France	China	Total
1945	6	0	0	0	0	6
1950	369	5	0	0	0	374
1955	3 057	200	10	0	0	3,267
1960	20,434	1,605	30	0	0	22,069
1965	31,982	6,129	310	32	5	38,458
1970	26,662	11,643	280	36	75	38,696
1975	27,826	19,055	350	188	185	47,604
1980	24,304	30,062	350	250	280	55,246
1986*	24,401	45,000	300	355	425	70,481
1990	21,004	37,000	300	505	430	59,239
1995	12,144	27,000	300	500	400	40,344
2000	10,577	21,000	185	470	400	32,632
2005	10.295	17,000	200	350	400	28,245
2010	8,500	11,000	225	300	240	20,265
2014	7,300	8,000	225	300	250	16,075

Sources: Hans M. Kristensen and Robert S. Norris, 'Nuclear Notebook', *Bulletin of Atomic Sciences* 62:4 (July–August 2006), 64–67, using data from the Natural Resources Defense Council; 2010: Shannon N. Kile, Vitaly Fedchenko, Bharath Gopalaswamy and Hans M. Kristensen, "World Nuclear Forces', *SIPRI Yearbook 2011* (Oxford: Oxford University Press, 2011), Table 7.1, 320; 'Nuclear forces reduced while modernization continue, says SIPRI', SIPRI Press Release, 16 June 2014; http://www.sipri.org/media/pressreleases/2014/nuclear_May_2014. Altogether, more than 128,000 nuclear warheads are estimated to have been built since 1945, with the US and USSR/Russia accounting for 55 and 43 percent of them, respectively.

*Peak Year Globally

the victims of the use of force by others, they had to be adequately armed themselves: 'if you want peace, prepare for war' is an even more common mantra. This increased the chances of defeat for any hostile state contemplating aggression and, even if victorious, raised the cost of victory.

The failed Hague Peace Conference (May–July 1899) was followed by the call in the League of Nations Covenant (Article 8) for 'the reduction of national armaments to the lowest point consistent with national safety and the enforcement by common action of international obligations'. Reflecting the conventional wisdom on the role of pacifism in the unchecked rise of Fascism, there was a relative downgrading in importance of arms control and disarmament from the League Covenant to the UN Charter (Article 26). Just weeks after it was signed in San Francisco on 26 June 1945, the United States conducted the world's first nuclear test at the Alamagordo Air Base in New Mexico on 16 July, and used the first atomic weapons in Hiroshima and Nagasaki on 6 and 9 August. The sheer destructiveness of the new type of weaponry had a profoundly conditioning impact on world leaders from the start of UN deliberations. The very first General Assembly resolution in January 1946 called for the newly established UN Atomic Energy Commission (AEC) to make proposals for the elimination of atomic weapons and other weapons of mass destruction (WMD).

Several giant normative steps forward have marked the UN's history since that time. Not surprisingly, Moscow and Washington as the two superpowers led the way both in advances and setbacks. The United States presented the Baruch Plan for the international control of atomic energy as early as June 1946, which led eventually to the establishment of the International Atomic Energy Agency (IAEA). The Soviet Union tested its first device in 1949. While the first proposal for a 'standstill agreement' on nuclear testing came from India's prime minister Jawaharlal Nehru in April 1954, the western allies submitted a working paper to the United Nations in August 1957 for a halt to nuclear testing and weapons production and the initiation of a reduction in nuclear weapons stockpiles as well as in general armaments.

Of greater import were a series of bilateral nuclear arms control agreements, including the Strategic Arms Limitations (SALT) and Anti-Ballistic Missile (ABM) treaties. The real momentum for the dramatic reductions in nuclear stockpiles and preparations came under Soviet and American presidents Mikhail Gorbachev and Ronald Reagan. The Intermediate Range Nuclear Forces (INF) Treaty of December 1987 was the first arms control agreement to ban an entire class of nuclear weapons. The Strategic Arms Reduction Treaty (or START I) of July 1991 committed the United States and the Soviet Union to halving their long-range nuclear forces; and, before the year was out, Washington and Moscow had also unilaterally withdrawn all US land and sea-based tactical nuclear weapons from overseas bases and operational deployments and stood down all Soviet strategic bombers on day-to-day alert status. Meanwhile, the US Congress passed the Nunn–Lugar Soviet Nuclear Threat Reduction Act to help Moscow destroy nuclear, chemical and other weapons. The START II Treaty, to reduce intercontinental ballistic missiles (ICBMs) still further, was signed in January 1993.

Many multilateral initiatives and achievements were recorded in parallel with the Moscow–Washington bilateral efforts. The Antarctic Treaty demilitarizing and denuclearizing the uninhabited continent was signed in 1959. The NPT, signed in 1968 and in force since 1970, established a robust nonproliferation and a weaker anti-nuclear norm. But even after its entry into force, the N5 conducted a large number of atomic-nuclear atmospheric and underground tests. The Partial Test Ban Treaty (1963) outlawed atmospheric, space and underwater nuclear testing. The Threshold Test Ban Treaty (1974) outlawed underground tests with more than a 150kt yield. But underground testing below this threshold was continued, for example in French Polynesia. The 1996 Comprehensive Nuclear Test Ban Treaty (CTBT), even though it is yet to enter into force, brought the end of the nuclear arms race to a statutory close and is the embodiment of the world's abhorrence of these weapons of mass destruction. The NPT was extended indefinitely and unconditionally in 1995, and the 2000 NPT Review Conference contained an ambitious forward-looking agenda. Although this stalled with the advent of the George W. Bush administration and its distinctive and dangerous agenda for remaking the world to its neoconservative liking, it was revived with the successor administration. In a major speech in Prague in April 2009, newly elected President Barack Obama pledged the United States 'to seek the peace and security of a world without nuclear weapons' and to 'reduce the role of nuclear weapons in [its] national security strategy'. He also undertook 'immediately and aggressively' to pursue US ratification of the CTBT and to support the negotiation of a fissile materials cut-off treaty (FMCT).[9] Later in the year, President Obama chaired a UN Security Council session which unanimously adopted US-sponsored Resolution 1887 'to create the conditions for a world without nuclear weapons'.[10]

China

The world's nuclear weapons holdings in 2014 are shown in Table 1.1. Of the N5, only China's nuclear arsenal is growing, albeit it has evolved and grown rather more slowly than was the case historically with the United States and the former Soviet Union. There is nothing to suggest that China is engaged in a 'sprint to parity' with Russia or the United States and plenty of evidence to conclude that it is not. China is modernizing and expanding its nuclear weapons systems, as the Second Artillery Force continues progressively to improve its missile force structure in both nuclear and conventional configurations and the Navy to enhance its strategic deterrence and counter-attack capability.[11] China has about 150 land-based missiles capable of carrying nuclear payloads, of which some 50 have a long enough range (7,000–12,000 km) to reach the continental United States. Its small stock of air-deliverable nuclear weapons are not believed to have any 'primary mission'.[12] China is reported to be working on a third generation ICBM equipped with multiple, independent targetable re-entry vehicles (MIRVs) and to be within years of establishing a 'near-continuous at-sea strategic deterrent' with the deployment of nuclear-powered ballistic missile submarines.[13] Heavily dependent on land-based missiles, China is actively modernizing them to increase the survivability and strengthen the retaliatory capabilities of its nuclear forces.[14] A 'credible sea-based nuclear capability' would significantly increase the survivability of its nuclear forces.[15]

China's nuclear weapons, declared doctrine and force posture and deployment patterns are said to be designed neither to coerce others nor to fight a nuclear war with the expectation of winning but to counter any attempt at nuclear blackmail. According to Li Bin, director of the Arms Control Program in Tsinghua University's Department of International Relations, China 'chooses to keep a small, off-alert nuclear force' as a means of 'countering nuclear coercion' but does not consider nuclear weapons to have any real military utility.[16] 'If China comes under a nuclear threat, [its] nuclear missile force will . . . get ready for a nuclear counterattack to deter the enemy from using nuclear weapons against China. If China comes under a nuclear attack . . . [it] will use nuclear missiles to launch a resolute counterattack'.[17] China remains committed to no first use of nuclear weapons 'at any time and in any circumstances' and has made an 'unequivocal commitment' not to use or threaten to use nuclear weapons against non-NWS and nuclear-weapon-free zones (NWFZ). That is, it would not use its nuclear weapons even in the extreme circumstances of its very survival being at stake under conventional attack. China holds that the NWS should abandon nuclear deterrence policy based on first use of nuclear weapons and instead conclude a treaty on no first use of nuclear weapons against one another.[18] That said, lack of transparency will continue to make it difficult to assess whether evolving force structures and postures do in fact accord with China's published statements of doctrine.

France

The 2008 French White Paper on defence and national security described nuclear deterrence as 'the ultimate guarantee of the security and independence of France'.[19] France no longer has a ground-based missile force. Its nuclear weapons are deployed on four submarines and a mix of land- and carrier-based aircraft. At any given time, at least one submarine is at sea, providing continuous deterrence. Despite recent cuts in the airborne component of France's nuclear deterrent, its nuclear arsenal is being modernized and upgraded with the progressive introduction of longer-range missiles and new warheads.[20] In December 2012, France denied that it was contemplating a change to its nuclear force posture such that it would no longer have a sea-borne deterrent 365 days in the year. This would happen if its fleet of submarines was reduced from four to three as a cost-cutting measure. France has pruned its warheads from more than 500 to 300 (Table 1.2). Nevertheless President Nicolas Sarkozy, in a speech in Cherbourg in March 2008, emphasized France's strong attachment to its nuclear deterrent as 'the nation's life insurance policy'.[21]

India

India conducted its first test, describing it disingenuously as a 'peaceful nuclear explosion', on 18 May 1974. On 11 and 13 May 1998, India conducted another five nuclear tests (one fusion and four fission bombs) and this time it proclaimed itself to be a nuclear weapons possessor state.[22] Like China, India and Pakistan too are increasing their nuclear arsenals. Although neither provides details of its nuclear arsenal, India is estimated to possess some 90–110 warheads.[23] Both are working to create survivable nuclear forces based on a mix of different launch platforms. Both have developed road-mobile nuclear capable ballistic missiles but neither's stockpile is fully deployed as yet. Indian plans to deploy nuclear weapons at sea are based on the development of a ballistic missile launched from a nuclear-powered submarine. Both elements are in the development testing phase and the capability may be deployed in coming years. India is developing and testing a mix of short-, medium- and long-range missiles and nuclear-powered ballistic missile submarines. India has ambitions to design and build multistage ballistic rockets, remote sensing and communications satellites and monitoring and guidance systems for putting different types of vehicles into space orbit.

India has not signed the CTBT but has maintained a voluntary moratorium on nuclear test explosions since 1998. Cold War experience indicates that 'the numbers of deployable weapons may be limited only by the fissile material production capacity on both sides rather than the number perceived to be needed for deterrence'.[24] Official information on India's fissile material production and holdings is sparse. India produces highly enriched uranium (HEU) and weapon grade plutonium, although so far HEU is thought to have been enriched only to levels of 30–45 percent for use in India's nuclear submarine propulsion program.[25] It is believed to be significantly increasing its fissile material production capacities with respect to both HEU and plutonium.[26]

The National Security Advisory Board published its draft report on nuclear doctrine in 1999, and it was officially adopted by the cabinet on 4 January 2003.[27] Its declared aim is to 'pursue a doctrine of credible minimum nuclear deterrence'. While 'credibility' is defined by retaliatory capability, command-control-communications survivability, and political will, 'minimum' defines size, cost, posture, doctrine and use. Taken together, 'minimum' cannot be defined in terms of numbers or capability but must remain flexible in order to accommodate and respond to changes in the size of the adversary's arsenal. India will not be the first to use nuclear weapons but would 'respond with punitive retaliation should deterrence fail'.[28] Confusingly and inconsistently, the 2003 policy qualified the 1999 absolute no first use formulation by opening up the possibility of using nuclear weapons in response to a biological or chemical weapon attack.[29]

Israel

Israel does not admit to the possession of nuclear weapons. Israel developed its nuclear weapons capability in the 1960s, but a policy of 'nuclear ambiguity' or 'opacity' makes any estimate of nuclear weapons numbers and capabilities essentially a matter of speculation. It is thought to have an arsenal of some 80 nuclear weapons (50 for delivery by ballistic missiles and 30 non-strategic nuclear weapons).[30] 'More than for any perceived security benefits, Israel's nuclear project was

8 *Introduction*

conceived for psychological comfort in face of the unthinkable quintessence of all Jewish and Israeli fears: a second Holocaust'.[31] In the 1960s, Prime Minister Levi Eshkol declared that Israel would 'not be the first to introduce nuclear weapons to the Middle East'[32] – nor the second, add some wags. The policy has served Israel well, providing 'the benefits of existential deterrence at a very low political cost' without directly opposing US nonproliferation objectives.[33] Israel sees an undeclared but barely disguised nuclear weapons capability as compensating for its small size and population, lack of strategic depth, and as an appropriate response to the multiplicity of existential threats confronting it in its region.

In the absence of a declared nuclear weapons capability, the circumstances in which Israel might be prepared to use such weapons have not been publicly documented. Its doctrine is shaped by two calculations. The so-called 'Samson Option' refers to the Jewish biblical hero who, refusing to die alone, brought down the roof of a Philistine temple, thereby killing his enemies along with himself. Israeli strategy rests also on the conviction that the acquisition of nuclear weapons by any regional adversary would constitute an existential threat to Israel that must be prevented using any necessary means. This is described as the Begin Doctrine after Prime Minister Menachem Begin, who bombed Iraq's suspected nuclear program at Osirak in June 1981. Contrary to standard deterrence theory, between them the Samson Option and the Begin Doctrine represent an asymmetrical model: Israel seeks to deter adversaries without itself being deterred by any of them being nuclear armed. Its hostility to Iran's suspected nuclear weapons program is explained by these twin imperatives.

North Korea

North Korea has only very recently joined the ranks of the nuclear-armed states, possesses a much smaller nuclear arsenal than the other eight and remains the subject of intense diplomatic efforts aimed at dismantling its nuclear weapons program. It effectively confirmed its withdrawal from the NPT in January 2003[34] – the only country so far to have done so – after being accused of operating a clandestine uranium enrichment program. It has conducted three nuclear weapon tests, one each in 2006, 2009 and 2013, and several rocket and missile launches but, as we shall see in Chapter 10, the capacity to target and hit other countries is still very limited. But the capacity of others to constrain North Korea's nuclear weapons ambitions is also very limited.

Pakistan

Pakistan is the only one of the nine nuclear-armed states where nuclear weapons were developed by the military, are essentially under military control and the decision to use them will be made by the military rather than civilian leadership. It has had a nuclear weapons program since the early 1970s. It followed India's nuclear tests with six of its own on 28 and 30 May 1998. Based on fissile material stock estimates and evidence of nuclear weapons design, Pakistan is currently estimated to have some 100–120 warheads for delivery by missiles and aircraft. Its nuclear arsenal is growing the fastest of any country in the world.[35] Like India, its nuclear doctrine is based on the principle of 'credible minimum deterrence', with resort to nuclear weapons envisaged only in response to an existential threat which need not be the result of an attack by any category of WMD (biological, chemical or nuclear weapons).[36] Pakistan's nuclear doctrine is India-specific, although, particularly after the US raid on Abbotabad in May 2011 that killed Osama bin Laden and in light of continuing strong differences of opinion on regional security issues, the expansion and modernization of Pakistan's nuclear arsenal may also be driven partly by fears of a US raid to capture or secure its nuclear forces.[37]

The development of tactical nuclear weapons as a counter to India's superiority in conventional arms, and to compensate for its lack of strategic depth, would seem to leave open the possibility of first use of nuclear weapons against India, particularly in the case of invasion. While battlefield nuclear weapons may be thought to give Pakistan the chance of denying 'victory' to India in a nuclear war by inflicting particularly severe damage, they would also expose Pakistan to a very high risk of nuclear retaliation and, if used against Indian forces inside Pakistan, to the certainty of partial irradiation of the homeland. Deployment of battlefield nuclear weapons requires the delegation of command and control to military units in the field. This increases the risks of miscalculation, accident, theft and infiltration by militant groups.[38]

Russia

Both Russia and the United States maintain a triad of land, air and sea-based nuclear weapons. Their deployed strategic offensive weapons (ICBMs, submarine-launched ballistic missiles [SLBMs] and gravity bombs) constitute formidable arsenals. Both countries also have inventories of 'tactical' or 'non-strategic' weapons. The United States deploys some 200 B-61 bombs at bases in five NATO countries, while 'Russia's non-strategic nuclear warheads are normally kept in central storage'.[39] US and Russian nuclear missiles are de-targeted. Re-targeting can be accomplished quickly, but a missile launched accidentally will land in an area of open ocean and an additional decision from the command authority is required prior to an authorized launch. New START entered into force on 6 February 2011 and commits the two countries to establish new limits on deployed strategic offensive nuclear weapons by 2018: 1,550 deployed strategic warheads (with each deployed nuclear-capable heavy bomber counting as just one warhead towards the limit) and a combined (deployed and non-deployed) limit of 800 strategic nuclear delivery vehicles (ICBMs, SLBMs, bombers), of which no more than 700 may be deployed.[40] Within these limits, each party is permitted to determine its own strategic force structure.

Russia is estimated to have some 8,000 nuclear warheads in total, including 4,000 retired strategic and non-strategic warheads awaiting dismantlement. It appears to be making changes to the deployment patterns of land-based strategic forces to increase their survivability, modernizing its nuclear submarine fleet and SLBMs and begun research and development work on a new strategic bomber.[41]

Russia reserves the right to use nuclear weapons in response to a WMD attack on it or its allies or if the country was under conventional attack and its very existence was under theat. According to its military doctrine, Russia's nuclear weapons are meant to prevent military conflict and, as such, have a potential role to play in regional and large-scale conflicts involving not only nuclear or other WMD but also conventional weapons. In February 2012 then-Prime Minister Vladimir Putin described Russia's 'robust nuclear deterrent' as a counterweight to US strength and a contribution to international stability. He ruled out any concessions on tactical nuclear weapons. Russia's armed forces were in fact 'preparing additional stronger weapons'. Final nuclear disarmament would only be possible when Russia had 'exceptionally accurate non-nuclear systems of similar effectiveness' to those under development in the United States.[42]

United Kingdom

British doctrine states that it will only consider using nuclear weapons 'in extreme circumstances of self-defence, including the defence of NATO Allies' but remains 'deliberately ambiguous about precisely when, how and at what scale [it] would contemplate their use'.[43] The United Kingdom's relatively small nuclear arsenal consists entirely of sea-launched Trident missiles deployed on four Vanguard-class submarines, one of which is always at sea. Missiles are de-targeted. The 2010 Strategic Defence and Security Review concluded that the United Kingdom's minimum credible deterrence needs could be met with fewer nuclear weapons. As a consequence, Britain announced that by the mid- 2020s, it would:

- Reduce the number of warheads on each of its submarines from 48 to 40;
- Reduce the requirement for operationally available warheads to no more than 120;
- Reduce the number of launch tubes on each submarine from 12 to 8; and
- Reduce its overall nuclear weapons stockpile to no more than 180.

The Vanguard-class submarines are due for replacement in the 2020s. While both the ruling Conservative and opposition Labour parties support the maintenance of a nuclear deterrent, a final decision on the configuration of the United Kingdom's future nuclear forces will not be taken until after the next general election in 2016. In the meantime, the government has already placed some GBP 4bn worth of orders for design and development of new submarines.[44] However, senior military commanders are reported to have private doubts about the wisdom of investing in a replacement for the Trident submarines at the cost of cutbacks in other areas that would adversely affect the operational combat capability of British armed forces.[45]

United States

The US aggregate nuclear weapons stockpile is a little over 7,000 warheads and reducing. The April 2010 *Nuclear Posture Review* (NPR) confirmed that the United

States would maintain its nuclear triad of ICBMs, SLBMs and heavy bombers. The US long-term nuclear modernization program currently includes twelve new nuclear-powered ballistic missile submarines, a new air-launched standoff nuclear missile and eventual replacement of the Minuteman III ICBM and B-52H strategic bomber.[46] The F-35 Joint Strike Fighter will also be made nuclear capable.[47] Thus 'planned reductions in deployed and Treaty-counted U.S. forces are . . . taking place in the context of an extensive Obama administration commitment to maintain and modernize the U.S. nuclear force and its supporting infrastructure for the long-term'. In 2010, senior US officials told hearings of the US Senate Foreign Relations Committee on New START that '[o]ver the next decade, the United States will invest well over $100bn in nuclear delivery systems to sustain existing capabilities and modernize some strategic systems. U.S. nuclear weapons will also undergo extensive life extension programs in the coming years to ensure their safety, security and effectiveness'.[48]

The 2010 NPR, the first comprehensive reassessment of US nuclear weapons policy in a decade (the previous NPR was in 2001), affirmed that the primary function of US nuclear weapons was to deter nuclear attack on the United States, its allies and partners. Although nuclear weapons would continue to have a role in deterring non-nuclear attacks (conventional, biological and chemical), this role had diminished and would continue to do so. While the United States was 'not prepared at the present time to adopt a universal policy that deterring nuclear attack is the sole purpose of nuclear weapons, . . . [it] will work to establish conditions under which such a policy could be safely adopted'.[49] Henceforth, non-nuclear systems could be expected to make an increasingly significant contribution to US deterrence and reassurance goals.

In 2011 the Department of Defense published a new National Military Strategy which affirmed 'the fundamental role' of US nuclear weapons in a nuclear armed world. It promised nonetheless to support 'the President's vision' by reducing 'the role and numbers of nuclear weapons, while maintaining a safe, secure, and effective strategic deterrent'. US nuclear forces would 'continue to support strategic stability through maintenance of an assured second strike capability', and the United States would 'retain sufficient nuclear force structure to hedge against unexpected geopolitical change, technological problems, and operational vulnerabilities'.[50] New strategic guidance published by the White House and the Department of Defense in January 2012 under the heading 'Sustaining U.S. Global Leadership: Priorities for 21st Century Defense' similarly commits the United States to 'field nuclear forces that can under any circumstances confront an adversary with the prospect of unacceptable damage, both to deter potential adversaries and to assure U.S. allies and other security partners that they can count on America's security commitments'.[51]

The June 2013 report on the US nuclear employment strategy noted that the United States 'seeks to maintain strategic stability with Russia', which remains Washington's 'only peer in nuclear weapons capabilities', by demonstrating the intent not to negate Russia's strategic deterrent.[52] Beyond this, the guiding principles from the 2010 NPR were repeated: the US policy 'is to achieve a credible deterrent, with the lowest possible number of nuclear weapons consistent with our current and future security requirements and those of our Allies and partners' by maintaining a nuclear triad of land-based ICBMs, SLBMs and nuclear capable heavy bombers. However, the Defense Department was directed to explore non-nuclear strike options in order to realize the president's goal of reducing the role of nuclear weapons in US national security strategy and moving towards deterrence of nuclear attack being the sole purpose of US nuclear weapons. However, a stockpile of additional non-deployed nuclear warheads would continue to be maintained, along with the ability to upload strategic delivery platforms, as 'a robust hedge against technical or geopolitical risk with fewer total nuclear weapons'. The ability to forward deploy nuclear weapons in support of extended deterrence would also be maintained.[53]

President Obama built on this in a major speech at the Brandenburg Gate in Berlin on 19 June 2013. He announced a multi-step strategy on nuclear weapons: a reduction of up to one-third of deployed strategic nuclear weapons; further negotiated cuts with Russia;[54] discussions with NATO allies for 'bold reductions in U.S. and Russian tactical weapons in Europe'; a fourth nuclear security summit in the United States in 2016; work to build support for CTBT ratification by the United States; and the initiation of discussions for a treaty to end the production of fissile materials for nuclear weapons.[55]

A nuclear renaissance?

According to the International Energy Agency (IEA), the world's energy consumption will increase, based on current trends and policies, by more than 50 percent from 2005 to 2030, with just China and India accounting for 45 percent of the extra growth in demand.[56] The IAEA's 2013 Nuclear Technology Review reported a total of 437 reactors in operation and another 67 new reactors under construction at the end of 2012. It anticipates 'significant growth in the use of nuclear energy worldwide' – between 23 to 100 percent by 2030.[57] Although most of the growth in nuclear energy is expected in Asia (Indonesia, Malaysia, Pakistan, Thailand and Vietnam), several Middle Eastern countries have also announced plans to explore the use of nuclear power and in July 2012 'the United Arab Emirates (UAE) became the first country in 27 years to start the construction of a first nuclear power plant'.[58]

The 437 reactors spread across 30 countries provide approximately 15 percent of the world's total electricity at present. After the well-publicized accidents at Three Mile Island (US, 1979) and Chernobyl (Ukraine, but at the time the former Soviet Union, 1986), public and political opposition to nuclear power was so strong that many existing reactor plants were shut down, plans for new ones were cancelled and virtually no new reactor was built over the last 15 years. With the escalating price of oil, caused by a spike in demand from booming major economies like China and India and disruptions to supply because of conflicts in the Middle East, the economics of even risk-discounted nuclear power has changed. With the accelerating threat of global warming caused by greenhouse gas emissions, the balance of public anxiety between energy sourced in nuclear power and coal and fossil fuel has changed dramatically. Combined with technological developments, the changed financial and environmental equations have also altered the politics of constructing and operating nuclear power reactors.[59]

At the same time, long lead times and high capital costs for nuclear construction mean that governments want to be assured that nuclear energy and plants are safe, secure, reliable and cost-effective. In this context, the IAEA concludes: 'The Fukushima Daiichi accident is expected to slow or delay the growth of nuclear power, but not to reverse it'.[60] All this throws up several clusters of concern:

1 How do we ensure that the plants are operated with safety, so that the chances of accidents are minimized, and mechanisms and procedures are put in place so that accidents are discovered immediately, their effects are mitigated and firewalls are constructed to prevent wider damage?
2 How do we secure the plants against theft and leakage of weapons-sensitive material, skills and knowledge? After all, the now notorious Abdul Qadeer Khan simply stole designs and material from places in the West he was working in, then returned to Pakistan and established a very effective global nuclear arms bazaar.[61]
3 How do we protect civilian use of nuclear power from being employed for weapons-related purposes?
4 How do we establish multinational regimes for the assurance of fuel supply, the management of spent fuel, the disposal of radioactive wastes and the decommissioning of old reactors?

These concerns relate not just to the countries in which the reactors are located but also to the international trade in nuclear material, skills and equipment. As IAEA Director-General Mohamed ElBaradei noted, 'Nuclear components designed in one country could be manufactured in another, shipped through a third, and assembled in a fourth for use in a fifth'.[62]

An agenda for action

In addition to proscribing nuclear proliferation, the NPT contains the only global treaty-level commitment to nuclear disarmament. Over the years, a number of international commissions[63] have drawn very similar conclusions about the all-encompassing nature of the threat posed by nuclear weapons, their dubious utility and the steps needed to get rid of them. The report of the International Commission on Nuclear Non-Proliferation and Disarmament (ICNND) introduced a number of new, including time-bound, elements to the nuclear disarmament agenda. It argued for the delegitimization of the role of nuclear weapons and for a two-phase approach to their elimination, recommending that 'minimization' be achieved between 2012 and 2025, and 'elimination' as soon as possible thereafter.[64] In 2009 the worldwide campaign organization Global Zero launched a four-phase action plan, much more ambitious than ICNND's, setting 2023 as the target date for negotiating a legally binding international agreement, signed by all nuclear capable countries, that would lead to the phased, verified and proportionate reduction of all nuclear arsenals, with complete dismantlement of all the world's nuclear weapons to be achieved by 2030.[65]

The credibility of the core arguments of both ICNND and Global Zero was reinforced by a study done for Global Zero by a panel under the leadership of retired US General James Cartwright, the former vice chairman of the Joint Chiefs of Staff, and including then-Senator and now Secretary of Defense Chuck Hagel. This recommended a dramatic drawdown over one decade of US and Russian nuclear forces to 900 total nuclear weapons (including both strategic and non-strategic) each, divided equally between deployed (450) and held in reserve on de-alerted status (450). The alternative deterrence construct would require a robust command, control, communications and early warning system that can withstand the shock of the initial strike and manage the transition to regenerated nuclear forces. The study argued further that once the two major nuclear powers had reduced their arsenals to these levels, China could be drawn into the negotiations followed by the other nuclear armed states.[66] With each new entrant into the multilateral arms control negotiations, it would become progressively more difficult for the remainder to stay outside the process.

The core arguments and structure of the book

The foregoing survey of the state of nuclear weapons throws up several challenging questions for analysts and policymakers. The chapters that follow approach the problem primarily as a normative and political project, more than as an analytical project. Part One looks at the broad outlines of the nuclear debate. Chapter 2 is an examination of the scholar–practitioner interface in trying to come to grips with the nature and magnitude of the challenge. The underlying assumption of the whole book, like that of the nuclear arms control and disarmament agenda, is that nuclear weapons are qualitatively different from all other classes of weapons in their destructive potential and in their inherently indiscriminate effects. With this in mind, looking back to and since their invention and use, Chapter 3 traces the main policy impact of the development of nuclear weapons on security strategy and on public discourse. This is followed in Chapter 4 by looking forward to the different collective nuclear futures from among which policymakers must choose: the status quo; reversal of the steady reductions in global warhead numbers; nuclear proliferation; and nuclear disarmament.

Part Two, spread over six substantial chapters (5–10), looks at several key regional challenges in West, South and East Asia and the South Pacific over the last three decades. As noted above, the bulk of the world's nuclear weapons – more than 90 percent – is held by Russia and the United States, who also conducted most of the nuclear testing. But in the 1980s and 1990s, world attention was focussed on nuclear testing in the Pacific by France as an established NPT NWS; then India and Pakistan as they broke through the NPT normative barrier, conducted nuclear tests in 1998 and have steadily consolidated their status since then as non-NPT nuclear-armed states; followed finally by North Korea, which became the first country to defect from and break out of the NPT to conduct nuclear tests in 2006, 2009 and 2013. While the world is trying to figure out how to coax North Korea back into the NPT bottle, it is simultaneously struggling with the challenge of trying to keep Iran in the NPT non-NWS box. Meanwhile, India has been accommodated as a de facto nuclear-armed state outside the NPT regime, with the September 2014 agreement for the sale of Australian uranium – foreshadowed in the discussion in Chapter 9 – being the latest example. The six chapters in Part Two address these challenges, spanning the last quarter century, in some detail, in all cases pointing to the dubious utility and questionable claims in defence of nuclear weaponization, as well as the added risks to national, regional and global security orders and other key goals.

The various regional challenges have tested and served to highlight both the indispensable utility for the foreseeable future but also some serious deficiencies in the existing normative architecture of the nuclear arms control and disarmament regime. Chapters 11–13 in Part Three deal with the international nuclear nonproliferation and disarmament machinery and regime, beginning with regional nuclear-weapon-free zones in Chapter 11. This is a topic that has been at the forefront of the nuclear arms control agenda in the last couple of years with the failure to convene a conference on a zone free of weapons of mass destruction in the Middle East; a failure that could damage the 2015 NPT Review Conference. Chapter 12 asks whether the treaty's considerable past achievements and present indispensability notwithstanding, the NPT's anomalies have become so many and so substantial that the treaty is incapable of functioning much longer as the anchor of the global nuclear arms control regime. The nuclear proliferation and terrorism agendas merged as a nightmare challenge in the minds of policymakers after the terror attacks of 11 September 2001 in New York and Washington. The resulting concentration of the world's attention on the challenge of nuclear security is discussed in Chapter 13.

The concluding Chapter 14 brings together the various disparate strands of the analysis to argue that it is time to break out of the sterile and unproductive debate over privileging nuclear nonproliferation or disarmament. Instead, both agendas, as well the effort to secure all the world's fissile material and nuclear plants and facilities in order to minimize the security risks of the peaceful uses of nuclear energy, must be pursued simultaneously. The book ends by outlining practical steps for moving towards a world of progressively reduced nuclear weapons in numbers, reduced salience of nuclear weapons in national security doctrines and deployment practices and an eventually denuclearized world anchored in a universal, legally binding and verifiable nuclear weapons convention.

Notes

1 Secretary of Defense, *Report on Nuclear Employment Strategy of the United States Specified in Section 491 of 10 U.S.C.* (Washington, DC: Department of Defense, RefID 6-9963D19, 12 June 2013), 2.

16 *Introduction*

2 'Remarks by President Obama at the Brandenburg Gate – Berlin, Germany' (Washington, DC: White House, Office of the Press Secretary, 19 June 2013); http://www.whitehouse.gov/the-press-office/2013/06/19/remarks-president-obama-brandenburg-gate-berlin-germany.
3 President John F. Kennedy, State of the Union speech, 11 January 1962, http://www.jfklink.com/speeches/jfk/publicpapers/1962/jfk07_62.html.
4 See Ramesh Thakur and Gareth Evans, eds., *Nuclear Weapons: The State of Play* (Canberra: Centre for Nuclear Non-Proliferation and Disarmament, 2013), Table 2.2, 104.
5 See Pauline K. Kerr and Mary Beth Nikitin, *Pakistan's Nuclear Weapons: Proliferation and Security Issues* (Washington, DC: Congressional Research Service, Report RL34248, 20 July 2011).
6 George P. Shultz, William J. Perry, Henry Kissinger, and Sam Nunn: 'A world free of nuclear weapons', 4 January 2007; 'Toward a nuclear free world', 15 January 2008; 'How to protect our nuclear deterrent', 19 January 2010; 'Deterrence in the age of nuclear proliferation', 7 March 2011; and 'Next steps in reducing nuclear risks', 5 March 2013.
7 Ivo Daalder and Jan Lodal, 'The logic of zero: Toward a world without nuclear weapons', *Foreign Affairs* 87:6 (2008), 81.
8 Center for Strategic and International Studies, *Toward a Grand Strategy for an Uncertain World: Renewing Transatlantic Partnership* (Washington, DC: Center for Strategic and International Studies, 2008).
9 'Remarks by President Barack Obama, Hradcany Square, Prague, 5 April 2009', Washington, DC: White House, Office of the Press Secretary, 2009; http://www.whitehouse.gov/video/The-President-in-Prague#transcript.
10 S/RES/1887 (24 September 2009).
11 *China Defence White Paper 2010*, http://www.china.org.cn/government/whitepaper/2011-03/31/content_22263885.htm.
12 Gregory Kulacki, 'China's nuclear arsenal: Status and evolution', *Union of Concerned Scientists* (October 2011), 1–2.
13 'China "is two years from arming its submarines with nuclear weapons," says U.S. report', *MailOnline*, updated 9 November 2012.
14 Li Bin, 'Tracking Chinese strategic mobile missiles', *Science & Global Security* 15:1 (2007), 4–5.
15 Wu Riqiang, 'Survivability of China's sea-based nuclear forces', *Science and Global Security* 19:2 (2011), 94–96.
16 http://www.armscontrol.org/act/2011_03/LiBin.
17 White paper on China's armed forces, *The Diversified Employment of China's Armed Forces* (Beijing: Information Office of the State Council, April 2013), http://news.xinhuanet.com/english/china/2013-04/16/c_132312681.htm.
18 *China Defence White Paper 2010*.
19 *The French White Paper on Defence and National Security*, http://www.ambafrance-ca.org/IMG/pdf/Livre_blanc_Press_kit_english_version.pdf.
20 Beatrice Fihn, ed., *The 2010 NPT Action Plan Monitoring Report* (Geneva: Geneva Centre for Security Policy, Swiss Federal Department of Foreign Affairs, and Reaching Critical Will, 2012), 28.
21 Speech by President Nicolas Sarkozy, Cherbourg, 21 March 2008, http://www.acronym.org.uk/docs/0803/doc09.htm.
22 See Sumit Ganguly, 'India's pathway to Pokhran II: The prospects and sources of New Delhi's nuclear weapons program', *International Security* 23:4 (Spring 1999): 148–77; and George Perkovich, *India's Nuclear Bomb: The Impact on Global Proliferation* (Berkeley, CA: University of California Press, 1999).
23 Tilman Brück, 'Summary', *SIPRI Yearbook 2013: Armaments, Disarmament and International Security* (Oxford: Oxford University Press, 2013), 12.
24 David O. Smith, *The US Experience with Tactical Nuclear Weapons: Lessons for South Asia* (Washington, DC: Stimson Center, 4 March 2013), 3.

25 International Panel on Fissile Materials, *Global Fissile Material Report 2013* (www.fissilematerials.org), 11–14, 21.
26 David Albright and Serena Kelleher-Vergantini, 'Construction finishing of likely New Indian centrifuge facility at rare materials plant', *ISIS Imagery Brief* (Washington, DC: Institute for Science and International Security, 4 December 2013).
27 See Shashank Joshi, 'India's military instrument: A doctrine stillborn', *Journal of Strategic Studies* 36:4 (2013): 512–40.
28 *Draft Report of the National Security Advisory Board on Indian Nuclear Doctrine*, 17 August 1999; http://www.fas.org/nuke/guide/india/doctrine/990817-indnucld.htm.
29 http://www.armscontrol.org/factsheets/indiaprofile.
30 S. H. Kile, P. Schell and H. M. Kristensen, 'Israeli nuclear forces', *SIPRI Yearbook 2012*, 341–42.
31 Dmitry Adamsky, 'Why Israel should learn to stop worrying and love the bomb: The case for a new nuclear strategy', *Foreign Affairs*, 31 March 2012, http://www.foreignaffairs.com/articles/137374/dmitry-adamsky/why-israel-should-learn-to-stop-worrying-and-love-the-bomb.
32 Noam Sheizaf, 'Clear and present danger', *Haaretz*, 21 March 2012.
33 http://www.nti.org/country-profilesd/Israel/nuclear/.
34 A state party has the right to withdraw from the NPT if it decides that 'extraordinary events, related to the subject matter of [the] Treaty, have jeopardized the supreme interests of its country' (Article 10). North Korea announced its withdrawal from the NPT on 12 March 1993 but then suspended it on 11 June 1993, the day before the decision would have taken effect. In January 2003, North Korea ended the suspension, which for all practical purposes meant withdrawal with immediate effect. Christer Ahlstrom, 'Withdrawal from arms control treaties', *SIPRI Yearbook 2004: Armaments, Disarmament and International Security* (Oxford: Oxford University Press, 2004): 763–77.
35 Andrew Bast, 'Pakistan's nuclear calculus', *Washington Quarterly* 34:4 (2011), 75–77.
36 http://www.globalsecurity.org/wmd/world/Pakistan/nuke-battlefield.htm.
37 Shyam Saran, 'Dealing with Pakistan's brinkmanship', *Hindu*, 7 December 2012.
38 http://www.globalsecurity.org/wmd/world/Pakistan/nuke-battlefield.htm.
39 Gaukhar Mukhatzhanova, *Implementation of the Conclusions and Recommendations for Follow-On Actions Adopted at the 2010 NPT Review Conference Disarmament Actions 1–22: Monitoring Report* (Monterey, CA: James Martin Center for Non-proliferation Studies, Monterey Institute of International Studies, April 2012), 29.
40 http://www.whitehouse.gov/blog/2010/04/08/new-start-treaty-and-protocol.
41 Mukhatzhanova, *Implementation of the 2010 NPT Review Conference Disarmament Actions*, 8–9.
42 'Strong Russian nuclear force deters conflict, Putin says', *Global Security Newswire*, 27 February 2012. This last statement is hard to reconcile with his deputy foreign minister's proposed prohibition of 'strategic offensive arms in non-nuclear configuration'. Putin's comments are, however, broadly consistent with current Russian military doctrine which 'assigns high-precision [apparently, conventional] weapons to the mission of strategic deterrence'; Nikolai Sokov, *The New 2010 Russian Military Doctrine: The Nuclear Angle*; http://npsglobal.org/.
43 UK Ministry of Defence, *Securing Britain in an Age of Uncertainty: The Strategic Defence Security Review*, Cm 7948 (London: HM Stationery Office, October 2010), 37.
44 Rachel Oswald, 'U.K. Defense Secretary says trident renewal is most cost-effective way to ensure deterrent', *Global Security Newswire*, 19 July 2012.
45 Oliver Wright and Kim Sengupta, 'Top military chiefs go cold on nuclear deterrent', *Independent* (London), 26 September 2012.
46 Ian Kearns, *Beyond the United Kingdom: Trends in the Other Nuclear Armed States*, Discussion Paper 1 of the British American Security Information Council (BASIC) Trident Commission (London: BASIC, November 2011), 4; http://www.basicint.org/publications/dr-ian-kearns-trident-commission-consultant/2011/beyond-uk-trends-other-nuclear-armed-s.

18 *Introduction*

47 US Department of Defense, *Nuclear Posture Review Report* (Washington, DC: April 2010), 27; http://www.defense.gov/npr/docs/2010%20nuclear%20posture%20review%20report.pdf.
48 Kearns, *Beyond the United Kingdom*, 11.
49 *Nuclear Posture Review*, 2010, viii.
50 US Department of Defense, *The National Military Strategy of the United States of America 2011: Redefining America's Military Leadership* (Washington, DC: February 2011), 7 and 19; http://www.army.mil/info/references/docs/NMS%20FEB%202011.pdf.
51 US Department of Defense, *Sustaining U.S. Global Leadership: Priorities for 21st Century Defense* (Washington, DC: January 2012), 5.
52 *Report on Nuclear Employment Strategy of the United States*, 3.
53 Ibid., 4–8.
54 For an exploration of the prospects for such talks, see Amy F. Woolf, *Next Steps in Nuclear Arms Control with Russia: Issues for Congress* (Washington, DC: Congressional Research Service Report R43037, 10 April 2013).
55 'Remarks by President Obama at the Brandenburg Gate'.
56 *World Energy Outlook 2007* (Paris: IEA, 2007).
57 IAEA, *Nuclear Technology Review* (Vienna: IAEA, GC(57)/INF/2, 22 July 2013), 1, paragraph 1; http://www.iaea.org/About/Policy/GC/GC57/GC57InfDocuments/English/gc57inf-2_en.pdf.
58 Ibid., 1, paragraph 2.
59 Those who remain sceptical of any nuclear solution continue to advocate renewables like wind and solar energy as well as increased energy efficiency.
60 IAEA, *Nuclear Technology Review*, 10, paragraph 27.
61 See Christopher Clary, 'Dr. Khan's Nuclear WalMart', *Disarmament Diplomacy* 76 (March/April 2004): 31–35; Douglas Frantz and Catherine Collins, 'Those nuclear flashpoints are made in Pakistan', *Washington Post*, 11 November 2007.
62 Mohamed ElBaradei, 'Preserving the non-proliferation treaty', *Disarmament Forum* 4 (2005), 5.
63 The Canberra Commission on the Elimination of Nuclear Weapons, 1996; the Tokyo Forum for Nuclear Non-proliferation and Disarmament, 1999; the UN Secretary-General's High-level Panel on Threats, Challenges and Change, 2004; and the Weapons of Mass Destruction (Blix) Commission, 2006.
64 ICNND (Gareth Evans and Yoriko Kawaguchi co-chairs), *Eliminating Nuclear Threats: A Practical Agenda for Global Policymakers*. Report of the International Commission on Nuclear Non-proliferation and Disarmament (Canberra and Tokyo: ICNND, 2009), 72–78.
65 Global Zero Action Plan, http://www.globalzero.org/files/pdf/gzap_3.0.pdf.
66 James Cartwright, *et al.*, *Modernizing U.S. Nuclear Strategy, Force Structure and Posture*. Global Zero U.S. Nuclear Policy Commission Report (Washington, DC: Global Zero, 2012); www.globalzero.org/en/us-nuclear-policy-commission-report.

Part I
The nuclear debate

2 Nuclear nonproliferation and disarmament*

Can the power of ideas tame the power of the state?

The nuclear arms control regime – centred on the 1968 Nuclear Non-Proliferation Treaty (NPT) – is under a fivefold challenge. There is disappointment at the failure of nuclear disarmament by the five NPT-licit nuclear powers (China, France, Russia, UK and US); anxiety about some non-nuclear signatories cheating on their NPT obligations, especially North Korea and Iran; dissatisfaction that three countries (India, Israel, Pakistan) remain outside the NPT regime; apprehensions about terrorists acquiring and using nuclear weapons; and concerns over the safety, security and proliferation risks of the increased interest in nuclear energy to offset the financial and environmental costs of fossil fuel.

The world faced a potential nuclear crossroads in 2010 with several milestones: a US Nuclear Posture Review that reduced the role of nuclear weapons and put additional restrictions on their use, a new Russia–US treaty that cuts their deployed strategic arsenals by about one-third, an April summit in Washington that pledged to tighten the security of nuclear materials and trade, and a five-yearly NPT Review Conference in New York in May. The calendar was ticking also on Iran's suspected weapons program and the best response to the challenge. Can policymakers draw on the expertise of scholars to address these challenges? Can scholars summarize their research into policy-relevant recommendations with the requisite crispness, clarity and implementability? How can the normally isolated worlds of ideas and action work together to produce policy proposals to take the world out of the seeming rut of a deadlocked nuclear arms control agenda?

Along with an interest in the normative framework for going to war and regulating the conduct of belligerents engaged in hostilities, analysts and policymakers have long been interested in regulating the weapons of warfare as a means of limiting the casualty toll of armed conflicts as well as lessening the temptation to go to war because of an abundant – some would say excess – supply of weaponry. This chapter will examine the relationship between the worlds of ideas and practice with respect to nuclear weapons organized along four questionss: the major theoretical approaches, the fit between scholarship and practice, the optimum engagement between them, and the likely directions in the foreseeable future.

Theoretical approaches: peace research vs. strategic studies

The dominant scholarly approaches can usefully be grouped under the contrasting broad headings of peace research and strategic studies. For example, nuclear disarmament fits more comfortably within the analytical framework of peace research than strategic studies. Conversely, a focus on nonproliferation to the neglect of disarmament reveals the strategic studies bias at the cost of peace research. Both approaches fall into 'applied research' stream and have been intellectually challenged for it.[1] Most countries seem to tap expertise in strategic studies institutes while ignoring much of the peace research and conflict resolution expertise.

Applied to the Cold War, the logic of realist analyses produced policy prescriptions of containment of the evil empire through a sustained posture of armed strength. The peace research community grew in strength, conviction and numbers in opposition to the logic of confrontation. Its adherents argued that the adversarial approach intensified mutual antagonisms, fed the conventional and nuclear arms race and increased the probability of war by design or accident. A true appreciation of the nuclear age Cold War would enlighten governments to the reality of structures of common security. The two major antagonists shared an interest in reciprocal self-preservation which was, or should have been, more powerful than their apparent enmity. In some ways the early peace researchers anticipated the politics of antagonistic collaboration that was to produce the period of detente in the 1970s–80s.

The 1980s witnessed growing interest in peace studies that was directly related to the heightened anxiety about the precarious state of the nuclear peace.[2] Both superpowers contributed to the militarization of international affairs. During the Cold War the literature was strongly weighted towards strategic studies. The balance tilted relatively more towards peace research with the end of the Cold War, both because of the diminution of the prospect of a transcendental war between the superpowers, and because the major powers were themselves now interested in cooperating to contain conflicts among others rather than exploiting regional conflicts to advance their own agendas. The substantial broadening of the definition of security after the Cold War to embrace non-traditional notions and threats fit comfortably within peace research but awkwardly in the national security analytical framework.

The two theoretical approaches have their own separate journals and publications. The International Institute for Strategic Studies (IISS) in London publishes books, monographs and journals, including the much acclaimed Adelphi Papers and the annual *Military Balance* and *Strategic Survey*. The annual *SIPRI Yearbook*, published by the Stockholm International Peace Research Institute (SIPRI) is just as acclaimed in the peace research and policy communities. The major scholarly journals in peace research are the *Journal of Conflict Resolution* and the *Journal of Peace Research*. *Security Dialogue* is normatively closer to peace research than strategic studies, reflecting its institutional links to the Peace Research Institute of Oslo

(PRIO). There are innumerable research institutions and think tanks that also illustrate the division into peace research and strategic studies. The Institute for Defence Studies and Analyses (IDSA) in New Delhi, the Strategic and Defence Studies Centre at the Australian National University in Canberra, the Department of Defence-funded Australian Strategic Policy Institute (ASPI) in Canberra, are complemented by peace research institutes in Copenhagen, Frankfurt, Oslo, Stockholm, Tampere, etc. alongside university departments at Notre Dame in the United States, Uppsala in Sweden, Bradford in the United Kingdom and University of Queensland in Australia. Northern Europe has the highest 'peace research density' of any region in the world.[3]

At any given time, most of the countries in the world are at peace but ready to go to war if necessary. Therein lies the key to the difference between peace research and strategic studies. Peace research aims to control the manifestation of arms and violence and question their utility in promoting societal values.[4] It is an etiology of conflict and conflict resolution.[5] It has a bias towards organized violence in conflicts between political actors, but is not restricted to international conflicts. Deaths can be caused by the direct application of force, as on the battlefield, and through "excess deaths" caused by conflict-related food scarcity, disease and damage to health infrastructure. They can also be caused, in greater magnitude and more pervasively, as the unintended consequences of structural inequalities in social systems. Poverty and malnutrition take a far deadlier toll on many more people each year than direct violence by their own or an enemy state.

Strategic studies is infused with realist assumptions that violence is endemic, inevitable and an instrument of statecraft in a relentless struggle for power among autonomous states. The task of strategic analysts is to predict courses of action that will enable states to maximize their own power while neutralizing or minimizing the national power of opponents, so that the conflict is resolved on one's own terms and not that of the enemy.[6] Peace research challenges the basic tenets of conventional analyses of violence and offers critical alternatives. How well do the conventional propositions stand up to facts? Does the evidence support the claim that if we want peace, we must prepare for war? Or do preparations for war cause war, or make it more likely? Strategic studies accepts and refines the instrumentality of violence; peace research questions and rejects it. Strategic studies focuses on the successful use of violence; peace research is concerned to reduce the frequency of latent and manifest use of force. Peace research changes focus from security of the state to welfare of individuals and the system: how everybody gains when parties in conflict avoid violence. For strategic studies, the most critical lesson of the interwar period (1919–39) is that pacifism and appeasement do not work against the Hitlers of the world. Few peace researchers would dispute this. But most would point to the injustice and inequity of the Treaty of Versailles, and the subsequent treatment of Germany from within the realist paradigm, as having spawned Hitler in the first place.

Unusually among academic disciplines, peace research 'triangulates' data, theory and values to insist upon the search for peace by peaceful means.[7] It argues that nonviolent alternatives are not given serious enough consideration, while the indirect costs and harmful legacies of the resort to armed violence are always underestimated.[8] An additional and enduring cost of war is the mimetic nature of violence, creating the conditions for the eruption of later violence by being emulated or mimed.[9] The problem is war; the approach is normative-philosophical or empirical-mathematical; the goal is the generation of a body of prescriptive propositions for nonviolent dispute resolution that can be put to practical use for improving the human condition, providing a better life in a safer world for all.

Possibilities for the breakdown of peace exist everywhere and at all times. The task for strategic studies is to identify them through the exploration of worst-case scenarios. Possibilities for building peace exist in every human crisis. The challenge for peace research is to identify them through the exploration of best-case scenarios. For strategists, the key question on Kashmir is how best to secure the province against the threat from India or Pakistan. So when India acquired nuclear weapons capability, from within the strategic studies framework Pakistan followed suit. For a peace researcher, it is equally legitimate to ask how best to protect the people of Kashmir from terrorists, security forces and an India–Pakistan nuclear war. The threats posed by the administrative, judicial, police, paramilitary and military structures of the state to individual and group rights, and by the bilateral nuclear equation to international and environmental security, are alien to strategic studies but central to peace research.

A radical conceptual shift – and the most significant for peace research – was from 'national security' with its focus on military defence of the state, to 'human security' with its emphasis on protecting the individual from life-threatening threats through direct and structural violence. The rise of human security – an essentially contested concept[10] – has been attributed to six factors.[11] The participants in armed conflict broadened from a narrow elite to mass conscripts. The industrial and scientific revolutions dramatically increased the range, lethality and accuracy of firepower, so that the state had to accept growing numbers of its own people being killed in the effort to protect them; the ultimate paradox came with nuclear weapons and strategies of mutually assured destruction. Many regimes took to murdering large numbers of their own people. In the wake of decolonization, many states emerged lacking the capacity to assure their citizens' security or exert authority over the resources, which were then captured by predatory groups who used the principle of sovereignty and the norm of nonintervention to shield themselves from external pressure. The collapse of the Soviet empire and the end of the confrontational, militarized and state-centric Cold War opened space for alternative conceptions of order and security. And finally, globalization has helped to reduce the salience of the state and of military threats and defences. Thus four of the six factors (the fourth and sixth being the two exceptions) grew directly out of developments related to national security.

National security is an artifice of the realists' imagination, a politically constructed concept. State security does not have privileged claim over such other needs for human beings as food, water and air. Human security helps peace researchers to translate the arid strategic studies language of 'countervalue targets', 'flexible response' and 'collateral damage' into human terms of civilians killed in the millions, food-growing soil poisoned for decades, and whole communities destroyed or displaced.

Given its historical evolution and normative mandate, the United Nations falls squarely into the peace research and human security camp. Going to war was an acknowledged attribute of state sovereignty and war itself was an accepted institution of the Westphalian system with distinctive rules, etiquette, norms, and stable patterns of practices to govern armed conflicts.[12] In that quasi-Hobbesian world barely removed from the state of nature, the main protection against aggression was countervailing power, which increased both the cost of victory and the risk of failure. Since 1945, the UN has spawned a corpus of law to stigmatize the act, threat and instruments of aggression and create a robust norm against it.

Fit between theory and practice

While many instinctive UN supporters might well embed the organization in the intellectual tradition of peace research, the historical fact is that the formal organization has its institutional antecedents in the wartime alliance led by the three 'Us': the UK, US and USSR. Hence the tension between idealism and realism that is integral to the UN identity and project and extends to its handling of nuclear weapons. The UN Charter was adopted at San Francisco six weeks before the use of atomic weapons in Hiroshima and Nagasaki. In time, the five permanent members of the Security Council coincidentally became the five licit nuclear weapons states (NWS) under the NPT. Given their privileged role in international law enforcement, they prioritized the legally binding and internationally enforceable nonproliferation obligations of the NPT while continually downgrading the Article 6 disarmament clause.

Thus the United Nations lies at the crossroads of the power of ideas and the power of the state. UNESCO's Preamble declares that if wars begin in the minds of people, then it is in their minds that the defences of peace must be constructed. That being the case, the primary forum for the transformation, from a culture of war among heavily armed states to a culture of peace among barely armed nations, must be the classroom and the laboratory. The principle that knowledge produced in universities and think tanks should be made available to the policy community is unexceptionable. In practice, the chief difficulty seems to be the lack of a common vocabulary for scholars and practitioners to engage in shared and informed discourse.

In the case of nuclear weapons policies, with the exception of highly formalized rational choice theories, this is less of a problem for strategic studies than for peace research. By its very nature, the former is more policy oriented while the latter can be highly 'theoretical'. Alternatively, when theoretical models or deeply intricate normative arguments are distilled into short policy recommendations, they become easy targets for dismissive remarks like a peacenik's manifesto, or Utopian dreams lacking in realism, or even for posing a threat to national security by trying to weaken national defence preparedness. In very few countries would peace research have a constituency inside the cabinet or bureaucracy. By contrast, departments of defence, the defence forces, the intelligence agencies and foreign services would be eager to recruit the best and brightest of strategic studies graduates. However, nuclear arms control and disarmament specialists are welcome in international organizations.

As John Asplund has noted,[13] decision-makers are often confronted by 'precarious ignorance' of inadequate information-cum-potentially disastrous consequences of the decision made on that narrow knowledge base. The description is applicable to the 2003 Iraq war, and potentially to a military strike on Iran to destroy its suspected nuclear weapons program. To be taken seriously by policy-makers, scholars have to learn to speak their language, to get and stay inside the dominant discourse. Many peace research scholars are hesitant to do so because, unlike counterparts in strategic studies, they fear being co-opted to serve the war-making agendas of political leaders. Many serious social scientists in general are reluctant to simplify their analyses and conclusions, airbrush their caveats and qualifications, and present recommendations with the degree of certainty that decision-makers demand. And so they end up sharing the fate of Cassandra: blessed with the gift of prophecy but cursed with not being believed.

In practice, perhaps the more significant impact that ideas have had on national and international public policy is firstly through a revolving door system of insider-outsider roles – Pierre Trudeau and potentially Michael Ignatieff in Canada,[14] Henry Kissinger, Condoleezza Rice, Stephen Krasner and Anne-Marie Slaughter in the US, and Francis Deng, Michael Doyle, John Ruggie, Jeffrey Sachs and Amartya Sen in the United Nations – and secondly as public intellectuals (with some overlap in the two groups). Many scholars are eager to lend their expertise for the public good and derive satisfaction from making a difference that cannot be given a monetary value. Certainly many good and great scholars worked for UN University projects – which generally fell under the peace research umbrella – for extremely modest honoraria.

Global governance: the terrain on which theory meets practice

Both the scholar and the practitioner are engaged in solving puzzles, albeit from different entry points. The crossroads at which they meet is global governance. The clearest way to comprehend the relevance of using the lens of global governance is by examining five 'gaps' between pressing global problems and feeble global solutions.[15] The first gap is that of knowledge. Often, there is little or no consensus about the nature, gravity, and magnitude of a problem with respect to the facts, theoretical explanation, and the best remedies and solutions.

Factually, is Iran's interest limited to nuclear energy or is it engaged in a clandestine pursuit of nuclear weapons and, if so, how many years away is it from acquiring the bomb? Is Pakistan's nuclear arsenal fully secured from being stolen by Islamists? What is North Korea's exact nuclear weapons capability? *Theoretically*, will the threat and imposition of sanctions or of air strikes, a combination of both, or neither, be effective in stopping Iran from acquiring nuclear weapons and rolling back North Korea's program? What is the best strategy for preventing the proliferation of nuclear weapons while also trying to encourage the elimination of existing stockpiles and avoiding their use in the meantime? Was the long peace[16] in Europe kept by nuclear deterrence, the integration of Western Europe, the democratization of Western Europe, or a combination of all three? To be of interest to policymakers in answering these questions, scholars would need both subject (nuclear proliferation) and regional (Iran, Europe, South Asia, Koreas) expertise.

Almost all empirical information on armaments is collected and stored by governments and international organizations. Few governments are prepared to release all information on their weapons inventories to others; most will publish some information; all are sensitive to how the information is presented and have laws punishing unauthorized access to classified military information. The main international repositories of information for nuclear and chemical weapons are the UN Secretariat, the International Atomic Energy Agency (IAEA), and the Organization for the Prohibition of Chemical Weapons (OPCW). Similarly, the UN Conventional Arms Register aims at the most authoritative data collection. It has the merits but also the shortcomings of relying on official reports from member governments. Some research institutions collect information from a variety of open sources and publish them in conveniently accessed compendiums like yearbooks or periodic reports. Analysts and commentators will look to these additional sources, including standard compilations from the Bonn International Center for Conversion (BICC), the IISS and SIPRI. Scholars and researchers are the mainstay of these databases.

Theoretical knowledge gaps are the provenance of researchers and there is a large literature on the various associations, correlations and causations between the variables of arms levels and the onset of war, or between military expenditures and economic development. Clearly there is no limit to the role of scholars in filling knowledge gaps. That said, past predictions from experts regarding the development and acquisition of arms have been notoriously inaccurate.[17]

We know the broad outlines of the inventories in the nuclear arsenals of the five NPT-licit NWS. But we can only make informed guesses about the two self-declared possessors of nuclear weapons, India and Pakistan; and less well-informed guesses about the deliberately ambiguous non-NPT nuclear power, Israel. With suspected NPT cheats such as Iran and North Korea, the situation becomes decidedly murky. The same is true of nonstate actors. The existence and extent of Abdul Qadeer Khan's underground nuclear bazaar – which came to light in 2003 only because Libya renounced the nuclear option and began cooperating in the verified dismantling of its clandestine infrastructure – caught everyone by surprise.[18] Conversely, most western commentators had assumed that Saddam Hussein had some level of nuclear weapons capability and were caught flat-footed by their complete absence.

Once a threat or problem has been identified and diagnosed, the next step is to help solidify a new norm of behaviour. Since 1945, the norm of nuclear abstinence has become firmly established. Norms more than the infrastructure and doctrines of deterrence have anathematized nuclear weapons to entrench the taboo against their use, even at the price of accepting defeat on the battlefield against non-nuclear enemies in Vietnam and Afghanistan.[19]

Four high-profile international commissions have reaffirmed and attempted to strengthen international nuclear norms. The Canberra Commission argued that the case for the elimination of nuclear weapons rested on three propositions: their destructive power robs them of military utility against other nuclear weapons states and renders them politically and morally indefensible against non-nuclear states; it defies credulity that they can be retained in perpetuity and never used by design or inadvertence; and their possession by some stimulates others to acquire them.[20] The 1999 Tokyo Forum for Nuclear Non-Proliferation and Disarmament repeated the alarm. The Weapons of Mass Destruction (WMD) Commission[21] is more likely to reinforce the anti-WMD norm than be remembered for major new policy recommendations. The report of the International Commission on Nuclear Non-Proliferation and Disarmament (ICNND) was more creative in trying to navigate its way through critical nuclear choices.[22] It integrates minimization of numbers, role and visibility of nuclear weapons in the short and medium term with their elimination in the long term; it bridges the gap between the NPT and post-NPT worlds by arguing for nuclear abolition to be enshrined in a universal, comprehensive, legally binding and verifiable nuclear weapons convention; it abandons the false distinction between the five NPT-licit NWS and the three non-NPT nuclear armed states (India, Israel, Pakistan), arguing that all eight belong in the same policy basket; and it strikes a balance between the desirability and inevitability of a move towards greater reliance on nuclear energy, on the one hand, and the safety, security and proliferation risks posed by increased nuclear power generation, on the other.

Blue ribbon international commissions seldom produce dramatic shifts in thinking. But, as the conduit for bringing ideas into intergovernmental forums, they do make a difference over the long term in various subtle and nuanced ways.[23] Scholars can be asked to join as commissioners or researchers. As Head of the federal government-funded Peace Research Centre, this author provided the background paper to the Canberra Commission on the case for a nuclear-weapon-free world.[24] Richard Falk of Princeton and Michael Ignatieff of Harvard were members of the independent commission that examined NATO intervention in Kosovo in 1999. Ignatieff, Gisèle Côté-Harper and Thakur were members of ICISS (the International Commission on Intervention and State Sovereignty), while Thomas G. Weiss was its research co-director. Stephen Stedman was the research director for the UN Secretary-General's High-level Panel on Threats, Challenges and Change in 2004. Scholars can also join practitioners to call for new commissions: the precursor to the Blix Commission on WMD was an op-ed written by Jayantha Dhanapala, UN Under-Secretary-General for Disarmament at the time, and Ramesh Thakur, Senior Vice Rector of the UN University (UNU) and UN Assistant Secretary-General at the time.[25]

With respect to institutional gaps, institutions in which norms and policies are housed include technical and material denial regimes like the Nuclear Suppliers Group (NSG); interdiction and enforcement regimes like the Proliferation

Security Initiative (PSI); ongoing negotiation and discussion arrangements like the Six Party talks on North Korea; and formal organizations like the IAEA, the OPCW and the Preparatory Commission for the CTBT Organization (CTBTO). Here scholars can study the effectiveness of design and identify facilitating or disabling conditions to explain successful or failed institutions. The actual creation and operation of the institutions is the preserve of practitioners. Thus researchers can explain what constitutes a nuclear-weapon-free zone (NWFZ) and explain why particular zones have been established and with what degree of success;[26] they can also debate the general proposition whether such zones serve any real purpose or are merely statements of good intentions; but the actual negotiations to create new zones can only be undertaken by officials. Similarly, scholars can identify implementation, compliance and enforcement gaps like the lack of verification machinery and compliance mechanisms for the disarmament obligations of the NPT, the lack of a credible and binding inspections regime for nonproliferation, and the lack of agreed criteria to assess proliferation threats. So too can former officials and government ministers constituted into an eminent persons panel and assisted by researchers identify various gaps and propose appropriate remedies.[27] But the task of filling the gaps has to be left to officials.

It is relatively easier to identify roles for scholars in the natural sciences. To promote arms control and disarmament, they can conduct research into managing the civilian nuclear fuel cycle, improving the physical security of nuclear material and facilities, verifying a fissile materials cut-off treaty (FMCT), and strengthening the Comprehensive Test Ban Treaty (CTBT).[28] Much of this can be done in advance in order to enhance the prospects of arms control and disarmament agreements. For example, the CTBTO has spent around one billion dollars over the last twelve years to build, operate and maintain the highly technical International Monitoring System that links 320 monitoring stations and 16 laboratories in nearly 90 countries. Its antecedents lie in the activities of the Group of Scientific Experts that was set up by the Geneva-based Conference on Disarmament and that developed and tested approaches to the seismic monitoring of nuclear test explosions from the mid-1970s onwards. Its work, undertaken even in the midst of the Cold War, was essential for laying the scientific groundwork for the CTBT negotiations.

Only the scientific community can identify the options and tradeoffs that will be required among levels of confidence, cost, complexity, vulnerability, uncertainties, adequacy and robustness of evidence, and the potential and limitations of technology. The Intergovernmental Panel on Climate Change (IPCC) provides one model for how the work of physical scientists can be communicated to and used by social scientists to study social, economic and political implications and policy requirements, despite the risks of 'politicization' of science. Norway's Foreign Minister has speculated about the creation of a matching Intergovernmental Panel on Nuclear Disarmament.[29] The two most prominent organizations of natural and health scientists acting as global pressure groups for arms control and disarmament are the Pugwash Conference and the International Physicians for the Prevention of Nuclear War (IPPNW), both of which have several national chapters and both are

Nobel Peace Laureates. Social scientists have to engage practitioners in one of the several more diffuse methods and forums discussed in this chapter.

A common mode of influencing public opinion and public policy is to become a public intellectual utilizing the growing media outlets to communicate one's views and prescriptions to the informed and engaged public. A regular column in the *New York Times* has given Paul Krugman, for example, a far larger readership than ever he could hope to have reached with his scholarly papers. To achieve public and policy impact, it is important that the op-eds be written for major national or international newspapers. The two global newspapers are the *Financial Times* and the *International Herald Tribune*.

In the annals of UN achievements, the author's biggest claim to fame might turn out to be publishing more than fifty op-eds for the *International Herald Tribune* as a serving senior official. Many were on the topic of nonproliferation and disarmament. Several of these attempted to clarify, explain and elucidate, while others were outright prescriptions. Were they influential? How do we measure impact? An article recommending adoption of the mine-ban treaty was published on the morning of the crucial vote on it at the Oslo conference in 1997.[30] Almost all countries would have settled on their national positions by then already; were even a few waverers brought back into the fold? An earlier article recommending an effort to trade a permanent Security Council seat for India's signature of the NPT was never even attempted.[31] On the other side, the accurate warning in 1996 that the effort to impose a test-ban treaty on India would be counter-productive was based more on a basic reading of Indian politics than prescience.[32]

As for practitioners reading what scholars have to say, desk officer-level national and international civil servants will follow the literature in their specialized areas of responsibility on a regular basis. In the case of arms control and disarmament, this includes *Arms Control Today*, *Bulletin of Atomic Scientists*, *Disarmament Diplomacy* published by the Acronym Institute in the UK, the *Disarmament Forum* published by the UN Institute for Disarmament Research (UNIDIR) in Geneva, and the *Nonproliferation Review* from the Monterey Institute of International Studies. These journals are important vehicles for scholars who want to communicate their research results, viewpoints and policy prescriptions to the policy community. Officials from the policy world are far less likely to read journals that focus solely on conceptual and theoretical debates, even if they are very highly regarded by the scholarly community itself. Thus *International Organization*, *International Security* and *International Studies Quarterly* are excellent outlets for publishing articles that will be read by serious scholars and enhance career advancement and reputation in academia, while *Foreign Affairs*, *Foreign Policy* and *The Washington Quarterly* – which avoid minutiae, acronyms and narrow debates conducted in the jargon of insiders – will reach a wider policy audience and help to make a difference in the world of practice.

The next few years

How we move forward in connecting scholars and practitioners can be discussed in the context of important changes in the theory and practice of diplomacy.[33] The typical international actors are states and the bulk of diplomacy involves relations among states directly, or between states, international organizations and other international actors. Yet we operate in a global environment vastly more challenging, complex and demanding today than a hundred years ago. As the world of diplomacy has changed from the older, exclusive and self-contained 'club' to the newer 'networked' model,[34] so the opportunities have multiplied for scholars to join and participate in the network at numerous points. Thus the modes, types and techniques of diplomacy include summit meetings among heads of state and government, shuttle diplomacy, Track Two diplomacy (unofficial and generally informal interaction between nongovernmental actors including NGOs, scholars, humanitarian organizations and former government officials), paradiplomacy (the use of private actors by states, for example personal representatives or envoys), multilateral diplomacy, celebrity diplomacy, public diplomacy, and conference diplomacy.

The different modes provide a variety of entry points for scholars interested in accessing and influencing the policy process. They can comprise the extensive networks that are created in the meticulous pre-summit preparations by national teams of diplomats and officials, most easily through think tank affiliations. They can be participants in Track Two diplomacy. In 1996, the Centre for Strategic and International Studies in Jakarta, the Stiftung Wissenschaft und Politik in Munich, and the Peace Research Centre in Canberra teamed up, under the sponsorship of the European Union and the governments of Germany and Australia, to organize a Track Two seminar on nonproliferation for the ASEAN Regional Forum (ARF). The seminar was held in Jakarta on 6–7 December and chaired jointly by Jusuf Wanandi, Winrich Kuehne and Ramesh Thakur from the three partner institutions. Its purpose was to discuss the challenge of nonproliferation of weapons of mass destruction in the Asia–Pacific region; the adequacy of the current available international and regional instruments for meeting the challenge; and measures that might be adopted to strengthen the barriers to proliferation and to encourage further disarmament.[35] Earlier, the Australian government had used the Peace Research Centre in background work for the successful negotiation of the Chemical Weapons Convention and also for the successful NPT Review and Extension Conference in 1995.

The Peace Research Centre was located in the Australian National University (ANU) but funded entirely by the federal government's Department of Foreign Affairs and Trade. This did not stop the Centre from advocating publicly for positions directly contrary to existing Australian policy. For example it was active in the public educational and advocacy campaign for a ban on antipersonnel landmines in the first half of the 1990s when Canberra strongly opposed the movement. It conducted seminars on the topic in parliament buildings and in July 1997, as Head of the Peace Research Centre, this author chaired the Canadian government-sponsored four-day regional seminar in Sydney on the anticipated Ottawa Treaty.[36] The largely civil society oriented seminar was given formal presentations by the Australian foreign ministry and the Australian defence forces opposed to the landmine ban, although in the end Australia did sign the treaty and implement its obligations.

International organizations have their own research units and many of these routinely involve scholars, sometimes recruited to join the organizations as officials, more commonly as consultants on project-specific contracts. The Peace and Governance Programme of UNU, for example, invited Christophe Carle, Stephen Cohen and Trevor Findlay to write chapters on South Asian nuclear issues and weapons of mass destruction.[37] It completed a major project in partnership with the New York-based International Peace Academy on the arms control implication of the 2003 Iraq War.[38] It would often bring back a selection of scholars after the completion of a project or on publication of the resulting book to briefing seminars in national, regional (e.g. Addis Ababa) or UN capitals (Geneva, New York). Its multi-partner project on the UN's role in regulating nuclear orders was completed in 2009.[39]

The main research body in the UN system charged with studying arms control and disarmament issues is the Geneva-based UNIDIR which maintains an active research and publications program. Its Director Patricia Lewis (who has since joined the Monterey Institute for International Studies[40]) and UNU Vice Rector Thakur wrote a joint article describing the complex system of the UN's role in nuclear arms control.[41] The UNU collaborated with the OPCW in a study examining the Chemical Weapons Convention[42] and worked with Under-Secretary-General Dhanapala in a joint China–UN arms control conference in Beijing in 2002.[43] The mantle of the UN University was useful in being able to write and publish articles relatively free of official control and vetting, including newspaper op-eds.[44]

Scholars can be asked to join governmental and intergovernmental advisory bodies, for example the UN Secretary-General's advisory group on disarmament. The author used to be a member of the Public Advisory Committee on Disarmament and Arms Control (PACDAC) in New Zealand, a statutory body to tender advice to the Minister for Disarmament, and of the National Consultative Committee on Peace and Disarmament which functioned as an advisory group to the Australian foreign minister. The German delegation to the 2010 NPT conference included Harald Mueller of the Frankfurt Peace Research Institute. All governments should tap into existing scholarly expertise by utilizing and expanding such structured opportunities for interaction between scholars and policymakers. This can be done ahead of the publication of official policy papers like the 2010 US Nuclear Posture Review or periodic defence white papers; in advance of international gatherings like the NPT five-year review conferences; and for briefing NGOs and citizens after such international gatherings, etc. Government departments often find it difficult to tolerate, let alone to encourage, contrarian thinking. To escape the policy rigidity of groupthink, they should sponsor and attend seminars and workshops on the pressing challenges of nuclear and disarmament with a diverse group of scholars, public intellectuals and officials attending in their personal capacity, much like the ARF Track Two seminar in 1996.

In turn, scholars should realize that, faced with time pressures and information overload, practitioners need policy-relevant advice with immediate urgency, shorn of confusing caveats and presented in clear and concise language and format. Practitioners are not and never will be interested in theories per se. It is up to scholars to link theories to actor behaviour and make policy recommendations on that basis to promote national security without endangering international security. And they will have to learn not to betray or abuse confidential information provided by such privileged access. Finally, professional bodies like the International Studies Association could also play their part by actively fostering joint scholar–practitioner panels at their annual conventions, including on the subject of nuclear arms control and disarmament.

Notes

* Originally published in *International Studies Review* 13:1 (2011): 34–45; reprinted by permission of Wiley–Blackwell.
1 Barry Buzan, *People, States and Fear* (Hemel Hempstead: Harvester/Wheatsheaf, 1982).
2 Pierre Allan and Kjell Goldmann, eds., *The End of the Cold War: Evaluating Theories of International Relations* (Amsterdam: Kluwer Law International, 1995).
3 *World Directory of Peace Research and Training Institutes* (Paris: UN Educational, Scientific and Cultural Organisation, 2000).
4 Matthew Evangelista, ed., *Peace Studies: Critical Concepts in Political Science* (London: Routledge, 2005); Paul Rogers and Oliver Ramsbotham, 'Then and Now: Peace Research – Past and Future', *Political Studies* 47:4 (1999): 740–54; Peter Wallensteen, ed., *Peace Research: Achievements and Challenges* (Boulder: Westview, 1988).
5 Walter Isard, *Understanding Conflict and the Science of Peace* (Cambridge, MA: Blackwell, 1992); Lester R. Kurtz, *Encyclopedia of Violence, Peace and Conflict* (Amsterdam: Academic Press, 2008).
6 John Baylis, James J. Wirtz and Colin S. Gray, *Strategy in the Contemporary World: An Introduction to Strategic Studies*, 3rd ed. (New York: Oxford University Press, 2010).
7 Johan Galtung, *Peace by Peaceful Means: Peace and Conflict, Development and Civilisation* (London: Sage, 1996).
8 Anders Boserup and Andrew Mack, *War without Weapons: Non-violence in National Defense* (New York: Shocken Books, 1975); Gene Sharp, *The Politics of Nonviolent Action* (Boston: Porter Sargent, 1973).
9 Rene Girard, 'Mimesis and Violence: Perspectives in Cultural Criticism', *Berkshire Review* 14 (1979): 9–19.
10 Walter Bryce Gallie, 'Essentially Contested Concepts', *Proceedings of the Aristotelian Society* 56 (1956): 167–220.
11 S. Neil MacFarlane and Yuen Foong Khong, *Human Security and the United Nations: A Critical History* (Bloomington: Indiana University Press, 2006), 6–9.
12 Kalevi J. Holsti, *War, the State, and the State of War* (Cambridge: Cambridge University Press, 1996).
13 Quoted in Håkan Wiberg, 'Peace Research: Past, Present and Future' (2005), http://www.uibk.ac.at/peacestudies/downloads/peacelibrary/peaceresearch.pdf. Published in Portuguese as 'Investigacao para a Paz: Passado, Presente e Future', *Revista Crítica de Ciências Sociais* 71 (June 2005), 6.
14 Ignatieff has since left Canadian politics and returned to academia at Harvard University.
15 Thomas G. Weiss and Ramesh Thakur, *Global Governance and the UN: An Unfinished Journey* (Bloomington: Indiana University Press, 2010).
16 John Lewis Gaddis, *The Long Peace: An Inquiry Into the History of the Cold War* (New York: Oxford University Press, 1987).
17 William C. Potter and Gaukhar Mukhatzhanova, 'Divining Nuclear Intentions: A Review Essay', *International Security* 33:1 (2008): 139–69.
18 Christopher Clary, 'Dr. Khan's Nuclear WalMart', *Disarmament Diplomacy* 76 (March/April 2004): 31–35.

34 *The nuclear debate*

19 Richard Price and Nina Tannenwald, 'Norms and Deterrence: The Nuclear and Chemical Weapons Taboos', in Peter J. Katzenstein, ed., *The Culture of National Security: Norms and Identity in World Politics* (New York: Columbia University Press, 1996): 114–52.
20 Canberra Commission, *Report of the Canberra Commission on the Elimination of Nuclear Weapons* (Canberra: Department of Foreign Affairs and Trade, 1996).
21 Hans Blix, *Weapons of Terror: Freeing the World of Nuclear, Biological and Chemical Arms* (Stockholm: WMD Commission Report, 2006).
22 ICNND, *Eliminating Nuclear Threats*. Report of the International Commission on Nuclear Non-Proliferation and Disarmament (Canberra: Department of Foreign Affairs and Trade, 2009).
23 Ramesh Thakur, Andrew F. Cooper and John English, eds., *International Commissions and the Power of Ideas* (Tokyo: United Nations University Press, 2005).
24 Ramesh Thakur, 'The Desirability of a Nuclear Weapon Free World', in Canberra Commission on the Elimination of Nuclear Weapons, *Background Papers* (Canberra: Department of Foreign Affairs and Trade, 1996): 74–88.
25 Jayantha Dhanapala and Ramesh Thakur, 'Let's get together against terrorism', *International Herald Tribune*, 4 June 2002.
26 Ramesh Thakur, ed., *Nuclear Weapons-Free Zones* (London/New York: Macmillan and St. Martin's Press, 1998).
27 HLP, *A More Secure World: Our Shared Responsibility*, Report of the High Level Panel on Threats, Challenges and Change (New York, United Nations, document A/59/565, 2004).
28 Royal Society, *Scientific Cooperation to Support Nuclear Arms Control and Disarmament* (London: Policy Document 03/10, March 2010).
29 J. Støre, 'Keynote Address to the 2008 Oslo Conference on Nuclear Disarmament', Oslo, Ministry of Foreign Affairs, Norway, 26 February 2008.
30 Ramesh Thakur, 'There's no need for weapons of slow-motion mass murder', *International Herald Tribune*, 17 September 1997.
31 Ramesh Thakur, 'Into the Security Council, out of the nuclear trap', *International Herald Tribune*, 1 February 1993.
32 'Without concrete disarmament on the part of the NWS, the world will slip back into real dangers of horizontal proliferation. So the choice is between progress and reversal, not between progress and the status quo': Thakur, 'Desirability of a Nuclear Weapon Free World', 85. 'Faced with US-led UN coercion, an isolated, sullen and resentful India is more likely to respond with an open nuclear programme, including a . . . series of nuclear tests': Ramesh Thakur, 'Nuclear India needs coaxing, not coercion', *Australian*, 6 September 1996.
33 R. P. Barston, *Modern Diplomacy*, 3rd ed (New York: Longman, 2006); G. R. Berridge, *Diplomacy: Theory and Practice*, 3rd ed (New York: Palgrave Macmillan, 2005); Christer Jönsson and Martin Hall, *Essence of Diplomacy* (New York: Palgrave Macmillan, 2005); Adam Watson, *Diplomacy: The Dialogue Between States* (New York: Routledge, 2004).
34 Jorge Heine, 'On the Manner of Practising the New Diplomacy', in Andrew F. Cooper, Brian Hocking and William Maley, eds., *Global Governance and Diplomacy: Worlds Apart* (Basingstoke: Palgrave MacMillan, 2008): 271–87.
35 Ramesh Thakur, ed., *Keeping Proliferation at Bay* (Jakarta: Centre for Strategic and International Studies, 1998).
36 Ramesh Thakur and William Maley, 'The Ottawa Convention on Landmines: A Landmark Humanitarian Treaty in Arms Control?' *Global Governance* 5:3 (1999): 273–302.
37 Christophe Carle, 'International Security in a Nuclear South Asia', in Ramesh Thakur and Oddny Wiggen, eds., *South Asia in the World: Problem Solving Perspectives on Security, Sustainable Development, and Good Governance* (Tokyo: United Nations University Press, 2004): 31–35; Stephen P. Cohen, 'Nuclear Weapons and Nuclear War in

South Asia: Unknowable Futures', in Thakur and Wiggen, eds., *South Asia in the World*: 39–57; Trevor Findlay, 'Weapons of Mass Destruction', in Edward Newman, Ramesh Thakur and John Tirman, eds., *Multilateralism Under Challenge? Power, International Order, and Structural Change* (Tokyo: United Nations University Press, 2006): 207–33.
38 Waheguru Pal Singh Sidhu and Ramesh Thakur, eds., *Arms Control After Iraq: Normative and Operational Challenges* (Tokyo: United Nations University Press, 2006).
39 Jane Boulden, Ramesh Thakur and Thomas G. Weiss, eds., *The United Nations and Nuclear Orders* (Tokyo: United Nations University Press, 2009).
40 Dr. Lewis is now with Chatham House in London.
41 Patricia Lewis and Ramesh Thakur, 'Arms control, disarmament and the United Nations', *Disarmament Forum* 1 (2004): 17–28.
42 Ramesh Thakur and Ere Haru, eds., *The Chemical Weapons Convention: Implementation Challenges and Opportunities* (Tokyo: United Nations University Press, 2006).
43 Ramesh Thakur, 'Defence, disarmament, and the United Nations', in *A Disarmament Agenda for the Twenty-first Century* (New York: United Nations Department for Disarmament Affairs, Occasional Papers No. 6, October 2002): 33–63.
44 Ramesh Thakur, *War in Our Time: Reflections on Iraq, Terrorism and Weapons of Mass Destruction* (Tokyo: United Nations University Press, 2007).

3 The nuclear debate*

It is a sobering reflection that an entire generation of people has grown up under the shadow of the mushroom cloud. Though some perhaps might dream of the wide blue skies beyond the cloud, for most people the nuclear reality has been an inescapable element of the strategic landscape. For over three decades, the majority of Americans and Europeans (we simply lack reliable information about the Chinese and Russians) have accepted nuclear deterrence as a proper and dependable cornerstone of Western security policies. Astonishingly, such a fundamental change in relations among different nations was put into place without serious public debate. Only in the 1980s has there been the sort of intensive and widespread call for justifying the strategy of nuclear deterrence that one would have expected at the start of the nuclear era. Today, not just a bunch of trendy intellectuals but a broad cross-section of concerned citizens have been scrutinizing nuclear policies closely and demanding answers from their governments as to the ethics, military necessity and political wisdom of constructing defence policies around 'the bomb'.

In this chapter I propose to develop the following arguments:

1. Nuclear weapons pose some genuine moral dilemmas, but political leaders cannot base their decisions solely upon ethical considerations;
2. The global nuclear balance is characterized by strategic parity or essential equivalence, rather than meaningful superiority by either side;
3. A nuclear war cannot be fought and won;
4. The need for controlling the arms race is urgent, but technical and political obstacles cannot be overcome easily.

Nuclear morality

Nuclear deterrence openly contemplates – indeed must be directly based on – the deliberate killing of people in the millions. In their famous pastoral letter of 3 May 1983, the Catholic Bishops of America expressed firm opposition to strategies of deliberate attack on large populations and strategies that would result in catastrophic loss of life as an 'unintended consequence' of weapons aimed at military targets. In the 'butchery of untold magnitude' caused by a nuclear war, it would not be very comforting to know that one had died an innocent victim of 'collateral damage'. (There is also something rather frightening about the way in which strategists talk of a nuclear war as a 'nuclear exchange', as though it was a commonplace transaction in the village market.)

The only goal of nuclear retaliation when deterrence has failed would be revenge. Many religions and moral systems have difficulty reconciling vengeful killings with proper conduct; the disproportionate and indiscriminate scale of nuclear retaliatory vengeance can surely not be reconciled with any self-respecting moral doctrine. Moreover, most of the people killed would be innocent noncombatants. Even Western leaders agree that in the Soviet bloc, ordinary citizens lack much say in the affairs of government. Indeed, Western political rhetoric has it that citizens behind the Iron Curtain are persecuted victims of their own governments. That being so, is it not immoral to visit nuclear punishment upon innocent people for the sins of their totalitarian leaders? And it is most certainly immoral to destroy peoples in neighbouring countries through radiation, and arrogant of the human race to destroy other species because we could not manage our own affairs.

In their thoughtful and weighty effort to apply religious and moral principles to nuclear weapons, the Catholic Bishops condemned nuclear war yet gave 'a strictly conditional moral acceptance of deterrence' in order to protect the independence and freedom of nations and peoples. The letter issued a profound challenge to contemporary US military policy and contributed to a delegitimization of nuclear doctrines. Its conditional acceptance of nuclear deterrence was consistent with Pope John Paul II's statement to the United Nations in 1982: 'In current conditions, "deterrence" based on balance, certainly not as an end in itself but as a step on the way toward a progressive disarmament, may still be judged morally acceptable'.[1] The conditions are more important than the fact of papal acceptability. Deterrence must be temporary and transient, pending but leading to progressive disarmament. It must also be 'based on balance', that is on parity or 'essential equivalence'. This does not require equality, let alone superiority, in every weapons category; it does require willingness to concede parity to the adversary as well. Fighting, winning or even prevailing in nuclear wars is therefore ruled out morally. Finally, the Pope argued that nuclear deterrence 'may still be judged morally acceptable' — meaning that it is not automatically nor always so.

The Catholic Bishops in 1983 similarly qualified acceptance of nuclear deterrence as a necessary evil with significant conditions. In particular even deterrence cannot evade the requirements of 'just war' doctrines. Thus deterrence must satisfy the principle of discrimination between combatants and noncombatants: civilians are immune to direct attacks. By this logic, the atomic bombing of Hiroshima and Nagasaki in 1945 was immoral, even if — and this is not a trivial 'if' — the bombing avoided still greater civilian deaths by shortening the war. A smaller evil cannot be justified by a greater good: it is still evil, and killing innocent noncombatants is murder. Secondly, deterrence to be moral must follow the rule of proportionality. The first requirement forbids the targeting of populations as nuclear hostages. The second places limits on the extent to which installations can be targeted, for even unintended damage may not justly exceed the evil to be avoided or the good desired to be achieved. Contemporary American targeting of 'military related' Soviet industry and utilities would inflict death and misery on millions of Soviet citizens as 'collateral' damage, and is therefore immoral.

Nuclear deterrence also poses a number of other moral challenges to our conscience. Deterrence rests on the threat to wage nuclear war. If a particular act is evil, the threat to do it must also be immoral; if nuclear war is evil, then threatening and preparing for such war is also morally wrong. 'Threaten No Evil' as a moral stricture is written into the United Nations Charter: 'All members shall refrain from the *threat or use* of force' (Article 2:4; emphasis added). The United Nations may not amount to much as an organization for world peace. Its Charter however does express the global consensus about certain ethical values and norms of behaviour in international relations.

Deterrence based on hitting population centres ignores too the moral distinction between ends and means. The position seems analogous to the taking of hostages by terrorists as a means of protecting themselves against capture, or in order to obtain other nefarious goals. We would rightly consider it immoral for the government to deter murder by threatening to kill any murderer's children. If this is not acceptable as proper public policy, why should nuclear deterrence be acceptable as proper foreign policy?

A related means – ends dilemma concerns one's own society and people. The whole ideological conflict is supposed to be about freedom versus totalitarianism. Those entrusted with the command of nuclear weapons – not just the military brass, but including also top civilian command around the president – must make compromises with their conscience in order to live in comfort despite holding the world to ransom. Those who have sacrificed their human values to masochistic conceptions of tough decisions in times of crisis are not likely to be impressed by the 'sentimental rubbish' of liberal humane values. At the same time, the very destructiveness of nuclear weapons means that a garrison state will be created rather than risks accepted of such weapons falling into criminal hands. This being so, what are the values for the defence of which Western society is being asked to make fundamental moral compromises? Nor are moral qualms stilled with the knowledge that the ruling elites of the nuclear powers, including the United States, build deep shelters and airborne command posts for themselves while offering their citizens as hostages. All this in the name of a policy supposed to guard citizens against enemy attack, a policy enunciated and devised by officials bearing the primary responsibility for protecting their citizens. What sort of morality can allow the privileged elite to be sheltered while leaving their wards unprotected?

Technological and military reality imposes yet another constraint on nuclear morality. Because the decision to retaliate must be instantaneous if deterrence has failed, there is no time for ordinary citizens or responsible officials to make the transition from nuclear deterrence to war only after thoughtful moral reflection. In other words, deterrence places a premium upon immorally casual decisions in its time of greatest need, and therefore amounts to moral abdication. Given the steadily diminishing lead-times before retaliatory weapons must be unleashed under automated launch on warning strategies, one may well ask: what price such computer-based morality?

The final moral difficulty involves the relationship between nuclear weapons and world poverty. It has been argued that policies of nuclear deterrence have entailed such heavy expenditure on arms that they amount to stealing from the poor. The statistics on the arms race are staggering. The World Health Organization (WHO) spent less than $100mn in its ten-year campaign to rid the world of smallpox; the money would not buy even one modern strategic bomber. Alternatively, the price of one aircraft carrier at $500mn would enable WHO to eradicate leprosy, malaria, trachoma and yaws. Funds are scarce to help 570mn malnourished and 1500mn people who lack adequate medical services, but the world can afford $35bn every year for trafficking in arms. The United Nations reckons that just one fifth of the world's annual military expenditures could abolish world hunger by the year 2000.

UN experts have identified military spending as an obstacle to economic growth. The arms race and development are therefore in a competitive relationship. Since 1945, 5–8 percent of the world's output has been allocated to the military. Yet the average military product is estimated to be twenty times as research intensive as the average consumer item for domestic use. A high defence outlay depresses economic growth directly by diverting investment funds and indirectly by diverting research and development skills and efforts. This is particularly true for developing countries whose need for external inputs like capital, trade and technology is usurped by military outlays. There has even been a proposal to increase financial flows to developing countries by adopting a 'disarmament dividend approach'. Under such a scheme, budgetary savings resulting from disarmament measures would be placed in a special fund for development. While the arms race imposes economic costs on everyone, it is most severe on the poorer countries and is therefore immoral in obstructing the alleviation of harsh miseries for millions of fellow human beings.

The above discussion presents the substantial moral doubts about nuclear weapons, war and strategy. Yet the moral dimension can be troubling in a second sense of being difficult to apply. The pursuit of morality, while wholly admirable in an individual, can still be indefensible in a statesman. The prophet can be wedded to absolute truth, the sage can devote his life to the search for ethical wisdom. Political leaders, however, are required to act according to political wisdom – not for them the search for truthful or ethical conduct as the sole or even dominant criterion. Nor am I easy at the prospect of world peace being dependent on 150 heads of government motivated by religiously fired morality.

This is not to assert that political leaders must actively pursue immoral courses of action. Rather, they must first accept the political realities of the world and their own country and then evaluate competing demands of moral and political choices within this framework. On occasions the moral issues themselves will be ambivalent and overlapping. Consider the distinction between nuclear war and nuclear weapons. Even if we are all agreed that nuclear war is evil, it does not follow that the nuclear weapons are themselves evil. (Can instruments ever be evil or good in themselves?) Also, determination of evil conduct must take place in relation to intent. The goal of nuclear deterrence is not to wage war, but to avert war and deter aggressive behaviour by the other side. The intention is not, therefore, immoral, and the consequences are partly determined by the actions of the other side. Conversely, if total unilateral nuclear disarmament led to the use of nuclear weapons by the other side, then one could plausibly argue that disarmament led to evil results. If nuclear war is evil, and if nuclear weapons on both sides help to deter their use in war by either side, then of course nuclear weapons and deterrence become strategies to combat evil.

Atomic weapons have been used only twice under conditions of war, at Hiroshima and Nagasaki. In both instances, an atomic power used the weapons against a non-atomic country. Considerations of a new morality or international reactions were insufficient to stop the Americans from using this terribly destructive bomb; why should they succeed in imposing unilateral restraint in future? But if the Japanese had possessed atomic weaponry too, the American government would have had greater cause to pause before escalating to the atomic level. The argument can be extended to conventional warfare too. In all the conflicts and killings since the Second World War, the two superpowers have successfully avoided a direct war between themselves. It is possible that the fear of uncontrolled escalation to nuclear horrors severely inhibits adventurous tendencies to risk direct confrontation. Of the several million deaths in battle since the Second World War, not one has been caused by a nuclear warhead. This is not a statistic to be lightly dismissed.

Yet another dilemma confronting the leadership of a nuclear power is how to reconcile the immorality of fighting a nuclear war with the acceptability of nuclear deterrence. Deterrence to be credible must convince the opponent that nuclear weapons will be used when put to the test. The threat to use nuclear weapons therefore needs to be backed up by contingency planning and preparations. Only a very small handful of policymakers could be privy to the secret that declaratory policy – to use nuclear weapons – was contrary to the operational policy. But even here leakage or espionage could wreck the policy over time. Nor would the public's conscience be assuaged, since one's own public is necessarily being duped by the declaratory policy. In addition, with increasing automaticity in nuclear planning, the decision to use nuclear weapons could well pass into the hands of leaders below the threshold of awareness of non-use in operational circumstances. Conversely, a country cannot possibly underwrite nuclear deterrence with an open policy of not using them. Nuclear weapons lose all deterrent power if it is known in advance that they will not be used, although paradoxically they still retain ultimate usability. A policy of 'possession without use' can thus easily be parodied or ridiculed as a policy of 'warmongering but no war'.

Nuclear balance and deterrence

In order to understand the military balance between the nuclear powers, it is first necessary to grasp the significant military changes brought about by nuclear weapons. The death and damage inflicted on Hiroshima on 6 August 1945 was comparable in scale to the destruction visited upon Dresden, Hamburg and Tokyo during the Second World War. But there was one important difference: Hiroshima was destroyed by a single bomb. In the American strategic arsenal today, the smallest nuclear warhead is still twice as powerful as the bomb dropped on Hiroshima; a single Trident submarine has enough arms to obliterate every Soviet city with a population of 100,000 or more.

The enormous destructiveness of nuclear weapons has produced four major changes in military strategy. First, modern delivery systems mean that there is no protection against nuclear bombs. On their most successful day in defending London against German 'buzz bombs' in the Second World War, on 28 August 1944, the British shot down 97 of 101 rockets. Had the four bombs that got away been nuclear, London would be a historical curiosity of rubble. The only defence against nuclear weapons is to be certain of destroying every enemy missile and bomber. Such certainty is not available today nor likely in the foreseeable future.

Second, nuclear weapons have not just made old fashioned defence impossible, they have also destroyed the gallantry of olden days which pitted soldier against soldier and left noncombatants alone if not in peace. The historical trend towards blurring the line between military and civilian sectors, already in evidence in the two world wars, has been completed by nuclear weapons. It is now possible to destroy the enemy society without defeating or even engaging enemy forces. While strategists bicker among themselves as to whether civilian populations should be primary or unintentional targets, the fact remains that civilians are the major targets of nuclear weapons.

Third, the destructiveness of nuclear weapons and the speed of their delivery systems mean that wars will no longer be protracted affairs. Where conventional wars can go on for years, the most important lines in a nuclear tragedy will be the opening words of the first act. Nuclear war could be over in days or even hours, denying leaders a chance to think again and change their minds. The final consequence results from the third fact as well. Because of the speed of nuclear war, a country cannot afford, as it could in the past, to mobilize fully only after or with the imminent onset of hostilities. Nuclear forces have to be in a state of constant readiness at full strength. Some analysts have argued that the cumulative impact of the four changes has been to make nuclear weapons devoid of any military use whatsoever; their only purpose can be deterrence.

Deciphering the strategic equation between the Western and Soviet alliances is one of the great pastimes of our era. Most of the people with specialist knowledge in the area are government employees, so their public contribution is made as part of partisan polemic rather than objective assessment. Of the few specialists who do not work for government, Soviet experts dare not dissent from the party line. Independent Western analysts who care to question their own side's official stance also risk a measure of denigration and denial of privileges flowing from access to those in power. Beyond the problem of expertise, there are difficulties arising from the lack of symmetry between the elements which make up the strategic equation: weapons category, technological quality, numbers, accuracy, lethality, geographic imperatives, and security interests. Because the two sides are not symmetrical, it is always possible to pick a category of weapons in which one side is superior to the other.

In the confrontation between the two superpowers in intercontinental nuclear weapons, the numbers involved are not in serious dispute, but there is considerable controversy over how best to interpret the numbers. Both powers declare their own purpose to be defensive while accusing the other of trying to achieve superiority or first strike capability. The numbers game can provide only a crude estimate of the military balance. Several further points should be noted.

First, the number of nuclear weapons and the sophistication of delivery systems have increased dramatically since the Second World War. In the 1950s, US warheads numbered less than 2,000, while the Soviets had fewer than 500 until 1965. Today by contrast the two superpowers have 9,000–10,000 intercontinental warheads each. Second, the relative balance between the two superpowers has changed enormously. In the 1950s, the US was generally invulnerable to Soviet attack; in the 1960s, the US still enjoyed nuclear superiority; since the 1970s, the most characteristic feature of the nuclear equation has been strategic parity. Third, the introduction of ballistic missiles in the 1960s degraded defensive capability even further. The fact of survivable ballistic forces on both sides means that both the Soviet Union and the United States are now vulnerable to second strike retaliation.

Fourth, given the numbers involved in the 1980s, all claims of superiority and inferiority should be treated with scepticism. Both sides have a huge margin of overkill. The Soviets with more launchers can deliver a greater megatonnage on the Americans, but the Americans have more strategic nuclear warheads. The accuracy of strategic missiles has increased tenfold over the last two decades, from 1000 metres in the 1960s (meaning half the missiles launched at a particular target would land within 1000 metres of it) and 500 metres in the 1970s, to 100 metres in the 1980s.

Fifth, the Soviet strategic force is relatively more vulnerable, whereas the American forces are more evenly balanced. Reflecting the continental interests of the Soviet Union in contrast to maritime US interests, 72 percent of the Soviet strategic force conglomerate is land-based and hence theoretically vulnerable (but more accurate). The Americans deploy half their strategic warheads on relatively invulnerable submarines, while Moscow has less than a quarter on its noisy (that is easier to pick up on sonar detectors) and comparatively vulnerable submarines. The Soviets have more concentrated industrial complexes than the Americans, which means that the US needs fewer warheads to achieve equivalent destruction. The Soviets lead in launchers and destructive power, and the Americans in warheads and payload.

Sixth, the US leads in lethality because of greater technological accuracy. Accuracy is more important than megatonnage, because a doubling of accuracy has the same lethal effect on targets as an eightfold increase in yield or explosive weight. American strategic missiles are a lot more accurate than their Soviet counterparts because of superiority in satellite-assisted and on-board computerized guidance systems. Any improvements in the already superior Western accuracy technologies must therefore be matched by disproportionate Soviet increases in megatonnage. Seventh, the US strategic force is in a greater state of readiness. At any given time, only 14 percent of Soviet strategic missile submarines are ready at their firing locales, as compared to 60 percent of American ones.[2]

Eighth, the Soviet Union is at a great geographical disadvantage vis-à-vis the United States. It lies in the middle of the world's biggest landmass and lacks adequate access to the oceans. It must contend with many more potential enemies in its immediate neighbourhood, its consciousness heightened by historical memories of major invasions and wars. The Soviets are not impressed with US claims that geographical handicaps are offset by proximity to Europe; they are much more inclined to see themselves as being flanked by antagonistic nuclear powers on three fronts. Finally two US allies, Britain and France, have modest nuclear capabilities. The Soviet Union lacks any ally with nuclear capability. (Given the nature of Soviet relations, there is always the danger that an East European country with nuclear capability would slip out of the Soviet bloc alliance.) The United States is prepared to station medium range missiles in Europe which can threaten Soviet command and control centres with minimal warning. An analogous deployment of Soviet missiles in Cuba or Nicaragua would arouse the worst of American bellicosity.

From MAD to NUTS

For all the destructiveness of nuclear weapons, nevertheless, and contrary to public mythology, wars have not been made obsolete. Indeed since the Second World War the number of people estimated to have died as a result of international conflicts and civil wars is twenty million. This belies the proposition that the advent of nuclear weapons means that war, far from being a continuation of policy by other means, is in fact the breakdown of policy resulting in mutual annihilation. Nuclear weapons have not deprived wars and the threat of wars of all political utility. Most international conflicts involve non-nuclear states, e.g. Iran and Iraq. Several of the more important conflicts of our time have seen non-nuclear nations fighting nuclear states, e.g. the United States in Vietnam and the Soviet Union in Afghanistan. The use of nuclear weapons in such wars is limited by the fact that their political and moral costs would be greater than the desired military and political objectives. Finally, in theory, even nuclear powers can engage in wars between themselves without using nuclear weapons. In practice however this has not occurred, not the least because of the danger that wars once started are difficult to keep limited to pre-determined levels of intensity – they tend to acquire a self-perpetuating logic of their own.

Despite the difficulties of military usability, therefore, nuclear weapons can still serve certain functions. The Harvard team identified seven goals of nuclear policy:

1 Basic Deterrence – to deter a Soviet nuclear attack upon the United States;
2 Extended Deterrence – to deter a conventional or nuclear attack on American allies by sheltering them under the US strategic umbrella;

3 Crisis Stability – to reduce incentives for either side to strike first in an international crisis;
4 War Fighting – to defeat conventional or nuclear aggression against the United States or its allies if deterrence fails, and to minimize damage;
5 War Termination – to end conventional or nuclear war if deterrence fails, with least damage to allied security interests;
6 Counter Deterrence – to prevent nuclear coercion of the United State and its allies;
7 Bargaining Chip – to provide support for US and allied negotiating strategies in arms control discussions.[3]

Each of these purposes places its own requirements on type and level of nuclear forces. Not all the requirements can be fully met and not all are consistent with one another. In addition, the United States must constantly keep to the fine line between nuclear forces that are useable enough to deter Soviet attack but not so useable that they invite a preemptive Soviet strike or tempt American commanders into launching them against the wishes of policymakers. The last worry has increased because of the seemingly greater emphasis placed upon goal (4), namely war fighting, under President Ronald Reagan's crusade against the Soviet Union. The Soviets do not have a military program that threatens the core of the US retaliatory capability. Reagan however is feared to have initiated a nuclear program directed at Soviet force survival prospects. Ironically, 'fightability' and 'prevailability' in nuclear war formed part of official Soviet doctrine and preparations in the 1960s. Such pronouncements were used to devastating effect by the US opponents of SALT II in the 1970s, just as official Soviet policy changed to believing that there will be no victors in a nuclear war.

A greater cause of the shift from MAD (Mutual Assured Destruction) to NUTS (Nuclear Utilization Theories or Nuclear Utilization Target Selection) is precisely the problem of nuclear weapons being militarily non-useable in Europe. The cornerstone of American foreign policy in the postwar period has been guaranteeing European security through extended deterrence. Nuclear weapons were to be substitutes for financial and manpower sacrifices considered politically impossible in Europe and they were to compensate for alleged Soviet superiority in conventional forces. Under the Eisenhower administration, the policy of massive retaliation envisaged that conventional forces in Europe would merely conduct a holding operation against a Soviet attack until nuclear strikes defeated the aggressor. In other words, the policy was that nuclear weapons would definitely be used in response to a Soviet attack in Europe.

The Kennedy administration replaced the policy of massive retaliation with that of flexible response where the use of nuclear weapons would be 'late and limited'. Their primary role was to deter a Soviet initiation of nuclear war and they were to be used by the West only as a weapon of last resort. The architect of flexible response, Robert McNamara, now argues that the policy has been rendered non-credible by Soviet achievement of parity in strategic and intermediate range forces. The scale of devastation that Soviet retaliatory strikes can inflict upon the United States makes it 'difficult to imagine any US President, under any circumstances, initiating a strategic strike except in retaliation against a Soviet nuclear strike'. In short, with 'huge survivable arsenals on both sides, strategic nuclear weapons have lost whatever military utility may once have been attributed to them'.[4] The only purpose of nuclear weapons, therefore, is to deter the other side from using them first. This takes away the credibility of US threats of retaliating against conventional Soviet aggression in Europe with nuclear weapons. To strengthen the credibility of its threat, the United States has built into the European situation an element of unpredictability and uncontrollability.

The global balance is maintained by deterrence, which depends upon an absolute non-use of nuclear weapons. The European balance is said to depend upon useable nuclear weapons. The chances are that a nuclear war if it occurs will be deliberate rather than accidental. There is always a statistical probability, nevertheless, that we could be destroyed by a nuclear war which no one intended to take place. The more the numbers of nuclear weapons in existence, the wider the area of their deployment, and the longer the chain of command and control over them, the greater is the probability of an accidental nuclear war. Such probability is higher during times of crisis, when the normal checks and balances could fail to work. In the tense 10–30 minutes flight time of a missile, both sides are required to analyze the flood of incoming information quickly. Some of the information could be wrong, some will be ambiguous, some misleading – but all must be processed before the point of 'use them or lose them' is reached. These moments of panic and confusion are clearly a recipe for a nuclear war by accident or at least without intent.

The probability of unauthorized use of nuclear weapons in peace-time is supposedly reduced by PAL (Permissive Action Link) codes. Their reliability is doubly undermined by the requirements that they must be 'hair trigger' responsive to political direction in order to strengthen enemy belief that nuclear weapons will be used, and that the codes will likely be released in times of tension (just when restrictions on access are most needed) to low-level commanders with operational control over nuclear weapons.

The Kennedy–McNamara strategy of flexible response was based upon nuclear retaliation in the last resort against Soviet conventional aggression in Europe. The policy was said to be credible because of the knowledge that American strategic superiority allowed the use of nuclear weapons to be limited to Europe and controlled in intensity, scope and duration. The achievement of Soviet strategic parity wrecked the policy of flexible response. The American policy now therefore is to threaten Moscow with the knowledge that because of lax American nuclear practices, a battlefield commander in Europe could use nuclear weapons on his own and that nuclear war so started could well get out of control and escalate to all out nuclear war. In other words, Soviet leaders must base their decisions not on the irrationality of US policy, but on battlefield realities and associated dangers of escalation where there is no 'firebreak' built into the nuclear equation. The NATO decision of December 1979 to deploy Pershing II and cruise missiles in Europe must be understood in this light. As if this was not discomforting enough, yet another disquieting element is the fact that the Soviet response to battlefield uncontrollability by NATO is to dismantle their own firebreaks. Thus Moscow has promised that deployment of the newer missiles will lead them into a 'launch on warning' disposition of nuclear forces in order to ensure their safety.

Reducing NATO's preparedness for conventional war is an adverse military consequence of Eurocentric NUTS. A more political consequence with implications for military defence is its divisiveness. It has been a most contentious policy from the beginning, dividing both the Western alliance as a whole and individual nations within the alliance. One of the great truths about nuclear weapons in general is that they terrify the enemy rather more than they comfort the possessors. Nuclear war fighting doctrines under Reagan have managed to terrify friends and foe alike with equal impartiality.

Proponents and defenders of NUTS argue that they are no more interested in fighting nuclear wars than proponents of MAD are interested in assuring mutual destruction. The debate rather concerns the best means of assuring deterrence, not the acceptability of nuclear war. Non-Americans might be forgiven for feeling happier when both the superpowers are equally deterred from contemplating the use of nuclear weapons.

Arms control or arms race?

It will be clear from the above discussion that the size of strategic forces on both sides makes the nuclear balance insensitive to minor changes in numbers of warheads or weapons systems. But a major imbalance in particular categories of weapons systems can be destabilizing. When faced with a military threat from an enemy, we can choose to respond by matching that threat. But there is an alternative, namely, to reduce and constrain the threat. Arms control measures are means of trying to constrain reciprocal threats. Unfortunately, the typical modern government displays a marked imbalance in its bureaucratic allotments to military defence and arms control. For example, the annual budget for the US Arms Control and Disarmament Agency (ACDA) is less than the cost of two F-16 fighter aircrafts.

The bureaucratic imbalance is further reinforced in the United States by a constitutional one. An American administration seeking increases in military spending must carry a majority in Congress with it. An American president who negotiates a complex and difficult arms control agreement with the Soviet Union must have the treaty ratified by a two-thirds majority in the Senate. In effect a Senate minority representing less than a third of US voters has the constitutional power to block ratification. Considering the diversity of interests represented in the US political process, obtaining a blocking minority in the Senate is not terribly difficult. Conversely, attempts to accommodate all such interest groups can seriously erode the credibility of arms limitation treaties. Certainly the history of US – Soviet arms negotiations since the Strategic Arms Limitation Treaty (SALT I) was signed in 1972 indicates that arms control efforts would have been substantially different in outcome had US presidents not been hampered by the pervasive fear of a Senate veto.

Arms control measures can contribute to peace and security in many different ways. The most prominent suggestions in the 1980s have been, in Europe, for regional nuclear disarmament and, in the United States, for unilateral freeze on nuclear weapons. Other possibilities include partial agreements (e.g. no atmospheric testing), tacit agreements (e.g. acting as if SALT II were in force even without its formal ratification), and stabilizing measures. Notable progress has been made since the Cuban missile crisis, with such agreements as the Partial Test Ban Treaty (1963), the Outer Space Treaty (1967), the Treaty of Tlatelolco (1967), the Non-Proliferation Treaty (1968), the Sea Bed Treaty (1971) and the Biological Weapons Convention (1972), as well as the SALT treaties. Good examples of stabilizing measures include the US – Soviet Nuclear Accidents Agreement of 1971, which provides for immediate notification of a nuclear accident or detection of unidentified objects by missile warning systems; the US – Soviet 1973 agreement on the prevention of nuclear war; the Document on Confidence Building Measures of 1975 which requires advance notification of major military exercises in Europe; and the Franco – Soviet and Anglo – Soviet Nuclear Accidents Agreements of 1976 and 1977 respectively, modelled on the US – Soviet one.

The value of arms control agreements can be measured against three criteria of stability: deterrence stability, that is do they enhance the credibility of retaliatory capability in order to deter risky adventures in foreign policy; crisis stability, that is do they diminish temptations to launch a first strike in times of great tension; and arms race stability, that is do they dampen the possibility of sudden dramatic changes in the relative military balance through weapons development. If we consider the motorway analogy, a generally obeyed traffic code ensures a smoother flow of vehicles with a diminished risk of accident. A highway code thus seeks to regulate traffic behaviour and make it more predictable, but does not eliminate it.

The potential for arms control agreements is limited by two factors, one technical, the other political. First, because of the mutual suspicion and distrust between the two superpowers, only those arms control agreements will be negotiated and ratified that are independently verifiable. Moscow and Washington will not rely upon each other's good faith; they require 'hard evidence' that cheating is not possible. Development of sophisticated verification technology in the 1960s, e.g. photoreconnaissance satellites, made it possible to negotiate SALT I. The achievement of SALT I was in turn limited to the technology of verification, such as delivery vehicles big enough to be seen from space, e.g. intercontinental ballistic missile (ICBM) launchers. Because of the importance of verification in sustaining confidence in the agreement, both sides promised not to interfere with each other's surveillance systems.

Technology marches on. Its march brings improved means of verification, so that weapons that lay beyond detection in the past will become verifiable in the future. But the march of technology has also meant that the arms race takes place in improving weapons capability rather than numbers, e.g. in accuracy. This complicates arms control negotiations. For example, cruise missiles present a special challenge to verification because they are so small and can easily be changed from conventional to nuclear warheads. The same difficulty arises with the triple-warhead

SS-20 missiles deployed by the Soviet Union in Eastern Europe. The intermediate range (4,000km) missiles are mobile and can be converted into an intercontinental 9,500km range missile simply by adding a booster rocket.

This is the stuff of which arms control negotiators' nightmares are made. Rapid advances in weapons technology are quickly blurring long-established distinctions between tactical, theatre and strategic nuclear weapons. At the same time, 'mini-nukes' or small nuclear weapons with yields around 1kt are eroding the 'firebreak' distinction between nuclear and conventional weapons. Let us take a specific example of verification difficulties. A freeze on all nuclear weapons systems requires procedures to verify the development, production, testing and deployment of about a hundred kinds of weapons and delivery systems, both offensive and defensive, across all levels of tactical, theatre and strategic forces. Such verification procedures must: (1) be devised; (2) be negotiated within the military – foreign policy bureaucracies of the two superpowers; (3) be negotiated between the two superpowers; (4) be ratified by them, which involves a major political battle to avoid a one-third Senate veto in the United States; and (5) they must then come into force in time to stop the arms race. The last requirement is necessary to avoid the agreement being technologically obsolete at birth or in infancy, and places a premium upon quick negotiation; the first four requirements highlight the difficulties involved in securing an agreement, and indicate elaborate, extensive and time-consuming negotiations.

At each stage, moreover, negotiators are required to make two difficult judgements. Absolute verification is impossible, so people must settle for 'reasonable' procedures. Negotiators must therefore decide, firstly, the likelihood of being able to detect different kinds of cheating. They must also assess, secondly, the risks to national security of different kinds of violation which escape detection. Risks of low-probability detection and high damage to security will not be acceptable. Risks of high-probability detection and low damage security must be taken, for the risks of an unchecked arms race are greater.

The technical hurdle to arms control agreements is thus verification negotiability. The political obstacle is the state of superpower relations. Throughout human history, arms races have reflected as well as shaped conflict between political systems. The SALT accord was made possible because of the prevailing climate of detente, and in turn contributed to a further relaxation of international tension.

Unfortunately, the United States and the Soviet Union had different perceptions of and interests in detente. As the differences began to re-emerge in the late 1970s, relations between the superpowers once again cooled down. American policy was hesitant and confusing after its retreat from Vietnam. Uncertain of its willingness and ability to continue playing a global role, the United States was caught off guard by the rapid shifts in local balance and diplomatic alignments across the African landscape, unsettled by the OPEC (Organization of the Petroleum Exporting Countries) grip on the nerves of the wealth of nations, and puzzled by inability to grasp the sudden resurgence of Islam within traditional frames of reference. The broad anxieties were matched by American suspicions of specific Soviet advances around the world. Moscow refused substantive concessions on human rights in the Helsinki agreements, transported Cuban expeditionary troops to Angola and Ethiopia, pressed ahead with advances in its nuclear weapons armoury, and seemed to be engaged in a relentless drive to encircle the Persian Gulf and its critical oil reserves, the 'crescent of crisis'.

The Soviet invasion of Afghanistan helped to crystallize a searching re-examination of the Carter administration's assumptions on foreign policy. In the 1980s, events such as insurgency in Central America, a growing Cuban role in Grenada, and the Soviet shooting down of a South Korean commercial airplane have served to confirm the Reagan image of the Soviet Union as the locus of all international evil.

Unease on the American side at the steady breakdown of detente has been matched by Soviet anger at provocative American strutting astride the world stage. President Jimmy Carter's trumpeting of human rights was seen by suspicious Soviet authorities as direct encouragement to the only opposition movement in their jurisdiction. American policy in the Middle East underwent puzzling changes, to the detriment of Soviet interests and the exclusion of any Soviet role. Washington was guilty of a more damaging sin of commission in the manner in which it played the China card. As architect of Carter's China policy, National Security Adviser Zbigniew Brzezinski appeared eager and impatient to intimidate the Kremlin with it. Finally, the entire arms control process had ground to a halt by the end of 1979, much to the evident dismay of Soviet leaders.

The deterioration of the Soviet international security environment accelerated under the Reagan presidency in the 1980s. Convinced of Reagan's malignancy, the Kremlin leaders have been alarmed at perceived American efforts to isolate and vilify the Soviet Union while denying it equality as a superpower. Reagan's military budgets forebode plans to alter the balance of global strategic forces as well as the European nuclear balance. The deployment of cruise and Pershing missiles in Europe is one of the most serious military setbacks to Soviet interests in recent years; the post-Vietnam fetters on US military action were thrown off to rousing popular acclaim in Reagan's invasion of Grenada; the Soviet strategic retreat in the Middle East after the Israeli invasion of Lebanon in 1982 was followed by the introduction of US marines and other NATO troops to Beirut; and US efforts to destabilize Nicaragua continue virtually unimpeded. Confronted with these multiple assaults upon their security – political interests, Soviet leaders appear to have concluded by the end of 1983 that 'appeasement' of Reagan's militarism would lead to disaster as it did with Hitler, and that efforts to improve relations with a Reagan-ruled USA were futile. So they withdrew from serious arms control talks.

In short, arms control cannot be separated from political problems in US – Soviet relations. Even while arms control agreements would improve political relations, the achievement of such agreements is also hostage to a moderation in tense relations. Peaceful relations make it possible to control the arms race more than the other way round. Soviet – American dialogue and agreements in the 1960s and 1970s built up a structure of cooperation which embodied the world's hopes for an avoidance of nuclear war. As the process of detente ground to a halt by the end of the 1970s and suffered reverses in the 1980s, the fruits of earlier cooperation began to decay and the two superpowers abandoned their postures as responsible managers of the world order. There are of course other sources of disorderly tendencies. But it is also true that, as the superpowers reconstructed a structure of confrontation, they lost virtually all claim to be regarded as the nuclear trustees for mankind: the circle of countries that still regard them as the 'great responsibles' has been a steadily narrowing one in the 1980s.

Notes

* Originally published in Ramesh Thakur, *In Defence of New Zealand: Foreign Policy Choices in the Nuclear Age* (Boulder, CO: Westview Press, 2nd Edition, 1986): 7–40. Reprinted by permission.
1 Quoted by Bruce M. Russett, 'Ethical Dilemmas of Nuclear Deterrence', *International Security* 8 (Spring 1984), 41.
2 Carl G. Jacobsen, 'MAD or NUTS?' *International Perspectives* (March/April 1983), 17.
3 Harvard Nuclear Study Group, *Living with Nuclear Weapons* (Cambridge MA.: Harvard University Press, 1983), chapter 7.
4 Robert S. McNamara, 'The Military Role of Nuclear Weapons', *Foreign Affairs* (Fall 1983), 67–68. McNamara was US Secretary of Defense, 1961–68.

4 Envisioning nuclear futures*

The paradox of war and peace is a constant refrain in human history. The incidence of war is as pervasive as the wish for peace is universal. The use and control of force, and so acquiring control over others, has preoccupied the minds of rulers and scholars alike since time immemorial. But so too have some of the most charismatic and influential personalities in human history – from Gautam Buddha and Jesus Christ to Mahatma Gandhi – dwelt upon the renunciation of force and the possibility of eliminating it from human relationships. At any given time, most countries are at peace and long to keep it so. Yet most are also ready to go to war if necessary. Only a few, however, have chosen to go down the ruinous path of acquiring and deploying nuclear weapons.

The tit-for-tat nuclear tests of May 1998 destroyed the Indian summer of complacency induced by the indefinite extension of the Non-Proliferation Treaty (NPT) in May 1995 and the adoption of the Comprehensive Test Ban Treaty (CTBT) in September 1996.[1] The 'in your face' tests were the first substantial breach in the nonproliferation regime established by the NPT in 1968. They were also a challenge to the great powers vis-à-vis their exclusive nuclear weapons status and to the family of nations with regard to the gap between international community norms and enforceable regimes; and they brought back the question of the linkage between nonproliferation and disarmament to the forefront of the international agenda. The linkage was clearly evident, for example, in the set of 51 resolutions on disarmament and international security adopted by the UN General Assembly at its 54th session on 1 December 1999. The rejection of the CTBT by the US Senate has ensured that the old debates on nuclear arms control and disarmament have been reignited on the threshold of the new millennium.

The two-month Kargil war in Kashmir in 1999, with over one thousand battle deaths (which thereby satisfies the commonly accepted definition of war), confirmed the folly of India–Pakistan nuclearization. Nuclear weapons failed to deter Pakistani infiltration or Indian retaliation and escalation to aerial bombardment. The West in effect called on both to act with the responsibility of nuclear powers while insisting that neither should be given the status, with the attendant privileges and perks. Equally, however, the war overturned two major hypotheses in the strategic literature: that democracies do not fight each other; and that nuclear powers do not go to war against one another. The implications of these resonate far more widely in the world at large.

Sustainable disarmament

The nuclear arms control agenda has three interlinked components: nonproliferation, arms control (for example de-alerting and de-mating), and disarmament (the partial, limited or total abolition of nuclear weapons). Arms control measures help to stabilize military relations, proliferation worsens the situation, disarmament improves it. The nuclear policies of many countries (including not just the five de jure and three de facto nuclear weapons countries, but also some non-nuclear allies) is riddled with contradictions. Unfortunately, the inconsistencies of others tend to be more readily apparent than one's own. Some countries focus solely on disarmament as the most urgent task in order to camouflage their own proliferation agendas. Suspicions multiplied in the international community, at least after the 1998 nuclear tests, that this is what lay behind India's opposition to the NPT and CTBT.[2] Others focus on nonproliferation as the immediate and most urgent priority while evading their responsibility for disarmament within a foreseeable timeframe. Many countries share such a view of the nuclear powers, but subscribe to the NPT despite it. Elements from both groups invoke arms control sometimes as a refuge from calls for nonproliferation and disarmament, and to obfuscate rather than clarify, let alone advance the anti-nuclear agenda. Pakistan promises nuclear disarmament if India does so first, but fails to see that India has a matching case vis-à-vis China.

Norms, not deterrence, have anathematized the use of nuclear weapons as unacceptable, immoral and possibly illegal under any circumstance – even for states that have assimilated them into military arsenals and integrated them into military commands and doctrines. Far from being anomalies, India and Pakistan have accentuated the flaws, contradictions and dangers that are inherent in the logic of nuclear rivalry. As we enter the new millennium, the international community faces stark choices: maintain the present course to a nuclear Armageddon, with the timing, locale, and date being beyond prediction but the outcome itself being almost certain; or abort the mutually assured suicide and embark urgently upon programs of real arms control and disarmament. 'Sustainable disarmament' requires the reduction of armaments to the lowest level where the security needs of any one country at a given time, or any one generation over time, are met without compromising the security and welfare needs of other countries or future generations. Such a holistic concept enables us to integrate a number of otherwise seemingly disparate threads in the peace research agenda. For it points to important linkages between disarmament, on one side, and nonproliferation, conflict resolution, environmental security, and development, on the other. It also sensitizes us to the need for a balance between geopolitical realism and normative idealism.

The relationship between war and arms buildups remains contested. Should those who want peace prepare for war, or does preparing for war increase both the means and the psychological disposition for waging it? To the extent that nations arm because they fear each other, rather than fear each other because they are armed, disarmament cannot be isolated from conflict resolution. The recent Kashmir war was indeed a good illustration of this. In terms of opportunity costs, heavy military expenditure is tantamount to stealing from the poor: arms instead of alms. Fifty years after independence, India had the biggest number of poor and illiterate in the world. As they said in the streets of Delhi in May 1998, 'No food, no clothing, no shelter? No worry, we have the bomb'.

In terms of equity, the NPT-N5 (the five nuclear powers recognized as such by the NPT) preach nuclear abstinence to others but do not practice it themselves.[3] President Bill Clinton lectured India and Pakistan that nuclear weapons capability is necessary neither to peace, security, prosperity nor national greatness[4] – seemingly unmindful of the fact that the US has conducted the largest number of nuclear tests, maintains the most lethal stockpile of nuclear weapons and insists on a continued program of subcritical testing that undermines the anti-nuclear norm. The US demands compliance with selected components of the anti-nuclear norm from others while rejecting the applicability of other, perhaps more significant, components to its own foreign policy and international conduct. The UN Security Council, dominated by the five permanent members (P5) who are also the N5, condemned eleven Indian and Pakistani tests – when not one of the over 2,000 previous tests had ever been so condemned by the Council. This was neither equitable, nor even politically prudent in that the apparent hypocrisy inflamed opinion in the subcontinent.[5] The stockpiles of nuclear weapons states (NWS) are in defiance of the World Court's 1996 Advisory Opinion of a legal obligation to pursue in good faith *and bring to a conclusion* negotiations leading to nuclear disarmament;[6] India and Pakistan breached no international treaty, convention or law by testing. The NWS imposing sanctions on the nuclear gatecrashers is tantamount to outlaws sitting in judgment, passing sentence and imposing punishment on the law abiding.

With these preliminary comments in mind, let us examine the four different paths – any more is hard to imagine – that the world might take over the next few decades: maintenance of the status quo; reversal to nuclear arms races between the N5; nuclear proliferation; and nuclear abolition.

Status quo

For over three decades, the world has lived with the unequal division between five legally recognized nuclear powers and the rest, without a nuclear war breaking out. Nevertheless, the equilibrium achieved with the indefinite extension of the NPT in 1995 was dynamic, not static.[7] The five NWS should have assessed the security gains of their nuclear weapons against the costs, risks and alternatives. In particular, they should have weighed the costs of the political chain reaction of nuclear weapons status against the likelihood of the usability of nuclear weapons.

The lack of compliance and enforcement of NPT disarmament obligations on the NWS delegitimizes its normative claims in the eyes of others and fuels the politics of resentment and grievance. The NWS are trapped in the fundamental paradox that while they justify their own nuclear weapons in national security terms, they seek to deny such weapons to anyone else for reasons of global security. After the Cold War, strategic threats to the United States are uncertain. Yet Washington, with the world's most powerful military arsenal at its disposal, insists on the right to deal with diffuse and uncertain threats with nuclear weapons. But it demands that India and Pakistan must forgo the option despite both countries facing clearly identifiable threats to their security from adversaries in the neighbourhood. The NPT status quo broke down in 1998 because of this basic asymmetry; India and Pakistan have raised the ante; it cannot simply be restored.

Trying to revert to the status quo ante in South Asia is about as realistic as demanding an immediate timetabled framework for the elimination of all nuclear weapons. Just as weapons that have been invented cannot be disinvented, so too that which has been tested may be detested, but cannot be de-tested.[8] For India and Pakistan the question is no longer if, but what kind of nuclear powers they are going to be. For the world the challenge is how to reconcile the two countries' legitimate security imperatives with equally legitimate international community concerns.

This poses the question of the gap between legal fiction and strategic reality. What might be the price we pay for retreating into a denial mode, vis-à-vis NPT legal definitions, on a subject as grave as nuclear weapons? Nuclear-armed India and Pakistan do not qualify as a NWS under the strange NPT definition because they did not test before 1 January 1967. The truly absurd situation would arise if one of the N5 was to give up nuclear weapons; under the NPT definition, it would still be a NWS. If the world is not to become a more dangerous place, it is imperative that the legal definition of a NWS in the NPT be reconciled with the reality of which country has and which does not have nuclear weapons. Otherwise, in time it is the NPT that will be seen to be seriously deficient. The problem, of course, is that if the NPT definition is opened for revision through a formal amendment of the treaty, the consequences regarding the status of existing states parties are anything but predictable. There is a real conundrum here that needs to be addressed more seriously than through finger-wagging at India's and Pakistan's nuclear naughtiness.

Arms control reverses

By pursuing genuine disarmament from the late 1980s, the NWS reversed confrontation, reconstructed cooperation in preserving the nuclear peace and restored perceptions of the superpowers as responsible managers of world order. The Cold War-related tensions of the nuclear balance relaxed as Russia became more introspective and concentrated on rebuilding a shrunken country and shattered economy. Nuclear weapons have a lesser role in shaping the nature of current relations between Moscow and Washington than at any time since World War II.

Still, the disarmament process could be reversed. Relations between any two or all three of Russia, China and the US could deteriorate to the point of a new

Cold War. Treaties already negotiated and signed could unravel through non-ratification or breakouts. The Conference on Disarmament (CD) could suffer a quiet death. The testing of nuclear weapons could be resumed by one of the N5 or non-NPT N3 (the three de facto nuclear powers not recognized as such by the NPT: India, Pakistan and Israel). Beijing was deeply unhappy with the open identification of China as the justification for India's testing in 1998. A year later, in response to the NATO bombing of the Chinese Embassy in Belgrade, calls were made from within the military for the resumption of testing as a gesture of defiance at NATO 'hegemonism'.[9]

The NATO action in Kosovo united Russians of all political persuasions in deep anger against the West. While the ailing and erratic Boris Yeltsin played Russian roulette with his prime ministers, wide swathes of people and politicians lost faith in the 'good faith' of liberal democracies in conducting foreign relations on the basis of justice, equality and non-use of force. Western criticisms of the Russian use of massive force against Chechnya in later 1999 drew angry reminders of NATO action in Kosovo: an international war, as opposed to Russia's actions within its borders, noted Russian commentators. What if in future the Russian military insist that their stewardship program is simply not credible and reliable any more without further testing?

China and North Korea were alarmed in 1999 with the use of force in an out-of-area operation against a country which had not attacked a NATO member. The leveraging role of nuclear weapons becomes salient for Pyongyang, while China's interest intensifies in their deterrent utility. NATO enlargement and the strikes on Kosovo also rubbed Russia's nose in the dirt of its historic defeat in the Cold War. The experience of a rampant Western coalition simply ignoring the rules of the game, namely the UN Security Council as the sole authorizing body for the use of international force, when the outcome did not suit them, has caused disquiet and unease in many countries and made them more determined to upgrade national defence preparedness. They too might become interested in nuclear warheads as leveraging weapons.

These developments, as well as heightened suspicions of China because of allegations of large-scale and long-running nuclear espionage, plus advances in missile delivery systems by North Korea, in turn stiffened opposition in influential pockets of the US political elite against existing arms control regimes. The world looks a lot bleaker than it did five years ago, and the prospects of a return to the nuclear arms race do not appear so fanciful any more.

Proliferation

The setbacks of the India–Pakistan tests and the US Senate rejection of the CTBT notwithstanding, the entire nonproliferation regime is not in grave danger of imminent collapse. The tests of 1998 did not lead to the emergence of fresh countries of proliferation concern. Most joined the NPT regime because they have no compelling security need for nuclear weapons, do not believe that these will confer any political benefits, and have concluded that the option is either too costly (technologically, economically and politically) or simply not relevant. The use of the word 'apartheid' by Indian critics of the NPT shows just far removed the terms of the nuclear debate in India are from international benchmarks. This emotive word entails entirely negative connotations. But in fact apartheid referred to a system where a minority imposed its order on a majority by coercion. The NPT has been signed by a majority of the world's countries exercising their free choice because they believe that, on balance, their security needs are better met through a rejection of the nuclear weapons option than by embracing it. Where for India the NPT is illegitimate because it is a denial of the equality of opportunity to proliferate, for most the regime is invaluable for providing security from proliferation and the promise of eventual disarmament.

We are still stuck with the same list of NPT rejectionists and cheats in 2000 as in 1998. To the extent that India and Pakistan have demonstrably suffered in terms of net security, economic development and status, their testing folly may, if anything, have made the nonproliferation regime correspondingly more robust and resilient. It is still likely that more widespread horizontal proliferation will occur because of the actions and inaction of the N5 rather than that of the non-NPT N3.

To many critics, the rejection of the CTBT by the US Senate falls into the last category. But even here the consequences need not necessarily be as dire as the fierce denunciations of the Senate vote suggest. Both Russia and China expressed disappointment, but also reaffirmed their own commitment to proceed with ratification. India made it clear that its decision on signing would be determined by calculations of its own national interests; the same stance was repeated after the military coup in Pakistan. As distinct from the NPT, the CTBT is almost a textbook example of a universal and non-discriminatory treaty: all its proscriptive and verification clauses apply equally to every country. Indian scientists have said that the 1998 tests have given them adequate data to be able to rely solely on nonexplosive experiments in laboratories and subcritical testing for development of a credible and reliable minimum nuclear deterrence capability. The only salience that the US Senate vote had for the Indian government was the vindication of the claim that a national consensus is necessary before a treaty with such grave consequences for national security can be signed.

The anachronistic belief that nuclear weapons are the currency of power is a generational overhang in the subcontinent. In evaluating the international respect or attention that China seems to command which India does not, it is easy but mistaken, by way of explanation, to point the finger at nuclear weapons. On the Chinese side, sustained economic growth, expansion and sophistication has helped Beijing to build and use market power. It remained on the margins of international affairs for many years after acquiring and deploying nuclear weapons, just as the ploy of nuclear brinksmanship has won North Korea few friends, little influence and no respect. Conversely, non-nuclear Japan and Germany have gained great influence through economic prowess. Japan, *the* emotional touchstone on nuclear policy for having been the only victim of the use of atomic or nuclear weapons, exerts more influence in the international nuclear debate than India. On the Indian side, persistent poverty, a sorry human development record, successive crises of government and an inability or unwillingness to confront hard policy choices have been more damaging to the country's international image than lack of nuclear weapons. Nuclear weapons are neither necessary nor sufficient to be an effective player in modern diplomacy.

It remains to be seen how the Kosovo war might lead to reassessments of the nuclear security equation. Kosovo is the terrain on which the rules of post-Cold War intervention were being written. Like the understandable but wrong nuclear tests by India, NATO's war over Kosovo, however understandable, was wrong, at least from the point of view of discouraging and restricting the use of force in world affairs. Over the course of the 20th century, the international community has sought to circumscribe the international use of force, firstly by narrowing the range of circumstances under which recourse to force is permitted, and secondly by subjecting the actions of states to the consent of the legitimate international authorities. The Kosovo war, *even if justified on balance*, was a major setback to this cause of progressively constricting the resort to force other than in self-defence. Bombing was the option of choice by an alliance overly confident of its overwhelming military superiority. A just war is still war, and can produce unjust consequences. The prospects of a world order based on the rule of law are no brighter as a result of Kosovo's 'liberation.' The overriding message is not that force has been put to the service of law, but that might is right. The symbolism of the United Nations as the institution for moderating the use of force to settle international quarrels was dealt a severe blow.

The national security calculations of many countries are likely to be affected in profound ways. It will surely have hardened the determination of security planners in Moscow, Beijing, Islamabad, New Delhi, Jerusalem and Pyongyang – not to mention Baghdad and Tehran – to put their faith in survivable nuclear forces rather than risk becoming the victims of the use of force by some future self-appointed guardians of world morality. According to William Pfaff, 'The affair provided a lesson in the utility of nuclear deterrence. Had Slobodan Milosevic possessed a nuclear deterrent, NATO would not have bombed his country'.[10]

If a prominent Western columnist can conclude thus, we should not be surprised that the same lesson will have been learnt by some government leaders alarmed at NATO triumphalism and interested in weapons to leverage NATO military action. This is especially so with the clear demonstration that the UN proscriptions on the use of force, and the authority of the Security Council as the sole legitimate custodian of international peace and security, can be so easily circumvented. At the Third Preparatory Committee (PrepCom) meeting of the NPT 2000 Review Conference in New York in May 1999, 'though the Chinese were the only ones publicly to wonder if NATO would have bombed Belgrade if Yugoslavia had also been nuclear armed, there were many in the corridors who made the obvious connection'.[11] Supporters of NATO action may well argue that this was an acceptable price to pay in the circumstances; what they may not do is to deny the price.

In the case of advanced industrialized countries, the flow of enabling technologies, material and expertise in the nuclear power industry can be used, through strategic prepositioning of materials and personnel, to build a 'virtual' nuclear weapons portfolio capable of rapid weaponization. Within the constraints of the NPT, a non-NWS can build the necessary infrastructure to provide it with the 'surge' capacity to upgrade to nuclear weapons within the timeframe of a crisis degenerating into conflict. Japan, for example, has followed a three-pronged policy. At the level of *rhetoric*, Japan is committed to nonproliferation and disarmament. At the level of *policy*, Japan is committed to the US alliance and quietly accepts the interpretation that the carrying of nuclear weapons into Japanese territory aboard visiting US warships does not violate the policy of 'no introduction' of nuclear weapons. At the level of *capability*, Japan has equally quietly built up the capacity to make and deploy nuclear weapons, missiles and delivery systems very quickly if and when a new consensus should emerge that such a course was necessary for national security.[12] The existing anti-nuclear consensus could erode with continuing strategic uncertainty in Northeast Asia.

Three critical events may mark 1998 as a watershed year in heightening the sense of urgency in Japan: the nuclear tests by India and Pakistan in May; the visit to China by President Bill Clinton in July, the refusal to stop in Japan en route to or from China ('Japan passing'), and the criticisms of Japanese economic policy while on Chinese soil ('Japan bashing'); and the test-launch of a missile/rocket by North Korea in August. Together, the three events unsettled the parameters of Japan's foreign and security policy. Further revisions of the US–Japan defence guidelines and the decision to take part in joint theatre missile defence (TMD) flowed from the triple shocks of 1998. The reaffirmation of Japan's importance to the US as a regional partner is interpreted either as an investment in or a hedge against the alliance. When Vice Minister for Defense Shingo Nishimura expressed a 'personal opinion' in October 1999 that Japan should evaluate the option of nuclear weapons, he was quickly relieved of his post. The suspicion remains that he may been voicing a sentiment more widely shared than the government is prepared to acknowledge.

In Northeast Asia as also in the Middle East, additional anti-nuclear barriers could be constructed through nuclear-weapon-free zones (NWFZ).[13] These are unacceptable to NWS if any effort is made to constrain their policies and practices instead of being a purely nonproliferation regime – NATO's three nuclear powers refused to sign the Protocols to the Treaty of Rarotonga (1985) for over a decade until after the Cold War ended. By maintaining the momentum for continued stigmatization, NWFZ sustain the structure of normative restraints on the acquisition, multiplication, deployment and use of nuclear weapons. They construct additional firebreaks against nuclear proliferation, and to that extent they deepen and consolidate global nonproliferation regimes at the regional level. They serve the purpose of strategic area denial to nuclear adversaries. For the sake of additional barriers to a new nuclear arms race, the NWS should endorse the Southeast Asian NWFZ and facilitate the establishment of a Central Asian NWFZ.

Abolition

If the NPT status quo is already history, and the risks of arms control reverses and proliferation are real, then the only remaining logical alternatives are to accept a world of more nuclear weapons and more NWS, or move to a nuclear-weapon-free world. The equilibrium established by the indefinite extension of the NPT and the adoption of the CTBT was dynamic, not static. The gravest nuclear danger thereafter was not war between Russia and the US, but the spread of nuclear weapons technology and materials beyond the N5. The danger of horizontal proliferation could not, cannot be contained indefinitely by maintaining the NPT status quo. Without concrete disarmament on the part of the NWS, the world was bound to slip into horizontal proliferation. The choice was between progress and reversal, not progress and the status quo: a progression down to zero for the N5, or the spread of nuclear weapons to others.[14]

The exhortations and the coercion of sanctions need to be buttressed, therefore, with the force of example. It is difficult to convince some states that the utility of nuclear weapons is nil when all who have such weapons insist on keeping them. Nuclear weapons are strategic equalizers that are more attractive to weaker sides in proliferating pairs. Because the United States insists on retaining nuclear weapons, Russia cannot reduce its stockpile to zero. So long as Russia and the US keep nuclear weapons, China will not eliminate its stockpile. Because China is the principal long-term security threat to India (but also because the United States has impinged adversely on Indian security interests in the past), India cannot be expected, despite repeated requests and commands, to roll back its nuclear program. Without Indian renunciation, Pakistan will not buckle to outside pressure or reason.

As argued throughout this chapter, the anti-nuclear norm is universal and applies with equal force to the N5, the non-NPT N3 and the non-nuclear NPT states parties. There is no normative reason to discriminate between India and the US. In addition, however, the retention of nuclear weapons by Washington can be questioned on utilitarian grounds. Alternatively, if the United States can justify a nuclear weapons capability on utilitarian grounds even while conceding the normative argument to anti-nuclear opponents and paying lip service to the *eventual* elimination of nuclear weapons, then the utilitarian justification for almost all other nuclear powers (perhaps with the exception of France and the UK) is stronger. For the security threats to them are greater and more readily identifiable, *and* their conventional arsenals are far less formidable than those of the United States. Of course, this argument will not be acceptable to those who believe in US exceptionalism, a belief that has kept Washington out of the Ottawa Treaty banning anti-personnel landmines and the Rome Treaty establishing the International Criminal Court (ICC).

The silver lining to the 1998 nuclear tests is that they re-energized the nuclear debate and agenda. The eleven steps back in May 1998 may yet help us to re-position ourselves on the springboard to nuclear disarmament. In present circumstances, there are some security arguments for the United States, Russia and China to keep nuclear stockpiles even while working more seriously to reduce their numbers. But the continued possession of nuclear weapons by Britain and France seems to be driven more by historical pride and a quest for status than by genuine national security concerns. Unilateral renunciations of nuclear weapons by one or both would underscore the break, brought about by India (ironically) and Pakistan, between permanent membership of the Security Council and possession of nuclear weapons.

Conclusion

An enduring resolution of any conflict must strike a balance between the two competing pulls of realism and justice. Peace cannot be grasped if it ignores current power relativities. Equally, however, peace cannot be maintained if it simply freezes current structural inequality. For then the so-called 'peace agreement' will be based on the passing inability of the dissatisfied and revisionists to challenge the status quo. For the agreement to hold across generations, it must be based on the acquiescence of the defeated to the terms of the settlement. That is, the accord must be legitimate, and legitimacy cannot be imposed by one side: it must be bestowed by both sides in a relationship. Until India and Israel realize this and act on it, there will be no lasting peace in Kashmir and the Middle East. Without peace, the risks of nuclear weapons in the two regions are magnified manifold.

Similarly, disarmament, to be sustainable, must somehow reflect both current international power realities and future international community needs. The NPT had become dangerously fragile because of the vertical proliferation of the NWS for two decades, before they reconstructed the structure of cooperation in nuclear peace, called a halt to their proliferating arsenals and began progressively to dismantle them under the virtuous cycle of mutually reinforcing unilateral, bilateral and multilateral arms control agreements and policies.

As shown by the difficulties with Iraq in 1998–99, the five permanent members of the UN Security Council are not united in their perceptions of the threats posed by nuclear proliferation and the best measures in response.[15] The disunity among the P5 on the question of punishing and reversing non-compliant behaviour heightens the nuclear dangers. In turn, however, the lack of unity reflects some of the ambiguities and complexities – political, moral and military – of the nuclear world which has moved beyond the simple dichotomy implied in the NPT.

The nonproliferation agenda having been more or less secured, the urgent requirement now is to emplace an increasing number of verifiable constraints on the policies, practices and arsenals of the NWS. The historic and favourable changes in the world strategic situation must be embedded in structures that consolidate, deepen and reinforce the nonproliferation, arms control and disarmament regimes in their normative, technical-denial and compliance-cum-enforcement attributes. All the regimes must be invested with the requisite political will, fiscal means and intelligence support. We should also endeavour to widen the adherence to these treaties. To the extent that the disarmament norm is embedded in the regimes, developing countries need to be drawn into their management bodies, else the normative consensus will decline. The challenge, as with the vexed issue of UN Security Council reform, will be to combine the representational and efficiency arguments; that is, to make sure that the management bodies do not become so large as to be unwieldy and inefficient. International agreement will be much easier to achieve on a zero than on a low-limit nuclear weapons regime.

Such a scenario typically provokes dismissive comments from 'realists.' Their own prescriptions are unrealistic, ahistorical and a counsel of despair. Realistically speaking, as distinct from refinements of essentially the same options, is there another option beyond those identified here? If not, then which is the most preferred option? As with Winston Churchill's famous aphorism on democracy, the abolitionist option may well be unrealistic; it is just that all other conceivable options are even more unrealistic. The conclusions of this article are compatible with a belief in the utility (as well as lack thereof) of nuclear weapons. But just as national security cannot a priori be privileged over other forms of security (economic, environmental, cultural, human), so the utility of nuclear weapons cannot be privileged over the costs, risks and alternatives.

The New Agenda resolution, adopted by the UN General Assembly on 1 December 1999, noted in the preamble that 'the contention that nuclear weapons can be retained in perpetuity and never used is not supported by the history of human experience ... the only complete defence is the elimination of nuclear weapons and the assurance that they will never be produced again'.[16] In most contexts, a step-by-step approach is the best policy. But such caution can be fatal if the need is to cross a chasm. In the case of nuclear weapons, the chasm that needs leaping over is the mental conditioning of national and world security resting on weapons of maximum insecurity.

Notes

* Originally published in *Security Dialogue* 31:1 (2000): 25–40. Reprinted by permission of Sage.
1 When those with recognizably Western names write articles on policy issues, they are not automatically assumed to reflect self-serving national perspectives. Judging by some of the reviewers' comments, this is not the case for those with recognizably Indian names. For the record: I am not Indian by nationality and suspect that, based on reactions to my past writings, most Indian officials and commentators would be horrified to discover that my views are in any way seen to reflect Indian thinking. On this subject I write more as someone who was a member of the Public Advisory Committee on Disarmament and Arms Control in New Zealand (1990–96), a member of the National Consultative Committee on Peace and Disarmament in Australia (1995–98), Head of the Peace Research Centre in Canberra (1995–98), a consultant to the Canberra Commission (1995–96), and joint organiser and co-chair of the ASEAN Regional Forum (ARF) Track Two Seminar on Non-Proliferation held in Jakarta in December 1996, as well as the editor of the papers from that seminar: Ramesh Thakur, ed., *Keeping Proliferation at Bay* (Jakarta: Centre for Strategic and International Studies in cooperation with the Peace Research Centre, 1998). As an expatriate Indian, on the one hand, if anything I probably subject Indian policy to a harsher analysis than the policies of other countries – a case of 'tough love' perhaps. See, in particular, Ramesh Thakur, 'India in the World: Neither Rich, Powerful, nor Principled', *Foreign Affairs* 76:4 (1997). Nevertheless, on the other hand, I do have difficulty with the proposition that the only villain in the piece, even with regard to the 1998 tests, is India.

2 My own views on the fallacy of Indian opposition to the NPT and CTBT and on why India should have renounced the nuclear option, published with terrible timing, are detailed in Ramesh Thakur, 'The nuclear option in India's security policy', *Asia-Pacific Review* 5:1 (1998): 39–60.
3 At the political level, I find it difficult to respond effectively when, reacting to my thesis about the essential irrelevance of nuclear weapons, Indians ask: if nuclear weapons are so useless, why has not one of the N5 given them up?
4 Office of the Press Secretary, the White House, 28 May 1998.
5 The larger question of compliance with and enforcement of anti-nuclear regimes is discussed in Ramesh Thakur, 'Non-Compliance: Who Decides, and What to Do?' *Australian Journal of International Affairs* 53:1 (1999): 71–81.
6 The normative status of the Court's Advisory Opinion is strengthened by the frequency of its recitation in UN General Assembly resolutions, for example Resolutions 54/54G, preambular paragraph 6; 54/54K, preambular paragraph 11; 54/54P, preambular paragraph 15; and 54/54R, specifically on the follow-up to the World Court's Opinion, which underlined the main conclusions of the Opinion (operative paragraph 1) and called on all states to fulfil their disarmament obligation by commencing multilateral negotiations in 2000 (operative paragraph 2); all of 1 December 1999.
7 I commented earlier that my argument advocating the renunciation of nuclear weapons by India was published with bad timing in the Spring-Summer of 1998. From another point of view, nonetheless, the nuclear tests of May 1998 vindicated the central thesis of that article, viz, while India's threshold posture had been stable for three decades, after 1995 (NPT extension) and 1996 (CTBT) 'the status quo of maintaining the option without proceeding to a program of tests and weaponization has become an unsustainable absurdity'. Thakur, 'The Nuclear Option in India's Security Policy', 54. My views on the unsustainability of the NPT status quo were similarly vindicated by the 1998 tests – however much I (and others) might regret the tests.
8 The cases of Argentina and Brazil show that the option can be given up, while that of South Africa proves that nuclear weapons status is reversible. But the security dynamics of the subcontinent are fundamentally different, and link up inexorably through China via serial bilateralism all the way to Russia and the United States. On this argument, it is easier to visualize Israel some day giving up the nuclear option because of dramatic changes in the local/regional security complex, than to see nuclear disarmament on the subcontinent without dramatic movement on the global front.
9 Willy Wo-lap Lam, 'China Takes Turn to the Right', *Japan Times*, 22 May 1999. Lam is China editor for the *South China Morning Post* (Hong Kong) and one of the most respected China-watchers in the region.
10 William Pfaff, 'No nonproliferation without nuclear reduction,' *International Herald Tribune*, 23 August 1999.
11 Rebecca Johnson, 'NPT Report,' *Disarmament Diplomacy* 37 (May 1999), 16.
12 This capability is the product of Japan being a modern technological economy, not of a clandestine pursuit of the nuclear weapons option.
13 See Ramesh Thakur, ed., *Nuclear Weapons-Free Zones* (London/New York: Macmillan and St. Martin's Press, 1998).
14 Of course, Pakistan tested because of India, not because of any of the N5. But if Pakistan tested solely because of India (since other proliferation pressures by Pakistan would almost certainly have been contained with India's accession to the NPT), and if India tested because of one or more of the N5, then Pakistan's tests too are directly linked to the N5 through a chain reaction of bilateral linkages.
15 For a fine analysis of the issues involved, see David Malone, 'Goodbye UNSCOM: A Sorry Tale in US–UN Relations', *Security Dialogue* 30:4 (December 1999).
16 A/RES/54/54G (1 December 1999), preambular paragraph 2.

Part II

Regional challenges in Asia, the Pacific and the Middle East

5 The last bang before a total ban*
French nuclear testing in the Pacific

On 13 June 1995, shortly after his election, President Jacques Chirac announced that France would conduct a series of eight further nuclear tests between September 1995 and May 1996. In the event, six tests were conducted over four months. The first, of a modest 8kt yield, was conducted at Moruroa Atoll on 5 September 1995. The sixth and final 120kt test was conducted at Fangataufa Atoll on 27 January 1996. This chapter addresses four substantial themes: the origins of French nuclear testing in the South Pacific; the heightened sense of anti-nuclearism in the South Pacific; the basis for the opposition to the resumption of nuclear testing by France; and the lines of action available to channel such opposition into policy measures designed to abort the testing.

Anti-nuclear sentiments in the South Pacific

The decision on the independent French deterrent was taken in the mid-1950s. The first French nuclear test was conducted in the Sahara in French Algeria on 13 February 1960 in defiance of a two-thirds vote in the UN General Assembly in November 1959 calling on France to refrain from testing. Upon independence in 1962, Algeria objected to such activities in the Sahara; Paris was given five years' grace to cease testing there. The tests were then shifted to French Polynesia from 1966 onwards. Having conducted 13 underground tests in Algeria, Paris decided to conduct atmospheric tests in the Pacific for reasons of lower costs, easier data collection on weapons performance and effects, and reduced political pressure because of the geographical remoteness of the new test sites. There are two test sites in French Polynesia: Moruroa and Fangataufa atolls. Both were uninhabited, located well away from commercial air and shipping routes, and fewer than 5000 inhabitants lived within a 1000km radius. Moruroa lies some 100km from the nearest inhabited island, 4000km from New Zealand and 6000km from Australia.

About 50 atmospheric tests were conducted between 1966–74, followed by over 150 underground tests from 1975–91. About eight different types of nuclear warheads were developed through these tests embracing the variety of weapons systems constituting France's independent *force de frappe* (strike force). Seven of the largest tests (with yields in the 80–150kt range) were conducted at Fangataufa, probably to avoid structural damage to Moruroa rock. Underground tests are conducted at the bottom of 500–1200 metre deep shafts bored into the basalt core of the atoll. While the shafts were originally drilled in the outer rim of the atoll, since the 1980s they have been drilled under the lagoon.

The history of the relationship of nuclear weapons use and testing in the Pacific area has sensitized Pacific peoples to the nuclear evil more deeply than others. The Pacific Ocean has created a sense of community in the same way in which the continental landmass has created the idea of Europe. In Europe and the Americas, land unites and seas divide. In the Pacific, oceans are a main source of livelihood and food for many communities and the principal means of linking small territories scattered across a vast seascape. By the 1980s there were six categories of nuclear issues of concern to the peoples of the region: vertical proliferation among the nuclear weapons states (NWS); the possibility of the breakdown of the nuclear peace; the spread of strategic weapons doctrines and nuclear weapons deployments to the South Pacific; nuclear testing in the South Pacific; facilities in the South Pacific which constituted part of the worldwide infrastructure of nuclear logistics; and environmental anxieties about possible dumping of nuclear waste in the South Pacific. All six concerns were sought to be addressed in the South Pacific Nuclear Free Zone (SPNFZ, 1985) which adopted the simple expedient of additional protocols for integrating the NWS into SPNFZ. Although China and the Soviet Union endorsed SPNFZ, none of the three Western NWS did. Yet Britain and the US do not in practice violate any of the zonal requirements. France's testing program at Mororoa continued unabated. The French attitude was that the bomb and the territory were French, the testing was done by France, so the choice of testing site was solely a French decision.[1]

Environmental concerns

The regional position was equally clear and simple. If the tests were harmful, they should be terminated. If they caused no harm, they should be transferred to metropolitan French soil. One reason why France has been dismissive of regional protests has been lack of proven environmental damage. Information on the effects of the tests is scarce, patchy and unreliable. Four different missions have been permitted to conduct strictly limited investigations between 1982 and 1990. All four were time-limited to between 3–5 days; had only restricted access to data, sites and samples (e.g. coral and sediment from site-specific or designated areas); and were not presented with adequate epidemiological data. Yet the reports of the four missions remain the most important source of publicly available information.

There are several fronts on which environmental damage is feared.[2] French defence personnel exposed to the nuclear tests have presumably been tested for radiation exposure; their results have not been released to the scientific or public community. Moreover, follow-up tests are not known to have been conducted on French military personnel. Fission products from the tests were expected to circle the globe in an eastward direction; sometimes they have been swept westwards when caught in cross-winds. This means that South Pacific as well as South American countries can be classified as 'downwind communities'.[3]

The short-term effects of underground testing include landslides, tidal waves (for example on 25 July 1979, when a test triggered an avalanche) and earthquakes caused by atoll surface fracturing; and radionuclides venting to the environment.[4] Cracks and fissures in the structure of the atoll are often thought to be caused, or worsened, by the nuclear tests. French scientists insist that the two atolls have a good 20 years' life left in them as test sites. Long-term effects include radioactive leakage to the biosphere and contamination of the food chain through plutonium that dissolves from the lagoon to the ocean.[5] Testing at Moruroa has created a vast repository of nuclear waste products under the atoll's surface, in effect turning Moruroa into a long-term waste dump. Yet Moruroa is not geologically suited to be a radioactive repository. Such a site should be inert and dry. Moruroa's structure is water-saturated, and fissures caused by explosions have been added to the many natural fractures in the lagoon and atoll.

The safety of the waste is dependent on the hydrology of the atoll, but the hydrology is affected by subsequent testing. France claims that the testing has not impaired the structural integrity of the atoll. The atoll is made up of three rock layers: reef limestones, a transitional sequence, and the volcanic layer. There is general agreement on all sides that the structural integrity of the limestones has been impaired. Therefore they do not constitute a barrier to potential leakage of radionuclides. The transitional zone varies considerably in thickness and composition and cannot be assumed to form an impermeable barrier to potential leakage. There is no evidence to suggest that the volcanic layer has been structurally damaged.

However, radionuclides take time to grow in the decay chain set off by an explosion. While anti-nuclear activists point to worst-case scenarios, French authorities prefer to draw attention to best-case scenarios. In the worst-case scenario, leached radionuclides could leak within five years. The transitional zone does not obstruct leakage. The reef limestones are porous and the tests have increased the potential channels for lateral and vertical flows. In the best-case scenario, leakage of leached radionuclides to the limestones would occur in about 500–4500 years and to the ocean in about 1000–10,000 years. The French authorities adhere to this conclusion: a slow leak into an environment where the total leak is small compared to the volume of the surrounding diluent to absorb and contain it. Besides, people and politicians cannot conceive of 500–10,000 year timeframes. Or so the French authorities must believe.

However, the indigenous people of the Pacific can and do think in such long historical timeframes: think of the importance of dreamtime in Australia's aboriginal folklore. According to some scientific models, 500 metre deep radionuclides could reach the cracks of the lagoon in less than 50 years instead of the 500–1000 years assumed by the French authorities. In lay terms, Moruroa is like a huge rock sponge sitting atop a radioactive undersea mountain. We put in place strict regimes for the storage of wastes from nuclear power stations. The arguments for equally strict regimes for the storage of wastes from nuclear explosions seem compelling.

For all this, it is worth emphasizing that to date, no conclusive evidence has been presented of significant health hazards resulting from French testing in the Pacific.

This is why Paris dismisses regional protests as irrational. A recent report commissioned by the Australian government from 18 leading scientists concluded that French testing at Moruroa was likely to pose only minimal risk to human health.[6] The most serious doubts about environmental effects are rooted in recent history. More than once, established opinion has been shown to be tragically defective in regard to the long-term effects of exposure to radiation, the time taken for some symptoms to develop and the slowness of recovery of the environment from radioactive contamination. In the minds of many people of the region, former testing sites in the Marshall Islands and on the Australian mainland constitute an archaeology of evil.

The 1995 Chirac decision

There are two main parts to the French case for renewed testing: need and safety. Both rest on the assumption that France is right to possess an independent deterrent. On the first point (need), Paris argues that it is necessary to update the current stock of ageing nuclear weapons and gather more data before shifting to an entirely computerized simulation. On the second point (safety), Paris argues that physical tests are the only way to verify the safety and reliability of weapons stockpiles.

The strategic justification for French nuclear testing in the South Pacific was always questionable. There was a time-lag of nine years between the first atmospheric and underground test at Moruroa in 1966 and 1975 respectively. The site was originally chosen because its isolation made it particularly suitable for atmospheric tests. The infrastructure built up after 1966 made Moruroa a convenient but not an essential site for underground testing. A technical report by Australian scientists in 1984–85 established that France can safely carry out nuclear testing on the Massif Central of mainland France and in northeast Corsica: they have the right geological and hydrological conditions in terms of underground watercourses and relatively sparse populations.[7] The main obstacle to conducting nuclear tests in France itself is the political price, not technical impediments, of relocating to the mainland.

At one level, testing will always add to the modernization, safety and reliability of weapons stockpiles. But these have to be assessed against costs, risks and alternatives. Stockpile safety can be adequately ensured with laboratory techniques using past nuclear test data and computer simulation modelling. With over 200 actual tests, some of the most sophisticated computer technology in the world, the possibility of access to US facilities, and the lack of any realistic threats to French national security, the marginal utility of each additional test is negligible. At a press briefing on 11 August Robert Bell, the president's special assistant for defence policy, confirmed that the US had offered to share its computer simulation with France.[8]

The potential damage to French security interests from an unravelling of the nonproliferation regime is higher. Even former President Francois Mitterrand had come to this conclusion in the 1990s and halted French testing. No closet peacenik he: France had conducted around 75 tests during his 14-year stewardship of the French ship of state, including a 150kt test on 9 May 1985. Mitterrand had become convinced that existing warheads could be married to new delivery systems as an alternative to carrying out further tests: adapt, don't develop, was his net policy conclusion. His predecessor Valery Giscard d'Estaing joined in the criticism, saying that with the collapse of the Soviet Union, France was surrounded on all sides by members of the European Union and there was no longer any justification for resuming nuclear tests.[9] Besides, India, Pakistan and Israel manage to pursue a policy of de facto deterrence without even admitting to having nuclear weapons, let alone testing them.

Why then did Chirac decide to resume testing? We can only speculate on the mix of motives that lay behind his decision.[10] From the vantage point of the South Pacific it seems to have had little to do with military efficiency and a lot to with national and personal prestige. Perhaps it was lofty indifference to the insignificant Australasians. Perhaps it was the same insouciance that led to the decision to decorate one of the intelligence officers responsible for the *Rainbow Warrior* outrage a decade ago:[11] France pursues its national interests around the world with total indifference to alien sensitivities. Perhaps it was simply French *elan*, a reaffirmation of France's status as a world power.

Whatever the reason(s), Chirac surely miscalculated the severity and extent of the reaction. A clue to understanding the strength of the regional opposition lies in the strategic state of the world in 1995, the 50th anniversary of Hiroshima and Nagasaki. Major progress had been made in reducing the nuclear arsenals of the superpowers and negotiating a chemical weapons convention. Most importantly, the Nuclear Non-Proliferation Treaty (NPT) was indefinitely extended at a conference New York in April–May despite unmet concerns of countries like Egypt, Indonesia and Mexico, reflecting faith in the reversal of the nuclear arms race since the end of the Cold War. In return, through the declaration on principles and objectives, the nuclear powers undertook to exercise the 'utmost restraint' in nuclear testing pending the entry into force of a comprehensive test ban treaty (CTBT) by the end of 1996.

Comprehensive test ban treaty (CTBT)

The NPT's extension removed the uncertainty and risk in long-term planning for national security and created a stable strategic environment for further reductions of weapons. The alternative would have left open windows of vulnerability. Yet critics of the NPT had cause to feel vindicated within days. China conducted its 42nd test on 15 May, just three days after the NPT conference finished, followed by another on 17 August. The Chinese test could only have encouraged the pro-test lobby in France. In turn, a resumption of testing by France gave further plausibility to the Chinese excuse and allowed them to resist pressures to cease and desist from further testing. Ideally, all testing should be banned by a CTBT which would be an embodiment of the world's abhorrence of nuclear weapons. It would enhance the NPT's legitimacy by being non-discriminatory, help to dissuade fresh entrants into the nuclear weapons club and upgrade the security of all states. Continued testing gives comfort to potential proliferators and poisons the atmosphere at the CTBT negotiations; 'It puts at risk our hopes for a post Cold War world which does not have the nuclear shadow hanging over it'.[12]

John D. Holum, Director of the US Arms Control and Disarmament Agency (ACDA), said on 18 January 1995 'it simply makes no sense to keep setting off nuclear explosions to further sift the finest particles of knowledge'.[13] The central purpose of a CTBT would be to end the qualitative arms race by constraining the development of more advanced nuclear weapons. Between 1991 and 1993 Moscow, Paris, Washington and London imposed and extended voluntary moratoria on nuclear testing. US President Bill Clinton noted on 2 July 1993 that additional nuclear tests could improve safety and reliability. 'However, the price we would pay in conducting those tests now by undercutting our own nonproliferation goals and ensuring that other nations would resume testing outweighs these benefits'.[14] On 11 August 1995, Clinton committed the US to a 'true zero-yield' CTBT, overriding the preferences of some in the military-defence establishment for a regime that would permit small, perhaps as low as 2kg yield laboratory nuclear weapons 'experiments' or up to 500 tonne yield tests. The US decision was announced just one day after France too had formally committed itself to a zero-yield CTBT upon the completion of its 1995–96 series of tests.

Robert Bell explained at a press briefing on 11 August that there was consensus in the policy community that once the science-based stockpile stewardship program was fully implemented about a decade out from now, there would be no requirement under any condition to envision any further testing. The critical question was how to close the window of vulnerability in the interim decade. Even within this timeframe, there was no proposal from the Department of Defense to conduct a nuclear test. Rather, the debate was one of contingency: what if a major problem is discovered with a particular nuclear weapons type? There was a suggestion that if a problem was discovered and fixed, confidence in its performance, safety and reliability would require a test of at least to the boost phase, that is up to 500 tonnes. The administration concluded that the prospect of negotiating a 500 tonne CTBT was negligible. The solution arrived at was to go for a 'supreme national interest' clause.[15] President Clinton said that safeguards would be established to conduct necessary testing, in consultation with Congress, if the safety or reliability of the US nuclear deterrent could no longer be certified. But because of the stockpile stewardship program that was being established, Clinton doubted that the right of 'supreme national interest' would ever need to be exercised, by him or any future US president, for US nuclear weapons are safe and reliable.[16]

Australian, New Zealand and Japanese governments immediately welcomed the French and US commitment to a zero-yield CTBT as a major policy breakthrough. Britain tests its weapons at the US test site in Nevada and is therefore automatically bound by the new US position. Its formal position was stated at the Conference on Disarmament (CD) in September 1995. China has repeatedly said that it accepts the idea of a comprehensive weapons test ban, but seeks an exemption for peaceful nuclear explosions. It remains to be seen whether the recent deterioration in Sino–US relations will make Beijing less cooperative on a range of international order management problems, including the terms of the CTBT. Russia is known to favour a regime that will permit tests in the range of 'tens of tonnes'. Holum commented that President Clinton's decision would help resolve 'by far the toughest nut' in the CTBT negotiations. The zero-yield decision, he said, makes the test ban negotiable by treating all countries the same.[17] The major point of negotiation at the CD in Geneva will thus will be the Russian position on a CTBT. Economic necessity has made Moscow so reliant on Washington in the last few years that Russia may not have much bargaining leverage over the substantive scope of CTBT clauses.

Options for opposing French tests

The options available to South Pacific governments and people to protest effectively against the Chirac decision range from in-country action to sub-regional, regional and global campaigns. All have been or will be tried. The prospects of success from any or all lines of action are not very high, for the countries of the region, acting either individually or in concert, lack significant diplomatic and economic leverage over France.

At the national level, the options were split between actions that governments could take and what the people could do directly. The thought of imposing sanctions was a non-starter: they have a bad history in terms of achieving success and they would damage those imposing sanctions more than the target countries. There have been many calls for Australia to halt uranium sales to France, an undeniable embarrassment. However, the sales are covered by long-term contracts regulating tonnage and price. Abrogating them would prove expensive for Australia directly, in compensation and penalty costs, and indirectly in reliability as a supplier in international trade. Moreover, the contracted price is at present about 60 percent above the spot market price of uranium. So, should Australia cancel uranium sales, France would be handed a financial reward for its decision to resume nuclear testing. The prospect of this is unlikely to cause President Chirac to change his mind on testing.

Governments in trouble domestically should treat public opinion as a voice to be heeded, not a problem to be managed. The Australian government has been perceived as a reluctant follower of public protests and as having been upstaged by the more robust reaction of the New Zealand government. Senator Gareth Evans' initial reaction – that it could have been worse – was intellectually defensible, yet fuelled public anger back home. His measured assessment gave priority to broader arms control objectives; the people demanded French blood (or its metaphorical equivalent). The foreign minister was conscious that strident opposition to the testing decision would be interpreted as attacks on the credibility of France's presence in the Pacific; on the credibility and authority of a newly-elected president who would be in office for at least another seven years; and on the credibility of France's national security policy based on the independent deterrent. On a wide range of international trade, economic, environment and security issues in which Australian interests are engaged, Paris exercises considerable influence. Moreover, France had made three important concessions. Testing would cease after eight new tests, France would sign a CTBT, and no new weapons systems would be developed.

In addition to such bilateral manoeuvres as recall of ambassadors, Canberra has also been trying to build coalitions in the South Pacific, Asia–Pacific and internationally. The South Pacific Forum (SPF) set up an anti-testing committee which held its inaugural meeting in Fiji in mid-July. It made two decisions: to send a high-level delegation to Paris, London and Washington to seek support for SPNFZ, and to make the UN General Assembly the focus of anti-nuclear sentiment.[18] Lending support to official protests, on 15 August Catholic bishops from 23 Pacific countries signed a rare joint statement calling on France to halt its testing, describing it as 'an act of theft from the poor of the world and from generations of people yet to come'.[19] Across the Pacific, a number of Latin American countries too planned to launch coordinated protest action against French testing. The development of a stronger Asian–Pacific identity allowed Australia and New Zealand to mobilize support at the meeting of the Association of Southeast Asian Nations (ASEAN) in Brunei. Criticism of France was especially pointed from Indonesia and Japan.

Japan is the emotional fulcrum on the subject of nuclear weapons. Japanese government leaders have issued a number of statements strongly critical of the French decision to resume testing. On 9 August, the 50th anniversary of Nagasaki, 'as the prime minister of the country that has experienced the devastation of atomic bombing', Tomiichi Murayama expressed 'intense anguish regarding nuclear weapons testing'.[20] The most worrying prospect for France would be a deepening of calls by some retailers to boycott French goods. For Japan represents a sizeable and affluent market.

In France itself, the Socialists publicly opposed the Chirac decision, calling for a referendum to be held on the issue. In a New Zealand television interview, former Prime Minister Michel Rocard described the decision to resume testing as 'a disaster' and Chirac's position as 'lonely and arrogant'.[21] By August opposition within France stood at 60 percent, with only 29 percent support for the Chirac decision.[22] But most observers believed that, having put his authority and France's credibility as a nuclear power on the line, Chirac would ride out the storm rather than back down. Such indeed proved to be the case, despite the continually plunging popularity of the Chirac administration in successive opinion polls.

European consumers did not launch a boycott of French goods. The strongest feelings among Europeans were expressed by Germans and Scandinavians. A number of European governments publicly criticized France to the clear dismay of French leaders. The effort by Paris to portray its nuclear weapons as the 'European deterrent' (or Euro-deterrent) failed to win many hearts and minds in Europe. But for Paris the key external countries of reference are Germany, Britain and the US. An opinion poll published on 7 July showed that a solid 95 percent of Germans opposed the French decision to resume nuclear testing. The German government expressed its reservations only in private. Bonn's dilemma was how to reconcile deep-seated fear of nuclear weapons with the need to maintain intimate relations with France. The British government was the most sympathetic towards the French decision, describing it as a matter for the Chirac government since it concerned French national security. Britain found itself quite isolated on the matter at the Commonwealth Heads of Government Meeting (CHOGM) in Auckland in November 1995. A number of US political leaders expressed moderately worded criticisms of Paris. The administration expressed its regret.

Legal challenges

New Zealand Prime Minister Jim Bolger expressed the hope that the International Court of Justice (ICJ) would issue a preliminary injunction stopping the French tests while the case against them was heard, but conceded that his own advisers were not optimistic about the legal challenge. Wellington was determined to use the very narrow window of opportunity available to it. New Zealand's case in 1973 had been based on broader contamination threats, while Australia's parallel case had been framed in the narrower terms of atmospheric testing. This is why New Zealand's option of reopening the case, which lapsed when France transferred its tests underground in 1974, was less unsoundly founded than Australia's. The difficulty was France had removed itself from the ICJ's jurisdiction in 1974. The application to reopen the old case was aimed at getting around this obstacle, since France had accepted the court's jurisdiction when that case began.

This posed a problem for Australia in particular, for only recently Canberra had defended itself successfully at The Hague against Portugal over the Australia–Indonesia Timor Gap Treaty. The main Australian legal defence was that as Indonesia did not accept the ICJ's compulsory jurisdiction, the case could not proceed. Raising a challenge to France in the same forum within a couple of months of that verdict would have exposed Australia to charges of inconsistency. But Senator Evans did promise Australian support to the revived New Zealand challenge.[23] The French spokesmen remained dismissive of the legal challenge, viewing it as emanating solely from domestic political compulsions. When the World Court rejected the New Zealand challenge, France felt vindicated.

The UN option

If the primary motivation behind President Chirac's decision to resume testing was political rather than military or technical, a possible means of influencing him to abort or curtail the testing was to raise the national, European and international political costs to France. Taking the issue of nuclear testing to the United Nations was one component in such a strategy of cost escalation. The General Assembly was the appropriate forum because it was there that the NWS had pledged to exercise 'utmost restraint' on testing pending the CTBT. As the Japanese put it, the French decision to resume testing was a 'betrayal' of the NPT deal agreed to in May 1995. The word was used by other Asian leaders too, for example the Indonesian and Philippine foreign ministers. It registered a characteristically Asian perception of diplomatic relations, in which trust and mutual understandings are at least as important as formal contractual provisions. On this interpretation,

France had violated the trust embodied in the NPT package deal. As the world's most representative forum, the General Assembly would also embarrass France by this reminder of anachronistic colonialism. As Prime Minister Paul Keating wrote, 'Inevitably, the decision to resume tests is seen as a regression to old colonial attitudes' and 'an assault upon the rights of small nations by a large one'.[24] Besides, France cannot veto a General Assembly resolution.

The French testing was scheduled to resume in September. Coincidentally, the General Assembly begins its session each year in September. The Philippines announced that, as chair of the 132-strong Group of 77 (G-77) developing countries, it would rally support at the General Assembly for a resolution condemning all nuclear weapons testing.[25] Australia and New Zealand joined other leading Pacific states, including Japan and Chile, in sponsoring and shepherding a resolution through the General Assembly. On 16 November the First Committee voted 95–12 in favour of a resolution deploring nuclear testing and calling for its immediate halt (the remaining countries either abstained or did not vote). On 12 December the full Assembly adopted the resolution by a vote of 85–18 (with 43 abstentions); support had declined mainly among Caribbean and African countries with colonial-era links to France.

Greenpeace as a non-governmental organization (NGO) actor

The French testing controversy raises another issue that may prove to be important in the long term, namely the relationship between democratically elected state governments and unelected, unaccountable, well-funded multinational organizations. The issue was first raised seriously in 1995 with the controversy over the Brent Spar affair in the UK. Shell had planned to dispose of a spent oil rig in deep sea. After publicity stunts by Greenpeace commandos led to threats of consumer boycotts across Europe, Shell, despite continued support from the British government, caved in and agreed to Greenpeace demands that the rig be dismantled on land. Yet the scientific consensus was that on environmental calculations alone, the deep sea option was the better one. The alternative is to bring the rig ashore, cut it up, dispose of the radioactivity and toxic material in an as-yet unspecified manner, and then bury the waste matter somewhere that will not attract a protest campaign. So neither elected governments, nor scientific experts, nor multinational corporations were able to withstand an emotive and sophisticated public relations war by the 'new multinationals': the NGOs. (Greenpeace subsequently admitted that it had a made a mistake on this issue.)

There was some danger of governments losing their way in a similar manner on the subject of French testing in the Pacific. New Zealand was embarrassed at the findings of a study by its own External Assessments Bureau that there is more background radiation in New Zealand than in Moruroa. Its move to reopen the legal case against France in the ICJ was against the considered advice of its own foreign ministry on grounds of costs, likelihood of success and the timeframe involved, since no verdict is likely until well after the tests have ceased.

Greenpeace is skilled in the art of picture bites for international television exposure. The *Rainbow Warrior II* sailed inside the 12-mile territorial limit of Moruroa with a cargo of TV journalists and sophisticated electronic gear for beaming pictures of the confrontation around the world instantly. The prestigious French daily *Le Monde* asked why Greenpeace had not protested as vigorously against China, the only country not to have joined the testing moratorium. Is Greenpeace 'morally justified in taking such actions only against open, transparent democracies', the paper asked.[26] Nevertheless, the world needs NGOs so that they can operate outside the framework of the states-system in order to put pressure on states on a variety of fronts such as human rights (Amnesty International) or the environment (Greenpeace). The world would be a less pleasant place to live in today had there been no NGOs holding governments to account over the past fifty years.

The issue of commensurate protests against China was a red herring. China is the only NWS not to have joined the moratorium on testing. Its biggest political argument is that the other NWS have carried out far more tests; China needs to catch up before joining them in the pause. Because China never joined the moratorium, the French decision was the first substantial *reversal* of the dramatic progress in nuclear disarmament in the 1990s. China has only one-fifth the databank of France in tests already conducted; its computer technology is well behind that of France; it does restrict testing to its own mainland; its continental testing site is neither as unstable geologically as the two atolls in the Pacific, nor as threatening to an integrated maritime environment; and it has identifiably real security threats. So yes, South Pacific countries do oppose continued testing by China. China's second test of the year in August, coming after the fierce controversy over the French decision to resume testing, did produce stronger and more forthright condemnations across the region than its first test in May. But no, South Pacific countries are not apologetic about opposing French testing at Moruroa with much greater strength of conviction.

Conclusion

Of the five NWS, China and France were the NPT holdouts until the 1990s. They were also the two testing recalcitrants. France continued to test nuclear systems in French Polynesia into the 1990s: a dramatic example of the seizure of the global commons.[27] For, legal niceties aside, Paris can have little moral claim to sovereign jurisdiction over its Polynesian territories. The depth, breadth and resilience of the opposition to French nuclear testing caught even the Australian and New Zealand governments off guard. It is not surprising then that it should have caught France and the rest of the official and journalistic world by surprise. The other distinctive feature of the protests across the region was that where in the past strong feelings had been confined to specific sectors of the population, in 1995 it embraced the full spectrum. Nor did regional unhappiness with France dissipate after the announcement from Paris in January 1996 that the sixth test was the last and France would now work towards concluding the CTBT negotiations in Geneva. Many Asian–Pacific governments remained angry that the French tests had eased international pressure on China and encouraged the threshold nuclear weapons states of India and Pakistan to harden their stance at the CTBT talks.[28]

The Chirac decision to resume nuclear testing may have been made in the mistaken belief that the anti-nuclear tide of public sentiment in the West had waned with the passing of the Cold War. The re-mobilization of anti-nuclear feelings throughout the world forced home the realization that many people had simply assumed that the nuclear arms race too had become a casualty of the end of the Cold War. Earlier public protests against French testing had not equalled the passion or the universal condemnation that poured forth in 1995. The French decision offended, antagonized and aroused people once more to the great cause of rolling back the nuclear arms race. To that extent, the decision-cum-reaction may have concentrated the minds of the major Western leaders on the continued deep hostility to any further nuclear testing and the political as well as technical merits for a zero-yield CTBT. Although Paris denied it (they would, wouldn't they?), the fury of the protests almost certainly influenced the French decision to terminate the testing program after six tests rather than the eight originally scheduled. The end-result may well represent a triumph of anti-nuclear hopes over military–nuclear realism.

Notes

* Originally published in *Pacific Research* (Canberra: Peace Research Centre, Australian National University, Working Paper No 159, 1995). Reprinted with permission.
1 In the wake of the furore created by the resumption of French testing in 1995, on 20 October France, the UK and the US announced their intention to accede to the SPNFZ Protocols 'in the first half of 1996'; *USIS Wireless File*, EPF508, 20 October 1995, 7.
2 These are discussed in detail in International Physicians for the Prevention of Nuclear War and The Institute for Energy and Environmental Research, *Radioactive Heaven and Earth: The Health and Environmental Effects of Nuclear Weapons Testing In, On and Above the Earth* (New York: Apex Press, 1991), chapter 9, 'French Testing'.
3 More recent data and analysis have documented the trail of grave environmental damage left by the earlier tests. Angelique Chrisafis, 'French nuclear tests "showered vast area of Polynesia with radioactivity"', *Guardian*, 4 July 2013.
4 Venting refers to the loss of radioactivity from the rocks surrounding the point of detonation at the time of detonation. Leaking refers to radioactivity transported by water after the material produced by the explosion has cooled.
5 On 23 January 1996 the French government acknowledged that radioactive materials had leaked into the sea from its nuclear test sites in the South Pacific, but in quantities too small to pose a threat to the environment; William Drozdiak, 'Paris admits radioactive leaks from atomic tests', *International Herald Tribune*, 24 January 1996.
6 Scott Emerson, 'N-tests health risk minimal: scientists', *Australian*, 17 August 1995.
7 'Background Paper on the French Nuclear Testing Program' (Canberra: Department of Foreign Affairs and Trade, 28 June 1995), 4.
8 USIS, *Wireless File*, EPF103, 14 August 1995, 5. Similarly, after the signing of the Partial Test Ban Treaty in 1963 banning atmospheric tests, President John F. Kennedy had proposed to President Charles de Gaulle that the US would assist in the development of the French nuclear program if Paris abandoned atmospheric testing. The offer was refused; Robert S. Norris, Andrew S. Burrows and Richard W. Fieldhouse, *Nuclear Weapons Databook, vol. 5, British, French and Chinese Nuclear Weapons* (Boulder: Westview, 1994), 206.
9 In an interview with *Le Figaro*, as reported in the *Canberra Times*, 13 October 1995.

10 For a preliminary account, see Shaun Gregory, 'Les Essais Nucléaires: France and the Nuclear Weapons Testing Resumption Decision' (Perth: Indian Ocean Centre for Peace Studies, Occasional Paper No. 44, 1995).
11 See Ramesh Thakur, 'A Dispute of Many Colours: France, New Zealand and the *Rainbow Warrior* Affair', *The World Today* 42:12 (1986): 209–14.
12 Paul Keating, 'Hiroshima a powerful reminder of our chance for a nuclear free world', *Weekend Australian*, 5–6 August 1995.
13 USIS, *Wireless File*, EPF410, 19 January 1995, 12.
14 USIS, *Wireless File*, EPF213, 6 July 1993, 35.
15 USIS, *Wireless File*, EPF103, 14 August 1995, 4–7.
16 USIS, *Wireless File*, EPF510 and EPF513, 11 August 1995, 10–13.
17 USIS, *Wireless File*, EPF104, 14 August 1995, 7.
18 Mark Bendeich, 'South Pacific to widen anti-nuclear struggle', Reuter News Service, Article Ref. 000679554945, 19 July 1995.
19 Reuter News Service, Article Ref. 000694712949, 17 August 1995.
20 Reuter News Service, Article Ref. 000691561401, 11 August 1995.
21 Reuter News Service, Article Ref. 000678481107, 17 July 1995.
22 *Canberra Times*, 3 August 1995.
23 *Australian*, 9 August 1995.
24 Paul Keating, 'A regression to old French colonial attitudes', *Australian*, 29 June 1995 (an edited translation of an article published the preceding day in *Le Monde*).
25 *Australian*, 10 August 1995.
26 Quoted in *The Economist*, 15 July 1995, 21. In fact Greenpeace did unfurl a protest banner against Chinese testing in Tiananamen Square in the week preceding the August test by China.
27 A prominent Australian columnist described the 1995 French decision to resume testing as 'extremely irresponsible', but 'consistent with its nuclear hooliganism in the Pacific in the 1970s'; Greg Sheridan, 'Why the French insist on attracting world outrage', *Australian*, 15 June 1995.
28 See Michael Richardson, 'Despite end of atomic tests, Asians remain angry with France', *International Herald Tribune*, 31 January 1996.

6 The nuclear option in India's security policy*

The nuclear arms control agenda has two components, nonproliferation and disarmament. The latter requires the actual reduction and abolition of nuclear weapons and can be pursued only by the five nuclear weapons states (NWS). In the Nuclear Non-Proliferation Treaty (NPT), the non-NWS gave up their right to nuclear weapons in legally binding form and subject to international safeguards. The nuclear powers promised to engage in arms control negotiations in good faith. Under the Intermediate-range Nuclear Forces (INF) and Strategic Arms Reduction (START) treaties, Moscow and Washington have been reducing their stockpile of strategic warheads by 2000 per year. A faster rate of destruction would compromise the safety of the process. The indefinite extension of the NPT in May 1995 reflected faith by 180 countries that the nuclear arms race has been halted and reversed.

Proliferation can occur with the spread of nuclear weapons to other countries, or with the increase in numbers or sophistication of nuclear weapons by the Big Five. Before the NPT was signed in 1968, many feared that more than twenty countries could have the bomb by the 1990s. Instead the NPT has become the embodiment of the nonproliferation norm (but not, importantly, of the disarmament norm) and has the widest membership of any arms control agreement in history. Today only four countries remain outside it: Cuba, India, Israel and Pakistan. India is crucial because it is the only one of the four NPT rejectionists to have exploded a nuclear device outside the exclusive club of the five NWS and also because its rejection in turn fuels the historic rivalry in South Asia.

India is a threshold NWS. It does not claim possession of nuclear weapons, has not forsworn the nuclear weapons option, produces significant amounts of its own nuclear material or equipment, and refuses to accept international control over them. The NPT extension, opposed by India, had two further consequences. The next most important item to come on the agenda of global arms control was the Comprehensive Nuclear Test Ban Treaty (CTBT). India suddenly realized that the CTBT would, in practical effect, severely circumscribe its long-held nuclear option. It would pose a technical barrier to the acquisition of new generations of weapons by the nuclear powers, but also to anything beyond India's existing rudimentary nuclear capability. India then set about trying, without success, to discredit and undermine the CTBT. Now India has four options: to become an overt NWS; to reject the NPT but sign the CTBT; to renounce the nuclear option; or to maintain the present threshold status while keeping open the nuclear option. Let us examine each in turn.

India as a nuclear armed state

Speaking to journalists in the Bihar state capital Patna on 29 September 1997, Madhavrao Scindia, a general secretary of the All India Congress Committee, advocated the deployment of nuclear weapons to bolster the country's security.[1] India could choose to join the nuclear club openly. For this it will have to calculate the domestic, regional and international political, economic and technological costs. The net security benefits will need to be demonstrably greater than the costs. This is far from self-evident.

Background

There are two thrusts to India's nuclear program: power generation and potential weapons production. From the start, alongside its quest for an autarchic industrial policy and a nonaligned foreign policy, India searched for nuclear self-sufficiency as a matter of conviction. India was lobbied hard during 1966–67 to sign the NPT treaty then being negotiated. A Secretaries' Committee examined the draft text in detail. Questions considered included evaluation of the likely impact of rejection on India's relations with the United States, Soviet Union and China; the economic consequences of rejection; and India's security needs. There was a consensus in the committee that India should not sign the NPT. Its views were supported by Foreign Minister M.C. Chagla and Prime Minister Indira Gandhi, and endorsed by the cabinet in May 1967.[2]

Indian objections to the treaty were noted early, remained consistent, but were not met. There was a pronounced imbalance of obligations between nuclear and non-nuclear powers, so much so that the NPT was directed at the wrong target. The treaty prohibited the actual manufacture of nuclear weapons, so all preparations short of final manufacture could be legitimately pursued. Parties joining the NPT would have a stricter supervision of fissile material and equipment for their production than those choosing to remain outside. The NPT was designed to prevent the proliferation of nuclear weapons or other nuclear explosive devices – but these were not defined. A NWS was defined, but mystically – as a state that had exploded a nuclear explosive device prior to 1 January 1967. The NWS were not required to provide positive security guarantees to those prepared to forswear the nuclear option.[3]

Furthermore, India argued, the existence of NWS within the NPT regime institutionalizes an international nuclear 'apartheid' and undermines the foundations of the nonproliferation normative order. Nonproliferation must begin with those who have done most of the proliferating in the first place. The total number of nuclear warheads possessed by the five NWS jumped after the NPT was signed in 1968.[4] With the refusal of the potential proliferators to accede to the NPT, its most important political consequence was to legitimize the possession of nuclear weapons for those who had it before 1 January 1967. The argument against the NPT was expressed at its bluntest by former Foreign Secretary M.K. Rasgotra at a conference in Islamabad on 2 September 1987. In his view, nuclear nonproliferation was a myth propagated by the NWS to perpetuate their monopoly of nuclear weapons and to retain control of the world market for peaceful applications of nuclear technology.[5]

Possible blurring of the line between nuclear power and nuclear weapons capability was demonstrated by India's 12kt 'peaceful nuclear explosion' on 18 May 1974. This was conclusive evidence of India's capacity to make nuclear explosives. Moreover, India has enough unsafeguarded plutonium for diversion to weapons production if it so decides. Punitive economic and nuclear energy measures instituted by Canada, the United States and others after the test complicated and delayed, but failed to abort, India's search for nuclear self-sufficiency. By the 1980s, India had developed an indigenous capability to produce its own uranium fuel, fabricate it, construct CANDU (Canada Deuterium Uranium) type power reactors, produce heavy water for their modulation, and reprocess the spent fuel into weapon grade plutonium. This was supported by a significant research and industrial infrastructure, and teaching and research institutions.

Until the mid-1980s, the Indian position on the nuclear option was open-ended. In the meantime, Pakistan had been following a two-track nuclear acquisition policy: a network of espionage and smuggling through front organizations and intermediaries in Europe and America, and collaboration with China. Reports on Pakistan's clandestine nuclear program and successful enrichment of weapon grade uranium gave fresh momentum to the debate in India. In an interview in 1993, retired army chief (1988–91) General Mirza Aslam Beg was to reveal that Pakistan carried out its first successful nuclear test in 1987.[6]

Arguments for weaponization

There are strong strategic, political and technical incentives to maintaining a nuclear option. Advocates of the nuclear option argue that nuclear weapons would enhance India's international status, ensure its strategic autonomy, erode great power hegemony, reinforce India's leading role in the third world and the Non-Aligned Movement (NAM), expand its diplomatic choices in global affairs and stabilize relations with China and Pakistan. The Indian military believe that the production and deployment of indigenous missiles will transform the traditional battlefield by their reach and firepower and thereby help to stabilize the situation in Kashmir without a war. More importantly, India perceives the nuclear option as a cost-effective 'political force multiplier' against China's nuclear weapons status and conventional superiority. The destabilizing effects of India's nuclear option on relations with Pakistan are regarded by New Delhi as a regrettable but acceptable 'collateral damage'.

The theoretical argument on the beneficial effects of 'the measured spread of nuclear weapons' was made by Kenneth Waltz. In essence he argued that the likelihood of war decreases as deterrent and defensive capabilities increase, and that the newer NWS would be socialized into the responsibilities of their new status.[7]

Stability-enhancing features of nuclear deterrence in general are given particular cogency in the case of India–Pakistan hostility by features distinctive to their relationship. For example, propinquity and the pattern of population distribution would leave either India or Pakistan vulnerable to fallout from its own weapons used against the other, thereby producing a measure of self-deterrence.[8] It is worth noting too that the wars between India and Pakistan have been exceptional in the degree of restraint shown by both sides. Neither has chosen to bomb civilian targets. The fact of partition is accepted by both countries. For these reasons, it is argued, a posture of nuclear deterrence could stabilize the status quo between the two leading powers of the subcontinent.

Despite sustained pressure over several years, the world has failed to persuade India and Pakistan to sign the NPT, open their nuclear programs to inspection or take part in regional talks on arms control. Now even the United States has effectively moved away from getting them to sign the NPT, to an attempt to cap a non-weaponized deterrence relationship between them. The goal of rolling back and eventually eliminating their nuclear capabilities can be postponed until the emergence of a more favourable political climate at a later, more distant date. To the extent that the security interests of both countries can be met without the acquisition of nuclear weapons, their actual deployment is unnecessary.

The NWS that established the NPT regime are trapped in the fundamental paradox that while they justify their own nuclear weapons in national security terms, they seek to deny such weapons to anyone else for reasons of global security. With the end of the Cold War, strategic threats to the United States are uncertain. Yet Washington, with the world's most powerful military arsenal at its disposal, insists on the right to deal with its diffuse and uncertain threats with nuclear weapons. But it insists that India must forgo the option despite facing clearly identifiable threats to its security from China and Pakistan.

The counter to India's position is best expressed by Japan. Ambassador Mitsuro Donowaki, head of the Japanese delegation to the 1990 NPT Review Conference, pointed to the paradox of Japan, as a 'victim' of NPT discrimination, urging China, a 'victimizer' NWS, to join the NPT. Japan too wants to end the discriminatory nature of the NPT: 'India . . . by staying outside of the Treaty . . . Japan . . . from within, by urging the nuclear weapons States to pursue disarmament'.[9]

Costs of weaponization

Weaponization would trigger a fresh round of conventional and nuclear arms escalation in the region and unleash diplomatic and military forces of unpredictable and uncontrollable consequences. The net gain to national security would be nil: India would simply be buying into insecurity at higher levels of military sophistication and expenditure vis-à-vis China and Pakistan.

There would be opportunity costs for development projects. Critics question claims of an economically inexpensive strategic posture that would produce miraculous tension reductions. Instead, the nuclear option could prove to be a major cost-multiplier if India found itself competing with the nuclear powers. To catch up with China, India would have to renounce the threshold status, conduct several tests and establish the entire supporting infrastructure of a NWS. India would have to compete with the nuclear powers in building up nuclear arsenals, modern delivery systems and survivable basing, command and control systems, all underpinned by a doctrine of deterrence that is yet to be developed. And a nuclear India would be a target of all other nuclear powers.

Kanti Bajpai has identified several domestic costs of the nuclear option.[10] Relying on secrecy and obfuscation, a nuclear program undermines the tradition of democratic accountability and contributes instead to a culture of lies and evasions. Shielding the program from public scrutiny hides the inefficiency, malpractice, mismanagement and dangers – and nuclear technology is unforgiving when things go wrong. The nuclear program encourages excessive centralization of political control as well as obsessive secrecy. In turn both exacerbate bureaucratization and militarization. And it soaks up large volumes of human, financial and material inputs. As well, the scale of the peaceful nuclear energy program is such as to have produced grave safety and environmental concerns.[11] India's safety record on nuclear plants operation is questionable.

The idea of nuclear deterrence is entrenched in the security discourse in the subcontinent. If not careful, India and Pakistan could find themselves in an unstable nuclear arms race, which drains scarce resources from economic development and further entrenches the Cold War mentality in the two countries. India's relations with other South Asian countries would also be seriously aggravated. The regional security environment would deteriorate greatly, accompanied by a rise in levels of fear and distrust. The other South Asian states could come to fear and loathe the regional bully.

India's political credibility would be damaged in the wider nonaligned and third world. India causes deep offence to many countries by implying that somehow everyone else has been duped by the nuclear powers. The South Pacific nations, having campaigned against French testing for thirty years, do not believe that the CTBT is illusory. It will end totally and forever testing and the associated health and environmental risks. There would be a powerful political, economic and technological backlash from around the world. Only the West and the major multilateral institutions dominated by the West (for example the International Monetary Fund (IMF) and the World Bank) can provide India with the necessary amounts of aid, credits and investment. India needs US money, business and technology to maintain the momentum of economic liberalization and modernization. The United States is India's most important trading partner and its largest foreign investor.

NPT no, CTBT yes

Second, short of full-fledged nuclear weapons status, India can stay out of the NPT but sign the CTBT. This would give up the nuclear option vis-à-vis China but preserve it vis-à-vis Pakistan. It would enable the two South Asian countries to acknowledge each other's de facto NWS. They could then move from moralizing about nuclear disarmament by others to engaging each other in meaningful arms control negotiations, conventional as well as nuclear. Speaking in Lahore on 6 September 1997, Prime Minister Nawaz Sharif asserted that 'the issue of nuclear capability is an established fact'.[12] The next day his counterpart across the border reaffirmed that India will keep the nuclear option open.[13]

India's opposition to the CTBT is caught in a time warp. The treaty should have been the crowning glory of the campaign begun by Jawaharlal Nehru back in 1954. Where India's position on the NPT was principled, logical and appreciated even by those who disagreed with it, its hawkish position on the CTBT is seen as based on sophistry and outdated power politics. In rejecting the CTBT, India is marching to a nuclear tune that no one else wants to hear any more. On balance the treaty meets more of India's longstanding concerns and imposes more constraints on the five nuclear powers than the other way round. The exception to this is the contentious entry into force formula. That would have been irrelevant had India signed. Indians are intensely irritated by US double standards in preaching nonproliferation while practising deterrence. The irritation is understandable. It is also irrelevant to a correct understanding of the merits of the CTBT and the dynamics of the nuclear equation today.

Domestic politics make it impossible for New Delhi to sign the CTBT. There is an overpowering national consensus against it. No one knows when the coalition government will collapse and the next election will be held. The pro-bomb Bharatiya Janata Party (BJP) is marking time until then. Given such political volatility, no party will commit political suicide by retreating on the CTBT. That said, there were three grounds to India's objections to the CTBT: its discriminatory nature; its failure on the disarmament front; and implications for India's national security. None withstands scrutiny.

Discrimination

India argues that the CTBT is discriminatory because it will entrench the dominance of the existing nuclear powers. This is disingenuous. *Every* CTBT clause will apply equally to *all* countries: a textbook example of a universal, non-discriminatory treaty. To argue that its effects are unequal is like arguing that the Olympics are discriminatory because they do not equalize for different opportunities between the rich and poor countries. Perhaps India, steeped in the culture of entitlement, should demand that one seventh of Olympic medals should be reserved for its athletes. Besides, virtually every facet of India's own public policy is based on discrimination on grounds of caste. India has also managed to live with a discriminatory United Nations system which confers permanent membership of the Security Council on just five countries, and with an Antarctic Treaty system which divides the world into members and outsiders.

Disarmament

Unquestionably, the CTBT is not linked to a timetabled commitment to total nuclear disarmament by the five NWS. Nor does it end crime in the world or corruption in India. . . Nonproliferation is worth pursuing in its own right. In doing so the CTBT does not jeopardize nuclear disarmament. It will permit the nuclear powers to keep their existing arsenals but prevent them from developing new generations of nuclear weapons. Wolfgang Hoffmann, head of the CTBT Organization being set up in Vienna, notes that according to the scientists he has consulted, even the United States cannot develop new weapons through laboratory tests alone. Peter Marschall, a British forensic seismologist and specialist on nuclear explosions, confirms: 'There is no substitute for actually testing the device'.[14]

The insistence on linkage is odd for another reason. As a bargaining lever or strategy for negotiation with the nuclear powers, its record is one of proven failure. The NWS engaged in a massive program of vertical nuclear weapons proliferation, as Indians have been only too keen to point out, during the years when India and some other key countries (for example South Africa) stayed outside the international nuclear restraints regime. Conversely, the most substantial progress in nuclear disarmament by Moscow and Washington was made after the end of the Cold War and the consequent improvement in the global security climate. Nonproliferation contributes to the enhancement of the international security environment. By insisting on linkage, India ensures that the best (a nuclear-weapon-free world) becomes the enemy of the good (an end to vertical plus horizontal proliferation). An end to proliferation and continuous weapons upgrading is worth a treaty in its own right pending nuclear disarmament. In the meantime, the CTBT could help in stabilizing the nuclear arms race in South Asia at the existing level.

National security

Government spokesmen insist that India cannot give up its nuclear option when such weapons were deployed across its borders on land and around its waters. A hard-headed assessment shows India's security interests as being better served by the CTBT. It does not take away India's option of a rudimentary nuclear weapons capability. It does rule out the option of developing a sophisticated capability. India could pursue the latter option only at the cost of a three-way nuclear arms race with Pakistan and China whose net result would be higher levels of insecurity.

Pakistan could scarcely conceal its glee at India's CTBT-related global discomfiture. All the moral opprobrium was heaped on India. Pakistan shielded its identical policy behind India's rejection, yet retained the nuclear option which alone gives it parity with India. Without the threat of nuclear weapons, Pakistan could not possibly counter India's massive conventional superiority. Frustrated with Pakistan's support for the terrorist insurgency in Kashmir, India could credibly threaten to launch punitive raids into Pakistan. Nuclear weapons, the great strategic equalizers, multiply Pakistan's ability to keep pricking away at Kashmir as an open sore.

International isolation

On 20 August 1996, India vetoed the adoption of the CTBT by the Conference on Disarmament (CD) in Geneva. Because the treaty requires the signature of all 44 countries that have nuclear research reactors, including India, to become operational, India also vetoed its transmission to the UN. Many countries were not prepared to let nearly three years of intensive negotiations be frustrated by one country. Australia took the lead in sidestepping India's veto and sent the draft text to the UN. Foreign Minister Alexander Downer argued that the world could not afford to miss, because of one recalcitrant, the unique opportunity to end nuclear testing definitively. Disarmament ideals have to be tempered by what is achievable and practical. The treaty's commitments and compromises reflect the best attainable balance of different countries' interests. It will stop testing, end the arms race, prevent proliferation and mark a milestone on the road to disarmament. Circumventing the CD did not damage it; the wishes of the world being thwarted by one country would have. Downer argued that failure to close on the treaty in 1996 would have meant the loss of the CTBT for the foreseeable future.

On 10 September the UN General Assembly approved the text of the CTBT that India had earlier blocked in the CD. When the final vote of 158–3 was announced, the normally staid Assembly broke out in applause. The cheers reflected, not pleasure at India's discomfiture, but deep conviction that the CTBT, imperfect as it is, marks an important milestone on the road to a nuclear-weapon-free world. Yet taking the CTBT directly to the UN General Assembly was wrong in principle, faulty in logic and bad politics.

The principled shortcomings of the procedure were two. First, it is manifestly unjust of those who continue to hold nuclear weapons to compel, rather than coax, any other country into testing abstinence. The linkage principle between the CTBT and nuclear disarmament is widely accepted and has been reaffirmed in the strongest possible terms in the World Court's Advisory Opinion of 8 July 1996. The Court said that the nuclear powers are legally obliged to bring to a conclusion, not merely engage in, negotiations on complete nuclear disarmament. On this the 14-judge Court was unanimous: judges from every NWS agreed with this fundamental obligation. Second, it is wrong to impose an international agreement on a sovereign state against its express wishes. The ramifications of empowering the United Nations to force an international treaty on a member state are profoundly subversive of the world order as we know it.

The logic was flawed because it confused results with process. The important goal is not India's formal signature of the CTBT, but compliance with it. If the world signs the CTBT, brings it into force and honours its provisions, it is inconceivable that India would be the only country to flout the no-test regime. In the two decades after the NPT's signing in 1968, when the five nuclear powers enlarged their nuclear stockpiles enormously and conducted very many tests, all that India managed to do was conduct one test in 1974. The imperatives of domestic and international politics prevented India from testing, making and deploying nuclear weapons. Now all nuclear powers have stopped testing, Moscow and Washington are reducing their nuclear stockpiles, and the world community is becoming stridently anti-nuclear. The pressure on India to refrain from testing would be insurmountable. India had committed itself to a policy of three noes: no signing, no veto, no testing. The most sensible course would have been to express regret at the no signature, happiness at the no veto and satisfaction at the no testing pledge. The logic of nonproliferation suggests therefore that the world should change the entry into force formula of the CTBT and bring it into force de facto for India and legally for every other country.

The politics of taking an unchanged CTBT to the UN was likely to produce the very opposite effect of that intended. Internally, there is an overwhelming national consensus, across the political, press and public spectrum, against the CTBT. Indian objections to the CTBT are wrong in almost every conceivable respect. But the fact of consensus, and the strength of nationalist passions underpinning it, represent ineluctable political reality. A second political reality is that the government is an unstable coalition of more than a dozen disparate political parties. Its demise, heralding fresh elections, could come any day. The biggest winners would be the pro-bomb BJP.

India is not alone in reacting to outside pressure with anger. Feelings against external interference are especially intense on issues of national security. Over the past three–four years, since around mid-1994, the nuclear hawks have gained ascendancy in the national security debate within India. Faced with US-led UN coercion, an isolated, sullen and resentful India is more likely to respond with an open nuclear program, including a two–three year series of nuclear tests, than to cave in to international pressure. For example General Sundarji, who remains one of the most influential commentators in the public debate on India's national security, changed his mind as a result of the UN manoeuvre. With the indefinite extension of the NPT and the CTBT being 'bulldozed through' in 1995 and 1996, he joined the calls for India to conduct 'a few more tests'. India, he believed, was resilient enough to withstand the adverse but temporary political, economic and technological repercussions.[15] Similarly K. Subrahmanyam, a retired high-ranking defence official and an equally influential commentator, argued that the UN vote was evidence, not of India's international isolation, but rather of the inability of almost all others 'to defend the principle of sovereignty of nations against the onslaught of nuclear hegemons'. He too concluded that 'The time has therefore come for India to declare itself as a nation with an operational nuclear deterrent capability'.[16]

India's objections to the CTBT are an alibi for keeping open its own nuclear ambitions. Equally, the insistence that India must ratify may have been an alibi for ensuring its failure, with India taking all blame. Australia and the United States were right to oppose this misguided formula in the first place. Instead of putting pressure on India, it can and should be ignored and isolated. If the entry into force formula is not altered, a majority vote at the UN does not change the essential dynamics. India's ratification is still necessary to make the treaty operational. Alternatively, if the treaty can be brought into operation de facto without India's signature, why not amend the formula to that effect? In due course India would come into the CTBT fold, just as China and France joined the NPT in the 1990s. Had we insisted on their ratification before the NPT became effective, the most important nonproliferation treaty would have been stillborn and there would be many more than just five nuclear powers today. Instead, very sensibly, those who found the NPT valuable brought it into force for themselves and its membership has progressively expanded. Far better for the CTBT to follow the same route to broad participation now and near universal success in the fullness of time.

By linking nonproliferation to disarmament, India undermines both. By making the CTBT conditional on India's ratification, the world jeopardizes the goals of imposing a legally binding end to testing by the threshold and the nuclear powers. If the CTBT falls, the military–nuclear lobby in all five NWS will be relieved. Pressure would also mount within India to join the nuclear club openly. The world and India would all lose. Perversely, the world was determined to reciprocate India's folly in not signing with a matching folly in demanding its signature, when that signature is irrelevant to the credibility and integrity of the test ban regime.

Renouncing the nuclear option

Third, India can decide that the military and political benefits of the nuclear option are illusory and give it up completely by signing both the NPT and the CTBT. There have been five sets of international developments which should moderate India's historical suspicion of the NPT. In 1992, France and China joined the NPT regime, thereby bringing all NWS within the fold. Second, the superpowers have at long last begun to fulfil their part of the NPT bargain in the reciprocal cycle of nuclear cuts. Third, Argentina and Brazil adhered to the Treaty of Tlatelolco establishing a nuclear-weapon-free zone (NWFZ) in Latin America. Fourth, in March 1993 President F.W. de Klerk confirmed that South Africa had manufactured six nuclear weapons, but they had been dismantled and destroyed in early 1990. South Africa has now signed the NPT and in 1996 it also signed the Treaty of Pelindaba establishing Africa as a NWFZ. Fifth and finally, with the breakup of the Soviet Union, Belarus, Kazakhstan and Ukraine agreed to the withdrawal of all Soviet nuclear weapons to Russia.[17] The policy implication of all this is that 'Increasingly isolated in its nuclear stance, India would do better to bend a bit with the winds of nuclear change than risk being cast as an international pariah'.[18]

Renouncing the nuclear option would enable India to focus its energies on economic growth as today's currency of power and reclaim the disarmament moral high ground. Indians still seem to regard nuclear weapons as the major currency of world power. Most countries have become convinced of their futility. Nuclear weapons did not deter enemies from attacking and defeating US and Soviet forces in Vietnam and Afghanistan respectively. Israel is a nuclear but not a world power; Japan is not nuclear but is a world power. By extending the NPT indefinitely, the world community showed that nuclear weapons are an increasingly debased international currency. Since then, Southeast Asia and Africa have adopted their own regional NWFZs, confirming that the nuclear currency is being taken out of circulation.

India's gravest security threats are rooted in internal social and economic problems. Nuclear weapons are of no use in helping India to combat terrorist violence in Kashmir, Punjab, Assam or Tamil Nadu. Ironically, India could probably maintain the nuclear option at greatly reduced political cost from within the NPT through acquisition of enabling technologies, material and expertise in the nuclear power industry to build the requisite infrastructure to upgrade to nuclear weapons with the imminent onset of a crisis.

Status quo of nuclear ambiguity

Fourth and finally, India can keep its present policy and face increasing international isolation without any of the security, political or moral benefits of the previous three options. This will be analogous to the economic policy of old, which kept India poor and isolated while the rest of the world moved on and simply passed India by. Had India decided to acquire nuclear weapons after its first test in 1974, by now the world would have come to live with it as the sixth nuclear armed state. Instead, in the 1990s India has had to bear the opprobrium of being an NPT rejectionist without having nuclear weapons.

The nuclear weapons debate in India itself remains inconclusive. The political and economic costs of nuclear weapons acquisition and the military costs of forswearing the nuclear option exceed the cost of sustaining the diplomatic, economic and military policies associated with a threshold NWS posture. A fundamental change in the equation could result from exogenous (war with China or Pakistan) and endogenous (internal party-political dynamics in India) stimuli. Until now, however, the 'strategy of ambivalence'[19] has permitted the effective development of nuclear weapons capability without incurring the adverse international penalties of open acquisition.

George Perkovich has argued that the strategy could be formalized into a posture of 'non-weaponized deterrence'.[20] This would require agreement between India and Pakistan on the permissible level of nuclear weapons preparation; a verification system to instil confidence that the level was not being exceeded; and the buttressing of crisis stability by injecting time buffers into the nuclear escalation process from the triggering crisis to the decision to build weapons and assemble, deploy and use them in first or retaliatory strikes. The threshold NWS status has been effectively stabilized for some considerable time in the subcontinent. The stance was politically sustainable because it appeased the nuclear hawks without arousing the ire of the nuclear pacifists. It was militarily sustainable because it was viable as a policy of minimum deterrence based on calculated ambiguity – a neat reversal of the standard deterrence theory which rests on the credible certainty of nuclear retaliation. The latter posture supposedly requires periodic nuclear testing; the former eschews it.

The nuclear option calculus has changed dramatically in the 1990s. Domestically, the political costs of *renouncing* the option have gone up steeply. With the end of the Cold War, financial and political incentives have increased to cooperate with the West, constrain nuclear programs and avert an arms race. Internationally, therefore, the costs of *exercising* the nuclear option have gone up equally steeply. In the meantime, the costs of *maintaining* an unexercised nuclear option are also mounting. 'Pretending that the Indian nuclear programme is entirely peaceful convinces no one; such rhetoric will only convey the impression of deviousness on

India's part'.[21] In return for these escalating costs, India fails to gain military parity with China. Instead, India pays the price for an option which 'assists Pakistan to level the military equation with India'.[22] Logically, therefore, the status quo of maintaining the option without proceeding to a program of tests and weaponization has become an unsustainable absurdity. For this reason, while the consensus behind the old option ensured that the equilibrium was a stable one, the equilibrium supporting India's present policy is dangerously unstable.

India's stockpile of weapon grade plutonium is quite small. There are also financial constraints on the size of the weapons program that India could embark on. For both reasons, India can afford only a modest survivable deterrent force, hoping that the small size will be offset by quality and reliability. The untested weapons capability that India already has is of military relevance against Pakistan only. To transform this into a reliable, effective and thus credible retaliatory deterrent against China, a limited series of tests will be necessary. Without further testing but with the maintenance of the nuclear option, India in effect vindicates the Western world's policy of bracketing it with Pakistan, the traditional military counterweight to India. The existing nuclear weapons capability ensures that the reach of India's military power is confined to the subcontinent and that its nuclear ambitions are held in check by Pakistan.

Brahma Chellaney and I draw opposite conclusions from this. He believes that the costs of merely maintaining the nuclear option are so high that India may as well exercise the option to derive the very substantial security benefits of nuclear deterrence at the minimal marginal costs of weaponization. I reverse the equation. The additional political, economic and technological costs of weaponization would be so high, and the net security gains so illusory and questionable, that India is better off renouncing the nuclear option and travelling down Japan's path to international influence. Thus India can break out of the straitjacket of being relegated to the minor league with Pakistan either by open testing and weaponization – joining the club of nuclear powers – or by renouncing the nuclear option and forcing Pakistan to do the same. India would then have to aspire to great power status like Japan and Germany, through economic prowess and market power.

Playing the UN card

We have looked at India's options. India is already subject to a raft of export control restraints on proliferation-sensitive materials and technology. Are there any carrots that might be offered as well? The most tempting would be for the existing five NWS to agree to a timetabled, unequivocal and binding commitment to the complete elimination of all nuclear weapons. That seems unlikely. India's long-term aspirations clearly include achieving the status of a great power. As the international political structure fragments from military bipolarity to political multipolarity, Indian security analysts see a nascent role for regional powers. In attempts to calculate the economies of India's nuclear program, observers often fail to appreciate the element of psychic national income produced by the status of being an acknowledged NWS.

Diplomatically and economically, nonaligned India was on the margins of the defeated and the losers in the Cold War. India's very prickliness on sovereignty issues – nuclear and economic nationalism – is evidence of fragile self-confidence and low world esteem. One possible solution to the impasse is for India to barter away its nuclear option in exchange for permanent membership of the UN Security Council.[23] The United Nations remains a prisoner of the past in the permanent membership of the Security Council which, rather unfortunately, is coterminous with nuclear weapons status. This gives rise to the mistaken but understandable perception that the possession of nuclear weapons confers the status of great power. One of India's most prominent defence commentators notes that the 'major players have missile and nuclear capacities and nuclear weapons are reaffirmed as the currency of power by restricting the veto power in the Security Council to the five nuclear weapons proliferators. Therefore, India needs to be a missile nuclear power'.[24] If non-NWS like Germany, Japan and India could be admitted to the hallowed ranks of the great powers on the Security Council, the international community would effectively divorce the status of great power from the possession of nuclear weapons.

The addition of India – which is a keen contender for permanent Security Council membership – could be tied to a renunciation of the nuclear weapons option. Permanent membership of the Security Council could tip the balance between incentives and disincentives in India's nuclear option calculus. It would confer global status. Without in any way diminishing national security, it would enhance India's international prestige. From the point of view of the world community, the gains would include widening the representational credentials of permanent members, separating the status of great power from the possession of nuclear weapons and achieving significant progress in nonproliferation objectives: all without any corresponding cost.

There would be many advantages to India in signing the NPT as part of a package deal. All other South Asian countries would be greatly reassured about India's nuclear intentions. Joint accession of the NPT by India and Pakistan would freeze the military balance more or less permanently in India's favour. Renouncing the nuclear weapons option would allow India to reclaim the moral high ground in moves towards nuclear arms control and disarmament. It would also facilitate access to nuclear technology for peaceful purposes under international safeguards. Permanent membership of the Security Council would make it possible for the Indian government to finesse nuclear hawks while delighting the nuclear doves by joining the NPT regime. It would also please the hawks, for permanent membership of the Security Council would put Pakistan in its place while giving India a seat alongside China at the high table in the UN system.

Conclusion

India has never received sufficient international credit for the good things it does. Its democracy has been taken for granted. Its defence expenditure is remarkably low on any reasonable criteria of threat assessment and legitimate security needs.

The wars between India and Pakistan have been 'civilized' affairs within the canons of the laws of wars. Civilians have not been deliberately targeted by either side. The nuclear self-restraints include no test since 1974, no declared nuclear weapons status, no sharing of nuclear technology with others and no overt deployment of missiles. India has also refrained, as a matter of deliberate policy, from exporting arms. India was happy to co-sponsor the UN resolution endorsing the 1993 Chemical Weapons Convention (CWC). India was neither a known nor a suspected possessor of chemical arms. Having ratified the CWC, India ended decades of silence and confirmed that it possesses stockpiles of chemical weapons and the production facilities to make more of them. As the *Washington Post* commented in an editorial, India's action was both 'an advertisement for the new treaty' and helped India to 'polish its arms control credentials'.[25] In the 1990s India has also invested much diplomatic capital in improving relations with its South Asian neighbours. This was accentuated after mid-1996 under the impact of the 'Gujral doctrine' which saw India make unilateral and non-reciprocal concessions. Relations with Bangladesh, Nepal and Sri Lanka are far better than they were a decade ago and fresh beginnings have been made even with Pakistan.

Notwithstanding its good international citizenship on arms control, India's ambiguous nuclear posture is a self-inflicted wound that will not heal so long as it neither acquires nor renounces nuclear weapons. What may originally have been principled and clever has degenerated into casuistry and indecisiveness. The current policy of maintaining the nuclear option is increasingly an anachronistic obstacle to the development of a sensible national security policy. Having passed its use-by date, it makes less and less military and political sense.

On most objective measures, India should be compared to China. Instead, the nuclear posture puts India on par with Pakistan. Most irritatingly, China is routinely suggested as a joint regional security manager in South Asia, in exasperating disregard of the fact that China is India's main security preoccupation on the nuclear front. In April 1997, China fractured the international coalition against it to stop the UN Human Rights Commission even debating its human rights record. Given the magnitude of the problem in China, this was a stunning demonstration of the importance of market power in today's world. India too should explore how best to enhance its market presence and expand its influence as a state actor in world affairs. India has generally seen itself as a world power in the making and conducted its regional and international relations on this basis. The result has been insignificance abroad, suspicion in the region and turbulence at home. India would be better advised to reverse the process. Stability and prosperity at home and in the region will enhance its international status and give credibility to its claims to global leadership.

Notes

* Originally published in *Asia Pacific Review* 5:1 (1998): 39–60. Reprinted by permission of Routledge.
1 *Times of India*, 30 September 1997.

92 Regional challenges

2   This paragraph is a distillation of chapter 17 of C. S. Jha, *From Bandung to Tashkent: Glimpses of India's Foreign Policy* (New Delhi: Sangam Books, 1983). Jha was Foreign Secretary at the time and a member of the Secretaries' Committee.
3   *Negative security assurances* are undertakings by NWS not to attack non-NWS; *positive security guarantees* are undertakings by NWS to render effective military assistance to non-NWS under attack.
4   Jasjit Singh, 'Prospects for Nuclear Proliferation', in Serge Sur, ed., *Nuclear Deterrence: Problems and Perspectives in the 1990s* (New York: United Nations, 1993), 69.
5   Maharajakrishna Rasgotra, 'Nuclear Non-Proliferation Issues in South Asia', in Eduardo Faleiro *et al.*, *Southern Asia–Pacific: Current Trends* (New Delhi: International Institute for Southern Asia–Pacific Studies, 1987): 38–42.
6   A Reuter report on *India News Network*, 27 July 1993. General Beg was deputy army chief in 1987.
7   Kenneth N. Waltz, *The Spread of Nuclear Weapons: More May Be Better* (London: International Institute for Strategic Studies, Adelphi Paper 171, 1981).
8   S. Rashid Naim, 'Asia's Day After: Nuclear War between India and Pakistan?', in Stephen P. Cohen, ed., *The Security of South Asia: American and Asian Perspectives* (Urbana: University of Illinois Press, 1987): 260–69.
9   Mitsuro Donowaki, 'Non-Proliferation Issues and the Future of the NPT', *Disarmament: A Periodic Review by the United Nations* 16:2 (1993), 73, 78.
10 Kanti P. Bajpai, *Nuclear Weapons and the Security of India: Giving Up the Bomb*, Peace Research Centre, Working Paper no. 161 (Canberra, September 1996), 13–18.
11 N. Gopal Raj, 'Issues Nuclear – The Safety Concerns', *Frontline*, 4–17 March 1989, 89–95.
12 Quoted in Shahid Ahmed Khan, 'Nawaz Sharif acknowledges Pakistan's capability', *Times of India*, 8 September 1997.
13 *Times of India*, 9 September 1997.
14 Both quoted in 'Treaty will stop N-weapons' development, say experts', *Times of India*, 2 August 1997.
15 K. Sundarji, 'India's best option', *Hindu*, 17 September 1996. The call for 'a few more underground nuclear tests' was repeated a fortnight later; K. Sundarji, 'India's post-CTBT strategy', *Hindu*, 30 September 1996.
16 K. Subrahmanyam, 'The world after CTBT', *Economic Times*, 19 September 1996.
17 In spring 2014, with the Russian annexation of Crimea and the tense crisis over Ukraine, many, rather mistakenly, concluded that if only Ukraine had kept it nuclear weapons in 1994, they would have effectively deterred Russia in 2014. See Ramesh Thakur, 'Ukraine and nukes', *Australian Outlook*, 24 April 2014, http://www.internationalaffairs.org.au/australian_outlook/ukraine-and-nukes/.
18 Leonard S. Spector, 'India's nuclear stance bombs out', *Asian Wall Street Journal*, 13 August 1992.
19 The phrase is from K. Subrahmanyam, 'An Indian Perspective on International Security', in D. H. McMillen, ed., *Asian Perspectives on International Security* (London: Macmillan, 1984), 165.
20 George Perkovich, 'A Nuclear Third Way in South Asia', *Foreign Policy* 91 (Summer 1993): 85–104.
21 C. Raja Mohan, 'Nuclear weapons and the Gujral Doctrine', *Hindu*, 22 September 1996.
22 Brahma Chellaney, 'Nuclear option: the unresolved issue', *Times of India*, 8 August 1997.
23 I first argued this in Ramesh Thakur, 'Into the Security Council, out of the nuclear trap', *International Herald Tribune*, 1 February 1993.
24 K. Subrahmanyam, 'Inscrutable India: disoriented dialogue with the US', *Times of India*, 6 October 1997.
25 'India sets an example', *International Herald Tribune*, 7 August 1997.

7 The South Asian nuclear challenge*

After sketching the background to the 1998 tests, this chapter discusses the South Asian nuclear developments through four questions: why did India and Pakistan resort to open testing; why were they wrong to do so; how can the fallout be contained; and what is the South Asian-global nuclear nexus? The answers will be helpful in drawing appropriate lessons.

Background

While both India and Pakistan were 'threshold' nuclear weapons states (NWS), there were two significant differences between their nuclear programs. India's was driven primarily by civilian applications of nuclear technology and was always under the firm policy control of the civil bureaucracy and government; Pakistan's was begun principally with military goals in mind and operated mainly under the control of the military. In May 1998 India's tests were planned and carried out by civilian operatives, Pakistan's were controlled by the military.

Independent India searched for nuclear self-reliance as a matter of conviction. The Atomic Energy Commission (AEC) was established in 1948 and eight years later Canada and the United States agreed to help India to build a nuclear research reactor for power generation without requiring oversight by the International Atomic Energy Agency (IAEA). India took a militant stance against the Nuclear Non-Proliferation Treaty (NPT) from the beginning for dividing the world into the nuclear haves and have-nots; Pakistan followed India's example in rejecting the treaty. The subcontinent became a much-touted region for nuclear weapons proliferation in the 1980s. Both India and Pakistan were assumed to have nuclear weapons *capacity*, but not nuclear weapons power status.[1] The knowledge that China had acquired nuclear weapons made it an attractive option for India; a reasonable supposition that Pakistan was acquiring the capability and material to make nuclear weapons made it imperative for any Indian government to make the bomb too. India's 1974 test may equally be said to have made it imperative for Pakistan to acquire the forbidden fruit of nuclear knowledge for the immediate protection of Pakistan's honour and the greater glory of Islam. Yet in fact Prime Minister Zulfikar Ali Bhutto had ordered the Pakistani nuclear capability to begin in 1972, that is, two years earlier.[2] The decision flowed from India's role in the secession of East Pakistan in 1971; India's 1974 test merely confirmed Bhutto in the correctness of his decision.

Pakistan followed a two-track nuclear acquisition policy: a network of espionage and smuggling through front organizations and intermediaries in Western Europe and North America, and collaboration with China. In January 1972 Bhutto directed the cream of the country's nuclear physicists to build the bomb and Pakistan set up a worldwide ring to buy, copy or steal nuclear weapons technology.[3] Reports of Pakistan's clandestine nuclear program and successful enrichment of weapon grade uranium gave fresh momentum to the debate in India. In 1986, army chief General K. Sundarji assured his soldiers that India was aware of a possible nuclear threat from potential adversaries and, in the event of a war, it would not be required to fight at a disadvantage.[4] In an interview with the Indian journalist Kuldip Nayar in 1987, the Pakistani scientist Abdul Qadeer Khan claimed that Pakistan had already made nuclear weapons. He dismissed such a thing as a 'peaceful' nuclear program, and boasted that whereas it had taken India twelve years to assemble the bomb, Pakistan had done it in seven. In the context of the US threat to cut off aid, he insisted that testing was not necessary.[5]

The Khan interview was probably directed at three different audiences. To the domestic Pakistani constituency, it signalled determination to resist being browbeaten by outsiders on an issue of national security. To Washington the statement conveyed the hint that, as a necessary conduit for the successful pursuit of US policy on Afghanistan, Pakistan had sufficient leverage to be able to afford to be independent in its nuclear policy. The final target of the disclosure was India. Pakistan feared that the Indian Army's Operation Brass Tacks exercises being carried out at the time could be the prelude to an invasion. Khan effectively upped the ante to the nuclear level. India responded by announcing that the emerging nuclear threat from Pakistan had made it imperative for it to review its own nuclear options.

US intelligence sources were reporting that Pakistan had recently completed a 'workable' nuclear bomb. The development presented the US with a 'hideous dilemma' in regard to the statutory requirement for a presidential certification that Pakistan did not possess 'explosive nuclear devices'.[6] Because nonproliferation concerns were subordinated to the policy of inflicting a bleeding wound on the Soviets in Afghanistan, intelligence evidence of Pakistan's nuclear weapons program was ignored and presidential certifications duly issued. Seymour Hersh has claimed that India and Pakistan were on the brink of a nuclear confrontation in May 1990. Pakistan had put together between six and ten nuclear weapons and the US-supplied F-16s were prepositioned and armed for delivery – ready to launch on command. The crisis was defused with the despatch of a high-level, blunt-talking US crisis management team to Islamabad and New Delhi.[7] In October 1990, following the standoff and after the Soviet withdrawal from Afghanistan, the Bush administration was unable to certify Pakistan's non-nuclear status.[8]

The nuclear option became a party-political issue in India's elections. On 24 September 1989, the manifesto of the Bharatiya Janata Party (BJP) opted for 'optimum defence preparedness, including production of nuclear bombs and delivery systems'.[9] The BJP has been the party to gain the most in all elections since then. Its share of seats in the Lok Sabha (House of the People – India's lower house of parliament) jumped from 2 to 85 in 1989, and then again to 119 in 1991, 161 in 1996, and 178 in 1998.[10]

Why the tests were understandable

India and Pakistan were thus caught in a self-ratcheting nuclear capability spiral which culminated in matching nuclear tests: five by India on 11 and 13 May 1998, and six by Pakistan on 28 and 30 May.[11] Pakistan's tests were conducted in the Chagai hills of Baluchistan near the Afghan border, India's at the old testing ground in Pokhran in Rajasthan (hence 'Pokhran-II'). Pakistan's tests were almost guaranteed after India's (although, in order to draw Pakistan inside the circle of international isolation, Indian cabinet ministers helpfully issued some inflammatory statements on Kashmir between 13 and 28 May). It will be useful, therefore, to examine India's calculations before looking at the resulting pressures on Pakistan. Why did India put itself on the wrong side of history? Unless we conclude that almost all Indians are irrational, it is important to try to come to terms with the strategic rationale behind India's tests. Explanations for the tests can be discussed at three levels of analysis: domestic, regional and global.

Domestic

Domestically, the Vajpayee government had little to lose and much to gain by tapping resurgent nationalist sentiment. The uneasy coalition of a dozen parties had been lurching from one crisis to another in negotiations before and after the formation of government. Its collapse often seemed imminent, threatening yet another election. The tests enhanced the government's and prime minister's authority and bought a period of political stability. Instant polls showed 91 percent approval rating against 7 percent disapproval, even though 80 percent of the people also believed that Pakistan would follow suit.[12] The BJP argued that only it had the courage of nuclear convictions that previous Congress and other governments demonstrably lacked.

Domestic politics therefore cannot be discounted. But nor should their importance be exaggerated. The quest for nuclear self-reliance was begun by Jawaharlal Nehru; the nuclear option was kept open by all successive governments; the 1974 test was ordered by Indira Gandhi; the infrastructural preparations for weaponization were authorized by Rajiv Gandhi in the late 1980s;[13] P.V. Narasimha Rao decided upon a test in December 1995 only to retreat under intense international pressure; and the CTBT was rejected by I.K. Gujral in 1996. The continuity across governments has been underpinned by a broad and durable national consensus. 'Had the tests been motivated simply by electoral exigencies, there would have been no need to test the range of technologies and yields demonstrated in May. In the marketplace of Indian public life, a simple low-yield device would have sufficed'.[14] In the immediate aftermath of the tests, the more telling criticism was not that the tests had been conducted in 1998, but that they had not been conducted in 1995–96 when China and France were doing the same. Criticisms directed at India (and Pakistan) under those circumstances would have been substantially more muted and refracted.

While the frame of reference for India's nuclear option includes the global strategic configuration and China as well as Pakistan, the latter's tends to be far more unidimensional. Once India tested, no government in Islamabad could afford not to provide a matching riposte unless it wished to commit instant political suicide. Opposition leader Benazir Bhutto of the Pakistan's People Party alternately goaded Prime Minister Nawaz Sharif for not having the courage to match India,[15] and called upon Washington to launch punitive air strikes on India for its rogue behaviour.[16] The world tried to counsel restraint through a mix of carrots and sticks. The imposition of sanctions on Pakistan would be as swift and thorough as on India, it was made clear. But if Pakistan abstained from testing, a considerably enhanced package of economic and military assistance would be forthcoming.

However, pressure mounted on Sharif from the public, opposition politicians and the military. A whispering campaign was begun questioning whether Pakistan had nuclear capability after all. The nuclear scientists joined generals in assuring the people that they could match India's tests within days; the government just had to give them the order. President Bill Clinton made several phone calls to Nawaz Sharif and sent high-level delegations to Pakistan. On 16 May, Sharif sent a letter to the economic summit of the G-8 expressing dismay at their lukewarm reaction o India's tests. A delegation was sent to Beijing, but reportedly failed to win positive security guarantees against India. New Delhi increased the pressure on Islamabad on 18 May when Home Minister Lal Krishna Advani (in charge of Kashmir) declared that Pakistan should come to terms with the new geopolitical reality and cease its militancy in Kashmir.[17]

In the face of such provocation from across the border and the lack of effective international action against India, the government was unable to withstand the domestic pressure despite international blandishments and threats. On 28 May, the government announced that Pakistan had conducted its first set of nuclear tests. Pakistan, said Sharif, had settled the score with India. On 11 June, following India's lead of 21 May, Pakistan formally announced that it too was imposing a unilateral moratorium on further testing.

Regional

If Pakistanis relied on strategic logic rather than emotion, they would realize that the pursuit of the nuclear option by India in itself was the firmest evidence of the lack of Indian designs on Pakistan. For Pakistan can achieve parity with India only through nuclear weapons. India faced strategic encirclement through nuclear-missile collusion between Pakistan, China and North Korea.[18] Condemnations of Pakistan's tests were tinged with appreciation of its dilemma after India's tests. In effect, India was penalized for its 34 years of restraint (1964–98) vis-à-vis China while Pakistan received understanding for its inability to abstain for more than a fortnight. After the signing of the CTBT in 1996, New Delhi faced the cruel choice of 'use it or lose it' on its long-held nuclear option. The threshold nuclear weapons status did not allow India to match China's conventional or nuclear capability. But it enabled Pakistan to neutralize India's conventional military superiority. Pakistan's test of the Ghauri missile on 6 April 1998 destroyed India's natural strategic depth and produced much crowing in Pakistan about having achieved parity with India.[19]

The missile, of North Korean origin, was but the latest in a long series of proliferation-sensitive assistance from China and North Korea to Pakistan. In 1983 a US State Department report, based on CIA (Central Intelligence Agency) information, concluded that there was 'unambiguous evidence', including a secret blueprint for a nuclear bomb, that Pakistan was actively pursuing a nuclear weapons program. Moreover, 'China has provided assistance to Pakistan's program to develop a nuclear weapons capability'; Pakistan's blueprint was in fact made in China. After the suspension of US aid in 1989, Pakistan built 7–12 nuclear warheads 'based on the Chinese design, assisted by Chinese scientists and Chinese technology'.[20] According to unclassified data compiled by the US Senate Governmental Affairs subcommittee on international security and proliferation, China sold proliferation-sensitive weapons technology to Iran and Pakistan at least nine times between 1995–97.[21] But Washington simply refused to act, always looking to fudge the issue because of uncertainty over just what could be done to rein in China and from a desire to avoid damaging the lucrative trade relationship. The sale of sensitive dual use technology by firms that contributed generously to Clinton's re-election campaign only increased the cynicism in India about Washington's ability or willingness to see, let alone address, India's rapidly worsening geostrategic environment.

India had almost institutionalized its position as the world's permanent nuclear dissident. As the nuclear calculus changed dramatically in the 1990s, New Delhi decided to break out of the dead end of an unexercised nuclear option. On most objective measures, India should be paired with China, not Pakistan. The scale of differences between India and Pakistan is vastly greater than that between India and China. Of the three countries, India is also the least militarized. Maybe there are good reasons why India should accept a permanent second class status vis-à-vis China and agree to being relegated to a mere subcontinental power while China is accorded the status of a major power globally. If so, the case has to be made. So far, not only has the case not been made; it has not even been asserted, merely assumed.

From the perspective of an Indian security planner, the world was firmly in a denial mode on two vital questions. Why was China providing such assistance to Pakistan in the 1990s? The most likely answer is that China wished to constrict India to the status of a subcontinental power. What was India to do? By testing three different types of nuclear weapons (fission, low-yield and fusion, with yields of 12, 0.2–0.5 and 45kt respectively), India confirmed levels of scientific, technical and organizational abilities that until then were merely suspected. New Delhi sent three different signals to Pakistan and China. Pakistan's indigenous nuclear capability is still considerably behind India's (although its borrowed technological sophistication may be in advance of India's). New Delhi can yet, if it chooses, match China on the nuclear world stage. And the collusion between Beijing and Islamabad will not go unanswered forever.

Global

The gravest nuclear danger after the end of the Cold War was not war between Russia and the United States, but the spread of nuclear weapons technology and materials to others beyond the five nuclear weapons states (NWS). But the danger of horizontal proliferation could not be contained indefinitely by maintaining the status quo of five NWS. The post-CTBT equilibrium was a dynamic equation. Without concrete disarmament on the part of the NWS, the world was bound to slip back into real dangers of horizontal proliferation. The choice was between progress and reversal, not between progress and the status quo: a progression down to zero for the existing NWS, or the spread of nuclear weapons to other states.

This is not wisdom with hindsight.[22] The Canberra Commission's core argument, that the possession of nuclear weapons by some stimulates others to acquire them,[23] has been vindicated.[24] As argued by Jaswant Singh, the government's senior defence adviser, in a world of nuclear weapons, India's national security 'lies either in global disarmament or in exercise of the principle of equal and legitimate security for all'.[25] India's old posture of nuclear ambiguity was increasingly seen as a sham. New Delhi was already paying the price through embargoes on high or dual use technology transfers. It seems to have concluded that the marginal costs of additional sanctions are outweighed by the real gains in national security and pride. The cunning plan to circumscribe India's nuclear option through the CTBT blew up in its sponsors' faces.

Why the testing was wrong

Impressed by the oft-repeated argument that nuclear deterrence was responsible for the long peace between the Cold War rivals, Indian and Pakistani strategists see no reason why the subcontinent should not enjoy a similar afterglow of weaponization. The putative benefits of universalized deterrence notwithstanding, India's security interests suffered substantial derogation in the aftermath of the nuclear tests. Its claims to nuclear weapons status and permanent membership of the UN Security Council were dismissed. Instead of breaking free from the subcontinent, India found itself bracketed even more tightly with 'arch-rival' Pakistan. The issue of Kashmir was internationalized as never before and Pakistan did its best to keep Kashmir on the world's front pages. Far from China being accepted as the point of departure for India's nuclear security policy, Beijing was actively courted by Washington as a co-manager to contain the nuclear situation in South Asia.[26]

This might suggest perhaps that Pakistan gained from the twin sets of nuclear tests. Such a conclusion would be erroneous. The tests by Pakistan set in train a chain of consequences whose net effect was to bring to a head the cumulative crises of governance and economy. Pakistan appeared set to become South Asia's first failed state. With insecure borders to the east and north, it was also being torn apart by armed sectarian and subnational groups whose violence threatened not just rival gangs but the nation as a whole. Costs were spiralling out of control, basic necessities were becoming unaffordable for ordinary people, the state was inadequate to the tasks of governance, and people-centred 'human security' had collided head-on with state-based 'national security'.[27] Pakistan had become 'a nuclear country with a begging bowl'.[28]

The nuclear crisis compelled Western policymakers to focus on the India–Pakistan security relativities in a way that they had not done before, with the result that for the first time the disparities began to register on their consciousness. They began to gain an inkling of why India is better paired with China than Pakistan. The latter's economic frailty was in sharp contrast to India's resilience. Pakistan's foreign exchange reserves were a paltry $1bn against almost $30bn for India. International sanctions severely dampened Pakistan's economic activity and risked its default on $30bn debts. The China–Pakistan chain of proliferation as the central cause of security concern for India began to be acknowledged. There is no satisfactory answer from Washington as to why an authoritarian country with an unimpressive human rights record that has been the major proliferator of nuclear technology, expertise and components to South Asia should be allowed to buy US satellites and other high technology[29] that is denied to the world's largest democracy with stringent export control regimes and no leakage of equipment or technology. Prime Minister Atal Bihari Vajpayee went so far as to claim, in a major foreign policy address to the Asia Society in New York on 28 September, that India and the US were 'natural allies' as the world's most populous and powerful democracies. However, the relationship was often damaged by Washington's unwillingness to 'appreciate and accommodate India's interests and concerns'. On South Asian issues, 'where our supreme national interests are involved, we encounter policy approaches from America that go contrary to our basic, irreducible security needs'.[30]

The deaths of a significant number of Pakistanis in the US air strikes on terrorist camps in Afghanistan in September further validated New Delhi's longstanding complaints about active Pakistani involvement in cross-border state sponsored terrorism in Kashmir.[31] Washington began to understand the complexities of linking Kashmir to any solution to the nuclear standoff. Where outsiders had worried that Kashmir would be the flashpoint for the next nuclear conflict, it transpired that nuclear testing had become the catalyst for raising the temperature over Kashmir.[32] In other words, while over the short term India suffered the setback of being bracketed with Pakistan, over the long term Pakistan risked the world waking to the realization that the two countries are in different leagues.

The flaws of subcontinental deterrence

The biggest immediate anxieties were of two types. First, there was fear of the widening of the breach in the nonproliferation normative barrier in East Asia (North

Korea), West Asia (Iraq, Iran) and North Africa (Libya). The repercussions for the drive to establish a nuclear-weapon-free zone in Central Asia were also negative. If South Asia's geostrategic environment was already bad, it could only get worse with the proliferation of nuclear weapons more widely around the region.

The second set of anxieties stemmed from the flawed analogy with the Cold War deterrence. Because that was itself more unstable than realized at the time, the thought of India–Pakistan relations being as stable as the Cold War deterrence is not very reassuring. The geostrategic environment of the subcontinent had no parallel in the Cold War. India and Pakistan share a long border; the US–USSR did not. This dramatically shortens the timeframe within which either country would have to decide, in the midst of a tense crisis or war, whether or not to use nuclear weapons. Contiguity permits India and Pakistan to meddle inside each other's territory in numbers and on a scale that was not an option during the Cold War. The entire province of Kashmir is in dispute; the US–USSR had no direct territorial dispute. India and Pakistan have fought three wars; Moscow and Washington fought none. India shares a long border with nuclear China which too is disputed. This introduces a three-way territorial conflict into the strategic equation which was never the case during the Cold War.

The infrastructure of Cold War nuclear rivalry was underpinned by a theory of deterrence. India and Pakistan are yet to develop doctrines that would provide the rationale for numbers, types, location, dispersal or use of nuclear weapons.[33] The stability of Cold War deterrence rested on credible second strike retaliatory capability. Stockpiles, command and control centres, and the military–political leadership were protected against a surprise attack that could destroy all of them in one strike. Neither India nor Pakistan has the most rudimentary survivable basing, command, control, communications and intelligence (C3I) systems in place. C3I systems are necessary for monitoring developments by the adversary through a widely dispersed and reliable surveillance and early warning system, establishing a fail safe chain of command for the launch of nuclear strikes, protecting the nuclear arsenal against unauthorized or inadvertent use, and constructing a secure defence communications system that is robust enough to withstand an enemy first strike with all functions intact and coordinate a retaliatory launch. Civilian defence infrastructure will also have to be created. All this will take many years to develop and install. Moscow and Washington spread their stockpiles across land, sea and air-based delivery platforms. The three-pronged dispersal added to detection and strike difficulties for the enemy and so buttressed second strike capability. India and Pakistan lack this stabilizing triad of weapons platforms. India's challenge is the greater since, by its own account, its primary point of reference is China; yet Pakistan cannot be ignored.

Because of the lack of survivable forces and command centres, both countries are vulnerable to a preemptive first strike. But there is an inherent asymmetry in risk calculation. Pakistan cannot match India's conventional superiority. But a successful first strike could destroy India's nuclear capability and paralyze its conventional superiority, thereby allowing Pakistan to avenge the 1971 defeat and wrest Kashmir from India: or so a government in Islamabad might conclude.[34]

Conversely, a government in New Delhi might conclude that since reciprocal nuclear capability rules out their actual use by either country, it is safe to launch a military strike against Pakistan in punishment for its provocations in Kashmir. There is nothing in the history of the US–Soviet relationship to indicate the eventual outcome of such an adventure. All these worries are exacerbated by political volatility and instability in both countries. Pakistan's government faces economic meltdown and political challenges from Islamist groups and the military. The Indian government is an unstable coalition of an intensely nationalist party sourcing legitimacy in religion and mythology, and a number of disparate parties pursuing different, and sometimes incompatible, regional agendas.

Economic growth as the currency of power and influence

Claims of an economically inexpensive strategic posture that would produce miraculous tension reductions are dubious. India's missile and space developments give it a substantial delivery system capability. Missiles can carry less explosives and are far less accurate than fighter bombers. But they are more difficult to intercept and so can breach enemy defences more readily and rapidly than non-missile alternatives. Because of their lesser payload and accuracy, they are an expensive extravagance unless mounted with weapons of mass destruction; they are not intended to deliver 'bouquets of flowers'. Weaponization could prove to be a major cost-multiplier if India found itself competing with the nuclear powers. India and Pakistan could find themselves in an unstable nuclear arms race which, as well as further entrenching the Cold War mentality in the two countries, drains scarce resources from economic development. In the fiftieth year of India's independence, India has the biggest number of poor and illiterate in the world. This gave rise to a distinctively Indian black humour: 'No water for the people to drink? Never mind, give them heavy water'.

India's and Pakistan's direct costs (even before counting the opportunity costs, especially for development projects) have barely begun. Between 1940 and 1996, the US spent $5.5tn (in 1996 prices) on nuclearization, of which only 7 percent was on the weapons; another 7 percent was on dealing with the effects of tests, storing radioactive wastes and cleaning up the environment; and 86 percent was on building delivery and C3I systems.[35] The most recent analysis projects an annual cost of $1.2bn.[36] Can India (let alone Pakistan) really afford to spend this much per year just on nuclear weaponry and associated infrastructure for the next ten years? A ten percent increase in the defence budget in real terms over the next decade would be a crippling burden for any country. It will likely be even worse for Pakistan, where almost one-third of central government expenditure is already spent on defence.

Diminished prestige

I have argued elsewhere that fifty years after independence, India in the world was neither rich enough to bribe, powerful enough to bully, nor principled enough to inspire. India should renounce the nuclear option, I suggested, and concentrate on regaining international influence as a moral exemplar of a stable and prosperous democracy.[37] Having been the targets of criticism at the annual meeting of the ASEAN Regional Forum (ARF) in Manila in July, India and Pakistan found themselves on the defensive also at the Non-Aligned Movement (NAM) summit meeting in Durban and the annual session of the UN General Assembly in New York in September. The Durban experience was particularly galling for India, the principal founding member of the anachronistic association.[38]

What can be done to contain the challenge? The futility of sanctions

The world could not allow India and Pakistan to defy the anti-nuclear norm with impunity. But what to do? The instinctive response was to impose sanctions. Under the Glenn–Symington Act, Washington had to apply sanctions on credits and credit guarantees, loans from US banks and military assistance; and oppose loans from the IMF and the World Bank. Japan, the subcontinent's biggest donor, also suspended all foreign aid. Other Western countries followed to varying lesser degrees. Unfortunately, sanctions faced three sets of difficulties: the historical record, moral equivalence and practical calculations.

The case against comprehensive generalized sanctions, based on a mass of historical evidence, appears to be very strong. They were discredited in the 1930s when imposed on Italy in punishment for its invasion of Ethiopia, and again when applied against the Ian Smith regime in Rhodesia in the 1960s. Sanctions do not work because the target country can choose from a range of sellers in the international marketplace: it is virtually impossible to secure universal participation in embargoes.[39] It is difficult to police their application even in countries that have agreed to participate. The incentive to make large profits by circumventing sanctions is usually more powerful than the motive for enforcing them and a variety of means and routes exist to camouflage sanctions-busting contacts. Sanctions can damage producer-groups in the countries imposing them, for example farmers. They can inflict considerable pain upon innocent countries in the neighbourhood. And the besieged country itself can actually emerge stronger overall, or in strategic sectors like defence, by pursuing a determined policy of import-substitution.

The moral premises of sanctions are open to serious question. The imposition of sanctions is frequently accompanied by sentimentality and sanctimony. Yet sanctions are neither effective, non-violent nor clean as a diplomatic tool. Rather, they are blunt and crude. They do cause death and destruction, sometimes on a large scale, through 'structural violence': starvation, malnutrition, the spread of deadly diseases and the lack of adequate supplies of medicine. Their primary victims are innocent civilians, mainly women and children. The five NWS, who preach nonproliferation but practice deterrence, have no moral authority to impose sanctions. The whiff of hypocrisy in statements from those who have nuclear weapons, or shelter under them, robs their condemnation of much value in shaping the nuclear choices of India and Pakistan.[40]

Pragmatically, outsiders' self-interest lies in assisting South Asia's economic growth. Pakistan's predicament after India's tests was better understood than India's before. Therefore there was little enthusiasm to impose sanctions on Pakistan. Yet it was far more vulnerable. India's size, resources and depth give it enough resilience to withstand sanctions to a much greater extent than Pakistan. Rajagopala Chidambaram, Chairman of India's AEC, argues that India is self-reliant, understood 'not as self-sufficiency per se but as providing immunity against technology-denial. I don't think sanctions will have too much of an effect'.[41] Moreover, at a time when the world community was mounting emergency rescue efforts in countries besieged by currency and stockmarket collapse, it made little sense to try to push Pakistan towards the same precipice of economic, social and political meltdown.

The dilemma faced by outsiders was this. A moderate response would be self-negating. The nuclear hawks would feel vindicated, saying that India was now being treated with respect because it had nuclear weapons, so these should be openly deployed in numbers. To accept India and Pakistan as NWS would reverse three decades of nonproliferation policy and victimize many countries that had signed the NPT and CTBT on the understanding that the number of NWS would be limited to five.[42] A harsh response would be self-fulfilling. The hawks would argue that a friendless India that is the target of hostile international attention needs an arsenal of nuclear weapons to defend its interests.

Lessons

The events of 1998 hold six important lessons. First, economics has not displaced geopolitics. Strategic calculations, raw politics and emotions have driven the nuclear policies of India and Pakistan even at the cost of economics. The old hard questions of nuclear proliferation, nuclear conflict and nuclear disarmament are back on the international security agenda.

Second, the vital interests of key actors have to be accommodated in any security regime, otherwise it will unravel. The world was dismissive of India's security concerns in drafting the clauses of the CTBT and of Pakistan's security dilemma once India tested. Outsiders underestimated India's and Pakistan's ability to break out of the attempted strangulation of the nuclear weapons option and overestimated their own capacity to coerce them into submission. International regimes, if they are to avoid falling into the feel-good trap, must rest on conjunctions of interests. If the possession of nuclear weapons is accepted in the arsenals of some states, nonproliferation cannot be forced on those who reject the treaties underpinning it: 'India cannot accept a semi-colonial and inferior status as a nation whose security prescriptions are determined for it by others'.[43]

Third, nonproliferation and disarmament are two sides of the same anti-nuclear coin. If India and Pakistan are committed to a nuclear free world, as they claim, they need to be told clearly that their tests were a major setback to the anti-nuclear cause. The five NWS also have to be called to account for their complacency and go-slow tactics on nuclear disarmament. The 1998 NAM summit meeting emphasized the need to work even harder to achieve the objectives of disarmament,

104 *Regional challenges*

'including the elimination of nuclear weapons'.[44] The norm is anti-nuclear, as embodied in the NPT including Article 6; the CTBT is the anti-testing expression of the broader norm; the self-serving conflation of the anti-nuclear norm into an anti-testing norm by the NWS does not withstand critical scrutiny. This is also the core of the abolitionist case. Even if we concede that nuclear weapons confer some security gains, these have to be assessed against the costs, risks and alternatives. In particular, the likelihood of the useability of nuclear weapons must be weighed against the costs of the political chain reaction of nuclear weapons status. That is why a group of eight non-nuclear countries, in contradistinction to the G-7, issued a joint foreign ministers' declaration to the five NWS *as well as* to India, Pakistan and Israel calling for an end to nuclear arms.[45]

Fourth, the consequences of the tests have finally registered the reality of what many have been arguing for years: nuclear weapons confer neither power, prestige nor influence. Fifth, sanctions are too blunt to be useful diplomatic instruments. The contrast between the policy of constructive engagement with China and destructive disengagement with South Asia was painfully obvious. Having imposed sanctions, Washington finds itself imprisoned in the classic termination trap:[46] how to lift sanctions without appearing to back down, on the one hand, or rewarding 'bad' behaviour on the other. Often, sanctions are maintained because policy-makers cannot decide on the best time to lift them. Having already paid the international price for testing, India sees no reason to revert to the status quo ante on high technology access in return for signing the CTBT and joining the global nonproliferation regime. Washington will find it difficult to lift restrictions on access to advanced technology without appearing to reward India.

Sixth, in the clash between new strategic realities and selective puritanism, the latter has to give way. Thus spake Jasjit Singh, co-convener of the national security task force: 'The Americans shouldn't waste time telling us to get rid of nuclear weapons. That decision has been made. The issue now is what kind of nuclear power we are going to be'.[47] The government's official paper tabled in parliament on 27 May declared simply but firmly: 'India is a nuclear weapon state. This is a reality that cannot be denied. It is not a conferment that we seek; nor is it a status for others to grant'.[48]

Conclusion

The new deal will have to be based on these six lessons. The challenge is 'to reconcile India's security imperatives with valid international concerns regarding nuclear weapons'.[49] The proliferation deed is done. Instead of demanding the impossible feat of untesting, it is better to accentuate the positive. Having come out of the nuclear closet, India and Pakistan can move from moralizing about nuclear disarmament by others to engaging each other in meaningful arms control negotiations.

The one-dimensional nature of Pakistan's security policy means that its nuclear posture lacks ballast and texture. The sense of nuclear drift in India is being replaced with a stress on responsibility and restraint. The rudiments of its strategic posture have begun to emerge since the shock tests of May: an acknowledgment of the nuclear reality vis-à-vis Pakistan; a 'minimum' deterrent against China; unilateral promises of no use of nuclear weapons against non-nuclear states and no first use against nuclear adversaries; unilateral moratorium on any further testing; a willingness to convert this into a binding obligation under the CTBT in return for a satisfactory outcome of discussions with 'key interlocutors', meaning largely the United States; and a commitment to work towards a universal, non-discriminatory nuclear weapons convention (NWC).

The genuine security concerns of India and Pakistan can be met without overt nuclear deployment: tested capability is enough to assure deterrence. Two important firebreaks can be constructed in the form of separating warheads from delivery systems and storing delivery vehicles separately from launch sites. In return for a tacit acceptance of the new reality and the lifting of sanctions, both India and Pakistan must sign the CTBT: unilateral moratoria are less helpful than legally binding accession. If they want the full range of dual-technology assistance, they can sign the NPT as well. The anti-CTBT consensus in India rests on a deliberate, but very successful, campaign of disinformation which discredited the regime. The domestic political difficulties are thus of their own making. Having carried out the tests, India need no longer have security worries about signing the CTBT. Both A.P.J. Abdul Kalam, head of the Defence Research and Development Organization (DRDO), and AEC Chairman Chidambaram have publicly said that further nuclear tests are not necessary from a scientific and technical perspective, and that signing the CTBT would not pose any problem for India's nuclear status.[50]

The world matched India's folly of testing with a reciprocal foolishness of instant condemnations. There was no serious analysis of either principles or justice, on the one hand; or efficacy and realism, on the other. In terms of principles, India's complaints are unanswerable by any country that has nuclear weapons. In terms of realism, condemnations that wilfully refused to acknowledge India's and Pakistan's minimum security requirements in their immediate geostrategic environment were always likely to aggravate rather than ease tensions. India's nuclear tests resulted, in addition to domestic political calculations, from the actions of China and Pakistan in the region, the inaction of the five NWS globally and a craving for international recognition.

The official Indian response to condemnation by the UN Security Council, whose five permanent members are the five NWS, was to point out that no other NWS had supported the World Court Advisory Opinion on the illegality of nuclear weapons; India's record of restraint on export of nuclear technologies and commodities was better than that of some of the five NWS; unlike India's unconditional commitment to a NWC, the five NWS were not prepared to commit themselves to decisive and irreversible steps towards nuclear disarmament; instead they were all engaged in programs of modernization of their nuclear arsenals; and India's tests had been restricted to 'the minimum necessary to maintain what is an irreducible component of our national security calculus'.[51] The Security Council's presidential statement of 14 May, strongly deploring India's tests, was rejected by New Delhi as 'completely unacceptable to us'. Security Council Resolution 1172

106 *Regional challenges*

(6 June 1998), condemning India's and Pakistan's tests and demanding that they stop, was similarly dismissed by Indian spokesmen as 'coercive and unhelpful in respect of the objectives it seeks to address'.[52] The world has to decide whether to engage with India as a responsible NWS or a rogue regime and, if the latter, then to accept the risk of a self-fulfilling prophecy.

Notes

* Originally published in John Baylis and Robert O'Neill, eds., *Alternative Nuclear Futures: The Role of Nuclear Weapons in the Post-Cold War World* (Oxford: Oxford University Press, 2000): 101–24. Reprinted by permission of Oxford University Press.
1 Other countries with comparable ambiguities in their nuclear postures include Iran, Iraq, Israel, North Korea and South Africa. The last signed the NPT in 1992. On 24 March 1993, President F. W. de Klerk said in parliament that South Africa had indeed possessed six nuclear bombs, but that these had been dismantled by his administration since coming to power in 1989. For the story of the transition of South Africa from a clandestine NWS to the key signatory of the African nuclear-weapon-free zone, see Julius O Ihonvbere, 'Africa – The Treaty of Pelindaba', in Ramesh Thakur, ed., *Nuclear-Weapon-Free Zones* (London/New York: Macmillan and St. Martin's Press, 1998): 93–116.
2 Neil Joeck, 'Pakistani Security and Nuclear Proliferation in South Asia', *Journal of Strategic Studies* 8:4 (1985): 86–87.
3 Tim Weiner, citing US officials and declassified US government documents, in 'U.S. and Chinese aid was essential as Pakistan built bomb', *International Herald Tribune*, 2 June 1998.
4 Quoted in Dilip Bobb and Raminder Singh, 'Pakistan's nuclear bombshell', *India Today*, 31 March 1987, 12.
5 Kuldip Nayar, 'We have the A-bomb, says Pakistan's "Dr Strangelove"', *Observer* (London), 1 March 1987.
6 *Asian Defence Journal*, January 1988, 102.
7 Seymour M. Hersh, 'On the Nuclear Edge', *New Yorker*, 29 March 1993: 56–73. The article is unusual both for its details and also for the number of senior former officials – including CIA director Robert M. Gates – who were prepared to be interviewed on the record.
8 Salamat Ali and Frank Tatu, 'Pakistan: nuclear fallout', *Far Eastern Economic Review*, 25 October 1990, 11–12.
9 *Statesman Weekly*, 30 September 1989, 4.
10 The long-term political changes in India are discussed in Ramesh Thakur, 'A Changing of the Guard in India', *Asian Survey* 38:6 (1998): 603–23.
11 The Western scientific and intelligence communities remain sceptical of the numbers and yields of the tests. The veracity of the claims made by both governments on these two points is not relevant to the analysis of this chapter.
12 *Hindu*, 13 May 1998.
13 K. Subrahmanyam, 'Politics of Shakti: new whine in an old bomb', *Times of India*, 26 May 1998.
14 Jaswant Singh, 'Against Nuclear Apartheid', *Foreign Affairs* 77:5 (1998), 49.
15 *Economist*, 23 May 1998, 27; Christopher Thomas, 'Bhutto adds to pressure for Pakistan nuclear test', *Times*, 21 May 1998.
16 Benazir Bhutto, 'Perspective on South Asia; punishment: make it swift, severe . . .', *Los Angeles Times*, 17 May 1998.
17 Harish Khare, 'Roll back proxy war, Pak. told', *Hindu*, 19 May 1998. Advani's remarks were widely condemned in the Indian media: if the BJP Government wished to be treated with the respect due to a nuclear power, it could begin by behaving like a responsible nuclear power, was the general tenor of the advice offered to him. See, for example, the editorial 'Need for caution', *Hindu*, 22 May 1998.

18 For details, published before the tests of May, see 'China's Missile Exports and Assistance to Pakistan', and 'China's Nuclear Exports and Assistance to Pakistan', Center for Nonproliferation Studies, Monterey Institute for International Studies, April 1998 and January 1998 respectively, at http://cns.miis.edu/archive/country_india/china/mpakpos.htm, and http://cns.miis.edu/archive/country_india/china/npakpos.htm.

19 Pakistan is also working on another missile named Ghaznavi. Both missiles carry powerfully belligerent connotations from Indian history. Mahmud of Ghazni (971–1030 AD) 'led no fewer than seventeen bloody annual forays into India . . . zealously smashing countless Hindu temple idols . . . and looting India's cities of as many of their jewels, specie, and women as he and his horde of Turkish cavalry could carry back across the Afghan passes'. Stanley Wolpert, *A New History of India* (New York: Oxford University Press, 1977), 107. And these are the words of an American historian. His sacking of the temple town of Somnath became part of Hindu folklore for centuries. His exploits were repeated a century and a half later by Muhhamad of Ghur (hence Ghauri), who led his first raid into India in 1175. The great university at Nalanda, home to over ten thousand monks, was sacked around 1202. 'The severity of the Turko–Afghan persecution directed against centers of Buddhist monasticism was so unrelenting that the religion of Buddha was now sent into exile from the land of its birth, never to return again in any significant numbers'; ibid., 108.

20 Weiner, 'U.S. and Chinese aid was essential as Pakistan built bomb'.

21 *Defense News*, 14–20 April 1997, 3, 26.

22 See Ramesh Thakur, 'The Desirability of a Nuclear Weapon Free World', in Canberra Commission on the Elimination of Nuclear Weapons, *Background Papers* (Canberra: Department of Foreign Affairs and Trade, 1996): 74–88.

23 *Report of the Canberra Commission on the Elimination of Nuclear Weapons* (Canberra: Department of Foreign Affairs and Trade, 1996), 18–22.

24 As an editorial in the *Japan Times* put it, 'Nuclear stockpiles must be reduced and then eliminated . . . as the cycle of action and reaction in South Asia has proven, nuclear stockpiles feed on themselves'; 'South Asia's Nuclear Chain Reaction', *Japan Times*, 30 May 1998.

25 Singh, 'Against Nuclear Apartheid', 41–42; or 'India, through a limited series of tests, has only reasserted that either the international nuclear security paradigm be reviewed or that it be made inclusive'; Jaswant Singh, 'For India, disarmament or equal security', *International Herald Tribune*, 5 August 1998. Singh is also the person conducting negotiations with US Deputy Secretary of State Strobe Talbott on how to bridge India's security needs and global nonproliferation concerns.

26 This provoked almost uncontrolled fury among Indian commentators: 'The President of the world's most powerful democracy has spent a remarkable nine days prostituting himself in the world's most powerful autocracy . . . when he is not coddling young women, he is coddling dictators. Mr Clinton's escape from Monicaland to dragonland helped put his character on public display: Not only did he coddle, he kowtowed and fawned'; Brahma Chellaney, 'Dealing with Beijing-Washington axis', *Pioneer*, 8 July 1998.

27 See Ramesh Thakur, 'From National to Human Security', in Stuart Harris and Andrew Mack, eds., *Asia-Pacific Security: The Economics-Politics Nexus* (Sydney: Allen & Unwin, 1997): 52–80.

28 A senior Pakistan government official quoted in Christopher Thomas, 'Nuclear power forced to rattle its begging bowl', *Times*, 26 August 1998.

29 Two weeks after the Indian tests, a US Senate panel released CIA analysis linking the sale of US high technology exports to China to long-range Chinese nuclear missiles, 13 of which are targeted at US cities; *Japan Times*, 23 May 1998. House Speaker Newt Gingrich commented that 'as the Indians watch the Clinton administration sell missile technology to the Chinese, it should not shock us that the Indians want to protect themselves'; *CNN* on the Internet, 19 May 1998.

30 Reports of the speech can be found in the *Hindu* and the *Times of India*, 29 September 1998.

108 *Regional challenges*

31 However, for a cautionary note on US denial mode in the past about Pakistan-based terrorism in the region, see Prem Shankar Jha, 'Supping with the devil', *Hindu*, 7 and 8 September 1998.
32 In my view, any solution to Kashmir will have to find a balance between four propositions: (i) Kashmir is not simply a territorial dispute between two states; rather, it is a symbol of three competing nationalisms: the territorial nationalism of the Kashmiris, the Islamic nationalism of Pakistan, and the secular nationalism of India; (ii) Pakistan has no interest in a bilateral solution if it can succeed in internationalizing the dispute; (iii) India can retain Kashmir indefinitely against the force of Pakistan; but (iv) it cannot do so forever against the wishes of the Kashmiri people. See Ramesh Thakur, *The Politics and Economics of India's Foreign Policy* (London: C. Hurst, 1994): 48–61.
33 For an account of just how unprepared India is with regard to the infrastructure of nuclear weapons and the panoply of nuclear doctrines, see, Manoj Joshi, 'Nuclear Weapons: In the Shadow of Fear', *India Today*, 21 July 1997: 62–65.
34 Against this, it might be argued that neither India nor Pakistan possesses the infrastructure of sophisticated targeting and precision delivery systems to provide credible first strike capability.
35 Stephen I. Schwartz, ed., *Atomic Audit: The Costs and Consequences of Nuclear Weapons Since 1940* (Washington DC: Brookings, 1998).
36 C. Rammanohar Reddy, 'The wages of Armageddon-III', *Hindu*, 2 September 1998.
37 Ramesh Thakur, 'India in the World: Neither Rich, Powerful, nor Principled', *Foreign Affairs* 76:4 (1997): 15–22.
38 For the argument why NAM is an anachronism, see Ramesh Thakur, 'India after Nonalignment', *Foreign Affairs* 71:2 (1992): 165–82.
39 In the case of India, the strongest reaction came from the United States, Australia, Canada, Japan and New Zealand. Russia resisted US pressure to terminate long established defence links with India. By September, France was ready to initiate a 'strategic dialogue' with India; C. Raja Mohan, 'India, France to start strategic dialogue', *Hindu*, 30 September 1998.
40 Thus an editorial in the *Japan Times* noted that Japan 'lived in peace under the U.S. nuclear umbrella: This might be called a sort of nuclear hypocrisy'; 'Leading the non-nuclear movement', *Japan Times*, 8 August 1998. See also C. Raja Mohan, 'Japan's nuclear hypocrisy', *Hindu*, 6 August (Hiroshima Day) 1998.
41 Interview with *Newsweek*, 14 September 1998, 58.
42 This is probably an exaggerated argument. Brazil signed the NPT and ratified the CTBT after the tests, on 14 July 1998.
43 Singh, 'For India, Disarmament or Equal Security'.
44 K. K. Katyal, 'India foils concerted move on nuclear tests', *Hindu*, 5 September 1998.
45 The eight countries are Brazil, Egypt, Ireland, Mexico, New Zealand, Slovenia, South Africa and Sweden. See David Andrews and Lena Hjelm-Wallen (the foreign ministers of Ireland and Sweden), 'Revive the Drive against Nuclear Weapons Now', *International Herald Tribune*, 22 June 1998.
46 See Kim Richard Nossal, *Rain Dancing: Sanctions in Canadian and Australian Foreign Policy* (Toronto: University of Toronto Press, 1994), chapter 10.
47 Quoted in John F. Burns, 'In nuclear India, small stash does not a ready arsenal make', *New York Times*, 26 July 1998.
48 Paper tabled in Parliament of India on 'Evolution of India's Nuclear Policy', Government of India, 27 May 1998, paragraph 14.
49 Singh, 'Against Nuclear Apartheid', 52.
50 *Times of India*, 22 September 1998.
51 India, 'Evolution of India's Nuclear Policy', 27 May 1998, paragraph 18.
52 This statement, along with other official Indian pronouncements since the tests of May, was found on the Internet at http://www.meadev.gov.in, a site no longer active.

8 The inconsequential gains and lasting insecurities of India's nuclear weaponization*

There is a curious India connection to the dawn of the nuclear age. Witnessing the first successful atomic test on 16 July 1945, J. Robert Oppenheimer, director of the Manhattan Project that developed the A-bomb, recalled the sacred Hindu text, the Bhagvad Gita: 'If the radiance of a thousand suns were to burst at once into the sky, that would be like the splendour of the mighty one'. Birth and death are symbiotically linked in the Hindu cycle of life. So Oppenheimer recalled too the matching verse from the Gita: 'Now I am become Death, the destroyer of worlds'.[1] On 18 May 1974, in a remote desert location in Pokhran, Rajasthan, India conducted its first test of a small and miniaturized nuclear explosive device in the inappropriately named Operation Smiling Buddha. The test drew international condemnation and generated a sequence of sanctions and a progressively greater isolation of India from global nuclear orders. Yet perversely, in insisting that Pokhran-I was a 'peaceful nuclear explosion', India ensured that it would get no military–political benefit from the test. Twenty-four years later, on 11 and 13 May 1998, Indian defence and nuclear scientists returned to the same location to conduct another five nuclear tests (one fusion and four fission bombs), code named Operation Shakti (force, power).[2] What did India gain with the second series of tests, now known as Pokhran-II? The short answer is: not much.[3]

I do not argue that India should pursue unilateral nuclear disarmament which is unlikely by any of the existing nine nuclear armed states – China, France, India, Israel, North Korea, Pakistan, Russia, the United Kingdom and the United States – and therefore unrealistic as a policy goal.[4] Rather, the main aim is to argue that a denuclearized world that includes the destruction of India's nuclear stockpile would favourably affect the balance of India's security and other interests, national and international interests, and material interests and value goals.[5] Although prospects for nuclear disarmament look dim, especially after the Ukraine crisis, the analysis rests on the belief that the goal of an eventually denuclearized world is both necessary and feasible. But universal nuclear disarmament will not happen if the nuclear armed states believe their security rests on the possession of nuclear weapons for which there is no substitute in any conceivable non-nuclear anchor of national security. An essential prerequisite for global nuclear disarmament, therefore, is persuasive analysis with respect to all nuclear armed states that nuclear weapons are not essential underpinnings of their national security. The primary purpose of this chapter is to demonstrate that the security benefits of nuclear weaponization have proven to be as illusory, dubious and fragile for India as they are for others, while the financial, developmental, political, humanitarian and even security costs, risks and dangers are only too real.

India has had an ambivalent relationship with several multilateral nuclear arms control regimes. With the Nuclear Non-Proliferation Treaty (NPT) and the Comprehensive Nuclear Test Ban Treaty (CTBT),[6] India was in the odd position of having been among the earliest initiators of the regimes in principle, but rejecting them because the main players were not prepared to accommodate India's priorities in the key terms of the treaties. With respect to others like the Nuclear Suppliers Group (NSG) and the Missile Technology Control Regime (MTCR), India viewed them essentially as technology-denial regimes. Because so many have been perceived as direct threats to India's core national security interests, its posture towards them is described as 'wary, almost suspicious, of specific multilateral efforts on arms control, while supporting multilateralism in the abstract'. The explanation for the disconnect is that India's initiatives typically 'were more aspirational than programmatic'.[7] The net result was to make India's nuclear diplomacy essentially defensive rather than entrepreneurial.

Bucking the global trend of falling numbers, India's nuclear arsenal is growing (Table 1.1 above). In 2005 India committed to continuing its unilateral moratorium on nuclear testing as part of the joint US–India statement establishing the basis for renewed bilateral peaceful nuclear cooperation. On 19 April 2012, India successfully tested a new missile whose 5,000km intercontinental ballistic missile (ICBM) capability puts Beijing, Shanghai and parts of Europe within range of Indian nuclear weapons for the first time. Indian plans to deploy nuclear weapons at sea are based on the development of a ballistic missile launched from a nuclear-powered submarine. The Agni-V test came shortly after the commissioning of the nuclear-powered attack submarine the *INS Chakra*. The launch in August 2013 of the indigenously developed aircraft carrier, *INS Vikrant*, expected to be operational by 2018, makes India one of only a handful of countries to have such capability. In the same month, the reactor on the 6,000 tonne nuclear-powered submarine *INS Arihant* with underwater ballistic launch capability went critical.

Mix-motive causes of nuclear proliferation

Prior to their 1998 tit-for-tat nuclear tests, both India and Pakistan were 'threshold' nuclear weapons states (NWS): non-NPT signatories that possessed nuclear breakout capability through plants, facilities, weapon grade fissile material and technical skills. Against this backdrop, why did India decide to go down the path of nuclear weaponization through testing in 1998? We saw in the last chapter how the 1995 NPT indefinite extension and the 1996 CTBT threatened to severely circumscribe India's long-held nuclear option. A former Indian governor on the IAEA Board has recently reiterated that 'The timing of the 1998 tests was determined more by the CTBT than by ideology. India chose to face sanctions for tests rather than for not signing the CTBT'.[8] Thereafter, India had four options: to become an overt nuclear armed state; reject the NPT but sign the CTBT; renounce the nuclear option; or maintain the threshold status while keeping open the nuclear option. India chose the first option. Prime Minister Atal Bihari Vajpayee's letter to President Bill Clinton justified the 1998 tests by pointing to China as an overt NWS that first, had committed aggression against India in 1962 and second, had materially helped Pakistan, guilty of three acts of aggression against India, 'to become a covert nuclear weapons state'.[9] Beyond the highly particularized local security dynamics, the permissive international environment of a globalized nuclear supply chain, and the precipitating factors that led to the twin series of tests by India and Pakistan, nuclear weapons can be sought for one or more of five reasons:[10] compellence of the enemy to one's preferred course of action; defence against attack; deterrence of enemy attack; leveraging adversary and great power behaviour; and status. Scrutinizing each one of these in turn shows that no matter how understandable India's nuclear breakout may have been in 1998, the bomb has little utility and many costs, risks and constraints.

Compellence

'Compellence' means the use of coercion, by threat or action, to force an adversary to stop or reverse something already being done, or to do something he would not otherwise do.[11] The belief that nuclear weapons permit a state to deploy coercive bargaining power that would not otherwise be available has little evidence in history. There is no demonstrable instance of a non-nuclear state having been cowed into changing its behaviour by the threat of being bombed with nuclear weapons. The normative taboo against this most indiscriminately inhumane weapon ever invented is so comprehensive and robust that under no conceivable circumstance will its use against a non-NWS compensate for the political costs. NWS have accepted defeat at the hands of non-NWS (US in Vietnam, Soviet Union in Afghanistan) rather than escalate armed conflict to the nuclear level. Some recent research suggests that the normative taboo against nuclear weapons use may be weakening among the American public.[12] But there remains a strong belief amongst those regularly engaged with the world's nuclear policymakers that the taboo has maintained its robustness.[13] More importantly for present purposes, Indian doctrine, backed by deployment patterns, explicitly eschews any intent to use nuclear weapons as tools of coercion.

Defence

By 'defence' I mean responses to an actual armed attack, conventional or nuclear, by a foreign power. It is hard to see any role for India's nuclear armaments as instruments of defence. Its doctrine disavows any intention to use nuclear weapons in response to conventional attacks. Nuclear weapons cannot be used for defence by nuclear armed rivals whose mutual vulnerability to second strike retaliatory capability means that any escalation through the nuclear threshold would be mutual national suicide. The use of nuclear weapons would also, almost certainly, be a violation of international humanitarian law, regardless of the type of attack and possibly even when the state was facing an existential threat.[14]

Given India's geographical position, size, weight and military capability, few countries could contemplate a military attack on it. India's nuclear arsenal offers no defence against a major conventional attack by China, Russia or the US – the only three countries with the *capability* to do so. As for *intent*, Russia is a diplomatic ally and friend of long standing. Relations with the US have warmed to a greater degree than anyone could have anticipated during the Cold War, including the key role that the India–US civil nuclear cooperation deal has played in helping India break out of the global nuclear isolation.[15] China's nuclear weapons, declared doctrine and force posture and deployment patterns are designed neither to coerce others nor to fight a nuclear war, but to counter any attempt at nuclear blackmail.[16] Indians may still suffer from the 1962 China syndrome when they were militarily humiliated by the People's Republic and their territorial dispute remains unresolved. But deepening and broadening bilateral Sino–Indian relations, and cooperation on several major international issues based on converging interests in forums like BRICS (Brazil, Russia, India, China, South Africa),[17] provide considerable substance, texture and ballast to the relationship today.

Deterrence

'Deterrence' refers to a threat intended to dissuade an adversary from starting hostilities or launching an attack that may be being contemplated but has not yet been initiated. The subcontinent's history since 1998 gives the lie to the then-hopes and expectations, on both sides of the border, that nuclearization would prove to be a largely stabilizing factor. India–Pakistan confidence building measures include agreements not to attack each other's nuclear facilities, an annual exchange of lists of such facilities and advance notification of missile launches within a specified range of each other's territories. But powerful domestic constituencies have grown up in both countries to identify a multiplication of threats that justify a matching expansion of a highly elastic posture of minimum credible deterrence. 'Pakistan and India have together introduced 17 new nuclear-weapon-capable delivery systems since 1998'.[18] Both have been developing, testing and inducting a triad of basing modes on land, sea and air platforms as well as families of ballistic and cruise missiles and short-range nuclear weapons for use 'at the forward edge of future battlefields'.[19]

Pakistan assembled its first nuclear bomb around 1987 and developed an unannounced doctrine under the nuclear umbrella in support of militant groups waging a low-cost war against Indian forces in Kashmir.[20] The low-cost and low-risk covert war in the shadow of the subcontinent's nuclearization had three attractions: it would weaken India by raising the human and economic costs of occupation; the fear of nuclear escalation would raise the threshold for cross-border Indian retaliatory raids; and it would help to internationalize the Kashmir dispute by highlighting the risk of nuclear escalation. India's nuclear weapons did not stop Pakistan from occupying Kargil in 1999.[21] The two countries came perilously close to a full-blown war in 2002, after the terrorist attack on India's Parliament in December 2001. Nuclear weapons have been doubly damaging to India vis-à-vis Pakistan. They have encouraged Pakistani provocations, be it incursions in Kargil in 1999 or cover for terrorist attacks as in Mumbai in November 2008.[22] And the fear of a nuclear war with catastrophic global consequences has increased international interest and involvement, something that suits Pakistan but agitates India.[23] The term 'nuclear flashpoint' soon became a staple of international media coverage of Kashmir.

Premeditated large-scale conventional attacks and preemptive nuclear strikes seem unlikely pathways to a nuclear exchange between India and Pakistan or between China and India. But the subcontinental rivalry is not free of the risk of a nuclear exchange triggered by acts of terror committed on Indian territory by individuals and groups linked to networks across the border in Pakistan. After the terrorist attacks on India's parliament in December 2001 and on Mumbai in November 2008, national leaders, assisted by constructive roles played by outsiders, managed to contain and then deflate escalatory pressures and defuse India–Pakistan tensions. Few can feel confident that such intentionally spectacular incidents will not be repeated, or that the escalatory pressures will be successfully contained in every provocation. That is, the brittleness of deterrence stability is a function of fragile crisis stability mechanisms.

India confronts two distinct sets of asymmetries vis-à-vis Pakistan. First, for Pakistan, nuclear weapons are a compensation for conventional weakness and hence its lack of interest in a no first use doctrine. By contrast, for India their sole purpose against Pakistan is deterrence against nuclear use. Second, Pakistan has also invested in terrorist groups as part of its unconventional inventory against India. In responding to a terrorist attack, any deliberate escalation by India through the nuclear threshold would be extremely high-risk. Uniquely among all nuclear armed states, Pakistan's nuclear policy, program and weapons are under military control; it hosts and supports terrorist and insurgent groups as instruments of security policy; and it is a revisionist and irredentist state. As a result, unlike other dyadic nuclear rivalries that focus on managing stability, Pakistan seeks 'managed instability' which is poorly understood, analyzed and theorized.[24] All this strengthens the argument, discussed in the last chapter, that the geostrategic environment of the subcontinent had no parallel in the Cold War.

Moreover, Pakistan is not a unitary actor and this poses a 'particular challenge for deterrence stability in the context of a disunity in the chain of command between top Pakistani authorities and actors who may commit violence against India ... of a scale that could lead to inter-state war with potential to escalate to potential use of nuclear weapons'.[25] So long as Pakistan is unable or unwilling to take effective preventive action to stop extremists based on its territory from planning and launching attacks on India, the latter's presumption of state–jihadists collusion will remain powerfully operative. Is India's institutional configuration robust enough to manage the transition, including the requisite strategic signalling, from a terrorist attack and through a conventional response to a nuclear exchange, depending on Pakistan's counter-measures? This is why Rear Admiral (ret'd) Raja Menon questions whether India's penchant for secrecy, opacity and ambiguity is adequate against a nuclear rival that is openly committed to a first use policy and is introducing battlefield nuclear weapons.[26]

The risks and potentially dangerous consequences of strategic signalling being 'lost in transmission' across the India–Pakistan border can be seen in the development of tactical missiles and battlefield nuclear weapons by the two sides whose utility is contingent on proximity to battlefields.[27] India's 300km supersonic Brahmos cruise missile could give it the capability to carry out prompt strikes inside Pakistan. Islamabad argues that its 60km Nasr/Hatf-9 ballistic missile serves three purposes: it counters India's superior and growing conventional capability financed by an escalating defence budget; it provides a riposte to India's offensive doctrines such as 'Cold Start' which postulate a limited but rapid conventional invasion of Pakistani territory; and it counters the development of India's ballistic missile defence. The chair of India's National Security Advisory Board, former Foreign Secretary Shyam Saran, responds that India would not be held to such nuclear blackmail: 'The label on a nuclear weapon used for attacking India, strategic or tactical, is irrelevant from the Indian perspective'.[28] If attacked by such weapons India would hit back with massive retaliation. This substantiates the argument by US intelligence expert Rob Williams that 'regardless of size, delivery system or yield . . . [or] the concept of employment', these tactical weapons 'carry strategic implications'.[29]

The challenging imperatives of proving credibility in relation to serial terrorist attacks have been highlighted by Rajaraman who notes that many Indian and foreign observers remain sceptical about the credibility of India's nuclear deterrent. If Pakistan were to use a small battlefield nuclear weapon delivered on its Hatf-9 missile, would India, a 'soft state',[30] carry through on its threat of massive nuclear retaliation knowing that this guaranteed mutual annihilation? Or would it simply absorb Pakistan's gamble of 'mini-escalation' (my words) that doesn't lead to mass casualties? To prove the credibility of its nuclear deterrent, Rajaraman argues, India will have to respond to a terrorist attack with 'a quick, focussed [conventional] strike on selected terrorist hideouts or support facilities in Pakistan'.[31] Perversely, then, the need to prove the credibility of its nuclear deterrent is increasing the pressure on India's policy-makers to launch a conventional military strike on Pakistan. This is a far cry from the naïve belief that the acquisition of nuclear weapons would deter Pakistani aggression.

The toxic mix of nuclear weapons and active jihadists raises questions over the robustness of Pakistan's nuclear security measures. The threat is obviously more grave for the state of Pakistan than India; it is still a threat to India as well. Pakistan insists that its stewardship of nuclear weapons and facilities is as secure as that of any other country's arsenal, and perhaps even more robust than Russia and the US which maintain some 2,000 weapons in a state of high operational alert ready for launch on warning or launch under attack. Thus most of Pakistan's warheads are not maintained in fully assembled condition, with warheads being physically separated from fissile material; they are subject to high-level authorization codes to guard against unintended, rogue and pilfered use; and they have three levels of physical security around the neighbourhoods in which stored, around the perimeter of the facilities, and around the weapons and related material themselves. In addition, the 40,000–70,000 personnel who have some maintenance and operational roles in the chain of custody from manufacture, transport, deployment, operations and protection of the nuclear weapons and infrastructure are subject to rigorous screening in recruitment, off-rotation, and ongoing intelligence surveillance.[32]

Nevertheless, Shaun Gregory lists three causes for concern. First, terrorist groups have shown a capacity to evolve in their targets and tactics of choice in attacking military bases, missile storage facilities and possibly even weapons storage facilities. While in the past the tactics have allowed them to penetrate base perimeters and hold space within them for some hours, further evolution in tactics might embolden them to attack known weapons storage facilities and gain access to storage bunkers. Second, some of these incidents indicate a worrying element of insider collusion in a context in which Islamist and terrorist sympathies are believed to exist within the armed forces. And third, the weapons and weapon-related materials are not quite as secure during transportation as when they are within hardened military facilities.[33] Another worrying scenario is that terrorists could seize weapons during a crisis, when they have been assembled for possible use – in fact the terrorists could initiate a crisis with exactly this aim.

Credible minimum deterrent

India became the proud possessor of nuclear weapons but projected little sophisticated sense of how to use them guided by strategic doctrines.[34] Its declared aim is to 'pursue a doctrine of credible minimum nuclear deterrence'. Just what is a 'credible minimum deterrent' that would dissuade nuclear blackmail and coercion and permit second strike nuclear retaliation? China and Pakistan are incommensurate in their national power, strategic frames and military capabilities, and therefore it is not possible to use them as a common benchmark. The requirements of numbers, reach, deployment patterns and locations, and distribution between land-based, air-launched and sea-borne assets, are mutually incompatible as between them: 'what is credible toward China will likely not be minimum toward Pakistan; and what is minimum toward Pakistan cannot be credible toward China'.[35] In the case of the China–India–Pakistan Asian nuclear triangle, the acquisition of nuclear capabilities and assets has outpaced the evolution of bilateral diplomacy and non-existence of trilateral strategic dialogue. The understanding of the point at which 'credible' and 'minimum' meet has morphed into the 'optimization point' that in Indian minds denotes roughly 300–350 warheads for China, 200–250 for India, and 150–200 for Pakistan[36] – figures that are already out of date in terms of the India–Pakistan relativity. Nuclear weapons constituencies have grown in size and influence in both India and Pakistan with the development, testing and induction of successive generations of nuclear weapons delivery vehicles. This 'nested security dilemma' has consequences for the deepening US military engagement with India as well. US military assistance to India can help to narrow the latter's gap with China – but only at the cost of exacerbating the India–Pakistan asymmetry and provoking stronger Chinese strategic support to Pakistan.[37]

The issue of credibility arises also with respect to the declared posture of 'no first use'. This strengthens the requirement for second strike retaliatory capability that can survive a surprise first strike. To give 'teeth' to this posture, India is committed to developing a land-air-sea triad of platforms, delivery vehicles and assets. However, the credibility of such a retaliatory capability is weakened with a de-alerted arsenal and posture. Can Indians be confident – and would the adversary be certain – that India would be able to bring together the various components of its nuclear forces and its top political and military leadership would survive intact and have the requisite cohesion and will to launch a punitive second strike?

K. Santhanam, director for the 1998 test sites preparations, and Ashok Parthasarathi, involved in the 1974 test as science adviser to Indira Gandhi, have claimed that the 1998 hydrogen bomb tests yielded less than half the amount of projected destructive energy: 15–20kt, not 45kt.[38] The reason for Santhanam's revelation may have been to put pressure on the government to conduct further tests for validating the design of India's hydrogen bomb.[39] Their claims were backed by some influential heavyweights, including P.K. Iyengar, former chief of the Atomic Energy Commission, and they agreed with the conclusions of some disinterested international observers who analyzed the test data at the time.[40] But the claims were rejected by Prime Minister Manmohan Singh, former president and then-scientific adviser to the Ministry of Defence Abdul Kalam, and Brajesh Mishra, the BJP government's national security adviser.[41]

Persisting doubts over the technical bases of credibility are reinforced by matching scepticism about the decision-making structure for authorizing the launch of nuclear weapons. Chari notes that there is a tension between the desire to assert civilian control until the last moment, and the operational requirements of a quick military response in the midst of a crisis. The Nuclear Command Authority (NCA) vests the ultimate decision-making power in the hands of the prime minister. The National Security Adviser links the political executive, headed by the prime minister, to the military command (the Strategic Forces Command). But the chain of succession in the political and military leadership in the event of disruption contingencies is opaque, raising questions about decision-making authority if the top leadership were to be decapitated in a first strike.[42]

Another consequence of a disassembled state of nuclear weapons maintenance is that India cannot maintain a 'launch on warning' or 'launch under attack' posture. Instead it must necessarily adopt a 'launch-after-hit' nuclear force configuration, which in turn increases the requirement of a still more robust command, control and communications system. India has decided against a strategy that requires launch on warning and has structured its nuclear forces accordingly. Its nuclear arsenal is said to be dispersed in different locations, with warheads separated from delivery systems. Different organizations have custody of weapons and delivery systems in peacetime. Its warheads are spread across land, air and sea borne platforms. 'Ownership' of most, if not all, of India's nuclear weapons is vested in the military. But, unlike other nuclear armed states, India does not have a Chief of Defence Staff (or Chairman of Joint Chiefs of Staff) who can be the interface between the executive, the NCA and the military. This is especially critical because India's nuclear arsenal is disaggregated, with warheads, core and ignition devices dispersed among the military, the Department of Atomic Energy and the Defence Research and Development Organization (DRDO) without a clear chain of command across the three. Moreover, there is a practical impediment to the decision to opt for mobile road and rail launch platforms. To put it politely, India lacks a robust, reliable and credible surface transportation infrastructure to move the separated warheads, missiles and cores from safe storage sites to the dispersed and secure launch sites.

Leverage

Weaker and poorer countries may seek to use nuclear weapons to shape the perceptions and alter the decision calculus of diplomacy and war of advanced military powers. Washington could have been the object of such a leveraging calculation as part of India's complex mix of motives in acquiring nuclear weapons. One of the most important incidents driving the symbolic politics of keeping the nuclear option open in India was the dispatch of the *USS Enterprise* to the Bay of Bengal during the 1971 Bangladesh War. That embedded fear of US military intervention against India has became obsolete after the Bush administration's policy of forging an entirely new, broad-based and deep relationship with India, in pursuit of which Washington negotiated a bilateral civil nuclear cooperation deal and used its considerable diplomatic weight to sway the Nuclear Suppliers Group (NSG) to endorse it.[43] In 2010 the US defence establishment welcomed India's rising military profile 'as a net provider of security in the Indian Ocean and beyond'.[44]

Status

Too many Indians (but not the security elite) were seduced by their own perception of nuclear weapons as the modern currency of power, prestige and influence. India could aspire to enhanced status like Germany through economic prowess and market power. Few analysts would take issue with the claim that currently, non-nuclear armed Germany has a higher status, weight and clout in Europe and the world than nuclear armed Britain and France. Tellingly, nuclear brinksmanship earns North Korea neither prestige, power nor friends; an unambiguous non-nuclear armed status has not prevented South Korea from doing better on all three counts.

India does have a higher international profile today than in 1998. This is despite, not because of nuclear weapons, and rooted in its economic and information technology credentials. No serious Indian analyst is likely to claim that Pakistan's profile has arisen alongside India's since 1998, despite Islamabad's more focussed efforts on expanding, deepening and broadening its nuclear weapons capability. Its political pathology of the military and civilian governments as competing centres of de jure and de facto power, the creeping Islamicization of the country and the penetration of jihadists deep into the state, and continuing economic travails have kept Pakistan's status at best static and at worst sliding downwards. By contrast India seemed to go from strength to strength buoyed by strong economic performance and resilience.

Conversely, more recently – starting perhaps with the 2010 Delhi Commonwealth Games fiasco as a showpiece shambles – Brand India has suffered a steady loss of global market value. In the fullness of time, the ten-year tenure of Manmohan Singh may well be judged to have been independent India's locust years as a personally amiable but politically ineffectual prime minister presided over an increasingly obvious paralysis of governance on every front, political and economic, domestic and international. As the reform agenda was neglected, the economy stuttered, job creation stalled, inequality increased, the share of manufacturing and agriculture in the GDP fell, the rupee collapsed, infrastructure creaked and crumbled, state governments exercised veto power over crucial foreign policy initiatives on Bangladesh and Sri Lanka, mega-corruptions mushroomed and social ills (dowry deaths, caste and communal violence, brutal gang rapes) festered from not being addressed.

India has the world's biggest pool of poor, sick, starving and illiterate. It fares poorly on the annual rankings by the World Bank on ease of doing business indicators, the UNDP's human development, and Transparency International's corruption indices. More than 16,000 farmer suicides have been recorded annually by the National Crime Records Bureau since 1995.[45] The inaugural Global Slavery Index reported a total of almost 30mn people worldwide living in conditions of slavery. India topped even this misery list with 14mn.[46] A Global Gender Gap Index by the World Economic Forum ranked India a lowly 101 out of 136 countries on gender parity.[47] Based on infanticide, child marriage and de facto slavery, India is the worst country in the G-20 in which to be a woman.[48]

In July 2012, almost 700mn Indians in 21 of India's 28 states were left without power as three major electricity grids collapsed for two consecutive days. Whole cities, hundreds of trains and other transport systems and industrial production ground to a halt. India's bureaucrats are rated the most inefficient in Asia by business executives with a score of 9.21 out of ten. Respondents also highlighted onerous and complex tax, environmental and other regulations and a time-consuming, costly and unpredictable court system.[49] In 73 countries tested on academic performance of 15-year old school students in maths, science and English (subjects in which Indians supposedly excel), India came second last.[50] Another study found 42 percent of India's children are underweight and 59 percent are stunted.[51] UNICEF reports that 58 percent of the world's population practising open defecation lives in India.[52] Meanwhile, India attracted global ridicule when the Archaeological Survey of India conducted a massive but futile treasure hunt in 2013 for 1,000 tonnes of gold in Unnao's Raja Rao Ram Bux Singh fort, based on a dream by seer Shobhan Sarkar.[53]

In the ill-fated Devyani Khobragade case that roiled India–US relations for a month,[54] the US diplomat expelled from India in retaliation and his wife were revealed to have posted several disparaging remarks about India on social media sites.[55] Such actions are highly ill-advised for serving diplomats. But the substance of their comments is nonetheless very revealing about what outsiders see in India and about Indians' denial of the reality of the economic ills and social pathologies all around them that evokes disgust and contempt among many foreigners.

The net impression abroad was of a corrupt super-elite looting the state's assets under the guise of a sclerotic shell of democracy while the country continues to be trapped in feudal and pre-industrial practices. If this trend continues, like Pakistan, the fact that India has nuclear weapons will add to international unease and worries rather than enhance India's global stature and international prestige. If India's economic future is mortgaged to bad governance rooted in populist politics, other countries will return India to the basket of benign neglect while offering ritual but empty praise for its rich civilization and culture.

Risks and costs

Against the contestable claims of utility, there is considerable historical evidence that a nuclear catastrophe was averted during the Cold War as much owing to good luck as wise management. In addition to an alarming number of close calls based on miscalculations and misperceptions and accidental near misses, the nuclear age has also left a trail of grave environmental damage.[56] There is also a significant economic cost. In terms of opportunity costs, heavy military expenditure amounts to stealing from the poor. India's US $47bn defence budget has doubled over the past decade and continues to rise sharply at an annual average of 5.7 percent. In 2011 India's core expenditure on nuclear weapons was US $3.8bn and the full nuclear costs amounted to US $4.9bn.[57]

For reasons of history, geography, topography and population distributions, the possession of nuclear weapons constrain the range of military options and shape the calculus of coercive diplomacy more for India vis-à-vis Pakistan, than for China vis-à-vis India. As demonstrated in the 1999 Kargil war, the possession of nuclear weapons by both sides in a conflict does not rule out either an initial military incursion across a disputed border or a conventional military retaliation. But it did dampen a full-scale conventional attack by India in order to avoid escalating to the nuclear threshold. If India is to retain the option of being able to respond to provocations in the form of border skirmishes and incursions or state-sponsored terrorist attacks with calibrated use of conventional military power, it must invest still more heavily in conventional military capability than would have been required in the absence of a nuclear overhang in the subcontinent.

In a convergence of Indian military–nuclear thinking with international norms, India's military doctrine has begun to emphasize offensive action, as with 'Cold Start' in 2004 for quick launch of division-sized battle groups upon provocation.[58] India's maritime strategy also increasingly emphasizes offensive action with power-projection capability both to the east and west across the Indian Ocean.[59] Indian weapons scientists are working on a successor Agni-VI missile with a 10,000km range (that is, covering all of China and Europe) with a projected test flight date of 2017.[60]

There are political costs of excessive centralization and secrecy, and grave safety and environmental concerns. There is the added risk of proliferation to extremist elements through leakage, theft, state collapse and state capture. To strengthen nuclear safety and security and reduce risks of accidents, India maintains its nuclear forces in a disassembled state in dispersed locations across the country, with warheads physically separated from delivery vehicles. But to buttress the 'credible' part of its doctrinal posture of assured retaliation, India must somehow increase its baseline readiness. The potential contradiction could intensify as India's nuclear arsenal grows. In July 2013 DRDO head Dr. Avinash Chander said that DRDO is 'working on canisterized systems that can launch from anywhere at any time' and 'making much more agile, fast-reacting, stable missiles so [that a] response can be within minutes' for all of India's nuclear missile systems eventually.[61]

In the absence of an official strategic defence (or nuclear posture) review, it is hard to discern where all this fits into the overall strategic picture and how India will ensure that a capability meant to deter does not in fact provoke, including additional assistance to Pakistan's nuclear capabilities. In other words, India is caught in an escalating cycle of increased nuclear and conventional military expenditures with no net gain in defence capability against the most likely threat contingencies. Internationally, India has shifted from being a disarmament champion to a nuclear armed state.[62] While the former was informed by a strategic vision, the latter has been ad hoc and episodic. As a disarmament crusader, India was the foremost critic of the NPT-centred nuclear regime. As a non-NPT nuclear armed state, India has been gradually integrating with the global nuclear orders while preaching nuclear abstinence to others like North Korea and Iran.[63]

Conclusion

South Asians are less secure today than before May 1998. India still lacks effective deterrent capability against China. History and geopolitics make the India–Pakistan nuclear equation more unstable than US–Soviet deterrence in the Cold War. Nuclear weapons failed to deter Pakistani infiltration and Indian retaliation and escalation in the two-month Kargil war in 1999, and a full military mobilization by both for all of 2002. Nuclear weapons are not going to help India combat internal insurgency, cross-border terrorism or parasitical corruption. Nor can nuclear weapons help to solve any of the real problems of poverty, illiteracy and malnutrition. And they are irrelevant to India's security needs against any other country. Contrary to facile claims of strategic, military or political utility and economic cost-effectiveness, once we drill down into the arguments, there is no persuasive need for India to stay nuclear armed.

While not advocating unilateral nuclear disarmament, such a conclusion should at least encourage India to be a champion of phased, regulated and verifiable global nuclear disarmament governed by a universal, non-discriminatory nuclear weapons convention (NWC). This would be in keeping with the legacy of Indian initiatives on nuclear arms control and disarmament, including the Rajiv Gandhi

Action Plan of 1988; with the fact that India was the most reluctant nuclear weapons possessor of all the nine nuclear armed states; and the somewhat incongruent reality that its official nuclear doctrine lists global nuclear disarmament as a national security objective.[64] On 2 April outgoing Prime Minister Singh affirmed that 'As a responsible' nuclear armed state, 'India supports the idea of a nuclear-weapon-free world because we believe that it enhances not just India's security, but also global security'.[65] He also called on all the nuclear armed states to join together to establish a global no first use norm.

A self-confident India would be a norm setter and rule shaper, not merely a passive norm and rule taker, in global affairs. 'The interactive web of multiple nuclear weapon capable states also creates a dynamic far more complex and unpredictable than that which prevailed during the Cold War, with an essentially binary nuclear equation between the two superpowers'.[66] Yet at the same time, while the probability of another use of nuclear weapons may have increased over the past two decades, and the gravity and magnitude of the threat posed by nuclear weapons remain undiminished, neither publics nor policy elites are as exercised now as they were during the Cold War by the fear of an imminent threat of nuclear Armageddon. This is why a state champion from within the group of nine nuclear armed states could play a particularly helpful role in breaking the prevailing complacency. The United States and Russia with more than 90 percent of nuclear weapons in their arsenals may have an extra-special responsibility. That is no reason for the other seven to abdicate their responsibility commensurate with their status as nuclear weapons possessor states.

Notes

* Originally published in *International Affairs* 90:5 (2014), 1101–24. Reprinted by permission of Wiley–Blackwell.
1 Robert Jungk, *Brighter than a Thousand Suns: A Personal History of the Atomic Scientists* (New York: Harcourt Brace, 1958), 201. This was later repeated in an interview for NBC television documentary *The Decision to Drop the Bomb* (1965). Available on YouTube: https://www.youtube.com/watch?v=ZuRvBoLu4t0. In fact there is a second connection alluded to by these quotes. The test was named Trinity. In Hinduism the Trinity refers to Brahma, Vishnu and Shiva: the three gods of creation, preservation and destruction.
2 See Sumit Ganguly, 'India's Pathway to Pokhran II: The Prospects and Sources of New Delhi's Nuclear Weapons Program', *International Security* 23:4 (1999), 148–77; and George Perkovich, *India's Nuclear Bomb: The Impact on Global Proliferation* (Berkeley: University of California Press, 1999). This was followed by six tests by Pakistan on 28 and 30 May. The number is of symbolic importance for making the total the same as India's tests in 1974 plus 1998. In announcing the tests, Prime Minister Nawaz Sharif remarked that '*hisab chuka diya*' (we have solved the equation – that is, the account is settled).
3 I am grateful for the many robust comments on an earlier draft of this paper from participants in a seminar at the Institute for Defence Studies and Analyses, New Delhi, 23 October 2013; and at the Jinnah Institute, Islamabad, 25 October 2013.
4 Although it is hard to think of any detrimental consequence for France and the UK were they to abandon nuclear weapons.

122 Regional challenges

5 The concept of a balance of interests is discussed in Ramesh Thakur, 'A Balance of Interests', in Andrew F. Cooper, Jorge Heine and Ramesh Thakur, eds., *The Oxford Handbook of Modern Diplomacy* (Oxford: Oxford University Press, 2013), 70–87.
6 See Arundhati Ghose (India's Ambassador for Disarmament at the time), 'Negotiating the CTBT: India's Security Concerns and Nuclear Disarmament', *Journal of International Affairs* 51:1 (1997), 239–61.
7 Rajesh Rajagopalan, 'From Defensive to Pragmatic Multilateralism and Back: India's Approach to Multilateral Arms Control and Disarmament', in Waheguru Pal Sidhu, Pratap Bhanu Mehta and Bruce Jones, eds., *Shaping the Emerging World: India and the Multilateral Order* (Washington DC: Brookings Institution Press, 2013), 198, 201.
8 T. P. Sreenivasan, 'More continuity, less change', *Indian Express*, 12 May 2014, http://indianexpress.com/article/opinion/columns/more-continuity-less-change/.
9 The text of the letter, released to the press by the Americans, was published in *The Hindu*, 14 May 1998.
10 Ramesh Thakur, 'Arms Control, Disarmament, and Non-Proliferation: A Political Perspective', in Jeffrey A. Larsen and Thomas D. Miller, eds., *Arms Control in the Asia–Pacific Region* (Colorado Springs: USAF Institute for National Security Studies, US Air Force Academy, 1999), 39–61.
11 The concept is associated with Thomas Schelling, *The Strategy of Conflict* (Cambridge MA: Harvard University Press, 1963).
12 Daryl G. Press, Scott D. Sagan and Benjamin A. Valentino, 'Atomic Aversion: Experimental Evidence on Taboos, Traditions and the Non-Use of Nuclear Weapons', *American Political Science Review* 107:1 (2013), 188–206.
13 Gareth Evans, 'Nuclear Deterrence in Asia and the Pacific', *Asia & the Pacific Policy Studies* 1:1 (2014), 91–111, http://onlinelibrary.wiley.com/doi/10.1002/app5.11/pdf. For another study of the continuing good health of the anti-nuclear norm, see Maria Rost Rublee, *Nonproliferation Norms: Why States Choose Nuclear Restraint* (Athens GA: University of Georgia Press, 2009).
14 Advisory Opinions and Orders of the International Court of Justice, *Legality of the Threat or Use of Nuclear Weapons* (8 July 1996), http://www.un.org/law/icjsum/9623.htm.
15 See Harsh V. Pant, *The U.S.–India Nuclear Pact: Policy, Process and Great Power Politics* (Oxford: Oxford University Press, 2011). The deal was not uniformly welcomed in India. See P. K. Iyengar, A. N. Prasad, A. Gopalakrishnan and Bharat Karnad, *Strategic Sellout: Indian–US Nuclear Deal* (New Delhi: Pentagon Press, 2009).
16 *China's National Defense in 2010* (Defence White Paper) (Beijing: Government of the People's Republic of China, Information Office of the State Council, 31 March 2010), chapter X, 'Arms Control and Disarmament', http://www.china.org.cn/government/whitepaper/2011-03/31/content_22263885.htm.
17 See Andrew F. Cooper and Ramesh Thakur, 'The BRICS in the New Global Economic Geography', in Thomas G. Weiss and Rorden Wilkinson, eds., *International Organization and Global Governance* (London: Routledge, 2014): 265–78.
18 Michael Krepon and Julia Thompson, 'Introduction', in Michael Krepon and Julia Thompson, eds., *Deterrence Stability and Escalation Control in South Asia* (Washington DC: Stimson Center, 2013), 12.
19 Ibid., 10.
20 Pervez Hoodbhoy and Zia Mian, 'Changing Nuclear Thinking in Pakistan', APLN/CNND *Policy Brief* 9 (Canberra: Asia Pacific Leadership Network and Centre for Nuclear Non-Proliferation and Disarmament, February 2014), paragraphs 28–30.
21 Peter R. Lavoy, ed., *Asymmetric Warfare in South Asia: the Causes and Consequences of the Kargil Conflict* (Cambridge: Cambridge University Press, 2009); Benjamin S. Lambeth, *Airpower at 18,000': The Indian Air Force in the Kargil War* (Washington DC: Carnegie Endowment for International Peace, 2012).

22 See Ramesh Thakur, 'Delinking Destiny from Geography: The Changing Balance of India–Pakistan Relations', *India Quarterly* 67:3 (2011), 197–212.
23 See Pauline K. Kerr and Mary Beth Nikitin, *Pakistan's Nuclear Weapons: Proliferation and Security Issues* (Washington DC: Congressional Research Service, Report RL34248, 20 July 2011).
24 Shaun Gregory, 'Pak toxic chaos plan changes nuke debate', *Times of India*, 6 March 2011, http://timesofindia.indiatimes.com/home/sunday-toi/all-that-matters/Pak-toxic-chaos-plan-changes-nuke-debate/articleshow/7637964.cms?referral=PM.
25 George Perkovich, 'The Non-Unitary Model and Deterrence Stability in South Asia' (Washington: Carnegie Endowment for International Peace, 13 November 2012), 3, http://www.carnegieendowment.org/2012/11/13/non-unitary-model-and-deterrence-stability-in-south-asia/eihm. For example, the 1999 Kargil operation was planned by a small group of officers in the Pakistan Army without foreknowledge of the country's air and navy chiefs, with dangerously high escalation potential; Lavoy, *Asymmetric Warfare in South Asia*.
26 Raja Menon, 'A mismatch of nuclear doctrines', *Hindu*, 22 January 2014.
27 See Shashank Joshi, 'Pakistan's Tactical Nuclear Nightmare: Déjà Vu?', *Washington Quarterly* 36:3 (2013), 159–72; Rajuram Nagappa, Arun Vishwanathan, and Aditi Malhotra, *Hatf-/IX/Nasr – Pakistan's Tactical Nuclear Weapon: Implications for Indo-/Pak Deterrence* (Bangalore: National Institute for Advanced Studies, July 2013).
28 Quoted in Rachel Oswald, 'South Asian Tactical Missiles Risk Dangerous Miscalculation, U.S. Intel Officer Says', *GlobalSecurityNewswire*, 6 June 2013, http://www.nti.org/gsn/article/work-s-asia-tactical-missiles-threatens-dangerous-miscalculation-intelligence-official/.
29 Ibid.
30 Gunnar Myrdal, *Asian Drama: An Inquiry into the Poverty of Nations*, 3 vols. (New York: Pantheon Books, 1968).
31 R. Rajaraman, 'Decisive action against any Pakistani misadventure is best way to establish nuclear credibility', *Times of India*, 20 September 2013.
32 Shaun Gregory, 'The Terrorist Threat to Nuclear Weapons in Pakistan', European Leadership Network, 4 June 2013, http://www.europeanleadershipnetwork.org/the-terrorist-threat-to-nuclear-weapons-in-pakistan_613.html.
33 Ibid.
34 Ashley J. Tellis, *India's Emerging Nuclear Posture: Between Recessed Deterrent and Ready Arsenal* (Santa Monica CA: RAND, 2001).
35 Vipin Narang, 'Five Myths about India's Nuclear Posture', *Washington Quarterly* 36:3 (2013), 144.
36 Confidential discussions with a former Indian foreign secretary and air force chief.
37 George G. Gilboy and Eric Heginbotham, 'Double Trouble: A Realist View of Chinese and Indian Power', *Washington Quarterly* 36:3 (2013), 137–38.
38 K. Santhanam and Ashok Parthasarathi, 'Pokhran-II thermonuclear test, a failure', *Hindu*, 17 September 2009.
39 Sachin Parashar, 'Pokhran II not fully successful: Scientist', *Times of India*, 27 August 2009.
40 Press Trust of India, 'AEC ex-chief backs Santhanam on Pokhran-II', *Hindu*, 25 September 2009.
41 Siddharth Varadarajan, '"Fizzle" claim for thermonuclear test refuted', *Hindu*, 27 August 2009; Press Trust of India, 'Pokhran II successful, insists Kalam', *Times of India*, 27 August 2009.
42 P.R. Chari, 'India's Nuclear Doctrine: A Critique', *Trishul* 16:1 (Wellington, India: Autumn 2003), 54–60.
43 Raja Mohan notes the irony that India worked hard for a decade to get the 2008 country-specific exemption deal. It then tied itself up in such knots of liability laws for reactor suppliers that six years later, Delhi is yet to sign a single commercial agreement for the supply of a nuclear reactor from any country; even Russia has baulked.

Meanwhile the India-specific NSG waiver was used by China to sell two additional nuclear reactors to Pakistan on the barely plausible claim that the sales were 'grandfathered'. C. Raja Mohan, 'Don't blame it on China', *Indian Express*, 17 October 2013.
44 Secretary of Defense, *Quadrennial Defense Review Report* (Washington DC: Department of Defense, February 2010), 60.
45 P. Sainath, 'Farm suicides rise in Maharashtra, State still leads the list', *Hindu*, 3 July 2012.
46 *BBC News*, 'New global index exposes 'modern slavery' worldwide', 17 October 2013, http://www.bbc.co.uk/news/world-24560937. Pakistan and India head the list on a per capita basis: 'Dry bones', *Economist*, 19 October 2013, 56.
47 Press Trust of India, 'India gets poor 101st rank on global gender gap index', *Times of India*, 25 October 2013.
48 Katherine Baldwin, 'Canada best G20 country to be a woman, India worst', *Guardian*, 13 June 2012.
49 'Indian bureaucrats have "terrific powers", rated worst in Asia', *Times of India*, 11 January 2012.
50 'Indian students rank 2nd last in global test', *Times of India*, 15 January 2012.
51 Aarti Dhar, '42 percent of Indian children are underweight', *Hindu*, 10 January 2012; Jason Burke, 'Over 40% of Indian children are malnourished, report finds', *Guardian*, 10 January 2012.
52 'With 58% figures, India tops in open defecation', *Times of India*, 2 October 2011.
53 Akshay Mukul, 'Seer's golden dream turning out to be nightmare for ASI in Unnao fort', *Times of India*, 30 October 2013.
54 See Ramesh Thakur, 'Rogue States Behaving Badly', *The Diplomatist* (January 2014), http://www.diplomatist.com/stories/story015.html.
55 Chidanand Rajghatta, 'Khobragade flap: US disavows social media postings by expelled diplomat and wife', *Times of India*, 15 January 2014.
56 Angelique Chrisafis, 'French nuclear tests "showered vast area of Polynesia with radioactivity"', *Guardian*, 4 July 2013.
57 Bruce Blair and Matthew A. Brown, 'World Spending on Nuclear Weapons Surpasses $1 Trillion Per Decade' (Washington DC: Global Zero, June 2011), http://www.globalzero.org/en/page/cost-of-nukes.
58 Walter C. Ladwig, 'A Cold Start for Hot Wars? The Indian Army's New Limited War Doctrine', *International Security* 32:3 (2008), 158–90.
59 Gilboy and Heginbotham, 'Double Trouble', 135.
60 'Following Agni 5 success India Plans Longer-Range Missile', *Global Security Newswire*, 18 September 2013, http://www.nti.org/gsn/article/pumped-over-success-agni-5-india-plans-even-longer-range-missile/.
61 Quoted in Narang, 'Five Myths about India's Nuclear Posture', 148. 'Canisterization' allows India to co-locate sub-components in hermetically sealed canisters for transportation and storage, whereby warheads can be 'pre-mated' to their delivery vehicles and kept one code away from being armed and released. This also reduces the visible signs of movement to outside observers as systems are fully assembled and readied for firing.
62 Rajiv Nayan, 'The Global Nuclear Non-Proliferation Paradigm and India', *Strategic Analysis* 35:4 (2011), 559–63.
63 The Indian hypocrisy argument is developed in Ramesh Thakur, 'North Korea Test as Spur to Nuclear Disarmament', *Economic and Political Weekly*, 21 October 2006: 4403–06.
64 Manpreet Sethi, 'Universal Nuclear Disarmament: What Can India Offer?' Global Consortium on Security Transformation, *Non-Proliferation and Disarmament Series* 3 (March 2011), http://www.securitytransformation.org/gc_publications.php.
65 Manmohan Singh, 'Inaugural Address', Conference on 'A Nuclear-Weapon-Free World: From Conception to Reality', Institute for Defence Studies and Analyses, New Delhi, 2 April 2014, author's notes from the event.
66 Sheel Kant Sharma (former Indian ambassador to the IAEA) and Shyam Saran, 'Deterrence is not a fantasy', *Indian Express*, 3 October 2013.

9 Follow the yellowcake road*

Balancing Australia's security, commercial and bilateral national interests against international anti-nuclear interests

In 2011 the Australian Labor Party (ALP) dropped a long-standing ban on the export of uranium to India, despite the latter not being a signatory of the Nuclear Non-Proliferation Treaty (NPT). The change in policy split the cabinet and divided analysts, some decrying it as a sell-out of Australian principles with potentially catastrophic consequences, others justifying it on grounds of updating Australian policies formed in a Cold War context in accord with changing contemporary world realities. Prime Minister Julia Gillard's visit to India in October 2012, during which she put an offer on the table to negotiate uranium sales,[1] was considered a success in both countries. Formal talks on a civil nuclear cooperation agreement began in March 2013.

This chapter does not take an explicit position on the merits and risks of exporting Australian uranium to India. Rather, the primary purpose is to question the utility of 'the national interest' as the framework for determining and assessing such a major and consequential foreign policy decision. I argue that 'the national interest' is an inadequate formulation to capture the breadth, texture and nuance of the full range of interests and values that must be weighed in an increasingly complex and interdependent world; and that 'a balance of interests' is a superior construct in describing, explaining and prescribing foreign policy. While the need to strengthen relations with India as a key emerging player in the shifting global geopolitical order, plus commercial considerations, might indicate the change in policy to be in 'the national interest', 'a balance of interests' compels an assessment of broader and wider considerations that must also be factored into the weighing of policy options. Those who view the topic primarily through the arms control lens have been opposed to the new stance on the grounds that it will reward rogue nonproliferation behaviour by India, aggravate tensions in the subcontinent, heighten the nuclear arms race between India and Pakistan, critically damage the global nonproliferation regime and increase nuclear safety risks.

The chapter proceeds in three parts. The first provides a brief background note on the origins and nature of Australia's uranium export policy. The second outlines the major interests involved in deepening bilateral relations with India and adjusting policy to changed geopolitical equations, and the potential economic benefits to be derived from lifting the ban on uranium sales. The third part changes the analytical focus to a balance of interests by first introducing the

126 *Regional challenges*

domestic political factor in the decision-making calculus and then examining in more detail the potential damage to the global nonproliferation architecture and the principle of a rules based order. It also introduces human agency into the calculation as a counterweight to the deterministic streak in the concept of the national interest.

Australia's uranium policy

While Australia holds 46 percent of the world's reserves of low cost uranium, its share of the global uranium market is under 16 percent.[2] The policy parameters that have until recently regulated the export of Australian uranium were set by the Liberal–Country party government of Malcolm Fraser in 1977:

- As an NPT state party, Australia is obligated under article 4 of the treaty to facilitate the peaceful uses of nuclear energy;
- Supply would be restricted to countries that could satisfy Canberra that the uranium would not be diverted to non-civilian purposes;
- The recipient countries had to be in good nonproliferation standing;
- In addition to International Atomic Energy Agency (IAEA) full-scope[3] safeguards (and subsequently also the IAEA Additional Protocol), the recipient countries would be required to conclude a bilateral safeguards agreement directly with Australia to account for the use of its uranium and any nuclear material produced from it.[4]

The policy settings satisfied even the ALP to the point where, when it came into office in 1983, it departed from the long-standing party opposition to any mining and export of uranium. Instead, its compromise formula accepted the status quo: the three mines already operating would be permitted to continue.

The next key shift in Australian uranium policy came with the change of government back to the conservative coalition under John Howard (1996–2007), guided by four considerations:

- A return to prioritizing bilateral relations over multilateralism as the bedrock foreign policy setting;
- The cultivation of diplomatic and trade relations with key regional and global geopolitical actors;
- The growing interest in nuclear energy under the pressure of increasing fossil fuel scarcity, rising oil prices and growing consciousness of climate change impacts; and
- Changing international market opportunities.[5]

On the basis of these considerations, in 2006–07 Australia announced in principle its willingness to sell uranium to China, Russia and India. During a four-day visit to the country in 2006, at a time when most countries were beating a path to New Delhi to affirm India's rising global profile, Howard said: 'Now is the time for a quantum leap in the relationship'. Prime Minister Manmohan Singh responded that since India was short of uranium, 'we would very much like Australia to sell uranium to India'.[6] In August 2007, when the India–US civil nuclear cooperation deal was facing difficulties in both countries and internationally, Howard endorsed India as a qualified potential recipient of Australian uranium, thereby buttressing the political position of the supporters of the deal in both India and the United States.[7]

In December 2007, with the return of Labor to office, the three mine restriction was lifted, but the other conditions regulating who could purchase Australian-sourced uranium remained intact. 'Good nonproliferation standing' now meant being party to the NPT. Accordingly, negotiations were successfully concluded with China in 2008 and Russia in 2010, as both were NPT states parties with safeguards agreements in place to permit international inspections of their civilian (though not military) nuclear facilities. But India, arguing the treaty fostered nuclear apartheid,[8] had remained outside the NPT and in 1998 crashed through the NPT barriers to joining the club of nuclear weapons possessor states.

Following the 2008 consummation of the India–US civil nuclear cooperation deal and the subsequent India-specific waiver by the Nuclear Suppliers Group (NSG), 14 of India's 22 reactors were to be designated as civilian and brought under IAEA safeguards. Eight would be designated as military and kept outside IAEA safeguards and oversight. India also retained the right to designate future reactors as either civilian or military. Whether or not they will be subject to international inspection would thus be determined solely by India.

Kevin Rudd's Labor government joined Washington in the NSG vote to rewrite the rulebook for India's benefit, leaving it with an illogical and untenable policy of supporting open access to global nuclear trade for India but not selling it Australian uranium. This apparently contradictory position reflected the willingness to do everything possible 'to support a rising India and the US alliance without breaching a domestic party political position'.[9] Against the global backdrop of growing commerce with India by a number of uranium suppliers (Argentina, Canada, France, Kazakhstan, Mongolia, Namibia, Russia, South Korea, the United Kingdom and the United States),[10] Australia's recalcitrance became a major hindrance to the broader bilateral relationship. The oddity of selling uranium to China, which though an NPT-licit nuclear weapons state (NWS) had a suspect record on nuclear proliferation to Pakistan and North Korea,[11] but banning its sale to India, which though a nuclear armed state outside the NPT had a demonstrable record of abstaining from nuclear proliferation to any third party, became a favourite Indian refrain undermining Canberra's claim that its uranium export decisions were based on norm reinforcing considerations. Manmohan Singh failed to attend the Commonwealth summit in Perth in October 2011, prompting media speculation that the continued ban on the export of uranium was a factor behind his decision to stay away.[12]

The non-visit concentrated the minds of Australians on the importance of the issue as an impediment to elevating the bilateral relationship to the next level and there was a concerted push in 2011 to change party policy. Resources minister

Martin Ferguson mused publicly that the ban had become 'a major concern in an otherwise close strategic relationship', and suggested that the ALP would have to modernize its policy and introduce the necessary 'flexibility and discretion' to permit uranium exports to India.[13] Bob Carr, a former Labor premier of New South Wales who in 2012 was drafted into the Senate and became foreign minister, supported the call for a party debate on the issue. A veteran journalist asked: 'How long will the obsolete and discredited ALP policy be allowed to prejudice Australia's ties with India, the emerging third biggest economy in the world?'[14] In November Gillard issued a strong call for a policy shift,[15] a call that was endorsed at the ALP national conference on 4 December. An Indian parliamentarian, speaking for the ruling Congress Party, responded with the statement: 'This may be the most important single step in the past three decades in furthering India–Australia relations'.[16]

Not 'the', nor 'national', nor even 'interest'

Lord Palmerston famously said Britain had no eternal enemies or allies, only eternal interests. But does 'the national interest' exist objectively and independently of the policy-maker and the analyst? The suggestion falls prey to the logical fallacy of affirming the consequent: that which should be proven by a process of reasoning and evidence based analysis is instead asserted to be true. If countries act only in the national interest, then it follows by definition that anything they do is in the national interest. Being axiomatic, this is tautological. Nor is it a satisfactory guide to policy. It is an exhortation, not a prescription. It produces the paradox that competing policy prescriptions are offered and justified in the name of the same national interest.

Realist scholars assumed and therefore failed to problematize state interests. Lacking a clear, unambiguous meaning, the concept 'the national interest' is empty of substantive content.[17] On what basis could the Vietnam War be said to be in the US vital interest (understood as the hard core of the national interest) when the US homeland was never threatened? Is the South China Sea a vital interest for China simply because Beijing has chosen to redefine it as a 'core interest'? Where do core political values and their promotion, ideological principles, a favourable world order and the long term fit into the scheme?

There are two problems with the word 'national'. In the domestic realm it implies a monolithic actor when in reality there are several competing actors. In international affairs, while states remain the primary unit, the diplomatic landscape is populated by a growing number of nonstate actors with an expanding role and increasing influence. Consequently 'the national interest' is neither 'the' (definitive), 'national' (few states are homogeneous and there are many nonstate international actors), nor 'interest' in the singular. States are multipurpose organizations pursuing multiple goals simultaneously. In most states there will be differences of perspectives, opinions and preferences among officials and cabinet ministers, reflecting their individual backgrounds, portfolios and philosophies. There will be just as substantial differences of opinion and policy preferences among the various sectoral groups, some of which will advocate policies diametrically opposed to those favoured by others. Arms sales and policies to protect national airlines are good examples of measures where the interests and values of citizens and consumers do not necessarily coincide with those of industry and employees.

An even bigger difficulty is who decides what the national interest is and how. If it is whatever governments proclaim it to be, scholars would have to accept at face value claims that Slobodan Milosevic's atrocities in Bosnia and Kosovo, Saddam Hussein's reign of terror in Iraq, the American and British decision to attack, invade and occupy Iraq, Iran's pursuit of nuclear weapons capability, Pakistan's Faustian pact with terrorist groups[18] – all were in the national interest of the countries concerned. Self-evidently, this is absurd. On this reasoning, based on the same objective factors, Australia's national interest not only flip-flopped but did multiple somersaults with changes of government from Howard to Rudd and Gillard. This is not a self-respecting cogent analytical construct but a theatre of tautology.

Only decision-makers have access to the relevant facts, albeit not necessarily all the facts. Outsiders lack access to the facts, thinking and motives of decision-makers. Their analyses and conclusions are necessarily speculative. But decision-makers will often be influenced by the lure of power and/or lucre for themselves, their families, clans/sects or political parties. They may accept monetary or other forms of inducement from domestic or multinational corporate lobbyists or from foreign governments, to advance the commercial or geopolitical interests of others while enriching themselves or denying political office to opponents. Does anyone believe that in an election year a US president's definition of the national interest is never 'contaminated' by electoral calculations? The justificatory rhetoric of the national interest often is invoked to cloak base motives with the mantle of collective legitimacy, since the national interest supposedly represents the social purposes of the political community. At other times, the language of the national interest will be used conscientiously in the firm belief that the chosen course of action is indeed in the best interests of the collective polity. But unless political decision-makers possess a measure of absolute infallibility that eludes even the pope, there are possibilities for error caused by incomplete or faulty information, or flawed analysis and diagnosis.

Hans Morgenthau conceded that leaders can make mistakes in calculating the state's real interests: 'As disinterested observers we understand his thoughts and actions perhaps better than he, the actor on the political scene, does himself'.[19] But who is this disinterested observer and what if there are several who disagree among themselves? Reynolds comments that government actions may be said to be in the national interest if they serve the 'real interest' of a community as determined by 'an omniscient observer'. Far from solving the problem, however, he notes, this merely raises additional difficulties, comparable to the problematic elements of Rousseau's 'general will'.[20]

What of former political leaders? Do they count as the voices of once authoritative policy-makers, or are they to be discounted as outside commentators? Former conservative Prime Minister Fraser, who approved the sale of Australian uranium in 1977, was dismayed by the changed policy, warning that it might have been smart politics by Gillard but was bad policy by Australia, likely to erode the global nonproliferation regime further and aggravate India–Pakistan tensions. 'At best, exporting uranium to India would allow use of more of its own uranium for weapons. At worst, Australian uranium could end up in nuclear weapons exploded in Pakistan or China'.[21] Former Labor Foreign Minister Gareth Evans responded that it was possible to share Fraser's anti-nuclear passion without being alarmed about uranium sales to India. In his view, after the 2008 NSG decision to endorse the India–US nuclear deal, it was better for Australia 'to cut its losses in its bilateral relationship that is going to matter hugely to us, both economically and strategically, in the decades ahead'.[22]

Analysts were similarly split. Andy Butfoy argued: 'Because it is the custodian of the world's largest reserves of uranium, Australia has a special responsibility to help protect the global rules containing' the danger of the 'the uncontrolled spread of nuclear weapons'.[23] The maximization of profits and jobs and the allure and advantages of closer ties with India as a future great power must be weighed against its past record as a nuclear rogue state. Moreover, playing 'the global warming card . . . mostly looks like tactical positioning rather than a genuine motive'.[24] Marianne Hanson was sceptical that the bilateral relationship with India was so frail and one-dimensional as to be vulnerable to damage on a single issue.[25] But Rory Medcalf concluded that selling uranium to India would be at least as justified as selling it to China and Russia.[26] Others argued that bilateral safeguards agreements can adequately protect Australian uranium from misuse, and that the exports will not unduly test the NPT regime but could open up additional opportunities to meet important safety concerns, help to stabilize potentially dangerous vertical and horizontal proliferation and also mitigate the region's burgeoning production of greenhouse gases.[27]

Bilateral relations with India

The above criticisms notwithstanding, the traditional framework put in place by the Fraser government could be used to justify the policy to sell uranium to India on grounds of deepening relations with a key player in a changing geopolitical framework, protecting trade interests and safeguarding Australian jobs. Australia's 1997 white paper on foreign and trade policy described bilateral relationships as 'the basic building block' of policy in these fields.[28] After taking into account the totality of Australian interests, the paper affirmed that the most significant bilateral relationships for Australia were those with the United States, Japan, China and Indonesia. 'Significant interests' were also engaged in relations with South Korea, other ASEAN countries, New Zealand and Papua New Guinea.[29] India was conspicuous by its absence, just as it was finally taking off. Since then India's attraction for Australia has grown – as a diplomatic actor of influence in shared major global problems and challenges, a policy and operational partner in managing the global commons of the high seas (for example, anti-piracy operations), climate, disaster relief (the 2004 tsunami), etc.;[30] as a partner in fighting international terrorism and Islamic fundamentalism; as a strategic counterweight to China; as a market for primary resources and services; and as a growing source of tourists, migrants and investments. The two countries have a shared strategic interest in a stable Indo–Pacific Asia that links them also to Indonesia and South Africa around the Indian Ocean rim. There are deepening trade, security, cultural, educational and services ties that, although not as deep as those that bind Australia to China, have fewer potential points of major friction compared to China.

While bilateral trade has grown rapidly and substantially, Australian investment in India has lagged behind. Other problems in the recent past have included controversies on and off the field in cricket, attacks on Indian students (numbers of whom plummeted from 120,000 in 2009 to 72,000 in 2011),[31] and occasional assaults on Australian tourists and missionaries in India. Noisy media in both countries can inflame popular passions and prejudices and complicate government-to-government relations. In 2011 India overtook China as the primary source of new migrants to Australia. Bad experiences mean that overseas Indians become carriers of grievance; good experiences means they function as force multipliers for traditional diplomacy. The rapid recovery in Australia's reputation among Indians was confirmed by polling data: Australia climbed from 35 out of 35 in 2010 to 8 out of 39 in 2012 in Indians' ranking of other countries.[32]

The most consequential mutual misperceptions arose from the failure of each nation to understand the principles and imperatives underpinning the other's nuclear policy. Each side was firmly convinced of its own intellectual and moral rectitude and smugly contemptuous of the other. Australia held India to have been deceitful in conducting a nuclear test in 1974 and a stubborn recalcitrant on the Comprehensive Nuclear Test Ban Treaty (CTBT), in the passage of which Canberra played a key role in 1996.[33] India considered countries like Australia and Canada to be grossly hypocritical in having permitted British atomic tests on their territory, sheltering under the US nuclear umbrella, hosting US military installations that are tightly integrated into the global US nuclear infrastructure and deeply implicated in global US nuclear doctrines and deployments, yet moralizing self-righteously to India about the virtue of nuclear weapons abstinence.[34]

Institutional memory as a key carrier of grievances within government bureaucracies is an insufficiently understood and theorized phenomenon.[35] The exceptionally strong reaction by Canberra to India's nuclear tests in 1998 still colours Indian foreign and defence officials' attitudes. Australian behaviour was considered erratic, crude and rude, and provoked anger and resentment that still linger. Peter Varghese, Australia's High Commissioner to India who took over as Secretary of Foreign Affairs in December 2012, argues that the history of trade and nonproliferation differences 'soured a generation of Australian and Indian diplomats towards each other', but that relations have now improved.[36] Several former senior Indian officials confirm the mutual disenchantment but remain sceptical about the claim that there has been a significant improvement. In an important study of mutual (mis)perceptions, both sides agreed on the reality of the 'lost decade' owing to a failure to invest in the effort to understand each other's differing circumstances, worldviews and interests, on the need to establish a broad base to a deep and meaningful relationship of reciprocal advantage in the foreseeable future, and hence on the need to invest resources in fostering diplomatic understandings and cultural and educational exchanges to build a vibrant and mutually beneficial relationship that is both robust and resilient.[37]

Geopolitical changes

That the global order is experiencing a major shift has become something of a cliché. The US National Intelligence Council's quadrennial report on global trends maps the world out to 2030 in the considered view of 16 intelligence agencies. The era of western ascendancy since 1750 and of US ascendancy since 1945, known as *Pax Americana*, is coming to an end. By 2030 Asia will be bigger in economic size and strategic weight than Europe and the United States combined, but the latter will remain the first among equals,[38] with the EU, China, India and Japan as the leading contenders to be counted among the equals. Its main theme is echoed in Australia's first-ever national security strategy paper: 'Australia's national security is intrinsically linked to the economic and strategic transformation in our region and in the world'.[39] This was preceded by a white paper on Australia's relations with Asia.[40]

Three drivers of the shifting global order are the re-emergence of China and of India as major nodes of global activity, and the relative US decline from dominance. All three trends were reflected in the India–US nuclear deal that left Australia trapped between a legacy national policy and a shifting global geopolitical and normative order. When Canberra cancelled the quadrilateral security dialogue among the four great democracies of Australia, India, Japan and the US in 2008, the quixotic nature of Australian policy was confirmed for many Indians amid suspicion that Mandarin-speaking Prime Minister Rudd was merely betraying his China leanings.[41]

Yet the public debate over the rise of China, its rapid military modernization and what this means for Australia's forward defence planning reveals considerable differences of opinion within Australia.[42] Are the time and circumstances right for Australia to accommodate itself to the realities of China's power? Would it be dangerous and unnecessarily provocative to develop an indigenous military capability to challenge China around Australia's approaches? Is it foolish to embrace the military relationship with the United States even more tightly as a hedge against rising Chinese military capability and nationalist assertiveness? Ironically, in the light of their respective Cold War diplomatic and security relationships, India's own turn to a strategic engagement with the United States this century makes Australia and India potential allies.[43] Washington supports a deepening of the strategic relationship between India and Australia.[44] The China angle was explicitly adduced by an influential Australian newspaper in an editorial endorsing India's test in April 2012 of its first intercontinental ballistic missile which puts most of China within range of India's nuclear warheads.[45]

Economic benefits

Commercial, nonproliferation and nuclear security interests can overlap or collide between industry and government stakeholders, and accountabilities in managing nuclear risks have to be shared between parliaments and boardrooms. The uranium industry, conscious of its image problem on both safety and proliferation concerns, is reluctant to promote nuclear energy aggressively in the absence of robust nonproliferation safeguards and a political consensus. Australia's production and export of uranium falls well below its potential. The industry–government Uranium Council has warned that restrictions on shipping uranium would jeopardize Australia's status as a major supplier as customers looked for alternative sources of supply.[46] Yet the anticipated economic gains are surprisingly modest. Compared to the A$ 63bn iron ore export industry, for example, uranium exports are worth only A$ 1bn a year, and the most optimistic projections would see them rise to just A$ 1.7bn.[47] While the fear of losing market share to competitors in the long run might be a relevant commercial consideration, the changed policy is more persuasively attributable to adjustments to changed geopolitical circumstances and efforts to consolidate and deepen bilateral relations with a key emerging power.

Balancing many interests

The construct of the national interest provides poor guidance to help us navigate our way through the changes in Australian policy. A state can be required to strike a balance among its different thematic interests (trade, national security, international treaty commitments, human rights), geographical orientations (transatlantic, Middle East, Asia–Pacific), national and international interests, and countries (India, Pakistan, China, US). A balance may be required even on one policy tool: should foreign aid be directed to the most needy, to those who will utilize it the most effectively, to countries in the donor's neighbourhood, region, or continent, to buttress allies, to reward defectors, or to punish norm violators by withholding it? Australia's interests did not change with the change of government in 2007; the internal party dynamics did. It took the ALP more than four years to shift the momentum of historical inertia and change its policy in late 2011. But domestic party political considerations are inimical to any assessment of 'the national interest' and explanations of foreign policy using its vocabulary.

In the 2010 federal election the Gillard-led ALP suffered significant losses but remained in power by entering into coalition with the Greens and with the support of several independent MPs. The Greens remain adamantly opposed to any uranium mining and export for three sets of reasons, each a powerful motivator in its own right with the party and its constituency: the potential proliferation risks and dangers of a consequent nuclear conflict; public health and environmental hazards posed by the risks of radiation pollution that are integral to any use of nuclear energy; and the unresolved and really long-term problem of nuclear waste disposal.[48]

Should the Greens win (or share) power in the 2013 general election, the full set of interests – let alone any such thing as the national interest – will remain exactly the same on 15 September as they were on 14 September (the date of the election). But the relative weight assigned to the different interests will change to tip the scales against the mining and export of uranium. To that extent, Palmerston's oft-quoted aphorism is not so much wrong as besides the point. It ignores the critical intervening role of human agency in calculating interests and values, weighing them in the balance and testing the political limits of the possible in tilting the scales in the favoured direction. The baggage of connotations that come with the phrase 'the national interest' makes it easier also to silence critical and dissenting opinion as somehow anti-national and to pretend to a degree of authoritativeness that belies the untidy mess of options and factors behind an apparently clean and neat policy decision.

Substituting the word 'a' in 'a balance of interests' for 'the' in 'the national interest' indicates that one particular balance is struck from among several possible options. It indicates human agency: individual people make specific decisions in the name of the entity concerned, be it an NGO, multinational corporation or state. And it includes the possibility of human fallibility and the prospect of course corrections.

The metaphor of the balance scales is accurate also in another important respect. Oftentimes, internal policy debates are the most fiercely contentious precisely because the opposing arguments and proponents are so finely balanced. It takes just one extra argument, consideration or policy-maker to tip the scales decisively on one side. 'The national interest' fails to do justice to this tipping-effect reality.

Global nuclear arms control and disarmament goals

'A balance of interests' can also better accommodate the interplay between national and international factors, and between interests and values, that must be weighed against one another in determining policy. For decades Australia has tried to delicately balance its identity as a reliable US ally with solid nuclear arms control credentials.[49] Hence the complex mix of factors determining whether or not a potential uranium recipient country was in good nonproliferation standing. The position *vis-à-vis* the NPT of India, Israel and Pakistan – the three countries with nuclear weapons that never signed the treaty – is just one of the anomalies undermining the credibility of the global nuclear nonproliferation regime.[50] The India–US nuclear deal followed by the NSG waiver and an India-specific IAEA safeguards agreement arguably created for India an informal status that mirrors the status of a recognized NWS under the NPT. The Bush administration's position, ultimately accepted by Australia and many other supplier countries, seemed to be that there were significant nonproliferation benefits to bringing India inside the tent of safeguarded nuclear commerce and export controls, that putting most of its nuclear reactors under international safeguards was better than having none under such controls, and that all evidence pointed to the conclusion that its nuclear weapons program would continue regardless of international civil cooperation. These international advances were complemented by an Indian statement in 2008 reaffirming its 'impeccable non-proliferation record' and credentials,[51] and highlighting its strengthened domestic and export controls, its posture of restraint on nuclear weapons doctrine and deployment (including no first use), the 'voluntary, unilateral moratorium' on nuclear testing, its openness to a fissile materials cut-off treaty (FMCT), and its continued support for total nuclear abolition through a universal nuclear weapons convention (NWC).[52]

Pakistan criticized the waiver on the grounds that it was country-specific and not criteria-based[53] and gave India worldwide access to nuclear material and technology and an assured fuel supply from any country looking for commercial sales. To Pakistan, Washington did not just compromise the integrity of the nonproliferation regime and endanger its existence; it also rewarded the very country that introduced nuclear capabilities into South Asia and in so doing fostered a regional nuclear arms race by accentuating Pakistan's anxieties and insecurities. By contrast, both Beijing and Islamabad argue that the 2010 Chinese announcement of the sales of two more nuclear reactors for the Chashma plant in Pakistan are covered by a general and generic agreement signed and 'grandfathered' before China joined the NSG.[54] But a US State Department official said the new reactors would violate undertakings made by Beijing when it was admitted to the NSG in 2004.[55]

Rules based order

Is the promotion of values also part of the national interest? The philosophical antecedents of 'the realist defense of the autonomy of the political sphere against . . . subversion' might well be said to lie in Thucydides' adage that 'the strong do what they can and the weak suffer what they must'. Consequently, 'Realism maintains that universal moral principles cannot be applied to the actions of states'.[56] Morgenthau may have been arguing for the need to separate the ethic of conviction from the ethic of consequences. Even if this distinction is accepted with respect to the personal beliefs of officials and leaders, what of the political community's collective and deeply held moral beliefs?

The dichotomous positioning of ethics as abstract and subjective, and the national interest as concrete and objective, is false. For it implicitly establishes a hierarchy of values in which the national interest becomes 'a doctrine of "higher allegiance", overriding – whenever necessary – not only the specific interests of individuals, but their common morality'.[57] Morgenthau concedes the point when he says that Realism has its own 'distinctive intellectual and moral attitude to matters political',[58] or, even more explicitly, when he speaks of 'the moral dignity of the national interest'.[59] To paraphrase the mantra of Realism, international politics, like all politics, is a struggle for normative ascendancy: the establishment and maintenance of the dominant normative architecture of international order, created and maintained by the interplay of power, ideas and values. Appeal to 'the national interest' by itself cannot determine the combination of – or the balance among and between – interests and values that the state ought to espouse in any given situation.[60]

Australia has a global train of interests as the world's thirteenth largest economy, sixth biggest landmass, third largest maritime zone and tenth biggest aid donor. With far-flung civilizational, commercial, strategic and environmental interests and links, Australia has a direct and big stake in a rules based global order. It is hard to think of an order more critical to Australia's and the world's future than the rules regulating and delegitimizing nuclear weapons. To the dismay of many, the India–US civil nuclear cooperation deal, the NSG waiver and the many bilateral uranium supply agreements that followed effectively drove a horse and cart through the NPT regime's prohibitions on trade in nuclear material with non-NPT countries.

Legality

Don Rothwell produced an analysis for the International Campaign to Abolish Nuclear Weapons (ICAN) questioning the compliance of any uranium sales to India with Australia's formal obligations under the 1985 Treaty of Rarotonga that established the South Pacific Nuclear Free Zone (SPNFZ).[61] Australia ratified this treaty in 1986. As a non-signatory of the NPT, India cannot legally be treated as a NWS. In article 4, the SPNFZ treaty stipulates that uranium sales by a SPNFZ state party, such as Australia, to a non-NWS, such as India, must be subject to the full-scope comprehensive safeguards required by article 3.1 of the NPT. To comply with this, India would be required to permit IAEA inspections of all its nuclear facilities. But under the India–US deal, endorsed by the NSG, India retained the right to declare some of its nuclear facilities to be dedicated to military purposes and as such exempt from IAEA inspection. This therefore presents 'an insurmountable legal obstacle' to Australia's selling uranium to India, and any such sales would expose Australia to the complaints procedure of annex 4 of the Treaty of Rarotonga initiated by any other SPNFZ state party. Rothwell's analysis is supported by Malcolm Fraser: 'selling uranium to India would breach our international treaty obligations'.[62]

But the interpretation is open to challenge. As India is not a party to the NPT, the obligations of article 3.1 do not apply to it. All three non-NPT nuclear armed states, India, Israel and Pakistan, have item-specific safeguards agreements with the IAEA over some of their nuclear facilities and materials which predate the NPT.[63] Material exported to recipient countries, including non-NPT states, must remain under INFCIRC/66 safeguards throughout the fuel-cycle progression. NPT article 3.1 safeguards are to be applied by the IAEA 'on all source or special fissionable material *in all peaceful nuclear activities*' (emphasis added). Non-NWS NPT parties must conclude INFCIRC/153 (corrected) (June 1972) safeguards agreements with the IAEA for *all* of their nuclear materials and facilities, including IAEA inspection of all nuclear facilities. Technically, therefore, one could argue that by separating its military and peaceful nuclear facilities and opening up the latter to the IAEA INFCIRC/66 safeguards, India, which is not a NPT non-NWS, is in compliance with article 3.1-type safeguards.[64]

Robertson buttresses this interpretation with a review of consistent state practice from the time the NPT entered into force in 1970 to the signing of the SPNFZ treaty, during which period several states were indeed supplying some nuclear material to various non-NPT countries. After all, that is partly how India conducted its 1974 test – by violating its bilateral undertakings to Canada not to divert the Canadian-supplied material to nuclear weapons. But there was no suggestion prior to 1974 that the Canadian supplies to India were in violation of the NPT article 3.1 requirements. In the context of established state practice, the drafters of the SPNFZ treaty copied instead of toughening the article 3.1 safeguards standard in their own article 4(a)(i). On this point, Robertson draws attention to the fact that annex 2 of the Treaty of Rarotonga explicitly cross-references INFCIRC/153, with its more restrictive safeguards for application to the SPNFZ states themselves, thereby adding weight to the interpretation of article 4(a)(i) safeguards – that it applies to all peaceful but not to military nuclear activities and thus the two sets of nuclear activities can coexist – to other states. And the 2008 NSG 'clean waiver' granted to India confirms this interpretation that NPT article 3.1 (and by extension the SPNFZ treaty, as Australia and New Zealand among the NSG are states parties to SPNFZ) does not prohibit trade in nuclear materials with India.[65]

Conclusion

The full spectrum of factors that have shaped, influenced and determined Australia's policy on exporting uranium to India include bilateral relations, with the impasse on uranium sales becoming symbolically important and holding up progress on a range of other foreign policy agenda items and challenges; geopolitical calculations, particularly in the light of the changing relative balance of power between China and the US against the backdrop of growing Chinese assertiveness and rising tensions in East Asia; economic benefits and commercial considerations, especially in view of the growing market power of India as the world's third biggest emerging economy; nonproliferation concerns and Australia's leading role in tightening loopholes and restrictions in the NPT regime; environmental considerations, with safety issues of nuclear power, especially since the Fukushima disaster of 2011, having to be offset by the reality of nuclear fuel being significantly cleaner than most other alternatives in the real world; domestic public and political party pressures; and bureaucratic inertia, with the weight of accumulated opinion and efforts in the senior ranks of western foreign affairs bureaucracies reflecting decades of dealing with India on nuclear issues as a problem child orphaned by the NPT. 'The national interest' just does not and cannot do justice to the richness, complexity and range of decision-making factors that must be weighed and evaluated against one another in this dynamic equation.

'A balance of interests' is a concept much better equipped for this analytical task of explanation and policy prescription. It is more accurate empirically and less dishonest in acknowledging the multiplicity of arguments and perspectives and the simple fact that the correct assessment will only become known in the fullness of time. Judgements are made on the basis of best-case assessments which inevitably are influenced also by utterly subjective factors, including individuals' experiences, values and preconceptions. 'The national interest' is erroneous as a description of the empirical reality, substitutes tautology for explanation and is unhelpful as a guide to policy. 'A balance of interests' is superior on all three counts of description, explanation and prescription. In addition, it captures human agency and allows for human error and multiple balances as weighed by different people reflecting their personal predilections, professional backgrounds, life and career experiences, and institutional interests and perspectives. Foreign policy and diplomacy involve a delicate balancing of interests, goals, issues, principles, values, demands and pressures from a diverse array of actors, domestic and international, governmental and nongovernmental.

Notes

* Originally published in *International Affairs* 89:4 (2013): 943–61. Reprinted by permission of Wiley-Blackwell.
1 Indian analysts interpreted this as 'a major, and much awaited, course correction' in Australian foreign policy towards India. See Sachin Parashar, 'Australia PM to sign N-trade pact during visit to India', *Times of India*, 14 October 2012.
2 World Nuclear Association, http://www.world-nuclear.org/info/uprod.html; and Australian Uranium Association, http://www.aua.org.au/content/resources.aspx.
3 This is now the standard IAEA safeguards under which all non-nuclear weapons states must declare all nuclear facilities and material to the Agency, maintain all nuclear accounting records and report any changes to the IAEA. The latter in turn can conduct inspections and verification activities, including installing cameras or carrying out environmental sampling to check the consistency of the state's records and reporting with the data.
4 Rory Medcalf, 'Australia's Uranium Puzzle: Why China and Russia but Not India?', *The Fearless Nadia Occasional Papers* (Melbourne: Australia India Institute, November 2011), 4.
5 Ibid., 4–5.
6 AAP, 'We'll buy your uranium: India', *Age*, 6 March 2006.
7 Medcalf, 'Australia's uranium puzzle', 11.
8 Ramesh Thakur, *The Politics and Economics of India's Foreign Policy* (London: Hurst, 1994): 87–110.
9 Medcalf, 'Australia's uranium puzzle', 11.
10 Ramesh Thakur and Gareth Evans, eds., *Nuclear Weapons: The State of Play* (Canberra: Centre for Nuclear Non-Proliferation and Disarmament, 2013), Table 2.2, 104.
11 See interview with Thomas C. Reed in Alex Kingsbury, 'Why China helped countries like Pakistan, North Korea build nuclear bombs', *US News and World Report*, 2 January 2009; Thomas C. Reed and Danny B. Stillman, *The Nuclear Express: A Political History of the Bomb and its Proliferation* (Minneapolis: Zenith, 2009); William J. Broad, 'Hidden travels of the atomic bomb', *New York Times*, 8 December 2008; R. Jeffrey Smith and Joby Warrick, 'A nuclear power's act of proliferation', *Washington Post*, 13 November 2009.
12 Hamish McDonald, 'A testing time for India – and Australia', *Age*, 3 September 2011.
13 Katherine Murphy, 'Sell India uranium, minister says', *Age*, 16 February 2011.
14 Paul Kelly, 'ALP needs to get over itself on uranium to India', *Weekend Australian*, 29–30 October 2011.
15 Phillip Coorey, 'Gillard's push for uranium sales to India', *Sydney Morning Herald*, 15 November 2011.
16 Manish Tewari, quoted in Greg Sheridan, 'India on highway to prosperity', *Weekend Australian*, 17–18 December 2011.

17 Scott Burchill, *The National Interest in International Relations Theory* (London: Palgrave Macmillan, 2005).
18 Sumit Ganguly and S. Paul Kapur, 'The Sorcerer's Apprentice: Islamist Militancy in South Asia', *Washington Quarterly* 33:1 (2010): 47–59.
19 Hans J. Morgenthau, *Politics Among Nations: The Struggle for Power and Peace*, 4th edition (New York: Knopf, 1967), 5.
20 P.A. Reynolds, *An Introduction to International Relations*, 3rd edition (London: Longman, 1994), 41–42.
21 Malcolm Fraser, 'Why Gillard's uranium-to-India policy is dangerously wrong', *Age*, 12 December 2011.
22 Gareth Evans, 'Nothing gained by treating India as an outlaw', *Age*, 15 December 2011.
23 Andy Butfoy, 'How Labor finished Bush's uranium script', *Inside Story*, 23 November 2011, http://inside.org.au/how-labor-finished-bush%E2%80%99s-uranium-script/.
24 Andy Butfoy, 'Australia is backing a nuclear rogue', *Age*, 20 August 2007.
25 Marianne Hanson, 'Selling uranium to India a blow to arms control', *Canberra Times*, 5 December 2011.
26 Medcalf, 'Australia's uranium puzzle'.
27 Devika Sharma, 'Uranium Trade and its Security Implications for India', *South Asian Survey* 17:1 (2010): 91–110.
28 Australia's Foreign and Trade Policy White Paper, *In the National Interest* (Canberra: Department of Foreign Affairs and Trade, 1997), 53.
29 Ibid., 57–64.
30 C. Raja Mohan, 'Rising India: partner in shaping the global commons?' *Washington Quarterly* 33:3 (2010): 133–48.
31 John McCarthy, Sanjaya Baru, Gopalaswami Parthasarathy, Maxine McKew, Ashok Malik and Christopher Kremmer, *Beyond the Lost Decade*, report of the Australia India Institute Perceptions Taskforce (Melbourne: Australia India Institute, 2012), 25, 42.
32 Ibid., 47.
33 Ramesh Thakur, 'Get test ban treaty operational and let India join later', *International Herald Tribune*, 9 September 1996.
34 G. Parthasarathy (India's High Commissioner to Australia at the time), 'Neither comprehensive, test ban nor a treaty', *Pacific Research* 9 (November 1996): 32–35.
35 For an analogous adverse impact on relations between Canada and India from their joint international service in non-UN peacekeeping in Vietnam, see Ramesh Thakur, *Peacekeeping in Vietnam: Canada, India, Poland and the International Commission* (Edmonton: University of Alberta Press, 1984).
36 Quoted in McCarthy et al., *Beyond the Lost Decade*, 8.
37 McCarthy et al., *Beyond the Lost Decade*.
38 National Intelligence Council, *Global Trends 2030: Alternative Worlds*, NIC document 2012–001 (Washington DC: Dec. 2012), http://www.dni.gov/nic/globaltrends.
39 Government of Australia, *Strong and Secure: A Strategy for Australia's National Security* (Canberra: Department of the Prime Minister and Cabinet, March 2013), 44.
40 Government of Australia, *Australia in the Asian Century*, White Paper (Canberra: October 2012). For my analysis of the paper, see Ramesh Thakur, 'Australia's Engagement with Asia: Strategic or Transactional?' *India Quarterly* 69:4 (2013): 335–50.
41 McCarthy et al., *Beyond the lost decade*, 12–15. Ironically, Australia's relations with China turned worse under Rudd than under any other prime minister of recent times before or since: see Jiang Zhang, 'Australia and China: The Challenges to Forging a "True Friendship"', in James Cotton and John Ravenhill, eds., *Middle Power Dreaming: Australia in World Affairs 2006–2010* (Melbourne: Oxford University Press, 2011): 71–93.
42 Ross Babbage, *Australia's Strategic Edge in 2030*, Kokoda Paper no. 15 (Canberra: Kokoda Foundation, February 2011); Hugh White, 'Power Shift: Australia's Future between Washington and Beijing', *Quarterly Essay* 39 (Melbourne, September 2010);

Paul Dibb, 'China: not about to attack Australia', *East Asia Forum*, 9 Aug. 2011, http://www.eastasiaforum.org/2011/08/09/china-not-about-to-attack-australia, accessed 31 May 2013; Malcolm Fraser, 'Australia–US relations in the "Asia century"', AsiaLink Series lecture on 25 September 2012, University of Melbourne; text supplied to the author by Mr Fraser.
43 McCarthy et al., *Beyond the Lost Decade*, 13–14.
44 David Wroe, 'Hillary Clinton encourages Australia–India relationship', *Age*, 13 November 2011.
45 Editorial, 'India's nuclear-capable missile', *Australian*, 30 April 2012.
46 Annabel Hepworth, 'Uranium opportunity "at risk", says secret report', *Australian*, 19 December 2012.
47 Medcalf, 'Australia's Uranium Puzzle', 9.
48 Ibid., 4.
49 Ramesh Thakur, 'Arms Control', in Fedor A. Mediansky, ed., *Australian Foreign Policy: Into the Next Millennium* (Sydney: Macmillan, 1997): 130–61.
50 See chapter 12 below.
51 While the claim to impeccability is true enough about official policy, and the government has continually tightened export control systems, a little bit of scepticism might still be in order about the quality and reliability of state capacity to monitor cross-border flows and activities.
52 Ministry of External Affairs, Government of India, 'Statement by External Affairs Minister of India Shri Pranab Mukherjee on the Civil Nuclear Initiative', 5 September 2008, http://www.mea.gov.in/in-focus-article.htm?18806/Statement+by+External+Affairs+Minister+of+India+Shri+Pranab+Mukherjee+on+the+Civil+Nuclear+Initiative.
53 For one effort to specify the criteria, see Pierre Goldschmidt, 'NSG membership: a criteria-based approach for non-NPT states', 24 May 2011, http://carnegieendowment.org/publications/index.cfm?fa=view&id=44147.
54 The so-called 'grandfather clause' refers to paragraph 4(c) of Part I of the NSG guidelines, which says that the fullscope safeguards requirement on trigger list items does not apply to agreements or contracts drawn up on or before 3 April 1992.
55 Bill Gertz, 'China, Pakistan reach nuke agreement', *Washington Free Beacon*, 22 March 2013, http://freebeacon.com/china-pakistan-reach-nuke-agreement/.
56 Morgenthau, *Politics Among Nations*, 10–13.
57 Roberto Toscano, 'The Ethics of Modern Diplomacy', in Jean-Marc Coicaud and Daniel Warner, eds., *Ethics and International Affairs* (Tokyo: UN University Press, 2001), 49.
58 Morgenthau, *Politics Among Nations*, 11.
59 Hans J. Morgenthau, *In Defense of the National Interest: A Critical Examination of American Foreign Policy* (New York: Knopf, 1951), 33.
60 See C. Raja Mohan, 'Balancing Interests and Values: India's Struggle with Democracy Promotion', *Washington Quarterly* 30:3 (2007): 99–115.
61 Donald R. Rothwell, 'Australia's Obligations under the South Pacific Nuclear Free Zone Treaty and Uranium Sales to India' (Melbourne: ICAN, 23 November 2011), http://www.mapw.org.au/files/downloads/ICANW~Legal%20Opinion~FINAL.pdf, or http://www.icanw.org/wp-content/uploads/2013/05/ICANWLegal-OpinionFINAL-1.pdf.
62 Fraser, 'Why Gillard's uranium-to-India policy is dangerously wrong'.
63 *The Agency's Safeguards System*, IAEA Doc. INFCIRC/66/Rev.2, 16 September 1968.
64 Kalman A. Robertson, 'The Legality of the Supply of Australian Uranium to India', *Security Challenges* 8:1 (2012), 28.
65 Ibid., 32–34.

10 Capping North Korea's weapons and Iran's capability

The last several chapters have looked at the challenge of nuclear weapons in India and Pakistan. Since the twin sets of nuclear tests in 1998, the only other country to have tested nuclear explosive devices is the Democratic People's Republic of Korea (DPRK or North Korea). The situation on the Korean Peninsula has posed many security challenges to the region and the international community. North Korea's nuclear and missile programs are a source of instability and tension in a region vital to global security and economic prosperity. The world has been at a loss on how to coax or coerce it back into the NPT box as a denuclearized state. It has been just as much at a loss on how to keep Iran from jumping out of the NPT box, with a potential risk of proliferation cascade across the Middle East and possibly beyond.

This chapter looks at these two cases. The Bush years (2000–08) proved to be calamitous for efforts to contain the nuclear weapons programs of both North Korea and Iran[1] which, along with Saddam Hussein's Iraq, were dubbed the axis of evil. Neoconservatives – who believed in using US power to transform the world, were openly disdainful of arms control treaties and diplomacy and believed in eliminating regimes rather than weapons – gained dominant sway in the administration. When President Bill Clinton left office Iran had a tentative nuclear research program with a few test centrifuges; by the end of Bush's two terms Iran had an industrial-sized uranium program and thousands of operational centrifuges. On North Korea the Clinton administration came very close to completing the agenda of changing the regime's behaviour and programs and left office hopeful that the task would soon be completed. Instead the open hostility from Washington drove Pyongyang in the opposite direction and led successively to its withdrawal from the Nuclear Non-Proliferation Treaty (NPT) – the only example of this to date – and to ballistic missile and nuclear weapons tests. The Bush administration's in-your-face belligerence as a substitute for diplomacy was also the major contributor to the failure of the 2005 NPT Review Conference and the rekindled interest of many other countries in hedging their bets on the boundary between peaceful and military uses of nuclear power.

Capping North Korea's nuclear weapons[2]

The DPRK regime is unique in the family of nations: a communist dynastic dictatorship (the third generation is currently in control) that has been a basket case for virtually its entire existence, guilty of acts of aggression and serial provocations against its more populous, prosperous and democratic southern kin state, of acts of state criminality in kidnapping Japanese citizens in Japan and smuggling them into North Korea, as well as acts of terrorism. It is hardly surprising then that the prospect of useable and deliverable nuclear weapons in North Korean hands sends shivers down many spines.

North Korea began its pursuit of nuclear weapons in the 1960s, accelerated the program in the 1980s[3] and withdrew from the NPT in 2003.[4] It cited the 'grave' threat to its security and sovereignty posed by the US 'tyrannical nuclear crushing policy toward the DPRK'.[5] This led also to the collapse of the 1994 Agreed Framework which had frozen Pyongyang's plutonium-based nuclear program for nearly a decade.[6] In 2005, in return for security assurances and the promise of economic cooperation, it promised to abandon all nuclear weapons and existing nuclear programs and return to the NPT under the International Atomic Energy Agency (IAEA) safeguards. North Korea revealed the presence of a uranium enrichment facility at Yongbyon in 2010.[7] It is developing a progressively more extensive range of ballistic missile capabilities, has close links with Iran and Syria and is a major proliferator of nuclear and ballistic missile technologies.

Pyongyang has repeatedly made commitments to abandon the weapons path in return for security assurances and economic assistance, shelved its nuclear ambitions temporarily and then broken its promises serially. Its 2006 and 2009 nuclear tests drew international condemnations and UN-mandated sanctions, prompting it to walk out from the Six Party Talks. Security Council Resolution 1718 (14 October 2006) imposed sanctions and demanded an end to all nuclear programs and weapons. Resolution 1874 (12 June 2009) prohibited any further test or launch using ballistic missile technology and toughened the sanctions. The Panel of Experts established pursuant to Resolution 1874 reported in 2012 that North Korea continued actively to violate Resolutions 1718 and 1874 using elaborate techniques to evade Security Council sanctions.[8] Pyongyang launched a long range rocket on 12 December and put a satellite into orbit. Japanese experts were impressed by the precision of the rocket technology and by the fact that the test was planned for and executed during adverse winter conditions.[9] The United States said the launch was a disguised ballistic missile test forbidden by previous Security Council resolutions and warned of unspecified consequences.[10] South Korean officials said the test would make them speed up plans for a comprehensive missile defence system.[11] A third nuclear test followed on 12 February 2013.

Nuclear weapons can be made from highly enriched uranium (HEU) or plutonium. HEU technology can be more easily disguised and concealed and is the route that Iran may be taking to build up its bomb-making capability. Plutonium bombs are easier to miniaturize for mounting warheads on missiles. North Korea's first two tests were plutonium-fuelled; we do not know whether uranium or plutonium was used in the 2013 test. North Korea already has between 25–40kg of plutonium, enough to make up to 8 more bombs, but it does not have much by way of a nuclear arsenal and even less of a delivery capability for hitting targets far (US, Australia, Europe) or near (Japan). It is not believed to have mastered the technology to miniaturize warheads and make them robust enough to withstand the rigours of a ballistic missile flight trajectory, such as high gravity forces, vibrations and temperature extremes. They pose no imminent threat therefore to the US mainland. Nor do they have the targeting accuracy to pose a threat even to Japan.

In the swiftly escalating cycle of harsh international reactions to the third test and toughening rhetoric of war from Pyongyang, North Korea invalidated the 1953 armistice agreement and enacted a new law enshrining its nuclear weapons status – which deepens the stake in keeping the bomb, creates a bureaucratic constituency for it and raises the political costs of changing policy. Pyongyang also announced that it would restart and readjust its uranium enrichment plant and plutonium producing reactor at Yongbyon, that had been mothballed in October 2007, for both power generation and bolstering the quality and quantity of its nuclear armed force. About 8,000 fuel rods are required to run the reactor; reprocessing spent fuel rods after the reactor has been operating for a year could yield 6–7kg of plutonium, enough to make one nuclear bomb.

In addition to a history of nuclear brinkmanship, North Korea has a long history of serial threats and provocations, including the sinking of the South Korean corvette *Cheonan* that killed 46 crew and the shelling of South Korea's Yeonpyeong Island in 2010. Kim Jong-il, who died in late 2011, was skilled at carefully calibrating tensions and cooling it in return for oil, aid or respect. But his son Kim Jong-un is a new, untested, young and inexperienced leader. He might be trying to reprise his father's and grandfather's tactics of ratcheting up tensions, winning additional concessions, distracting attention from domestic problems, and then winding down tensions again. A good clue to the episode being more theatre than crisis was the calm with which the citizens of Seoul went about their quotidian lives while the world watched tensely to see what would happen next. The risk of a war that neither side wanted lay more in the possibility of miscommunication, misperception and miscalculation that could have seen the cycle of provocation and escalation spin out of control.

Possible motives

The timing of the last crisis may have been related to annual joint military exercises by Seoul and Washington that in 2013 included practice runs by US B-52 bombers, nuclear capable B-2 stealth bombers and F-22 stealth fighters – exercises that mimic nuclear strikes against the North and worry Beijing as well by giving concrete expression to the US 'pivot' to Asia. Most Western media reports amplified the North's bellicose rhetoric without highlighting the joint military exercises that provoked them, thereby feeding public perceptions of a crazed young leader and regime.

We cannot be confident of Kim's motives. He might have wanted to ward off a genuinely feared threat; to bolster domestic leadership credibility by projecting himself as tough; to ensure that he has the continuing support of the military; to strengthen domestic cohesion; to try and position himself to extract economic concessions; etc. It is part of established theories of strategic deception to make your enemy believe that you will act irrationally and vindictively when your vital interests are attacked. The unfavourable comparisons with the South further intensify the North's anxieties. The asymmetry between North and South Korea is very stark on just about every dimension: population, 24mn and 50mn; GDP, $12bn to $1.2tn; per capita income, under $506 against $23,000. Nuclear weapons help North Korea to offset the loss of the Cold War-era Soviet strategic counterweight, the infinitely greater economic dynamism of South Korea and a perceptible diminution of Chinese enthusiasm for its troublesome ally. They serve as a hedge against US attack: would Saddam Husssein and Muammar Gaddafi have suffered their horrible fates if they had acquired and held on to nuclear weapons? It also sees a nuclear weapons capability as a means of maximizing positive outcomes from negotiations with its adversaries; the test and the crisis could be a means of prepositioning Pyongyang to extract more benefits from future talks. 'Provoke then negotiate' has been a staple of North Korea's strategy.

What to do?

Outside confidence is not high that Kim Jong-un can play the same game as his father and grandfather with matching skill. He could miscalculate Seoul's, Tokyo's and/or Washington's response to his provocations. He could misjudge his own escalatory and negotiating skills or power. Another cause of worry was the leadership transitions in Beijing, Seoul and Tokyo along with the relatively new North Korean leader himself. The world seems unable to decide on an appropriate strategy for defusing the tension. Condemnations by the UN Security Council of North Korea's nuclear weapons and ballistic programs have become so ritualized that they corrode the UN's credibility as its demands are continually and serially defied. Unilateral punitive measures are impractical because of China's fault tolerance for Pyongyang. The path of still more punitive sanctions and isolation seems to lead nowhere. The possible solutions would seem to be either a return of North Korea to the NPT as a non-nuclear weapons state (NWS) under full IAEA safeguards and inspections; or an acceptance of its nuclear armed status subject to binding commitments to observe the same disciplines on export, transfer and disciplines as the other NWS.

Why should a strategy of deterrence not work against North Korea (or Iran)? It worked against the far more formidable and powerful Soviet threat in the Cold War. We managed to live with thousands of nuclear weapons being added to the Soviet arsenal year after year; why should the sky fall if a few more bombs are built by some additional countries? Some answer by branding Iran and North Korea 'rogue regimes'. Such demonization has two negative consequences. It adds to their paranoia and deepens their determination to strengthen nuclear weapons capability in order to complicate the calculus of anyone seeking regime change (the leveraging argument for nuclear weapons discussed in chapter 8). And it makes it difficult for outsiders to craft political responses to the security dilemma or seek a reconciliation based on some compromise and mutual accommodation: the only acceptable goal is complete rollback, not containment based on deterrence.

Japan and South Korea may not be willing to accept a nuclear armed North Korea under any circumstance and would be tempted to get the bomb themselves under that scenario. Lawmakers from Seoul's governing party began openly canvassing the possibility of redeploying US tactical nuclear weapons or even South Korea acquiring its own independent nuclear deterrent. In 2006, the Japanese government commissioned an internal confidential report on the possibility of producing its own nuclear weapons.[12] Internationally, the NPT constrains the weapon option, the US nuclear extended deterrence bolsters Japan's security confidence and weaponization could rupture relations with Washington. Domestically, the three non-nuclear principles (no manufacture, possession or basing of nuclear weapons); the very strong nuclear allergy in public opinion; and the atomic energy basic law that limits nuclear activity to peaceful purposes are powerful constraints on the weapons option. Even so, while Japan's nuclear weaponization taboo may survive intact for now, the threshold for debate about it has been progressively lowered with serial North Korean provocations and Chinese belligerence.

Beijing as the key

The key to any solution is Beijing. On the one hand, there are many costs and risks to China from the nuclear brinkmanship practised periodically by Pyongyang. The repeating cycle of nuclear brinkmanship could lead to a war that neither side wants, seeks or expects. That would destabilize the whole region and set back China's development goals. A report for the Carnegie–Tsinghua Center for Global Policy noted that Beijing often believes Washington hides behind the rhetoric of nonproliferation in order to engage in provocative and destabilizing acts of its own with a view to containing China economically and militarily. Therefore China seeks to strike a balance in its own policy between keeping the US preoccupied but dissuading it from an extreme response.[13]

China frets that North Korea's seemingly unstoppable provocations could strengthen nationalist sentiment in Japan and South Korea to develop nuclear weapons, thereby nuclearizing China's neighbourhood and increasing the prospects of a nuclear war along its borders. It could provoke a preemptive strike against the North by a US under pressure from Japan and South Korea. As an NPT and P5 (the five permanent members of the UN Security Council) status quo power, China has a strategic stake in the NPT and does not want it to unravel. For this reason, the export of nuclear and missile technologies and material by North Korea is unwelcome. Even short of war, rising tensions on the Korean Peninsula strengthen the military alliance between Seoul, Tokyo and Washington and could produce an increased US resident military presence or deployments and joint exercises with its allies.

On the other hand, the worst possible outcome from Beijing's point of view is a collapse or defeat of the North Korean regime. This would cause a flood of refugees to stream across the border into China and bring South Korean and US forces right to China's borders – precisely the trigger that provoked China to counter-intervene in the Korean War in the 1950s in the first place. A collapse of North Korea could also risk its nuclear bombs falling into the hands of rogue groups or else being secured by South Korea. The presence of a communist regime in Pyongyang is critical to ensure a buffer state, no matter how unpredictable, independent minded and exasperating it might be. Besides, a nuclear North Korea might be a nuisance to China but it seriously complicates Washington's military planning in East Asia.

There is an acute moral hazard in making concessions in return for nuclear brinksmanship: a reward for serial provocations. The appetite for concessions has diminished with each new outburst of brinksmanship. However reluctantly, nevertheless, sooner or later North Korea will have to be brought back to the negotiating table. Hence the interest in the alternative strategy of engagement that, rather than rewarding it for each test in return for unenforceable and no longer credible promises of no more tests, instead tries to moderate North Korea's behaviour as a nuclear armed state. Denuclearization may no longer be a practical goal. Arms control may be the only realistic option. A 'solution' would limit the size of North Korea's nuclear arsenal and put firm restrictions on its export and transfer policies. The line could still be held at four 'Nos': no addition to the nuclear arsenal; no more tests;[14] no quality upgrades in sophistication of its bombs; and no export of nuclear or missile material, components or technology.

Capping Iran's capability short of the bomb

Suspicions about Iran's interest in using its peaceful nuclear program as a cover for clandestine weapons acquisition have persisted for a long time. The acquisition of nuclear weapons by Iran would have a series of negative consequences for almost every component of the nuclear arms control agenda, from increasing pressures on other states in the regions, and beyond, to proliferate, to heightened risks of nuclear terrorism, use of nuclear weapons, and setbacks to efforts to cut global nuclear stockpiles and reduce their role and salience in national security doctrines. Also, like both North Korea and Pakistan, Iran too is widely believed to be a state sponsor of terrorism.

That said, it is important to note several specific features about Iran that distinguish it both from Northeast and South Asian regional security drivers. To start with, the Iran Islamic revolutionary regime can in no sense be compared to the Kim dynasty of North Korea. It is also a few centuries since Iran committed acts of aggression against anyone else. It is one of the more democratic states of the Middle East, especially in comparison to the Arab monarchies, sheikhdoms and dictatorships that dot the region. Nor, secondly, can it be compared in any realistic sense to Pakistan with its history of an unresolved territorial dispute with a nuclear neighbour and security policy firmly in the hands of the military that functions as a state within a state. The third distinctive feature of Iran's regional security complex is the importance of the Shia–Sunni schism that seems to have hardened all around the Islamic crescent in recent years, and the way this intersects both with Arab–non-Arab sectarian politics and US–Russian/Chinese global politics. Fourth, Israel as an unacknowledged nuclear armed state since the 1970s has no parallel in either South or Northeast Asia. It is a state imposed on the region by the Western powers in the dying days of their colonial dominance but now backed without qualification by the United States, surrounded by many enemies unreconciled to its existence and sworn to its destruction. Finally, there is little appreciation in the West that unlike the DPRK and Pakistan which evoke no sympathy, there is considerable sympathy in the rest of the world towards Iran which is perceived more as a victim of Anglo–American interventions, attacks, interferences and hostility than a perpetrator of belligerence.

November 2011 IAEA report

The November 2011 IAEA report on Iran's alleged nuclear weapons program effectively raised the global threat level.[15] The agency faced the daunting challenge of making a judgment on how far Iran's nuclear program had advanced and its potential for weaponization on the basis of suggestive but dated, inconclusive and possibly fake evidence (hundreds of pages of evidence were sourced to one laptop of unproven provenance given to the IAEA by a Western intelligence agency).[16] The IAEA is the UN's technical but neutral nuclear watchdog. Mohamed ElBaradei, the IAEA director general during the 2002–03 Iraq crisis, successfully protected the agency's independence and credibility and was awarded the Nobel peace prize for his international public service and courage in resisting national agendas.

The agency faced three difficult dilemmas in the preparation of the 2011 report. If indeed Iran is weaponizing and the IAEA failed to detect this in time and register its suspicions, the credibility of the agency would be seriously damaged. But if the report were to exaggerate the threat from Iran, it would risk playing into the hands of those hawks in Israel and Washington who favour a military attack on Iran in order to terminate its nuclear program. The agency's credibility would be damaged by the perceptions of the political bias of the new director general. In time, the report would rebound on the IAEA itself, cross-infect it with the slow but steady erosion of US credibility in the Middle East and discredit it as an impartial agency serving the international community. The third and final dilemma concerned the possible impact on Iran itself. On the one hand, if it was engaged in the clandestine pursuit of nuclear weapons, the continual soft-pedalling of the risk and threat could serve to embolden it. Alternatively, if it was seeking nuclear weapons capability but had not, as yet, made the crucial decision to acquire useable nuclear weapons, a harsh IAEA report could, counter-productively, tip it over from capability into weaponization.

At the end of ElBaradei's term in December 2009, we know – courtesy of WikiLeaks – that Japanese career diplomat Yukiya Amano was Washington's and the West's choice to succeed him. Although acknowledging the need for concessions to developing countries for political reasons, Amano was reported as being 'solidly in the US court on every strategic decision, from high-level personnel appointments to the handling of Iran's alleged nuclear weapons program'.[17] Without solid and reliable evidence, suspicions would arise that the damning conclusion is explained more by the change of leadership at the IAEA than by fresh evidence.[18] On the basis of the same evidence, ElBaradei's reports had concluded that there was no conclusive proof of Iran having crossed the weapons threshold, but his successor Amano concluded there is no definitive proof that Iran's nuclear program is peaceful. The IAEA 'is unable to provide credible assurance about the absence of undeclared nuclear material and activities in Iran, and therefore to conclude that all nuclear material in Iran is in peaceful activities'. It is on this basis that it 'has serious concerns regarding possible military dimensions to Iran's nuclear program'.[19] But this is *not* a finding of non-compliance.

The only authority for enforcing NPT obligations is the UN Security Council. Since the P5 are also the N5 (NPT-licit five NWS), the conflict of interest is clear between their pursuit of enforcement of the NPT nonproliferation obligations on the non-NWS and their tardiness in implementing the NPT disarmament obligations themselves. But it is difficult in present circumstances to think of a realistic alternative to the Security Council as the enforcement arm of the international community.

Iran's nuclear program

As a sovereign state, Iran has the legal ('inalienable') right to enrich uranium which the NPT does not abridge for any non-NWS state party. It might have an interest in doing so for weapons-related purposes precisely because it lives in a particularly threatening environment that includes five nuclear armed states (Israel, Pakistan, India, Russia, China). Non-Arab Shia Iran is also surrounded by a string of deeply hostile Sunni-ruled Arab regimes. Additionally, American ground troops are deployed in large numbers in Iraq and Afghanistan and US warships ply the seas around Iran. A substantial military presence will be maintained both in Iraq and Afghanistan even after the withdrawal of US combat troops. Britain and the US also have intervened repeatedly in Iran and have a record of almost unbroken bellicose rhetoric against the Islamic republic. During the bitter eight-year Iran–Iraq war (1980–88), the international community refused to help Iran as the victim of Iraqi aggression that included use of chemical weapons by Saddam, instead imposing a de facto moral (immoral?) equivalency between them. Iranian nuclear scientists have been assassinated. The country's nuclear program has been subjected to cyber-attacks by the Stuxnet computer worm. Iran may be paranoid but, as the saying goes, even the paranoid have real enemies.

In 2003, a UN-disarmed Saddam was attacked by a US-led coalition. In 2011, a nuclear-disarmed Libya was attacked by NATO. But a nuclear armed North Korea has not been attacked. In 2011, referring to Gaddafi, Iran's Supreme Leader Ayatollah Ali Khamenei said: 'this gentleman wrapped up all his nuclear facilities, packed them on a ship and delivered them to the West and said, "Take them!" . . . Look where we are, and in what position they are now'.[20]

Given this history, geography and strategic reality, the pursuit of nuclear weapons by Iran may well be irreversible, unless its nuclear-weapon-free status can be embedded in a broader Middle East nuclear-weapon-free zone (NWFZ) that includes Israel, or else in a universal nuclear weapons convention (NWC) that abolishes nuclear weapons for everyone. Indeed the program was begun by the Shah in 1974 when he announced an ambitious nuclear power program, but it was not deemed a threat to Western interests because he was an ally. Washington even foreshadowed the installation of more than 20 nuclear power plants in Iran by 2000.

There is no firm evidence that Iran has actually tipped over into weapons production. The IAEA report lists efforts by Iran's military to procure nuclear related and dual use material and equipment; to develop ways and means of producing undeclared nuclear material; to tap into clandestine networks for obtaining weapons related information and documentation; and to work on an indigenous nuclear weapons design. Importantly, however, almost all these activities took place before 2003.[21] Hence its surprisingly limp conclusion that there are 'indications that some activities relevant to the development of a nuclear explosive device continued after 2003, and that some may still be ongoing'.[22]

Iran today can no more prove a negative – that it is not conducting hidden proliferation activities – than could Iraq in 2002–03. On 10 March 2011, James Clapper, the US director of national intelligence, testified in Senate that according to the consensus view of 16 US intelligence agencies, Iran had not as yet decided to restart its nuclear weapons program that was halted in 2003 (with some mopping up activities continuing into 2004).[23] Even the pre-2003 assessment referred to weapons-relevant research by Iranian scientists, not to constructing a bomb factory. In an article in *The New Yorker* in 2011, investigative journalist Seymour Hersh quoted ElBaradei's firm view that Iran does not constitute 'a clear and present danger'. During his time as director general, he had not seen 'a shred of evidence' like the building of nuclear weapons facilities or the use of enriched uranium to suggest that Iran was actually weaponizing.[24]

But Iran is positioning itself to be able to weaponize at a later date. The world's dilemma is that it would be virtually impossible to take any effective action after the fact. It is not clear what the world can do before the fact either. Given the reality of the serious economic malaise afflicting almost the whole of the Western world, any imposition of economic sanctions on Iran would be self-damaging. Trade with Iran is based not on altruism or charity but economic self-interest and comparative advantage. Therefore imposition of sanctions would mean that politics would cut across the economic logic of trade based on the most efficient terms of exchange and trading partners.

Israel, itself an NPT-illicit nuclear power, has been demanding that Iran be forcibly prevented from acquiring the bomb. Israel's attack on Iraq's Osirak reactor in 1981, instead of destroying an existing capability, may have spurred Saddam into the search for nuclear weapons. Accepting that Iran has been building up its technical and material capacity to weaponize, threats of military action will almost certainly strengthen the hawks in Tehran who will want to get as many bombs as quickly as possible. Carrying out the threat may ensure that all post-attack regimes would pursue the weapons option with grim determination as the most urgent national security priority.

Perceptions in some quarters of a creeping politicization of the IAEA is leading to a backlash. In September 2010, the 117-strong Non-Aligned Movement (NAM) expressed concerns about 'the possible implications of the continued departure from standard verification language' in Amano's report on Iran.[25] The NAM countries were also displeased by the director general's uncritical acceptance of Western-sourced intelligence on Iran's nuclear activities that the agency itself cannot verify independently. The enduring legacy of the Iraq war in 2003 is a deep international mistrust of the intelligence assessments and conclusions offered by Western governments. Iran convened a special meeting of NAM on 8 November in response to the IAEA report and answered 20 questions, noting that after 4,000 days of the most intensive inspection in the agency's history, it had failed to detect 'even one gram of uranium being diverted for military purposes'.[26]

Western responses

In 2003, Britain and the US fixed facts and intelligence to justify the pre-determined policy to go to war. But Hans Blix, the chief UN weapons inspector and ElBaradei's predecessor at the IAEA, and ElBaradei himself, held firm to their institutional integrity.[27] That in turn gave added weight to the assessments and reports of the IAEA as a credible arbiter on the state of Iran's nuclear program. Now critics fear that Amano is leveraging that institutional legitimacy in a way that could make the IAEA an instrument for justifying aggression against Iran. On 8 November 2011, *The New York Times* reported that Amano had met with top White House officials 11 days previously to discuss the contents of his forthcoming report on Iran with the National Security Council. Alert to the political sensitivity of the visit, the White House declined to confirm that it had taken place.[28]

There is a critical gap in the US policy process. Reza Marashi, a former Iran desk officer in the state department, has written about the 10 percent rule: intelligence should make up only 10 percent of the information on which to base policy, with 90 percent coming from open sources and classified embassy reporting.[29] Lacking an embassy presence in Tehran, Washington is over-reliant on intelligence to the neglect of diplomatic resources for analyzing happenings and formulating a sound and coherent policy that reflects balanced judgment and an appreciation of the broader context. If intelligence, meant to be the missing piece, is the only piece of the puzzle, it can be cherry-picked to support predetermined policies and prejudices. The lack of an embassy presence has been especially crippling for dealing with a country that is crucial for US policy goals on Afghanistan, Iraq, the wider Israeli–Palestinian conflict, nuclear proliferation, terrorism, and energy security.

Because the new report is relying essentially on information about pre-2003 activities, its evidence base is more or less the same as that used by ElBaradei in his reports. ElBaradei was far more cautious and circumspect, and concentrated more clearly on scientific and technological side of the equation, possibly because he was extra careful about not providing any ammunition to those who want to attack Iran. The new report is still verifying the non-diversion of Iran's uranium stockpiles.

Disturbingly reminiscent of 2003 in some respects, parts of the new IAEA report rely on innuendo and insinuation rather than verifiable evidence and facts. Section C of the report deals with indicators of nuclear explosive development in Iran. In section C.6, the report provides a commentary on the design concept of a multipoint initiation system for detonating a nuclear explosive device. In paragraph 44, the report mentions 'strong indications' that Iran's development of such a system and associated activities 'were assisted by the work of a foreign expert who was not only knowledgeable in these technologies, but who, a Member State has informed the Agency, worked for much of his career with this technology in the nuclear weapons program of the country of his origin'. The IAEA had also verified that this unnamed person was in Iran from about 1996 to about 2002, 'ostensibly to assist Iran in the development of a facility and technique for making ultra-dispersed diamonds' and during this time, 'he also lectured on explosion physics and its applications'.

This sounds ominous. But a plausible counter-narrative is provided by Gareth Porter, an investigative historian and journalist specializing in US national security policy.[30] The 'member state' feeding this information to the IAEA is Israel which has its own clear agenda (and does not allow IAEA inspectors access to its nuclear facilities). The scientist concerned has been identified as Vyacheslav Danilenko. His 'country of origin' is Russia. During the Soviet era, he worked at the Scientific Research Institute of Technical Physics in Snezhinsk, Russia. The institute is indeed famous for its work on the development of nuclear warheads. But it also has a unit that specializes in the synthesis of diamonds which is where Danilenko worked. He is not a nuclear weapons scientist but one of the world's top specialists in the production of nano-diamonds by explosives. Apparently Iran has an aggressive program to develop its nanotechnology sector, including a major focus on nano-diamonds.

There has been speculation in several recent news reports that the Israeli cabinet is assessing the option of attacking Iran, in which event Washington will have no choice but to back Israel, and that Britain is examining how best to support the United States in such circumstances. In other words the drums of war are becoming louder once again as they did in 2002–03. And, as with Iraq, the justification is no more persuasive, but the risks of wider unintended consequences are even more grave and the moral authority of those seeking to go on the attack is even more suspect. Some argue that the war option is unlikely as President Barack Obama prefers leading from behind, will not act without an unobtainable coalition of the willing and is more concerned about the dire economic predicament and the damaging economic consequences of a war with Iran.

The aim of stopping Iran from developing a nuclear *capability* may well be a lost cause. The real policy challenge is how Iran can be retrofitted into the region's security landscape to discourage overt weaponization: that is, to accept it is nuclear capable but not accept it as, or provoke it into becoming, nuclear armed. This is a strategy described as nuclear hedging: 'a national strategy of maintaining a viable option for the relatively rapid acquisition of nuclear weapons, based on an indigenous technical capacity to produce them within a relatively short time frame ranging from several weeks to a few years'.[31] A RAND study comes to a similar conclusion: 'Looking out over the next few years, Iran is not projected to develop a nuclear weapon, although Iran will likely continue working on its domestic enrichment and nuclear energy program, which will move Iran technologically closer to a weapon'.[32]

Is the distinction between capability and weaponization specious, mere sophistry, or is it tenable in the real world? If we recall the case of India, it demonstrated its capability and the existence of a nuclear program with its so-called peaceful nuclear explosion – a fine example of legalistic sophistry – in 1974, but did not overtly weaponize until 1998: a gap of 24 years that, in the nuclear field, is an eternity. Similarly, Iran has spent billions of dollars on its nuclear program stretching over at least three decades and has a sizable scientific establishment. Like Sherlock Holmes' comment about the hound that did not bark, the really interesting question is not whether Iran has a nuclear program or an interest in nuclear weapons – the answer to both is an unambiguous 'yes' – but rather, why does it not already have the bomb? And, following from that, how can we keep it on the peaceful side of the threshold?

The answer to these two questions is not an obsession with the latest twists and turns in technological progress and development, but the national security calculus. Ultimately, whether in the case of Britain, China, France, Russia and the United States, or India, Israel, Pakistan and Iran, the critical decision to acquire, forswear or keep alive the option but not exercise it yet as a half-way compromise, is a political one made by the real centre of political power (the military in Pakistan, the theocracy in Iran). Rather than the simplistic, vacuous and misleading concept of 'the national interest', the choice has to reflect a balance of interests in the plural:[33] temporally, between immediate, short-term and ultimate, long-term goals; vertically, between domestic, regional and international considerations; and horizontally, between personalities, institutions, national needs and regime compulsions.

Iran has made many offensive and belligerent threats both against the Jewish nation and the state of Israel. It has sponsored acts of terrorism. It has nurtured and supported anti-Western factions in Iraq, Afghanistan and Lebanon. For all this, there is as yet no consensus in Tehran on getting the nuclear bomb. There is nothing to suggest that the religious elite is not serious when it declares – as it has for three decades – that the nuclear bomb is un-Islamic because of its inhumane, indiscriminate and devastating lethality. Ayatollah Khamenei, the final authority on Islamic law and arbiter of government policy, said in February 2012: 'Iran is not seeking to have the atomic bomb, possession of which is pointless, dangerous and is a great sin from an intellectual and a religious point of view'.[34] (The Iranian and Catholic clergy would seem to be in agreement on this point of the immorality of nuclear weapons from within their respective theologies.) There would also be additional risks and costs of weaponization, including military strikes by Israel and the United States.

The best – perhaps the only – way to make Iran forswear the bomb in the short term is to forswear talk and threats of imminent military action. Ratcheting up bellicose rhetoric, especially in tandem with threats from Israel, or, heaven forbid, carrying out attacks on Iran, would be guaranteed to ensure nuclear weaponization sooner rather than later. Conversely, maintaining a tough watch-and-inspect regime, based on an adaptation of the ultimately successful containment strategy against the former Soviet Union that would allow enough time for Iran's many internal contradictions to cause the regime to collapse from within, might help to keep Iran in the box of a nuclear capable but not nuclear armed state. The best way to eliminate Iran's nuclear weapons capability entirely would be to push for a credible and verifiable Middle East NWFZ; to be followed by the abolition of nuclear weapons for everyone under a universal NWC. In the meantime, only the nuclear pure have the right to cast stones at Iran's nuclear program.

Epilogue

Efforts to negotiate a resolution of the standoff with Iran had made no substantive progress in 2012. But an opening was provided in September 2013 on the margins of the start of the annual session of the UN General Assembly. US Secretary of State John Kerry and Iran's Foreign Minister Mohammad Javad Zarif – both new to their jobs – met in the company of diplomats from Britain, China, France, Russia and Germany, the P5+1 countries that have been engaged in years of talks with Tehran that previously had gone nowhere. This was the highest-level meeting between US and Iranian officials since the traumatic hostage crisis of the 1970s. The parties agreed to begin talks in Geneva in mid-October. A phone call between Presidents Barack Obama and Hassan Rouhani followed on 27 September – the first direct conversation between the two countries' presidents since 1979.

A 'historic breakthrough' deal was announced in on 24 November 2013: an interim deal whereby Iran agreed to scale back its weapon-sensitive material and activities under IAEA oversight in return for some sanctions relief. Negotiations for a follow-up agreement were to have been concluded in July 2014. However, at the time of writing, the complex negotiations had not been concluded and on 18 July all sides agreed to a four-month extension of the deadline until mid-November. Meanwhile there seemed to be a growing risk that the Russia–West standoff over the escalating Ukraine crisis would provoke Moscow into backing away from pressure on Tehran in retaliation for US and Western sanctions on Russia.[35]

The accord was neither a historic breakthrough nor a historic mistake (as characterized by Israel), merely an interim agreement.[36] It was an important and welcome first step that stopped well short of the final step. It was welcome because it paused Iran's march towards weapons and the West's march to another war. With neither a regime collapse imminent nor an effective military strike on Iran realistic, the Geneva deal was an acceptable stop-gap measure. The perceived threat from Iranian enrichment was reduced without crossing Tehran's red line. The interim deal neither explicitly accepted nor disavowed Iran's right to enrichment. It halted enrichment above 5 percent, neutralized the stockpile of near-20 percent enriched uranium, and halted progress on Iran's enrichment capacity. As quid pro quo, Iran was granted about US $7bn of sanctions relief (out of a total of

$80bn–$100bn) and the promise of no more UN, European Union (EU) or US sanctions for six months. Because of doubts about Iran's good faith and other possible undeclared facilities beyond IAEA reach, critics in Israel, Saudi Arabia and the United States were spoiling to wreck the deal for allegedly putting Iran on the same path as led to North Korea's eventual nuclear breakout. This is hyperbole. The limitations on proliferation-sensitive material, stockpile and facilities will lengthen the time required for Iran to weaponize, currently estimated to be about six months (although some, including Kerry during Senate testimony on 8 April 2014, fear it could be as low as two months[37]). Iran will not be any closer, but further away from the bomb because of the deal. Even if the interim agreement lapses, the Geneva accord will still have slowed Iran's march to nuclear weapons.

The most propitious time for ending a conflict is when it ripens to the point of a mutually 'hurting stalemate',[38] when both sides realize they are not going to prevail on the battlefield but are paying high costs while the conflict continues. There is little question but that the tough sanctions have hurt Iran. But America too has paid a heavy price militarily, financially and reputationally for its addiction to invading countries in and around the Middle East. As Washington geared up for yet another war of choice in August 2013 in Syria, the warmongering policy elite and commentariat was shocked into sobriety by the collapse of domestic, Congressional and global support.[39]

Porter argues that US and Israeli leaders and officials have subordinated an objective assessment of available indicators of Iranian motives and intentions to their own political interests. They wrongly concluded in the early 1990s that Iran was actively pursuing a full-scale, clandestine nuclear weapons program, whereas, in Porter's view, the weapons component of the largely civilian nuclear program did not amount to more than some weapons-related research from the late 1990s to 2003.[40] Earlier deals offered by Tehran had been turned down by Washington. The result? Iran's centrifuges multiplied from 164 in 2003 (when Iran's offer of a freeze as part of a grand bargain was spurned by the Bush administration) and 3000 in 2005 to 19,000 in 2013 (although only 11,000 were useable) and a stockpile of 8000kg of enriched uranium. Some success for sanctions. Hossein Mousavian, a former spokesman for Iran's nuclear negotiators, said the deal did not represent Iran's capitulation under crippling sanctions. Rather, it was the result of the election of a new president in Tehran keen to explore a rapprochement with the EU and US, and the shift in the US red line from 'no enrichment' to 'no bomb'.[41] Similarly, another informed Iran observer Trita Parsi also argues that it was reaching out to Tehran, not crippling it through sanctions, that brought about the nuclear deal – and it could have happened much earlier. The self-validating belief that the pain of sanctions was responsible for the Iranians' election choice of the moderate Rouhani is even more fanciful:

> The idea that the United States has the ability to engineer the outcome of elections in a country that is thousands of miles away, with which it has no trade, where it has had no diplomatic presence for 35 years, and where only a handful of current U.S. diplomats have ever served or even visited, expands

the concept of arrogance to new and exciting frontiers . . . The fact that the pragmatic faction within the Iranian government has on numerous occasions offered more attractive nuclear proposals to the West – prior to the crippling economic sanctions imposed by Obama – fundamentally undermines the notion that sanctions were needed to reach a deal.[42]

It may be, too, that Iran's nuclear program has matured from a nascent to an advanced capability since 2003–05, to the point where Tehran felt comfortable enough to pause it rather than keep absorbing the high costs of the sanctions regimes. In February 2014 the IAEA reported that Iran's stockpile of uranium enriched to just under 20 percent – the threshold for HEU and just a short technical step away from weapon grade HEU – had fallen to 161kg from 196kg in November: the first decline in four years.[43] Iran's 20 percent-enriched uranium stockpile had fallen to half by mid-April.[44]

But the agreement was fragile. It was possible still for Iran to withdraw from the NPT, expel IAEA inspectors and use its bomb-capable nuclear infrastructure to make nuclear weapons. However, most of the sanctions and the entire sanctions architecture remained in place. Because the sanctions relief was limited, temporary and reversible, the incentives for Iran to implement the interim agreement were stronger than the potential rewards of violating it; because it slowed and reversed the decade-long trend of an expansion of Iranian enrichment stockpile and capacity, the West had a strong incentive against breaching the deal – a useful benchmark for assessing a negotiated outcome.

The key challenge ahead was to define the precise terms of the nuclear program Iran is permitted to keep. The final step of the comprehensive solution envisaged in the interim deal would see the complete lifting of all UN, multilateral and national nuclear-related sanctions on Iran. The next set of demands included efforts to cut back the number of centrifuges substantially; dismantle the heavy water reactor at Arak that is regarded as unnecessary for civilian purposes and destabilizing because it can be used for reprocessing and plutonium separation as precursors to weaponization; closure of the enrichment facility at Fordow; and broader guaranteed IAEA inspections at Parchin.

If the West's goal is to verifiably and irreversibly roll back Iran's nuclear breakout capability, the quest is likely to prove futile. For reasons of security – history and geopolitics give both Iran and Israel a nightmarishly bad neighbourhood – as much as national pride, Iran will insist on maintaining material and infrastructure that give it some minimum capability to weaponize in future if necessary. Rather, the real challenge will be to widen the technological and detection gap between capability and weaponization, to cap Iran's capability at a point that provides the necessary reassurance to regional states and the international community by aligning the detection probability with the time required for effective international intervention to stop any attempted breakout. As Perkovich argues, demanding zero enrichment from Iran makes zero sense. Rather, the international community's focus should be on the timeframe of Iran's capacity to make a nuclear weapon.[45]

That said, containing Iran's nuclear weapons program will not complete the agenda of lifting the shadow of the nuclear weapons threat from the Middle East. To most people, the threat to regional and international security posed by Iran possessing 100 to 200 nuclear weapons and their means of delivery would be considerably greater and more real than with Israel having that capability. Nevertheless, it is fanciful to believe Israel can be permitted to keep its nuclear arsenal indefinitely but no other Middle Eastern country will ever get the bomb. Either the region will be verifiably denuclearized and Israel folded into a NWFZ, or Iran will break out some day.

The Geneva agreement buys time by freezing Iran's nuclear program for six months while a comprehensive permanent deal is negotiated. Should that eventuate, it might prove to be a game changer for the entire Middle East. For Iran, this is a bold effort to reset relations with the West by breaking cleanly with the volatile Ahmadinejad administration. The bitter enmity between Iran and the US has framed Middle East geopolitics since 1979. The Geneva agreement has the potential to unlock that frame. By ending Iran's isolation and bringing it back into the international fold, the West could help to rebuild Iran's once powerful secular middle class, dilute the influence of the radical clergy and turn Tehran into an ally to defeat the Taliban and al Qaeda. A successful end-state agreement could also unlock the potential to begin negotiations with Iran on regional issues like Afghanistan, Syria, Iraq and Lebanon. Washington needs to bring closure to the 34-year conflict with Iran also in order to focus on China's assertiveness in the Asia–Pacific and Russia's return to influence in the Middle East.

Notes

1 See especially Joseph Cirincione, *Nuclear Nightmares: Securing the World before It Is Too Late* (New York: Columbia University Press, 2013), chapter 2, 'Legacy'.
2 The core of the North Korean analysis was published as two op-eds: Ramesh Thakur, 'North Korean nuclear crisis', *Japan Times*, 11 June 2013, and 'Alternatives to North Korea's denuclearization', *Japan Times*, 16 June 2013.
3 W.C. Clemens, ''North Korea's Quest for Nuclear Weapons: New Historical Evidence', *Journal of East Asian Studies* 10:1 (2010): 127–54. The new evidence is the newly-opened archives of North Korea's former Warsaw Pact allies in Eastern Europe.
4 A state party has the right to withdraw from the NPT if it decides that 'extraordinary events, related to the subject matter of [the] Treaty, have jeopardized the supreme interests of its country' (Article 10). North Korea announced its withdrawal from the NPT on 12 March 1993 but then suspended it on 11 June 1993, the day before the decision would have taken effect. In January 2003, North Korea ended the suspension, which for all practical purposes meant withdrawal with immediate effect. Christer Ahlstrom, 'Withdrawal from arms control treaties', *SIPRI Yearbook 2004: Armaments, Disarmament and International Security* (Oxford: Oxford University Press, 2004), 763–77.
5 Korean Central News Agency (KCNA), 22 January 2003.
6 George Bunn and John B. Rhinelander, 'NPT withdrawal: time for the Security Council to step in', http://www.armscontrol.org/act/2005_05/Bunn_Rhinelander.
7 S.S. Hecker, 'What I Found in North Korea', *Foreign Affairs*, 9 December 2010, 4; http://www.foreignaffairs.com/articles/67023/siegfried-s-hecker/what-i-found-in-north-korea.
8 http://www.un.org/ga/search/view_doc.asp?symbol=S/2012/422.

9 Ayako Mie, 'Significant leap for Pyongyang missile tech', *Japan Times*, 13 December 2012.
10 Some anti-nuclear activists asked why North Korea was singled out for worldwide condemnations while tests by India (Agni), Pakistan (Nodong-derived Ghauri) and the United States (Minuteman III) over the preceding weeks in November and December were hardly mentioned by anyone.
11 Kim Eun-jung, 'Seoul says N. Korea's satellite circling Earth "normally"', Yonhap News Agency, 13 December 2012, http://english.yonhapnews.co.kr/national/2012/12/13/63/0301000000AEN20121213005153315F.HTML.
12 'Nuclear arms card for Japan', *Japan Times*, 29 April 2013; an abridged translation of an article from the April issue of *Sentaku*.
13 Lora Saalman, *Balancing Chinese Interests on North Korea and Iran*, 1 April 2013, http://carnegieendowment.org/2013/04/01/balancing-chinese-interests-on-north-korea-and-iran/fvbm.
14 On 28 May 2014, reacting to reports that Pyongyang may be preparing for another nuclear test, South Korean President Park Geun-hye warned that this could spark a regional nuclear domino effect; 'S. Korean Leader Warns of "Nuclear Domino" if North Conducts Test', *Global Security Newswire*, 30 May 2014, http://www.nti.org/gsn/article/south-korean-president-warns-regional-domino-effect-if-north-detonates-nuke-device/?mgs1=9be0g4aKbL.
15 The rest of this section on Iran was originally published as 'To Stop Iran Getting the Bomb, Must We Learn to Live with Its Nuclear Capability?', *Strategic Analysis* 36:2 (2012): 328–34. Reprinted by permission of Sage.
16 Gareth Porter argues that the IAEA was manipulated into putting out reports suggesting that Iran had a covert weapons program based largely on forged and fabricated documents that originated mainly in Israel. Even US intelligence on the Iranian nuclear program was systematically distorted by political hostility. Gareth Porter, *Manufactured Crisis: The Untold Story of the Iran Nuclear Scare* (Charlottesville VA: Just World Books, 2014).
17 Scott Peterson, 'WikiLeaks cable portrays IAEA chief as "in US court" on Iran nuclear program', *Christian Science Monitor*, 2 December 2010, http://www.csmonitor.com/World/Middle-East/2010/1202/WikiLeaks-cable-portrays-IAEA-chief-as-in-US-court-on-Iran-nuclear-program; Seymour M. Hersh, 'Iran and the IAEA', *New Yorker*, 18 November 2011, http://www.newyorker.com/online/blogs/comment/2011/11/iran-and-the-iaea.html#ixzz1e6eFgZ37.
18 According to former IAEA inspector Robert Kelley, the IAEA continues to attract allegations of pursuing a political agenda to target Iran rather than performing the functions of technical analysis, 'leaving itself open to a serious loss of credibility as a technical organization'. Quoted in Yousaf Butt, 'IAEA conduct complicates Iran nuclear deal', Reuters, 22 February 2014, http://blogs.reuters.com/great-debate/2014/02/21/iaea-conduct-complicates-iran-nuclear-deal/.
19 *Implementation of the NPT Safeguards Agreement and relevant provisions of the Security Council resolutions on the Islamic Republic of Iran – Report by the Director General* (Vienna: IAEA Board of Governors, GOV/2011/65, 8 November 2011), paragraphs 52–53.
20 Quoted in James Risen, 'Seeking nuclear insight in fog of the Ayatollah's utterances', *New York Times*, 13 April 2012.
21 *Implementation of the NPT Safeguards Agreement*, paragraph 43.
22 Ibid., paragraph 45.
23 The transcript of his statement and discussion can be downloaded from http://armed-services.senate.gov/testimony.cfm?wit_id=9990&id=5038. See also Jeffrey Lewis, 'Clapper on Iran NIE', *Arms Control Wonk*, 19 March 2011, http://lewis.armscontrolwonk.com/archive/3703/clapper-on-iran-nie.
24 Seymour M. Hersh, 'Iran and the Bomb', *New Yorker*, 6 June 2011, 35.
25 Kaveh L. Afrasiabi, 'Non-Aligned Movement backs Iran', *Asia Times*, 17 September 2010, http://www.atimes.com/atimes/Middle_East/LI17Ak02.html.

158 *Regional challenges*

26 'Iran provides 20 answers to clarify ambiguities about its nuclear program', *Tehran Times*, 10 November 2011, http://tehrantimes.com/index.php/politics/4362-iran-provides-20-answers-to-clarify-ambiguities-about-its-nuclear-program.
27 For their own stories, see Hans Blix, *Disarming Iraq* (New York: Pantheon Books, 2004), and Mohamed ElBaradei, *The Age of Deception: Nuclear Diplomacy in Treacherous Times* (London: Bloomsbury, 2011).
28 David E. Sanger and William J. Broad, 'U.S. hangs back as inspectors prepare report on Iran's nuclear program', *New York Times*, 8 November 2011, http://www.nytimes.com/2011/11/07/world/middleeast/united-states-hangs-back-as-inspectors-prepare-report-on-irans-nuclear-program.html.
29 Reza Marashi, 'America's real Iran problem', *New York Times*, 10 November 2011. WikiLeaks cables proved how assiduous, good and sometimes even elegant US embassy cables are.
30 Gareth Porter, 'IAEA's "Soviet nuclear scientist" never worked on weapons', *Inter-Press Service* 10 November 2011, http://ipsnews.net/news.asp?idnews=105776.
31 John Carlson, 'Iran nuclear issue – considerations for a negotiated outcome', Institute for Science and International Security, 4 November 2011, http://isis-online.org/isis-reports/detail/iran-nuclear-issue-considerations-for-a-negotiated-outcome/.
32 Eric Jesse, *Forecasting the Future of Iran: Implications for U.S. Strategy and Policy* (Santa Monica: RAND, 2011), 130, 170.
33 This is elaborated in Ramesh Thakur, 'A Balance of Interests', in Andrew F. Cooper, Jorge Heine, and Ramesh Thakur, eds., *The Oxford Handbook of Diplomacy* (Oxford: Oxford University Press, 2013): 70–87.
34 Quoted in Risen, 'Seeking nuclear insight in fog of the Ayatollah's utterances'. See also Hossein Mousavian 'Globalising Iran's Fatwa Against Nuclear Weapons', *Survival: Global Politics and Strategy* 55:2 (2013), 147–62.
35 Josh Rogin, 'Putin poised to retaliate against Obama by trashing Iran deal', *Daily Beast*, 18 July 2014, http://www.thedailybeast.com/articles/2014/07/18/putin-set-to-retaliate-against-obama-by-trashing-iran-deal.html. For another analysis of the complex interlinkages between the two crises, see Alexei Arbatov, 'Iran, Russia, and the Ukrainian Crisis', *The National Interest*, 17 July 2014, http://nationalinterest.org/blog/the-buzz/iran-russia-the-ukrainian-crisis-10902.
36 See Yousaf Butt, 'Eight ways you're wrong about Iran's nuclear program', *The National Interest*, 17 January 2014, http://nationalinterest.org/commentary/eight-ways-youre-wrong-about-irans-nuclear-program-9723.
37 Patrick Migliorini, David Albright, *et al.*, 'Iranian Breakout Estimates, Updated September 2013', 24 October 2013, http://isis-online.org/uploads/isis-reports/documents/Breakout_Study_24October2013.pdf; Patricia Zengerle, 'Kerry says Iran nuclear "breakout" window now seen as two months', Reuters, 8 April 2104, http://www.reuters.com/article/2014/04/08/us-iran-nuclear-usa-breakout-idUSBREA3719I20140408.
38 See Richard Haas, *Conflicts Unending* ((New Haven CT: Yale University Press, 1990); William Zartmann, 'Ripeness: The Hurting Stalemate and Beyond', in Paul C. Stern and Daniel Druckman, eds., *International Conflict Resolution after the Cold War* (Washington DC: National Academy Press, 2000).
39 In an *NBC News/Wall Street Journal* poll at the end of April 2014, despite the three-month Ukraine crisis, 47 percent of Americans said the US should cut down its activity in foreign affairs, 19 percent said it should be more active, and 30 percent were satisfied with the current level. By way of comparison, after 9/11 in 2001, 40 percent had supported greater overseas engagement against just 14 percent wanting to reduce the overseas US role. Carrie Dann, '47% Say U.S. Should Reduce Role in World Affairs', *NBC News*, 30 April 2014, http://www.nbcnews.com/politics/first-read/47-say-u-s-should-reduce-role-world-affairs-n92871.
40 Porter, *Manufactured Crisis*.

41 Hossein Mousavian, 'It was not sanctions that brought Iran to the table', *Financial Times*, 19 November 2013.
42 Trita Parsi, 'No, sanctions didn't force Iran to make a deal', *Foreign Policy*, 15 May 2014, http://www.foreignpolicy.com/articles/2014/05/14/sanctions_did_not_force_iran_to_make_a_deal_nuclear_enrichment.
43 Fredrik Dahl, 'Iran's most sensitive uranium stockpile falls after nuclear deal', Reuters, 21 February 2014, http://www.reuters.com/article/2014/02/21/us-iran-nuclear-iaea-idUSBREA1K1B920140221 (26 Feb 2014). About 250kg is needed for the core of one nuclear warhead.
44 Reuters, 'UN: Iran cuts nuclear assets despite slow progress on uranium site', *Global Security Newswire*, 17 April 2014, http://www.nti.org/gsn/article/un-iran-curbs-key-atomic-assets-despite-slow-progress-uranium-site/.
45 George Perkovich, 'No Endgame in Sight', *Foreign Affairs Snapshot*, 15 January 2014, http://www.foreignaffairs.com/articles/140650/george-perkovich/no-endgame-in-sight.

Part III
The nuclear regime

11 Stepping stones to a nuclear-weapon-free world*

Nuclear-weapon-free zones (NWFZs) are legal mechanisms for buttressing nuclear nonproliferation and political stepping stones towards nuclear disarmament. The worldwide outrage and disbelief provoked by the French decision to resume nuclear testing in 1995 confirmed both the public revulsion against nuclear weapons and their associated infrastructure, and the general belief that they are problems left over from the Cold War. There is a growing strategic disconnect between the unaltered theology of nuclear deterrence, on the one hand and, on the other, the military and political reality of reduced nuclear stockpiles and increasing normative constraints on the usability of nuclear weapons.

We are at a crossroads on the international strategic landscape. The past decade has seen great progress in nuclear disarmament. The threat of nuclear war between Moscow and Washington has receded. Yet the United States continues to deploy over 8,000 nuclear weapons and Russia over 11,000. The two erstwhile Cold War enemies have reduced nuclear delivery vehicles but have not yet agreed to dismantle nuclear warheads. France, China, Britain, Israel, India and Pakistan too have active nuclear weapons programs. The gravest nuclear danger now is not war between Russia and the United States, but the spread of nuclear weapons technology and materials beyond the five nuclear weapons states (NWS). The danger of horizontal proliferation cannot be contained indefinitely by maintaining the status quo of five NWS. The existing balance of nuclear weapons status is a dynamic equilibrium, not a static equation. The world cannot accept forever a power hierarchy frozen in terms of the nuclear weapons divide of 1968. The only two policy options are a progression down to zero for the existing NWS, or the spread of nuclear weapons to many other states.

NWFZs, meant to forestall the latter eventuality, signify 'disarmament before the fact'. They are undertaken by those who do not possess nuclear weapons but fear being ensnared in outsiders' nuclear webs. The concept predates and supplements the Nuclear Non-Proliferation Treaty (NPT). Ten years before the NPT, Poland's Foreign Minister Adam Rapacki proposed the establishment of a NWFZ in Central Europe (Poland, Czechoslovakia, East and West Germany) as a means of forestalling the nuclearization of West Germany and the deployment of Soviet nuclear weapons on the territory of Warsaw Pact allies. As well as manufacture, the stationing and stockpiling of nuclear weapons and delivery vehicles would be prohibited in the zone. Ironically, even though a NWFZ has yet to be established in Central or any other part of Europe, it has been established in many other parts of the world and the meaning of the concept has been greatly clarified and refined since the Rapacki Plan of 1958.

The Antarctic Treaty of 1959 denuclearized the uninhabited continent; the Outer Space Treaty (1967) and Moon Agreement (1979) denuclearized the heavens, while the Sea Bed Treaty (1971) did the same with the ocean floor. The first NWFZ in a populated region was set up in Latin America by the Treaty of Tlatelolco in 1967. This was followed by the Treaty of Rarotonga in the South Pacific in 1985, the Treaty of Bangkok in Southeast Asia in 1995 and the Treaty of Pelindaba in Africa in 1996. The number of states parties to have signed and ratified the four zones, and details of NWS signature of the zonal protocols, are shown in Tables 11.1 and 11.2. The total number of states parties of the five NWFZs spread across four continents is almost one hundred (that is, more than half the world's countries).

NWFZs have developed cumulatively. The South Pacific Nuclear Free Zone (SPNFZ) built on and adapted the Latin American zonal provisions to suit the conditions and circumstances of the South Pacific. Southeast Asia and Africa in turn borrowed from both models available to them, namely Tlatelolco and Rarotonga. Like Rarotonga, for example, Bangkok and Pelindaba extend their proscription not just to nuclear weapons but to 'nuclear explosive devices' that release nuclear energy, irrespective of peaceful or aggressive purposes.

In many ways the more interesting case studies are those regions for which NWFZs have been proposed but without success. Why does the idea of NWFZs for the Middle East, South Asia and Northeast Asia continue to attract some policy analysts or academic commentators? Conversely, why does it fail to attract key groups of players in each of these regions? The Korean peninsula was in fact denuclearized in 1991, while an authoritative UN report on a NWFZ for the Middle East was published in 1990.[1] With respect to the three zones of conflict rather than zones of peace, there exists a

Table 11.1 The world's nuclear-weapon-free zones

Zone	Opened for signature	Entry into Force	No. of States Parties
Latin America (Treaty of Tlatelolco)	14 Feb 1967	25 Apr 1969	33
South Pacific (Treaty of Rarotonga)	6 Aug 1985	11 Dec 1986	13
Southeast Asia (Treaty of Bangkok)	15 Dec 1995	27 Mar 1997	10
Africa (Treaty of Pelindaba)	11 Apr 1996	15 Jul 2009	37
Central Asia	8 Sep 2006	21 Mar 2009	5

Source: http://www.un.org/disarmament/WMD/Nuclear/NWFZ.shtml.

N.B. The five NWS have recognized Mongolia's self-declared national nuclear-weapon-free status and have provided Mongolia with negative security assurances and pledged to respect its nuclear-weapon-free status.

Table 11.2 Dates of NWS ratification of NWFZ treaty protocols

	China	France	Russia	UK	USA
Tlatelolco[a]					
Protocol I	N/A	24.8.1992	N/A	11.12.1969	23.11.1981
Protocol II	12.6.1974	22.3.1974	8.1.1979	11.12.1969	12.5.1971
Rarotonga[b]					
Protocol I	N/A	20.9.1996	N/A	19.9.1997	Not yet
Protocol II	21.10.1988	20.9.1996	21.4.1988	19.9.1997	Not yet
Protocol III	21.10.1988	20.9.1996	21.4.1988	19.9.1997	Not yet
Pelindaba[c]					
Protocol I	10.10.1997	20.9.1996	5.4.2011	12.3.2001	Not yet
Protocol II	10.10.1997	20.9.1996	5.4.2011	12.3.2001	Not yet
Protocol III	N/A	20.9.1996	N/A	N/A	N/A

Source: http://www.un.org/disarmament/WMD/Nuclear/NWFZ.shtml.

Notes

[a]**Tlatelolco** (Latin American NWFZ): Parties to Protocol I agree to apply key provisions of the treaty to their territories within the zone. Parties to Protocol II agree to respect the treaty's aims and provisions and provide negative security assurances to states parties.

[b]**Rarotonga** (South Pacific NFZ): Parties to Protocol I agree to apply key provisions of the treaty to their territories within the zone (open to France, the UK and US). Parties to Protocol II agree to respect the treaty's aims and provisions and provide negative security assurances to states parties (open to the five NPT NWS). Parties to Protocol III agree not to conduct nuclear tests anywhere in the SPNFZ (open to the five NPT NWS).

[c]**Pelindaba** (African NWFZ): Parties to Protocol I agree to respect the treaty's aims and provisions and provide negative security assurances to states parties (open to the five NPT NWS). Parties to Protocol II agree not to conduct nuclear tests or assist or encourage nuclear testing anywhere in the African NWFZ (open to the five NPT NWS). Parties to Protocol III agree to apply key provisions of the treaty to their territories within the zone (open to France and Spain).

In addition:

Bangkok (Southeast Asian NWFZ): The treaty's one protocol is open to the five NPT NWS but has not yet been signed by any of them, chiefly due to NWS concerns about the treaty's geographical scope. As with other NWFZs, the parties to the protocol would agree to respect the treaty's aims and provide negative security assurances to states parties.

Central Asia: The treaty's one protocol is open to the five NPT NWS but has not yet been signed by any of them. A prominent concern for some NWS is that the treaty does not affect rights and obligations of the parties under international treaties concluded prior to entry into force of the CANWFZ, so may allow Russia to station nuclear weapons in Central Asia under the 1992 Tashkent Collective Security Treaty. As with other NWFZs, the parties to the protocol would agree to respect the treaty's aims and provide negative security assurances to states parties.

formidable range of technical, geographical, historical, domestic, regional and global obstacles to the attainment of NWFZs in these troubled theatres.

Nature and goals of NWFZs

A NWFZ denotes an area established by a group of states by a treaty which defines the status of the absence of nuclear weapons from the zone and sets up a system of verification and control to guarantee compliance. A NWFZ is characterized by 'four Noes': no possession, testing, deployment or use of nuclear weapons. Thus it differs from the NPT in one crucial respect. The latter permits the stationing of nuclear weapons on the territory of states parties as long as they do not exercise jurisdiction and control over them; a NWFZ prohibits such stationing. A NWFZ goes beyond the NPT also in requiring commitments from the NWS not to use nuclear weapons against zonal members – unlike unilateral declarations of non-use, treaty commitments are legally binding on the NWS; and in setting up regional verification machinery to complement the work of the International Atomic Energy Agency (IAEA) in preventing cheating.

All NWFZs share the elements of prohibiting forever the acquisition, deployment, use and testing of nuclear weapons on territorial land, sea and airspace; requiring no use assurances from the NWS; setting up verification systems; and obtaining the endorsement of the international community through a UN General Assembly resolution. They differ on whether the scope of the prohibitions extends to peaceful nuclear explosions (permitted by Tlatelolco but prohibited by the others), delivery systems (none), nuclear facilities and research and development (Pelindaba), and the disposal of radioactive wastes (Rarotonga and Pelindaba);[2] on whether the area of application includes exclusive economic zones (Bangkok) and the high seas (Tlatelolco); on the entry into force and denunciation provisions; and on subjecting protocol obligations of the NWS to compliance procedures (Pelindaba) and linking the latter to international mechanisms like the IAEA and the UN Security Council (all except Rarotonga). In the main the differences reflect disparate geostrategic circumstances.

Article 7 of the NPT accepts that 'Nothing in this Treaty affects the right of any group of states to conclude regional treaties in order to assure the total absence of nuclear weapons in their respective territories'. The article implicitly acknowledged that the NPT itself had failed 'to assure the total absence of nuclear weapons' in the territories of states parties. When the NPT was indefinitely extended in 1995, the 'Principles and Objectives for Nonproliferation and Disarmament' adopted by the NPT Review and Extension Conference (NPTREC) expressed the conviction of the participants that regional denuclearization, including NWFZs, enhance global as well as regional security.[3] The Principles and Objectives have been described as 'politically binding' by NPTREC President Jayantha Dhanapala, reflecting the political bargain and encapsulating the political will of the conference participants.[4] They 'comprise a rolling text with a program of action geared towards eventually achieving total nuclear disarmament'.[5] While comprehensive disarmament remains a long range goal of the international community, the conviction has grown that immediate and partial measures, which would increase confidence and create a more favourable atmosphere for overall disarmament, should be pursued. Arms control efforts look too much to the past and are reactive and curative. For a region which seeks to perpetuate the status quo of isolation from nuclear weapons strategy and deployment, the greater need is for measures that are anticipatory: prophylactic, not therapeutic.

NWFZ proposals concentrate on nuclear weapons rather than the underlying causes of conflicts and the impossibility of reversing scientific knowledge and technological capability. The ostensible goal is to insulate a region totally from the destructive effects of nuclear warfare in general and nuclear weapons deployment and testing in particular. Subsumed within this broad objective are subsidiary goals of lowering the costs and burdens of the nuclear arms race, reducing the probability of war and decreasing the harmful effects if war should nevertheless occur.

Regional initiative

There is no consensus on the requirements of a NWFZ. The closest approximation to a widely acceptable articulation of the criteria and nature of NWFZs are contained in two comprehensive expert studies under UN auspices in 1975 and 1985.[6] First, the initiative should come from the countries of the region. This avoids charges of an outside power imposing its preferences on regional actors. In Latin America, the South Pacific, Southeast Asia and Africa the initiative was pursued through the appropriate regional organizations. The attainment of NWFZs in all three was facilitated by the regions' experience of multilateralism. Conversely, the Middle East, South Asia and Northeast Asia are seriously lacking in inclusive experiences of multilateralism. The Middle East and Northeast Asia lack the formal institutions, while the South Asian Association for Regional Cooperation (SAARC) lacks the history and experience of successful regional cooperation on political and security issues. The obstacle could potentially be circumvented in Northeast Asia by nesting security explorations in the ASEAN Regional Forum (ARF), and in the Middle East by nesting NWFZ discussions in the Arms Control and Regional Security multilateral working group. SAARC has neither the status nor unifying role of a major regional organization similar, for example, to the Association of Southeast Asian Nations (ASEAN), the Organization of American States (OAS), the Organization of African Unity (OAU) or the South Pacific Forum (SPF) which set up NWFZs in Southeast Asia, Latin America, Africa and the South Pacific respectively.

Regional organizations have the advantages of closeness to the conflicts, deeper familiarity with the issues underlying the conflict and the social and political contexts encasing them, and awareness of the urgency to deal with the crisis to hand. The handicaps under which they operate include local rivalries, partisanship, the tendency to replicate local power imbalances within the regional organizations, and the fear of establishing precedents for intervention in the internal affairs of member countries.[7] In order to take on the role of initiating zonal talks, regional organizations would firstly need to possess the requisite financial, institutional and military capacity to play a regional conflict management role. Second, they would need to be synchronous with the regional security complexes which emphasize the 'interdependence of rivalry as well as that of shared interests'.[8] That is, for regional arrangements to have real meaning, all the parties that are central to a regional security complex must be included. However, if all relevant regional actors are included, the regional arrangements can be rendered impotent because of the refusal of the parties to permit security discussions for fear of derailing regional cooperation on non-security issues, as is the case with SAARC.[9] India rejects Pakistan's efforts at the UN for a

South Asian NWFZ in part on the procedural objection that there is no authority of a regional organization behind them. The question of China–Taiwan relations could play a similar spoiling role in Northeast Asia. Taiwan remains one of the most likely flashpoints in Asia. But, insisting that it is an internal affair and not a regional or international problem, China will not permit any discussion of the Taiwan issue in any regional or international, intergovernmental or second track forum.

Treaty

Second, the specific provisions of the NWFZ should be codified in a multilateral treaty establishing the zone in perpetuity. This ensures that the zone is established in a legally binding form, the commitments of zonal members are transparent, and outsiders as well as members can have reasonable confidence in the value and durability of the zone. All four zones have been established by treaty, with Rarotonga being the shortest and Tlatelolco the longest. All four have been established in perpetuity and none is subject to any reservations. Bangkok is the only one that contains a provision for a review, to be conducted ten years after the treaty has entered into force. The entry into force clauses are the simplest for Rarotonga and Bangkok, requiring eight and seven ratifications respectively. Pelindaba needs 28 ratifications to come into force, while Tlatelolco was the most complex. It was contingent upon certain conditions (adherence by all regional and protocol states, and conclusion of safeguards agreements with the IAEA), but these could be waived by the states parties and were waived by most. Tlatelolco and Pelindaba permit withdrawal upon three and twelve months' notice respectively when the supreme interests of a party are jeopardized by extraordinary events. Rarotonga and Bangkok are more restrictive in limiting denunciation to material breaches of the NWFZ treaties themselves and requiring 12-month periods of notice.

Membership

Third, adherence to a treaty by sovereign states has to be voluntary. Even if all relevant regional states were supportive of a zone in principle, the difficulty would remain of how best to convert support for a NWFZ in the abstract into signature of a NWFZ treaty in the particular. Regional countries will have different approaches in respect of the content of a treaty. Conservatives will want to reject measures which impact upon existing security policies and practices; they might prefer to leave open the option of the stationing of nuclear weapons of a protector-NWS in the region at a future date. Radicals might favour banning all types of nuclear involvement in the region – port calls, transit facilities for nuclear capable aircraft, command, control, communications, computers, and intelligence facilities, movement of nuclear capable warships in regional waterways – and extending the zonal boundary to bring contiguous NWS within its scope.

In the case of Rarotonga, all who were eligible in 1985, when the treaty was concluded, had signed by 1997. Three countries – the Federated States of Micronesia (FSM), Marshall Islands and Palau – joined the SPF after 1985. All three have been self-governing in compacts of free association with the US since 1986 which leaves the latter in charge of their defence and security. Therein lies the problem. The compacts permit the United States to transit territory and overfly airspace with nuclear weapons, and to store nuclear weapons on these territories in times of national emergency, state of war or as necessary to defend against actual or impending attack. The application of SPNFZ obligations would be inconsistent with these US rights.

A NWFZ deepens and extends the NPT. What happens then in a region where important local actors are not party to the NPT, like Israel in the Middle East and India and Pakistan in South Asia? All the potential signatory states to a Northeast Asian nuclear-weapon-free zone (NEANWFZ) are already members of the NPT.[10] Yet the international community has been suspicious of the fidelity of North Korea to its NPT obligations. The Korean case illustrates just how difficult it is to implement a NWFZ successfully when proliferation risks are high, political relationships are strained, verification procedures are both critically important yet difficult to agree on, and no patient process of treaty negotiation has been undertaken by an expert working group. What this means is that progress towards a NEANWFZ will require the prior resolution of the issue of North Korea's nuclear weapons program. Similarly, a South Asian NWFZ cannot precede but must follow the renunciation of the nuclear weapons option by India and Pakistan. A NWFZ is not the means but the symbol of forswearing nuclear weapons and precluding any future departure from the non-nuclear status.

To be credible, a NWFZ must include all militarily significant states in the region. This immediately raises the question of how the determination is to be made as to which states are 'militarily significant' for any particular zone. In the case of a NEANWFZ, for example, this would mean the inclusion of the two Koreas, Japan and Taiwan. But what of China and Russia? And should China be included or excluded from a South Asian NWFZ? Should it be subject to the restrictions of any future South or Northeast Asian NWFZ as a full-fledged state party, or should it be a protocol, de facto extra-regional NWS whose zonal obligations are not subject to monitoring and verification mechanisms? China argues that it is a global NWS and should be involved in discussions alongside the other four NWS, not as a regional member of the relevant zone. In other words, how can we square the familiar circle of a NWFZ symbolizing nonproliferation to the NWS but disarmament to the threshold NWS?

Existing security arrangements

Fourth, a NWFZ must satisfy the principle of undiminished security for all countries in the region as well as the global powers. States will become parties to a NWFZ only if convinced that it will, on balance, advance rather than threaten their security interests. Countries of Latin America, the South Pacific, Southeast Asia and Africa agreed to zonal arrangements when so convinced. Conversely, zonal proposals for the Middle East and South and Northeast Asia have not borne fruit so far because important states in these regions suspect that a NWFZ would seriously degrade their security.

170 *The nuclear regime*

Similarly, states are unlikely to enter into NWFZ arrangements if their existing treaty relationships will be jeopardized by zonal obligations. This is why it is accepted that security treaty relationships within a zone should not be disturbed. In South Asia, many Indian analysts believe Pakistan to be a de facto nuclear ally of China and some even suspect that China has conducted one or more nuclear tests as a proxy for Pakistan. In the Middle East, the problem may lie in the de facto and non-reciprocal US security guarantee of Israel. In the Middle East, Turkey is a member of the North Atlantic Treaty Organization (NATO). The possession and deployment of nuclear weapons are integral to NATO doctrine and command structure. How can this be reconciled with Turkey's membership of a Middle East NWFZ? Alternatively, how meaningful would be a Middle East NWFZ if Turkey was not included?

The prospects of establishing NWFZs in the Middle East, South Asia and Northeast Asia may have become more difficult in the 1990s because of several interlinked and overlapping processes that are underway and render the strategic environments in all three regions very fluid. There is no stable regional geostrategic environment that can be 'frozen' in a NWFZ. The election of Binyamin Netanyahu as prime minister arrested and diverted the flow of Israeli-Palestinian relations after the Oslo accords. The collapse of the Soviet Union in 1991, the indefinite extension of the NPT in 1995 and the adoption of the Comprehensive Test Ban Treaty (CTBT) in 1996 have fundamentally impacted on India's security calculations in South Asia. In Northeast Asia, the collapse of the Soviet Union, the passing of Kim Il-sung, the status of China as the emergent superpower and the outwards reinterpretation of the US–Japan security alliance have unsettled the basic parameters of the regional order. Precisely because NWFZs are confidence building measures (CBMs), that is stability *enhancing* measures, they are inappropriate instruments for use in fluid geopolitical environments.

As with so much else in human society, timing can be critical with respect to the catalyst that propels regional countries towards a NWFZ and determines success or failure of zonal negotiations. Initiatives, negotiations and the terms of NWFZs cannot be divorced from the regional and international political environment, including the number, identity and state of major power relations; the state of arms control; and the prospect of deployment of nuclear weapons in new and sensitive areas. In such circumstances, a NWFZ can institute a safe corridor between the nuclear weapons of contending rivals. The threat of having Soviet missiles based in Cuba, which led to the 1962 missile crisis, was critical in concentrating the minds of the people and governments of Latin America on the realization that they could have been the victims of a nuclear war despite no country in the continent possessing any nuclear weapons.

In the South Pacific, French nuclear testing provided the focal point of coordination of anti-nuclear concerns and the tensions of the second Cold War in the 1980s concentrated the minds of nations on the merits of a NWFZ. The absence of the appropriate conjunction of regional interests aborted the NWFZ initiative in 1975 but vested it with success in 1985. The anti-nuclear coalition was galvanized by New Zealand's determination to shed its previous security identity that had tied it firmly to the ANZUS (the Australia–New Zealand–US security treaty) alliance. New Zealand accepted being cast into the security wilderness by the US rather than permit ship visits under the ambiguous formula of neither confirming nor denying the presence of nuclear weapons on board. The way in which the regional zone was drafted avoided the stark choice between irreconcilable alternatives that New Zealand had drifted into in its national policy. Because SPNFZ was crafted in such a way as to harmonize its obligations with existing ANZUS practice, Australia was able to sign SPNFZ and remain an active defence partner of the US with no curtailment of any existing security interactions.

The attainment of the African NWFZ was delayed for several decades pending the right political conditions and balances needed for the continent's denuclearization. The twin developments of black majority rule and ex-post facto revelations of white South Africa having been an undeclared NWS were powerful boosts to the NWFZ campaign. Also important is the timing and sequencing of changes in the local nuclear dynamics. Australia was lukewarm, if not opposed, to the South Pacific initiative in 1975 but actively led the zonal movement in 1984–85. The rise of a powerful domestic anti-nuclear movement in the interim was not coincidental.

Verification

Fifth, in order for everyone to have confidence in the credibility and effectiveness of a NWFZ, it should have a two-tier system for verifying the non-diversion of nuclear material from peaceful nuclear activities. Regionally, bureaucratic machinery should be established to facilitate on-site challenge and spot inspections. Internationally, a NWFZ should require submission to fullscope IAEA safeguards on all fissionable material in all peaceful nuclear activities within the territory of a party, under its jurisdiction or carried out under its control anywhere. With such a compliance and control system in force, applied to the complete nuclear fuel cycle for each party to ensure that any diversion of fissile material would be detected in good time, regional states as well as outsiders will have reasonable assurance that the NWFZ status is not being violated.

All four zones require IAEA fullscope safeguards. Tlatelolco, Bangkok and Pelindaba created organizations specifically for monitoring compliance with the regional NWFZs. The Agency for the Prohibition of Nuclear Weapons in Latin America and the Caribbean (OPANAL) holds regular sessions and can call special sessions if required. It has its own fulltime Secretary General and a five-member Council that must be able to function continuously. Under the original Article 16 of the Treaty of Tlatelolco, special inspections of suspicious activity could be arranged either by OPANAL or the IAEA. After an amendment in 1992, the right to conduct special inspections was vested exclusively in the IAEA. The implementation of the Treaty of Bangkok is to be overseen by a Commission for the Southeast Asian NWFZ (SEANWFZ) composed of all states parties, with an Executive Committee also comprising all parties. Pelindaba requires the establishment of a 12-member African Commission on Nuclear Energy (AFCONE) for ensuring compliance with zonal obligations.

AFCONE can request IAEA inspections accompanied by its own representatives. SPNFZ has no standing verification machinery or officials of its own, only an ad hoc Consultative Committee with the power to appoint special inspection teams.

Breaches of the zonal treaties *must* be reported to the OAS *and* the UN Security Council and General Assembly in the case of Tlatelolco; they can be handled by the OAU *or* referred by the latter to the UN Security Council under Pelindaba; are left entirely to the discretion of the South Pacific Forum in Rarotonga; and *may* be referred by the SEANWFZ Commission to the IAEA and, if international peace and security is threatened, to the UN Security Council and General Assembly. The Treaty of Bangkok is doubly distinctive. It requires the Executive Committee to convene a special meeting of the Commission to decide on appropriate measures in the event of a breach of the non-use protocol by a NWS; and it provides for the referral of disputes over the interpretation of the treaty to the International Court of Justice (ICJ).

The protracted negotiations on the CTBT threw up many problems, among them the political difficulty caused by the widening technological gap between the intelligence capabilities of the advanced industrial states and the developing countries. This remains a potential area of tension in the two-tier verification machinery of regional NWFZs as well. There is a qualitative discrepancy between the ability of developing countries and the US to detect possible violations of arms control agreements which can trigger international inspection. Countries like India have become suspicious that the United States has begun to transform disarmament instruments into nonproliferation modalities by exploiting its technological edge. Another potential gap in a NWFZ regime is the lack of machinery for policing NWS compliance with the protocols. A control system can be established for verifying the behaviour of treaty parties, but is more problematical for monitoring the behaviour of nuclear powers within zonal limits.

The IAEA can be entrusted with the responsibility of verifying compliance of peaceful nuclear activities with non-weaponization obligations. The prospects of credible NWFZs in Asia would brighten with the establishment of a counterpart to the European Atomic Energy Community (EURATOM).[11] 'ASIATOM' could be given ownership of all fissile material and, in partnership with the IAEA, enhance transparency and cooperative control to guarantee the peaceful uses of nuclear energy.

Peaceful nuclear development

Sixth, peaceful nuclear development should be permitted. In keeping with the NPT bargain, a NWFZ cannot proscribe peaceful nuclear development. But in order to pre-empt this becoming the pathway to a 'peaceful nuclear explosion', Rarotonga was unequivocal in prohibiting the manufacture, acquisition, control or testing 'of any nuclear explosive device', defined as 'any nuclear weapon or other explosive device capable of releasing nuclear energy, irrespective of the purpose for which it could be used'. Zonal parties can be forbidden to transfer material or equipment, even for peaceful purposes, to states not subject to NPT and

IAEA safeguards. That is, parties would be enjoined to ensure that any transfer of nuclear technology or material conformed to strict nonproliferation measures in order to provide assurance of exclusively peaceful use.

Geographic scope

Seventh, the zone should have clearly defined and recognized boundaries. But how this can be achieved is not always obvious. The perimeter enclosing a zone can be a patchwork covering only the territories of member countries, or it can be a 'picture frame' incorporating all enclosed space within the zone. In the latter event, in the case of maritime zones the 'zone of application' of the treaty clauses becomes separate from the 'zone' as such, since they cannot extend to the high seas. For example, the major portion of SPNFZ comprises international waterways. Under customary international law codified in the 1982 UN Convention on the Law of the Seas (UNCLOS), all states have the right to enter and use such waterways. A group of states can agree among themselves to impose restrictions on their own activities, but not on that of others. (Although they can invite other states to sign relevant protocols containing similar restrictions.)

Zonal prohibitions should encompass the total land, territorial sea and airspace of states parties. The status of exclusive economic zones (EEZ), archipelagic waters and straits is more contentious. SEANWFZ obligations extend to the continental shelves, archipelagic waters and EEZ of states parties, but without prejudice to the freedom of the high seas and rights of innocent passage and transit. The problem arises in that coastal states enjoy full jurisdiction only over internal territorial waters; all states enjoy rights of 'innocent passage' in territorial seas and archipelagic waters. Coastal states have no jurisdiction over the naval vessels or weapons of other states in EEZ or on the high seas. Another problem arises with respect to territories inside the zone (such as colonies or dependencies) belonging to extra-regional countries. The clearest example in recent times of such a situation arose with respect to French Polynesia, the site of nuclear testing by France from 1966 to 1996.

A third problem area is the status of members who join a regional organization after a NWFZ is already in place. Typically, a zone extends to the total membership of the regional organization that has been the formal forum for discussions and negotiations leading to the establishment of the NWFZ. A treaty should be made open for signature by any future member of the regional organization, but should accession be a mandatory requirement? A fourth and related problem concerns accession to the regional organization and zone by a new member whose territorial boundaries extend beyond the existing geographical scope of the NWFZ.

The fifth and final difficulty arises with respect to territory in dispute between two or more countries. In the case of Tlatelolco, Argentina claims sovereignty over the Islas Malvinas/Falkland Islands which are physically under British control. In the case of Pelindaba, the British dependency of Chagos Archipelago/Diego Garcia is claimed by Mauritius and as such included within the African zone, but without prejudice to the question of sovereignty. The settlement of the territorial disputes, it is assumed, are separate from and independent of the

NWFZ and do not affect the management of the latter. Argentina and Britain are signatories to the treaty and protocols of Tlatelolco; the Treaty of Pelindaba does not invite Britain to sign Protocol III on dependencies. In a South Asian NWFZ which did not include China, what would be the status of territory claimed by India but occupied by China? Tlatelolco and Pelindaba provide useful precedents for how the difficulty might be resolved or shelved without affecting the integrity of the regional NWFZs.

Between them, the established zones offer models for continental as well as maritime strategic environments. The zonal prohibitions under the treaties of Tlatelolco and Bangkok extend to maritime areas adjoining the territorial waters of member states. The South Pacific zone adopted a 'picture frame' rather than an 'incomplete patchwork' approach. It drew the outer boundaries of the zone and included the total enclosed space as the nuclear free zone. But in fact the denuclearization provisions do not apply beyond territorial waters; only the anti-dumping clauses do. The picture frame approach may not be relevant to the Middle East and Northeast Asia. But it could be relevant to South Asia, bearing in mind that India has island possessions to the east (the Andaman and Nicobar group) and west (the Lakshadweep group). If however a picture frame approach was to be adopted for South Asia, then India might well try to push the frame outwards to incorporate Diego Garcia within the zonal boundary. This would then set up a clash of interests with the United States.

Freedom of the seas

Eighth, in defining the territory of the zone, members must respect the freedom of the high seas and straits used for international navigation, and of international airspace. A holistic picture frame zone immediately raises the spectre of infringement of well-established rules of international law with regard to naval navigation. However, unlike 'innocent passage' which is accepted by all four zonal regimes, 'hostile passage' – transit of vehicles carrying prohibited weapons in an active mode through the NWFZ for use against targets beyond it – is unlikely to be acceptable to any of the four zones. As confidence building more than arms control measures, NWFZs strengthen the nonproliferation norm epitomized in the NPT. The most significant component of a normative world order is international law. Parts of the legal order may well be flawed, parts archaic and parts ineffectual. The remedy is to modify, codify and develop legal principles and enforcement mechanisms, not to violate them. Imposing restrictions on established maritime rights would not be proper because ultimately it would be damaging to the goal of creating a civilized world ruled by law and reason. A NWFZ must therefore function within the existing law of the seas.

NWS support

Finally, NWFZs should have the support of the NWS. The existing zones seek to integrate the NWS through protocols to the treaty. This is not always successful.

China and Russia endorsed the South Pacific zone fairly promptly; France, Britain and the US did so only a decade later, after the Cold War had ended and French nuclear testing in the Pacific had ceased. This despite the fact that SPNFZ negotiators had engaged in early and frequent consultations with the US in drafting the treaty in such a way that it did not impede any existing US activity. With the Soviet profile barely visible in the South Pacific and proliferation not a threat in the region, Washington did not see any of its goals being advanced by SPNFZ. Conversely, the zone did have a negative impact on NATO ally France. It could also have set a precedent for the spread of the anti-nuclear 'allergy' to other regions, and the cumulative impact of NWFZs could create obstacles to the free movement of US nuclear forces around the globe.

The United States signed Protocol I of the Treaty of Tlatelolco, applying the denuclearization provisions to its territories within the zone, under the Carter administration in 1977, and ratified it under the Reagan administration in 1981. Washington excluded Guantanamo Base in Cuba from its coverage until such time as Cuba itself joined the treaty. Cuba signed in 1995 but did not ratify until 2002, the last to do so. Protocol II, containing the negative security assurances on neither using nor threatening zonal members with nuclear weapons, was signed by the US in 1968 and ratified in 1971. This was the first example of the US entering into an obligation restricting the use of its nuclear weapons.[12] Washington concluded that the treaty marked a significant contribution to its security interests by prohibiting the type of nuclear weapons deployment that had provoked the Cuban missile crisis in 1962, instituting regional compliance machinery, requiring IAEA safeguards by member states, and promoting the cause of a universal non-proliferation treaty. Nevertheless Washington attached a unilateral interpretation setting conditions to the protocol, namely US obligations would cease in the event of an attack by a party with the assistance of a NWS.[13] This was to set the pattern for conditions attached by almost all the NWS to the negative security assurances of almost all the NWFZs. A second set of reservations sometimes noted by the NWS, for example China and the UK with respect to SPNFZ, concerns material breach of the zonal treaties by members. Finally, none of the NWS has signed the SEANWFZ protocols because of the infringements on rights of innocent passage and freedom of the seas. The problem with zonal arrangements for South Asia and Northeast Asia will be that NWS are major regional actors: China *vis-à-vis* South Asia, China and Russia in Northeast Asia.

The utility and limitations of NWFZs

NWFZs are integral components of the mosaic of international action on denuclearization and delegitimization of the entire edifice of nuclear weapons (possession, testing, deployment, doctrines and strategies). The traditional – mostly US – argument against NWFZs was that they encouraged the 'nuclear allergy' and in so doing undermined deterrence. In the post-Cold War era this argument is no longer relevant. Instead, anti-proliferation goals are now accorded higher priority. NWFZs can play a modest role in the global campaign against nuclear proliferation precisely by heightening the nuclear allergy. By maintaining the momentum for the continued stigmatization of this weapon of mass destruction, NWFZs sustain the structure of normative restraints on the acquisition, multiplication, deployment and use of nuclear weapons. They contribute to the marginalization of nuclear weapons as tools of national security. They institutionalize nonproliferation norms, consolidate nonproliferation successes and maintain the momentum to denuclearization ahead of the willingness of the NWS to renounce their own nuclear arsenals.[14]

The search for a NWFZ for the Middle East, South Asia and Northeast Asia can be justified on grounds of the risks which attend the rivalry between the nuclear powers, the proliferation propensity of regional actors and the dynamics of interaction between local and international actors. It is a sobering fact that all three threshold NWS are in the Middle East and South Asia and three of the five NPT-licit NWS (China, Russia and the United States) are engaged in a competitive rivalry in Northeast Asia. The Middle East has been a cauldron of regional conflict for the entire period since World War II. The axis of the regional conflict has often intersected with that of global rivalry. The region has been the setting for the acquisition and use of weapons of mass destruction (WMD): Israel is a threshold NWS, Iraq is known to have been pursuing a clandestine but well-advanced program of nuclear weapons acquisition, and chemical weapons were used during the Iran–Iraq war (1980–88).

The world interest is engaged in South Asia because of the numbers of people involved – some one-fifth of humanity – and because of the risks of a nuclear conflict. India and Pakistan have a rivalry as intense and long as the Israeli–Palestinian conflict. It has led to three wars in the past and could escalate to a nuclear cataclysm in the future. By the mid-1990s relations between India and Pakistan had deteriorated to the most dangerous level since 1971. India's strategic environment is unique in that it has major border conflicts with a NWS on one side and a threshold NWS on another.

The North Pacific remains a potentially unstable zone of confrontation. History does not inspire confidence that major power interactions will remain forever harmonious and free of a clash of interests. The Korean peninsula is located in a strategic zone, subject to the pulls and pressures of relations between China, Japan, Russia and the United States. The *unification* of the peninsula may be a purely internal decision for the people of Korea and a product of negotiations between the two parallel sets of authorities north and south of the demilitarized zone (DMZ). The *stability* of the peninsula will be a function of the interaction between local dynamics and major power relations. This gives rise to the question of how Korea might be removed from the zone of strategic confrontation. The great powers could seek to establish a de facto concert to stabilize the peninsula; or they could seek to promote neutrality or impose neutralization on the Koreans as a condition of unification; or they could try to develop subregional and multilateral forums for security dialogues.

The Treaty of Tlatelolco helped to embed and institutionalize the nonproliferation norm in Latin America, and thereby raised the cost of violating the regional-cum-global norm. That is, regional NWFZs can assist in ensuring higher levels of compliance with the nonproliferation regime. In addition, and just as importantly, compliance with the nonproliferation norm has in turn contributed to the redefinition of national security interests by the major Latin American players. Argentine and Brazilian nuclear aspirations were 'socialized' and successfully contained within the framework of the Latin American NWFZ. The institutional components of regional NWFZ arrangements help to absorb nuclear strains and stresses and to undermine the strategic and political utility of nuclear weapons.

NWFZs as CBMs

The relationship between the process and substance of negotiating the modalities of a NWFZ in each of the contested zones remains unclear. Who should initiate and organize the discussions – the principal rivals in the region or the relevant regional organization? How can Israel enter into talks with countries that refuse to sign peace agreements with it? How can India and Pakistan engage in meaningful talks on nuclear issues when neither acknowledges the possession of nuclear weapons? As these questions indicate, there is a symbiotic relationship between process and substance. Some commentators argue that NWFZ arrangements can only come after a general improvement in the security atmosphere in presently volatile and conflict riven regions. Nations do not distrust each other because they are armed; they are armed because they distrust each other. Therefore a NWFZ in regions of high conflict intensity may have to follow rather than cause the end of conflicts. Furthermore, premature insistence on a regional NWFZ could heighten regional tensions and instability. On the other hand, it is possible that NWFZs can themselves comprise CBMs on the road to peace. The confidence built among regional states through a NWFZ can spill over into other areas of regional interactions. For all proponents of NWFZs, the difficulties raised by countries from within potential zones heighten the suspicions of others in the region and the world about their nuclear intentions.

There is a two stage paradox of trust with regard to NWFZs. The more intense the suspicions and hostility between regional rivals and the greater the likelihood that one or more of them are engaged in nuclear weapons programs, the greater is the need for a regional NWFZ as a means of lowering tensions and building trust. Peace and security cannot be consolidated in Northeast Asia, for example, without the prior resolution of nuclear issues. But negotiations, perhaps even pre-negotiations, towards a NWFZ will prove stillborn unless there is a minimum level of trust among the regional countries. Once this minimum condition is satisfied, however, the very experience of working together in negotiating a zonal arrangement, and then working together once the zone is operational, generates habits of cooperation and sustains mutual confidence which are necessary conditions for resolving other regional security issues. This is a variant of the familiar functionalist spillover argument from the old integration theories. In other words, the vicious cycle of fear, mistrust and hostility sustaining open or ambiguous nuclear weapons programs and postures can be replaced by the virtuous cycle of unequivocal non-nuclear status sustaining mutual confidence and cooperation.

Some of the criticisms of NWFZs arise from a confusion between arms control agreements and CBMs. Unlike the NPT, NWFZs are regional CBMs, not simply in the obvious sense of being a legal mechanism for member states to assure each other of their peaceful intentions, but also because the very process of creating a NWFZ necessitates mutual regional cooperation. A NWFZ may be defective if viewed as an arms control agreement; it can be valuable as a CBM which expands the area of peace. It may not eliminate the possibility of nuclear weapons use in the region; it can promote security and raise the threshold of nuclear initiation in the region by reducing instabilities, and diminishing uncertainties about military arrangements by facilitating exchanges of information on nuclear-related military activity. A NWFZ is a useful means of influencing the nature of peacetime relations between the NWS. Non-nuclear NPT parties are legally committed to their non-nuclear status. A NWFZ constructs a legal barrier to the introduction of the nuclear weapons of other states into the region. Most importantly, it takes away nuclear weapons from any future security architecture being drafted for the region.

Should the prohibition against stationing extend to other installations that are integral components of nuclear weapons systems, such as the so-called joint Australian–US facilities in Australia, concerned with military communications, navigation, and satellite tracking and control, which are integrated into the global US nuclear infrastructure? During the Cold War they collected vital military intelligence, spied on Soviet missile sites, detected nuclear explosions, helped verify arms limitation agreements and were meant to provide the Americans with early warning of any Soviet attack. Not including such installations within the scope of prohibited items will inevitably dilute the effect and credibility of a NWFZ. However, efforts to include them may abort negotiations on the establishment of the zone.

Conclusion

Success or failure in efforts to establish NWFZs depend in part upon the right mix of structural, locational and perceptual variables, and timing. It would be prudent to recognize the very real difficulties on the road to establishing any more NWFZs. In the Middle East and Northeast Asia, there is no existing subregional organization to initiate and guide negotiations, no subregional dialogue process that can form the backdrop to a NWFZ negotiation. The Israeli, Pakistani, Indian and North Korean nuclear status must somehow be resolved before any meaningful discussion can begin on NWFZs. There is the politically sensitive issue of how China and Taiwan might be integrated into a regional NWFZ. Nor is the overall political environment very propitious for the conclusion of a NWFZ treaty in any of the three regions. A NWFZ is more likely to be established as a CBM among states that have already forsworn the nuclear option. It is less likely to be established as an arms control or disarmament measure to constrain the future potential of states that retain the nuclear option in their national security calculus. That is, it can entrench a non-nuclear status and make future nuclear breakout less likely, but it cannot circumvent determined opposition to the NPT.

The central purpose and utility of NWFZs can be demonstrated with an analogy. In recent years, the movement to create an expanding circle of smoke free zones has become quite powerful in many countries. Such zones would be meaningless in practice if they applied only to non-smokers. On the other hand, smokers are required neither to give up on their addiction totally and in all places, nor to hand over their packets of cigarettes to gatekeepers when entering a smoke free zone. The zone is fully effective if smokers refrain from lighting up while they are inside the zone. Similarly, in itself a NWFZ is an agreement by non-NWS to sanctify their status within a regional treaty based zone. But its core provisions should have the support of the NWS with respect to their activities within the zone.

Until such time as a reliable system of international security is in place, a NWFZ is a useful collateral substitute for global arms control. But it is a policy neither of global disarmament nor of national defence. States will be attracted to one only when convinced that their vital security interests will be enhanced and not jeopardized by participation. Zones have been established in Latin America, the South Pacific, Southeast Asia and Africa because countries of these regions believe their security environment can be stabilized through NWFZs. Conversely, zones have proven difficult to negotiate for other regions because states there remain sceptical of substantial security benefits.

Epilogue

The above analysis was published in 1998. The first NWFZ was established in (uninhabited) Antarctica in 1959. Since then, five more have been established in Latin America and the Caribbean, the South Pacific, Southeast Asia, Africa, and Central Asia. Mongolia has also declared itself a national NWFZ in law. New NWFZs have been proposed for the Middle East, Northeast Asia and the Arctic. The status of all the world's NWFZs as of spring 2014 is shown in Table 11.1. The most substantial gap in relation to existing NWFZs is the failure of the relevant NWS to accede to the various protocols that commit the nuclear powers not to use nuclear weapons against zone members, although this remains incomplete in some key cases (Table 11.2). That said, on 29 April 2014 the five NWS announced at the NPT PrepCom meeting in New York that they would sign the one protocol of the Central Asian NWZ pledging not to attack or threaten members with nuclear weapons and also to respect its other provisions.[15]

Additionally, there is the question of proposed new zones for regions such as Northeast Asia and the Middle East. The 2010 NPT Review Conference requested the UN Secretary-General, Russia, the UK and the US to convene a conference in 2012 on a Middle East WMD-free-zone. Efforts to convene a conference in 2012 ultimately stalled in the face of growing regional instability and the absence of agreement on what the conference might reasonably be expected to achieve. All existing NWFZs have confirmed and consolidated the non-NWS status of regional countries. It is far from clear that new zones can be created as the means of achieving the denuclearization of an existing nuclear armed state (North Korea, Israel). Circumstances are particularly unpropitious for a Middle East NWFZ where key states are in a formal state of war and/or non-recognition, convulsed in a brutal civil war, not NPT members, host to nuclear weapons of a NWS (NATO member Turkey), pursuing a breakout capability, (or in Northeast Asia have already conducted several nuclear tests), etc.[16] Moreover, as an NPT nonstate party, Israel is particularly wary of the proposal's origins in a document to which it did not subscribe and which singled out Israel for criticism.

Notes

* Originally published in Ramesh Thakur, ed., *Nuclear Weapons-Free Zones* (London/New York: Macmillan and St. Martin's Press, 1998): 3–32. Reprinted by permission of Macmillan.
1 *Towards a Nuclear-Weapon-Free Zone in the Middle East* (New York: United Nations, 1990), Document A/45/435.
2 While Rarotonga prohibits the dumping of wastes at sea, Pelindaba prohibits it anywhere in the zone.
3 1995 NPTREC document NPT/CONF.1995/32/DEC.2.
4 Jayantha Dhanapala, 'The Role of NWFZ and the NPT', Address delivered at the International Conference on Central Asia Nuclear-Weapon-Free Zone, Tashkent, 15–16 September 1997.
5 Tariq Rauf, 'Proliferation of Nuclear, Chemical and Biological Weapons after the Cold War', in Ramesh Thakur, ed., *Keeping Proliferation at Bay* (Jakarta: Centre for Strategic and International Studies, 1998), 43.
6 *Comprehensive Study of the Question of Nuclear-Weapon-Free Zones in All of its Aspects* (New York: United Nations, Special Report of the Conference of the Committee on Disarmament, 1976), Document A/10027/Add.1; and *Study on the Question of Nuclear-Weapon-Free Zones*. The latter was never finalized, and officially may not exist, but it forms an annex to a letter of 9 February 1985 from the chairman of the Group of Experts, Klaus Törnudd of Finland, to the United Nations Secretary-General.
7 See S. Neil McFarlane and Thomas G. Weiss, 'Regional Organizations and Regional Security', *Security Studies* 21 (1992), 7, 11, 31.
8 Barry Buzan, *People, States and Fear: An Agenda for International Security Studies in the Post-Cold War Era* (Boulder: Lynne Rienner, 2nd ed. 1991), 190.
9 Mohammed Ayoob, *The Third World Security Predicament: State Making, Regional Conflict, and the International System* (Boulder: Lynne Rienner, 1995), 156.
10 Taiwan's position is anomalous. It has signed the NPT but is often not treated as a state party to the treaty since it is not considered by many to be a state. Taiwan's nuclear facilities are, however, under IAEA safeguards.
11 For a recent proposal, see John Carlson, 'An Asia–Pacific Nuclear Energy Community', APLN/CNND *Policy Brief* No. 4 (Canberra: Asia Pacific Leadership Network and Centre for Nuclear Non-Proliferation and Disarmament, June 2013).
12 *Arms Control and Disarmament Agreements* (Washington DC: US Arms Control and Disarmament Agency, 1982), 63.
13 Proclamation by President Richard Nixon on Ratification of Protocol II of the Treaty of Tlatelolco, 11 June 1971; ibid., 78.
14 Zachary S. Davis, 'The Spread of Nuclear-Weapon-Free Zones: Building a New Nuclear Bargain', *Arms Control Today* 26(1) (February 1996), 16, 18.

15 Rachel Oswald, 'Five powers agree to respect Central Asian Nuclear-Free Zone', *Global Security Newswire*, 30 April 2014, http://www.nti.org/gsn/article/five-nuclear-powers-agree-sign-protocol-central-asian-nuclear-free-zone/.

16 See Pierre Goldschmidt, 'A Top-Down Approach to a Nuclear Weapons Free Zone in the Middle East', and Ariel Levite, 'Reflections on The Regional Security Environment and Basic Principles for the Relations of the Members of the Zone': papers presented at the EU Nonproliferation Consortium seminar, Brussels, 5–6 November 2012, http://carnegieendowment.org/2012/11/05/top-down-approach-to-nuclear-weapons-free-zone-in-middle-east/ece2 and www.nonproliferation.eu/documents/backgroundpapers/levite.pdf.

12 NPT regime change*
Has the good become the enemy of the best?

As will be clear from almost all previous chapters, the Non-Proliferation Treaty (NPT) is the 'mother-lode' of all nuclear treaty based regimes, embraced by virtually the entire family of nations. An important and integral component of the broader NPT regime is the treaty to prohibit the testing of nuclear explosive devices. The requirement for the development and modernization of a large number of nuclear weapons designs was justified during the Cold War by the need to maintain a technically credible deterrent posture. The justification became less persuasive after the Cold War and another vital element was added to the nonproliferation structure with a ban on nuclear testing that is comprehensive, universal and verifiable. As of 21 July 2014, 183 countries had signed and 162 had ratified the Comprehensive Nuclear Test Ban Treaty (CTBT). This still leaves eight countries, out of the 44 with nuclear reactors listed in Annex 2 of the treaty, whose signatures (India, North Korea, Pakistan) and ratifications (China, Egypt, Iran, Israel, USA) are needed to bring it into force.[1] Since the treaty's adoption, just a handful of nuclear weapon test explosions have been conducted, five by India and six by Pakistan in 1998, and three by North Korea in the past decade (2006, 2009 and 2013). The policies and doctrines of the nine nuclear armed states with regard to nuclear testing was described in chapter 1. A related treaty based regime that does not yet exist but many deeply desire would prohibit additional production of fissile material for nuclear weapons use. Unfortunately, Pakistan has consistently blocked the adoption of any program of work in the Conference on Disarmament (CD) in Geneva because it will not agree to a fissile materials cut-off treaty (FMCT) negotiations in the absence of prior agreement to include existing stocks of weapon grade fissile material, where it believes itself to be at a disadvantage vis-à-vis India.

The last chapter showed how regional nuclear-weapon-free zones buttress the global NPT regime. The next chapter will examine the growth of nuclear security as a supplement to the NPT to better reflect the security agenda of the 21st century, including the fear of nuclear terrorism. This chapter looks at the congenital flaws and accumulating anomalies of the NPT itself.

There were two great pillars of the normative edifice for containing the nuclear horror: the doctrines of strategic deterrence which prevented their use among those who had nuclear weapons; and the nonproliferation regime, centred on the NPT that both outlawed their spread to others and imposed a legal obligation on the nuclear weapons states (NWS) to eliminate their own nuclear arsenals through negotiations – their only explicit multilateral disarmament commitment. The NPT was signed in 1968 and came into force in 1970 as the centrepiece of the global nonproliferation regime that codified the international political norm of non-nuclear weapons status.[2] It tries to curb proliferation by a mix of incentives and disincentives. In return for intrusive end-use control over imported nuclear and nuclear-related technology and material, non-NWS were granted access to nuclear technology, components and material on a most-favoured-nation basis. The NPT regime also includes a number of treaties restricting nuclear testing. The Partial Test Ban Treaty (1963) outlawed atmospheric, space and underwater nuclear testing. The Threshold Test Ban Treaty (1974) outlawed underground tests of more than 150kt yield. The elusive goal of a total ban on nuclear testing was seemingly realized in 1996 with the endorsement by the General Assembly of the CTBT. But, in part due to the rigid entry into force provisions of the CTBT, and in part owing to changed administrations in Washington and the altered climate of arms control after 9/11, the CTBT is unlikely to enter into force in the foreseeable future.

Today both pillars are at risk of crumbling. Some commentators fear that arms control is at an impasse and disarmament could be reversed. Kofi Annan noted in 2005 that the NPT 'faces a crisis of confidence and compliance born of a growing strain on verification and enforcement'.[3] Revelations, that on 29 August 2007, a B-52 bomber carrying six air-launched cruise missiles armed with nuclear warheads had made an unauthorized flight from North Dakota to Louisiana, did nothing to diminish the sense of crisis afflicting the nuclear weapons agenda.[4] A quartet of American national security heavyweights caution that 'The accelerating spread of nuclear weapons, nuclear know-how and nuclear material has brought us to a nuclear tipping point'.[5]

The lengthening list of proliferation-sensitive concerns includes North Korea's weaponized nuclear capability and its nuclear test of 2006,[6] worries about Iran's nuclear program,[7] reports that Saudi Arabia may be contemplating an off-the-shelf purchase of nuclear weapons,[8] evidence of mild misdeeds by South Korea,[9] Taiwan[10] and Egypt,[11] apprehensions of a new uranium enrichment plant that would give Brazil a nuclear breakout capability,[12] dismay at Russia's retreat from a no first use policy, anxieties about the 27,000 nuclear warheads with a total yield of 5,000 megatonnes held by the five NWS (with Russia and the US holding more than 26,000 warheads), fears that Washington is lowering the threshold of normative barriers to the use of a new generation of nuclear weapons, evidence of an extensive multinational nuclear black market that demonstrated the inadequacy of the existing export controls system, and the prospect of terrorists acquiring nuclear weapons. Rounding out this list of concerns, Pakistan is often dubbed the most dangerous place on earth because of the lethal nexus of an unstable military dictatorship, Islamist groups bitterly hostile to the West, terrorists and nuclear weapons. Concerns persist about the potential leakage of 'loose nukes' from Russia to terrorists. Worst case scenarios see terrorists using nuclear or radiological weapons to kill hundreds of thousands of people. Fortunately, no terrorist group is known to have the competence to build nuclear weapons and there is no evidence so far that nuclear weapons have been transferred to terrorist organizations.

These anxieties are hardly allayed by multilateral action. Washington announced its commitment to negotiate a legally binding FMCT, but without verification provisions. Space talks remain blocked. The Six Party Talks make but fitful progress in keeping North Korea from establishing a fully functioning nuclear weapons program. Iran sends conflicting messages on compliance with NPT commitments and its pursuit of a nuclear energy program for peaceful purposes. For four decades, the world has lived with five (Britain, China, France, Russia and the United States), followed by eight (Israel, India and Pakistan) and then nine (North Korea), nuclear powers. Can we live with a tenth, if that be Iran? The disquieting trend of a widening circle of NPT-licit, NPT-illicit and extra-NPT nuclear weapons powers in turn has a self-generating effect in drawing other countries into the game of nuclear brinksmanship. The only good news stories are that Libya walked away from that path in December 2003,[13] Iraq does not have them and North Korea shut down its plutonium production in July 2007 under international inspection.[14]

The global governance mechanisms for nonproliferation and disarmament are in a sorry state. The CD has been immobilized, unable even to agree on an agenda for a decade. In a speech on 23 January 2008, Secretary-General Ban Ki-moon could only declare helplessly that he was 'deeply troubled' by its 'impasse over priorities' and warned that it was 'in danger of losing its way'.[15] The UN reform summit in 2005 failed to agree on a single sentence on the hot subject. Reliance on the Security Council as the forum of choice for enforcing compliance is deeply problematical, since the five permanent members (P5) are the five NPT-licit NWS (N5), the council is severely unrepresentative and unaccountable, and the P-5/N5 have been amongst the most arms-exporting and war-prone countries since 1945.

The rising anxieties about nuclear weapons are rooted in two major and parallel developments: the so-called renaissance of nuclear power and a resurgence of old-fashioned national security threats that supposedly had ebbed with the end of the Cold War. Between them, the developments highlight how all three legs of the NPT's triangular linkage – nuclear power for civilian use, nuclear nonproliferation and nuclear disarmament – are straining the regime. The NPT's inherent contradictions and tensions have ripened and the regime's weaknesses have become increasingly apparent. When we factor in also its many anomalies, we begin to understand why the regime seems to be so close to breaking point. Can it be repaired and continue as the centrepiece of global nuclear arms control policy? Or is it destined to go the way of Humpty Dumpty, in which case would it better to abandon the NPT and look to a new nuclear weapons convention (NWC) as the chief cure for the world's nuclear ailment? This chapter begins by reviewing the two sets of concerns that form the roots of the growing nuclear anxieties. It then highlights the weaknesses, deficiencies and anomalies of the NPT before postulating the need to move beyond the sclerotic regime.

Security threats

We would be foolish to believe that the renaissance of nuclear power is explained fully and solely by the interest in nuclear energy for civilian uses. On the supply side, a major challenge is the globalization of the arms industry, the flooding of the global arms market and a resulting loosening of supplier constraints. Under modern conditions of globalized trade, instantaneous and voluminous electronic information exchanges, interlinked financial systems and the sheer diversity of technology, the control of access to nuclear weapons technology and material has grown vastly more complex and challenging. Proliferation refers to the dispersion of weapons, capabilities and technologies. There are eight categories of proliferation-sensitive actors:

1. **Vertically proliferating NWS**: Those who increased their nuclear stockpiles and upgraded their nuclear lethality from inside the NPT regime;
2. **NPT-irresponsible NWS**: those who export nuclear/missile materials, technology and expertise in violation of international commitments;
3. **Fragmenting NWS**, or NPT splinters: when the old Soviet Union broke up, for instance, we faced the prospect of an additional three NWS (Belarus, Kazakhstan, Ukraine). Fortunately, they were persuaded to forego the nuclear option;
4. **NPT cheats**: those who have signed the NPT but are engaged in activities in violation of their obligations;
5. **Threshold NWS**: those who do not possess nuclear weapons but have not forsworn the option and have the material and capacity to do so. With India and Pakistan coming out of the nuclear closet in 1998, and few left to deny Israel's nuclear weapons capability, the threshold status is effectively obsolete;
6. **Nuclear terrorists**: It defies credulity that nuclear weapons and materials can be kept secure in government inventories and never be obtained by any terrorist group. While a government's nuclear capability can be seized and destroyed, it is impossible to capture or kill every single terrorist and his/her last piece of dynamite, Semtex or timing mechanism;
7. **'Virtual' NWS**: Countries can acquire and maintain all the materials and skills required to make nuclear weapons quickly once a decision is made to do so. Thus Ichiro Ozawa of Japan's Liberal Party warned China not to forget that Japan could easily make 3,000–4,000 nuclear weapons;[16]
8. **Missile proliferators**: Missiles are an acutely destabilizing form of weaponry because little defence is available against them. Armed with biological, chemical or nuclear warheads, they can be lethal.

The challenge on the international security front is thus fourfold. First, the N5 have simply disregarded their NPT Article 6 obligation to disarm. As argued in chapter 1, their nuclear arsenals, doctrines and modernization plans indicate the retention and expanded use of these weapons for decades to come. Second, three states lie outside the NPT and have gone down the weapons path: India, Israel and Pakistan. The stop-start India–US civil nuclear cooperation deal proved extremely contentious. Supporters argued that it serves the strategic goals of both countries while also advancing the global nonproliferation agenda more realistically than any conceivable alternative. Yet it caused despondency among the arms control community for its breach of the NPT regime even as it made some Indians uncomfortable for drawing India into the American strategic embrace and others for constricting India's future nuclear options.[17] The constitutional and political crisis in Pakistan in 2007–08 spread alarm in many sectors about how safe and secure its nuclear arsenal was from Islamists within and jihadists outside the military. Third, the NPT is an intergovernmental agreement and therefore does not cover nonstate groups, including terrorists, who might be pursuing nuclear weapons. It is not at all clear how the international normative architecture can be extended to cover them on legislative, operational and compliance dimensions. And fourth, some NPT members may be trying to cheat on their nonproliferation obligations and be pursuing the weapons option through stealth.

Because of the robust international norm against nuclear weapons and the legal obligations of the NPT that has been signed by all countries other than India, Israel and Pakistan, countries planning to cross the line from civilian to weapons programs do so clandestinely. For example, few believe Iran's professions of peaceful intent in their uranium enrichment drive. Yet the consequences of using military force to try to stop the drive may be worse than learning to live with the new reality. For far too many, the drumbeats of warnings and threats being sounded in Washington on Iran – US President George W. Bush has even spoken of World War III! – brought back memories of 2002–03. During the presidential primary campaign, Hillary Clinton threatened to 'obliterate' Iran if it dared to attack Israel with nuclear weapons.[18] This is an all too familiar story. Most did not like the ending the first time around in Iraq and are unlikely to like it any better the next time. In the same vein, there is the familiar discrepancy between the assessments of the International Atomic Energy Agency (IAEA) and of some Western countries regarding the gravity and urgency of the threat of a nuclearized Iran.

NPT weaknesses

There are several major gaps in the arms control and disarmament regime:

1 Lack of NPT universality;
2 The continuing existence of stockpiles of nuclear weapons;
3 Lack of a NWC outlawing the possession and use of nuclear weapons by all actors;
4 Lack of verification machinery and compliance mechanisms for the NPT Article 6 disarmament obligations;
5 Lack of a credible and binding inspections regime for nonproliferation;
6 Lack of agreed criteria to assess proliferation threats;
7 Lack of a basis in international law to enforce nonproliferation norms for states outside the treaty regimes; and
8 Inapplicability of norms and regimes to nonstate actors.

Some NPT weaknesses are not just intrinsic, but were intentional. For example the wording of Articles 1 and 2 deliberately permits the NWS to transfer nuclear weapons to other countries (Cold War allies at the time) – that is, engage in geographical proliferation – as long as control of the weapons remained in NWS hands. The subsequent popularity of regional nuclear-weapon-free zones owed much to the desire to plug this loophole. Such zones cover virtually the entire southern hemisphere but are conspicuously scarce north of the equator. The desire to marry two possibly incompatible goals – President Dwight Eisenhower's vision of 'atoms for peace' and nonproliferation – produced the odd juxtaposition of Articles 3 and 4, and opened the door for developments in North Korea and Iran. For nuclear energy for peaceful purposes can be pursued legitimately to the point of being a screwdriver away from a weapons capability.

Other NPT weaknesses became apparent with the benefit of hindsight. By failing to include clearly timetabled, legally binding, verifiable and enforceable disarmament commitments, it temporarily legitimized the nuclear arsenals of the N5. The imbalance of reporting, verification and compliance mechanisms between nonproliferation and disarmament in the NPT regime has also over time served to erode seriously the legitimacy of this centrepiece of the global arms control effort. By relying on the promise of signatories to use nuclear materials, facilities and technology for peaceful purposes only, it empowered them to operate dangerously close to a nuclear weapons capability. It proscribed non-nuclear states from acquiring nuclear weapons, but failed to design a strategy for dealing with non-signatory states parties. It permits withdrawals much too easily. Because there is no standing agency or secretariat, the NPT depends on five year review conferences for resolving implementation problems. These operate by the consensus rule, which does not make for decisive resolution of contentious issues. Verification and enforcement are one step removed to the extent that the IAEA acts as a buffer between the NPT and the Security Council.

The Iraq experience shows the enormous difficulty of ensuring compliance with international norms and commitments, even with respect to one of the world's most odious regimes pursuing the world's most destructive weapons.[19] The failure to find weapons of mass destruction (WMD) since the war cannot eradicate the known historical record of Saddam Hussein's past pursuit of them, nor his will to use them against outsiders as well as Iraqis. Moreover, there is an inherent tension between the IAEA's mandate for promoting peaceful nuclear energy use and the overall strategic goal of nonproliferation. This is best illustrated by the fact that India and Pakistan, outside the NPT regime, are on the IAEA Board of Governors. It is also increasingly a problem because more and more of nuclear technology, materials and equipment are dual use. When the chief distinction between peaceful and offensive use rests on intent, there is a problem.

Strengthening treaty regimes requires national legislation and measures on criminalization of proliferation activities, effective protection of proliferation-sensitive personnel, materials and equipment, control and accounting systems for monitoring materials and stocks, and regulation and surveillance of dual use transfers. The NPT could be strengthened by making the IAEA Additional Protocol mandatory for all states parties, toughening up or even eliminating the exit clause and making clear that withdrawal from the NPT will be treated as a threat to peace and security.[20] But these cannot be done without also addressing gaps on the disarmament side of the NPT and reform of the composition and procedures of the UN Security Council. A body that is itself seen as increasingly illegitimate by many members of the international community will have difficulty enforcing global norms in the name of that community.

The IAEA's reluctance to cite Iran for noncompliance with the NPT may indicate weaknesses in the treaty structure and procedures which reflect the world of 1968 rather than 2008. Moreover, Tehran joins Pyongyang in throwing down the gauntlet, yet again, to a basic inconsistency in our definition of the problem. Is it the very destructiveness of nuclear weapons that somehow makes them so evil that they should be proscribed for all, including the N5? Or is it rogue states, whose behaviour is so bad that they cannot be trusted with weapons which are tolerable, if not desirable, in more mature and responsible hands?

NPT anomalies

The many internal inconsistencies and tensions notwithstanding, the NPT has been the symbol of the dominant arms control, disarmament and nonproliferation paradigm. Over the course of four decades, however, six significant anomalies have accumulated and now weigh it down close to the point of rupture.

First, the definition of a NWS is chronological – a country that manufactured and exploded a nuclear device before 1 January 1967. India, Pakistan, Israel, North Korea – even Iran – could test, deploy and even use nuclear weapons, but cannot be described as nuclear powers. Conversely, Britain and France could dismantle their nuclear edifice and destroy their nuclear arsenals, but would still count as nuclear powers. This is an Alice-in-Wonderland approach to affairs of deadly seriousness. But can the NPT definition be opened up for revision through a formal amendment of the treaty with all the unpredictable consequences?[21]

Second, even as the threat from nonstate actors has grown frighteningly real, multilateral treaties like the NPT can regulate and monitor the activities only of states. A.Q. Khan's underground nuclear bazaar that merrily sold nuclear technology, components and weapons designs to Iran, Libya and North Korea showed how porous is the border between private and state rogue actors. Protestations of innocence by the Pakistan government are simply not credible. They were either actively complicit, connived in and facilitated, or at the very least knew about and tolerated the existence and activities of the network. The 'hero of the nation' was placed under a comfortable version of house arrest by his 'friend' General Pervez Musharraf. Moreover, it is at the very least arguable that the Khan network still exists and is active, and that Pakistan's nuclear weapons are not safe.[22]

A robust and credible normative architecture to control the actions of terrorist groups who can acquire and use nuclear weapons must be developed outside the NPT. The problem of non-parties and nonstate actors could be taken care of by accepting the suggestion that the fruitless search for universal membership should be replaced by 'universal compliance' with the terms of arms control regimes. The Carnegie Endowment for International Peace lists a set of six obligations to make this a reality: making nonproliferation irreversible; devaluing the political and military currency of nuclear weapons, including the steady, verified dismantlement of nuclear arsenals; securing all nuclear materials through robust standards for monitoring and accounting for fissile materials in any form; enforceable prohibitions against efforts by individuals, corporations and states to assist others in secretly acquiring the technology, material and know-how for nuclear weapons; a commitment to conflict resolution; and persuading India, Israel and Pakistan to accept the same nonproliferation obligations as the NWS signatories to the NPT.[23]

Third, North Korea's open defiance, spread over many years, shows that decades after a problem arises, we still cannot agree on an appropriate response inside the NPT framework. It becomes increasingly difficult to defang tyrants of nuclear weapons the day after they acquire them. The UN seems incapable of doing so the day before. If international institutions cannot cope, states will try to do so themselves, either unilaterally or in company with like-minded allies. If prevention is strategically necessary and morally justified but legally not permitted, then the existing framework of laws and rules – not preventive military action – is defective. In other words, where for decades countries like India argued that the NPT, although legal, was illegitimate because of the nuclear 'apartheid' built into it, can the 'good cops' now turn the legality-legitimacy argument on its head?

The fourth anomaly is lumping biological, chemical and nuclear weapons in one conceptual and policy basket. They differ in their technical features, in the ease with they can be acquired and developed and in their capacity to cause mass destruction. Treating them as one weapons category can distort analysis and produce flawed responses. There is also the danger of mission creep. Justifying nuclear weapons as a useful tool in countering biological and chemical weapons may be one step too far. If nuclear weapons are accepted as having a role to counter biochemical warfare, then how can we deny a nuclear weapons capability to Iran which actually suffered chemical weapons attacks from Saddam Hussein?

Fifth, not a single country that had nuclear weapons when the NPT was signed in 1968 has given them up. Their behaviour fuels the politics of grievance and resentment. Can the country with the world's most powerful nuclear weapons rightfully use military force to prevent their acquisition by others? From where do the president and prime minister of nuclear armed France and the United Kingdom derive the moral authority to declare that a nuclear Iran is unacceptable and must be stopped by force if necessary?

The final anomaly concerns the central doctrine underpinning the contemporary Westphalian system, which holds that sovereign states are equal in status and legitimacy. In reality, states are not of equal worth and significance, neither militarily, economically, politically nor morally. It seems unlikely that in the eyes of most people and countries, nuclear weapons in the hands of Britain and North Korea are equally dangerous.[24] This is why President George Bush warned of the threat of the world's most destructive weapons falling into the hands of the world's worst regimes: it is the conjunction of the two that is especially dangerous. Granted, the Iraq war has been a disaster richly foretold. But was there any moral equivalence between Saddam Hussein and George W. Bush, Tony Blair, and John Howard – leaders of three countries that waged the war?

Similarly, how reasonable or logical is it to lump India, Iran, Israel, North Korea and Pakistan together without discriminating between their respective records, yet continue to distinguish between nonproliferation and disarmament? A decade after India and Pakistan gate-crashed into the nuclear club, any effort to roll back their nuclear weapons capability amounts to nuclear disarmament, not nonproliferation. Analyzing the problem from within the conceptual lens of nonproliferation is simply inappropriate. The logical policy implication is either to condemn nuclear weapons for everyone, or to distinguish bad and rogue from responsible behaviour and oppose regimes, not the weapons. But that threatens the core assumption of the NPT, that nuclear weapons are immoral for anyone. This has been the central bone of contention between the proponents and opponents of the India–US civil nuclear cooperation deal: that it acknowledges India's responsible nuclear stewardship or that it threatens the core integrity of the NPT.

Making the NPT history

As argued in chapter 4, we face four nuclear choices: status quo, proliferation, nuclear rearmament, or abolition. India's, Pakistan's and North Korea's tests confirmed the folly of believing – in defiance of common sense, logic and history – that a self-selecting group of five powers could indefinitely retain their monopoly on the world's most destructive weaponry. It truly is remarkable how those who worship at the altar of nuclear weapons threaten to excommunicate for heresy others wishing to join their sect. The first country to engage in nuclear breakout in 1998, India deplored North Korea's test in 2006 as a threat to regional peace and stability and for highlighting the dangers of clandestine proliferation. Thus did India, quickly followed by Pakistan, join the ranks of the nuclear powers preaching nuclear abstinence for others while engaged in consenting deterrence themselves. Other members of the nuclear club condemned North Korea's test as 'brazen', 'grave', 'provocative, 'intolerable', etc. That test and Iran's ongoing defiance are symptoms, not the cause, of the NPT being a broken reed. It is time to return with some seriousness and urgency to the dream of a nuclear-weapon-free world.

An eminent group of former US secretaries of defence and state – George Shultz, William Perry, Henry Kissinger – and Senator Sam Nunn, former chairman of the Senate Armed Services Committee, published an article that electrified disarmament activists by calling on Washington to take the lead in the abolition of nuclear weapons.[25] They did not dispute that nuclear weapons confer many national security benefits. Rather, they argued that these were subordinate to the threats posed to US security by the uncontrolled proliferation of nuclear weapons. They followed a year later by publishing a second article noting the worldwide positive response that their call had evoked and the serious and substantive work that it had produced among a coalition of Americans aiming to marry the vision of a nuclear-weapon-free world to a series of progressive steps to pull the world back from the nuclear precipice, such as reducing warhead numbers and limiting the role of nuclear weapons in security policy.[26]

Ironically, therefore, sections of the admittedly retired national security elite are coming around to embracing and championing the nuclear-weapon-free cause in a decade in which the formerly energized popular movement has been largely dormant. But their views are not universally shared. A group of retired NATO generals argued recently for an alliance 'policy of deterrence by proactive denial' that includes both pre-emption and prevention. They put forward the concept of 'interactive escalation' based on 'escalation dominance' that can use 'all instruments of soft and hard power, ranging from the diplomatic protest to nuclear weapons'. In their view, 'nuclear weapons – and with them the option of first use – are indispensable . . . and nuclear escalation continues to remain an element of any modern strategy'.[27] In this context, it is worth recalling that the dramatic reductions in nuclear arsenals in the first half of the 1990s resulted from unilateral initiatives (reinforced by the power of positive reciprocity) by Mikhail Gorbachev and George H.W. Bush, not from verifiable agreements signed after protracted negotiations. They reflected and in turn contributed to improved political trust and the dismantling of 'the vast apparatus of ideological hostility that had been built up' over four decades.[28]

The NPT can fairly be judged to have been the most brilliant half-successful arms control agreement in history. The number of countries to sign it embraced virtually the entire family of nations. Yet at the same time, the nuclear arsenals of the N5 expanded enormously. With four decades having elapsed since 1968, the N5 must be deemed to be in violation of their solemn obligation to disarm, reinforced by the Advisory Opinion of the World Court in 1996 that Article 6 requires them to engage in *and bring to a conclusion* negotiations for nuclear abolition. Despite this history and background, a surprising number of arms control experts focus solely on the nonproliferation side to demand denial of technology and materiel to all who refuse to sign and abide by the NPT, and punishment of any who cross the threshold. The term 'nonproliferation ayatollahs' is applied pejoratively to them.

The symbiotic link between nonproliferation and disarmament is integral to the NPT. Most countries gave up the weapons option in return for a promise by the N5 to engage in good faith negotiations to eliminate nuclear weapons. It was expected that nuclear disarmament could take some time. Accordingly, unlike the nonproliferation obligations, the Article 6 disarmament obligation was not brought under international monitoring and enforcement. The logics of nuclear disarmament and nonproliferation are inseparable. Iraq was attacked when it did not have nuclear weapons (having been disarmed not by American bombs but by UN inspectors) while North Korea, which had nuclear weapons but not oil, was spared.[29] The unintended but entirely predictable consequence for any regime that feared US attacks was: if you wish to avoid Saddam Hussein's fate, don't cooperate in efforts to disarm but instead get the bomb as quickly as possible. By worsening regional and global insecurities, the Iraq war increased the attractiveness of the nuclear option and strengthened the motivation to get them by any means necessary.

There is a marked contradiction between rhetoric and example. The Bush administration has justified new weapons and additional uses by shifting US nuclear posture from deterrence to use, redefining their mission from a nuclear stalemate with a superpower peer to waging and winning wars against countries that cannot fight back in kind. To paraphrase Donald Rumsfeld apropos of coalitions, the existence, numbers and lethality of nuclear weapons will determine missions, not the other way round. Refining and miniaturizing nuclear weapons, developing new doctrines and justifications for their use and lowering the threshold for their use weaken the taboo against them and erode the normative barriers to nuclear proliferation.

How do we move from analysis and prescription to action and nuclear abolition? To begin with, some practical and concrete measures are long overdue: bringing the CTBT into force, negotiating a verifiable FMCT, retrenching from launch on warning postures, standing down nuclear forces, to name but a few. That is, reviving, implementing and building on existing agreements for reducing the role, readiness and numbers of nuclear weapons and introducing further degrees of separation between the possession and launch of nuclear weapons by modifying the doctrines and practices of deployment. But these amount to tinkering, not a bold and comprehensive vision of the final destination. What we need are rules based regimes anchored in the principles of reciprocity of obligations, participatory decision-making and independent verification procedures and compliance mechanisms. In the words of a former US deputy secretary of defence, 'America is sleepwalking through history, armed with nuclear weapons. The Cold War left us with a massive inventory of weapons we no longer need, an infrastructure we can no longer use or maintain, and no thought of where our future lies'.[30] The three policy imperatives are to encourage the reduction of nuclear inventories among the NWS, strengthen controls over nuclear stocks and material among them and minimize the attraction of the nuclear option to those who do not have these weapons.

Annan argued that the unique status of the NWS 'also entails a unique responsibility' and they must do more, including further and irreversible reductions in non-strategic nuclear arsenals, reaffirmation of negative security assurances, swift negotiation of an FMCT and the maintenance of the moratorium on nuclear testing until the entry into force of the CTBT. He strongly urged states to agree on these measures at the 2005 NPT Review Conference. On the nonproliferation side, he urged a strengthening of the IAEA verification machinery through universal adoption of the Model Additional Protocol and the creation of incentives for states to forego uranium enrichment and plutonium separation capacities, with the IAEA to act as a guarantor for the supply of fissile material to civilian nuclear users at market rates.[31]

In the end, the 2005 NPT Review Conference ended in complete collapse. It failed to address the vital challenges or offer practical ideas for preventing the use, acquisition and spread of nuclear weapons. The first half of the conference was dogged by procedural wrangling, while the second half was equally rancorous. The exercise ended in acrimony and recriminations over where the primary blame lay for the lost opportunity to bolster the NPT. Washington, which has historically led international efforts to reinforce the NPT regime, faulted the international community, yet again, for failure to confront the reality of the threat of proliferation by countries like Iran and North Korea. Arms control advocates countered that the US delegation had come intent on focusing on the proliferation side of the equation and was totally intransigent with regard to previously agreed-to commitments on arms control and disarmament measures by the existing nuclear powers. In an echo of communist systems, the information booklet produced by the US government during the conference blanked out milestones no longer popular with the current administration, including the 1996 CTBT and the 2000 NPT Review Conference. Joseph Cirincione commented that 'official disdain for these agreements seems to have turned into denial that they existed'.[32] Most countries concluded that the NWS had no intention of fulfilling their NPT-based disarmament obligations and agreed commitments from the 1995 and 2000 conferences. This had a triple negative effect: it eroded support for US proposals for strengthening the nonproliferation elements of the treaty, weakened support for strong action against possible Iranian and North Korean transgressions and may soften adherence to NPT obligations over the long run.

The 2005 world summit similarly failed to come to any agreement on nonproliferation and disarmament, a failure described as 'inexcusable' and 'a disgrace' by Annan and blamed on 'posturing' getting in the way of results.[33] Some senior diplomats blamed the 2005 summit's failure to tackle the nuclear threat effectively on Washington. The US refusal to countenance any form of disarmament blocked attempts to adopt measures that would prevent regimes seeking to develop a nuclear capability. One diplomat remarked that Washington refused to accept the 'logical premise' that it must engage in disarmament if it wants to discourage a 'new nuclear arms race'.[34]

The NPT may be creaking beyond repair even with respect to its nuclear energy bargain as the nexus of security, economic, energy and environmental imperatives can no longer be adequately nested within that one old regime. More countries are bumping against the nuclear weapons ceiling at the same time as the world energy crisis is encouraging a move to nuclear energy. The bulk of the international market is controlled by the P-5/N5 and their allies like Australia, Canada, Germany and Japan. As western as well as eastern Europeans have discovered, Russia is an unreliable supplier of energy, not averse to using it as a political weapon. But so too is Washington prone to imposing sanctions on regimes it dislikes which constitutes a threat to security of nuclear supplies. There is therefore growing interest in creating a new international market under the auspices of multilateral nuclear arrangements in order to assure the continued supply of nuclear fuel and services even without ownership that would raise suspicions about motives and complications about civilian–military firewalls.[35] Internationalizing the nuclear fuel cycle and entrusting supply to a body like the IAEA would simultaneously ensure security of supply divorced from political hostilities and reduce-cum-eliminate the need for enrichment and reprocessing plants in countries interested in acquiring nuclear power for civilian use.[36]

Too many have paid lip service to the slogan of a nuclear-weapon-free world but have not pursued a serious program of action to make it a reality. The elegant theorems, cogent logic and fluent reasoning of many authoritative international commissions have made no discernible dent on the old, new and aspiring nuclear powers. A coalition between nuclear armed and non-nuclear countries – for example India, which has crossed the threshold from a disarmament leader to a hypocritical nuclear power, and Japan, the only country to have suffered an atomic attack – might break the stalemate and dispel the looming nuclear clouds. Critical introspection and self-reflection is required also on the part of civil society actors and arms control NGOs: does the focus on the NPT play into the hands of the nonproliferation hawks, divert attention and effort from nuclear disarmament and in effect thereby undermine the pursuit of nuclear abolition? That is, has the good – nonproliferation via the NPT – become the enemy of the best: nuclear abolition?

A cross-national survey of public attitudes in the three Western nuclear armed countries shows some interesting and surprising features (Table 12.1). First, people are clearly convinced of the failure of the NPT regime. Second, they are just as firmly convinced that nuclear weapons make the world more dangerous rather than safer. And third, they are willing to see this belief translated into policy by supporting with almost equal conviction the twin goals of preventing further proliferation and eliminating nuclear weapons entirely through an enforceable agreement.

Time is running out for the contradictions, hypocrisy and accumulated anomalies. Either we will achieve nuclear abolition or we will have to live with nuclear proliferation followed by nuclear war. If the nonproliferation end of the NPT bargain collapses, the regime will become obsolete. If the disarmament goal of the NPT is realized, the regime is completed but also becomes redundant. Either way, the NPT regime as we have known it has passed its use-by date. Better the soft glow of satisfaction from the noble goal realized of nuclear weapons banned, than the harsh glare of the morning after these weapons are used.

Table 12.1 Public opinion on nuclear weapons (percentages)

	France	UK	USA
NPT has been effective	22.0	25.0	15.9
NPT has been ineffective	47.6	40.4	46.3
Strongly/moderately agree that non-nuclear states should be prevented from developing them	88.3	84.9	82.3
Eliminate NW worldwide	39.0	50.9	48.7
Reduce global numbers of NW	44.6	39.7	33.6
Maintain current number/develop new weapons	13.5	5.8	8.9
Eliminate nuclear testing worldwide	58.8	60.8	52.8
Nuclear weapons make world safer	11.6	18.2	10.2
Nuclear weapons make world more dangerous	76.9	73.4	79.3
Support eliminating NW through enforceable agreement	86.6	84.5	73.5
Oppose eliminating NW through enforceable agreement	6.5	8.5	16.7

Source: *Global Public Opinion on Nuclear Weapons* (Vancouver: The Simons Foundation in partnership with Angus Read Strategies, September 2007). The other countries included in the survey, which asked a total of 15 questions, were Germany, Israel, and Italy.

Notes

* Originally published in Jane Boulden, Ramesh Thakur and Thomas G. Weiss, eds., *The United Nations and Nuclear Orders* (Tokyo: United Nations University Press, 2009): 273–97. Reprinted by permission of UN University.
1 http://www.ctbto.org/the-treaty/.
2 I use the term 'regime' to refer to norms, rules and behaviour around which actor expectations converge in the issue-area of nonproliferation even in the absence of formal international organization. The nonproliferation regime includes the norms of international nuclear behaviour as well as the network of international treaties, institutions, export controls and nuclear trade agreements.
3 Kofi Annan, *In Larger Freedom: Towards Development, Security and Human Rights for All* (New York: United Nations, document A/59/2005, 21 March 2005), paragraph 97.
4 For the *New York Times* editorial on the incident, see 'The wake-up flight of a wayward B-52', *New York Times*, 15 February 2008.
5 George P. Shultz, William J. Perry, Henry A. Kissinger, and Sam Nunn, 'Toward a nuclear free world', *Wall Street Journal*, 15 January 2008.
6 See International Institute for Strategic Studies, *North Korea's Weapons Programmes: A Net Assessment* (London: Palgrave Macmillan, 2004); *North Korea: Where Next for the Nuclear Talks?* Asia Report No. 87 (Brussels: International Crisis Group, 2004).
7 *Iran: Where Next on the Nuclear Standoff?* Middle East Briefing (Brussels: International Crisis Group, 2004).
8 Jonathan Power, 'Turning a blind eye to nukes: The US and Saudi Arabia?' *International Herald Tribune*, 4 August 2004.
9 'South Korea says it enriched uranium four years ago', *Japan Times*, 3 September 2004; 'ROK enrichment tests conducted "3 times"', *Daily Yomiuri*, 5 September 2004.
10 'Taipei held nuke experiments as late as mid-1980s', *Japan Times*, 14 October 2004 and 'Concern over Taiwan nuclear ambitions', *Japan Times*, 17 October 2004.
11 'Egyptian scientists produced nuclear material: diplomats', *Japan Times*, 6 January 2005.
12 Larry Rohter, 'If Brazil wants to scare the world, it's succeeding', *New York Times*, 31 October 2004.
13 The Bush administration was quick to claim the Libyan renunciation of the nuclear option as a tangible success of its Iraq war policy. It is just as plausible to link the Libyan decision to domestic political compulsions, the adverse impact of the international sanctions imposed on it in the 1980s, and the trend line for a negotiated end to the stalemate visible since the Clinton administration. See Thomas E. McNamara (a former ambassador and Assistant Secretary of State who developed and implemented the UN sanctions policy against Libya as a special assistant to President George H. W. Bush in 1991–92), 'Why Qaddafi turned his back on terror', *International Herald Tribune*, 5 May 2004; Flynt Leverett, 'Why Libya gave up the bomb', *New York Times*, 23 January 2004; Geoff D. Porter, 'The faulty premise of pre-emption', *New York Times*, 31 July 2004; and Thomas E. McNamara, 'Unilateral and Multilateral Strategies against State Sponsors of Terror: A Case Study of Libya 1979–2003', in David Cortright and George A. Lopez, eds., *Uniting Against Terror: Cooperative Nonmilitary Responses to the Global Terrorist Threat* (Cambridge MA: MIT Press, 2007). Many Arabs believe that as a result of the difficult insurgency in Iraq after the war, it is Washington that became more receptive to longstanding Libyan overtures and signals for an end to the confrontation. Thus both versions agree on the war being the deal maker, but for opposite reasons.
14 Having said that, on 19 September 2008 North Korea said it had stopped disabling the Yongbyon nuclear reactor and was making 'thorough preparations' to restart it. Foreign ministry official Hyun Hak-bong said that Pyongyang had suspended work to put the plant out of action because the US had not fulfilled its part of a disarmament-for-aid deal. http://news.bbc.co.uk/2/hi/asia-pacific/7624601.stm.

15 'Statement to the Conference on Disarmament in Geneva', *UN News Centre*, http://www.un.org/apps/news/infocus/sgspeeches/statments_full.asp?statID=174.
16 As reported in the *Japan Times*, 6 April 2002.
17 See Ramesh Thakur, 'US–India nuclear accord a win-win outcome for all', *Daily Yomiuri*, 27 November 2005 and Jayantha Dhanapala and Daryl Kimball, 'A Nonproliferation Disaster', *Proliferation Analysis* (Washington DC: Carnegie Endowment for International Peace, 2008).
18 Ewen MacAskill, '"Obliteration" threat to Iran in case of nuclear attack', *Guardian*, 23 April 2008. See also Norman Podhoretz, 'The Case for Bombing Iran', *Commentary* 123:6 (2007): 17–23.
19 See Waheguru Pal Singh Sidhu and Ramesh Thakur, eds., *Arms Control After Iraq: Normative and Operational Challenges* (Tokyo: United Nations University Press, 2006).
20 This will always be problematic, in that all countries insist on exit options in international treaties.
21 See Jenny Nielsen, 'Engaging India, Israel and Pakistan in the Nuclear Non-Proliferation Regime', *Disarmament Diplomacy* 86 (Autumn 2007): 13–28.
22 See Adrian Levy and Catherine Scott-Clark, *Deception: Pakistan, the United States, and the Secret Trade in Nuclear Weapons* (New York: Walker, 2007); David Armstrong and Joseph J. Trento, *America and the Islamic Bomb: The Deadly Compromise* (Hanover, NH: Steerforth, 2007); International Institute for Strategic Studies, *Nuclear Black Markets: Pakistan, A.Q. Khan and the Rise of Proliferation Networks – A Net Assessment* (London: IISS Strategic Dossier, May 2007); and Selig S. Harrison, 'What A.Q. Khan knows', *Washington Post*, 31 January 2008.
23 George Perkovich, Jessica Tuchman Mathews, Joseph Cirincione, Rose Gottemoeller and Jon Wolfsthal, *Universal Compliance: A Strategy for Universal Compliance* (Washington DC: Carnegie Endowment for International Peace, March 2005).
24 Thus the conservative columnist Charles Krauthammer: 'During the Cold War, we worried about Soviet nukes, but never French or British nukes. Weapons don't kill people; people kill people'. 'Deterring the undeterrable', *Washington Post*, 18 April 2008.
25 George P. Shultz, William J. Perry, Henry A. Kissinger, and Sam Nunn, 'A world free of nuclear weapons', *Wall Street Journal*, 4 January 2007.
26 Shultz, Perry, Kissinger and Nunn, 'Toward a nuclear free world', *Wall Street Journal* 15 January 2008. They were joined by Madeleine Albright, James Baker, Zbigniew Brzezinski, Frank Carlucci, Warren Christopher, Melvin Laird and Colin Powell – all former secretaries of state and defence and national security advisers – as well as a number of scholars in a project housed at Stanford University's Hoover Institute.
27 Klaus Naumann, John Shalikashvili, Lord Inge, Jacques Lanxade, and Henk van den Breemen, *Towards a Grand Strategy for an Uncertain World: Renewing Transatlantic Partnership* (Lunteren, Germany: Noaber Foundation, 2007), 96–97. For a contrary view of what NATO should be doing with nuclear weapons, see *Visible Intent: NATO's Responsibility to Nuclear Disarmament* (New York: Middle Powers Initiative Briefing Paper, 2008).
28 David Cortright, 'Overcoming Nuclear Dangers', *Policy Analysis Brief* (Muscatine, Iowa: Stanley Foundation, November 2007), 10.
29 The hindsight verdict on Israel's attack on the Iraqi reactor at Osirak in June 1981 is kinder than the contemporary condemnations. Yet as a counterpoint, it is worth noting the judgment of a retired senior Egyptian ambassador that Egypt's ratification of the NPT in February 1981 would have been seriously imperilled if the attack on Iraq had preceded it. Mohamed I. Shaker, 'An Egyptian Perspective', in Sidhu and Thakur, *Arms Control After Iraq*, 257.
30 John J. Hamre, 'Toward a nuclear strategy', *Washington Post*, 2 May 2005.
31 Annan, *In Larger Freedom*, paragraphs 97–100.
32 Joseph Cirincione, 'US "rewrites history" of arms-control deals in conference brochure', *Japan Times*, 26 May 2005.

33 William M. Reilly, 'Analysis: The U.N.'s document', United Press International, 14 September 2005, http://about.upi.com/products/upi_scitech/UPI-20050914-052229-8545R.
34 Mark Townsend, 'Summit failure blamed on US', *Observer*, 18 September 2005.
35 Downstream agenda would have to include also the conversion of existing national facilities to international control while ensuring that new facilities being constructed are multinational from the start.
36 See John Thomson and Geoffrey Forden, 'Multilateralism as a Dual-Use Technique: Encouraging Nuclear Energy and Avoiding Proliferation', *Policy Analysis Brief* (Muscatine, Iowa: Stanley Foundation, March 2008).

13 The global governance architecture of nuclear security*

Since the terrorist attacks of 11 September 2001, nuclear security concerns have been heightened owing to several developments: fears that terrorist groups with cadres of suicide bombers not deterred by the thought of their own deaths are interested in acquiring nuclear weapons, radioactive and fissile material, or in attacking nuclear facilities; revelations of illicit trafficking in nuclear materials, components, and technology; unresolved security vulnerabilities at nuclear facilities in Russia and some other former Soviet republics; and several nuclear incidents in recent times.

In his visionary speech in Prague on 5 April 2009, President Barack Obama announced the start of 'a new international effort to secure all vulnerable nuclear material around the world within four years'.[1] The justification was to reduce the risk of nuclear terrorism, described as both the most immediate and extreme threat to global security. This chapter will first state the problem, then describe global governance of nuclear security, including components of the UN system, bilateral US–Russia and other cooperative arrangements, and the nuclear security summits. In the third part, it assesses the state of nuclear security governance against four global governance disconnects.

The problem

Terrorists need only to identify and exploit the weakest link in the chain of international nuclear security to acquire enough fissile material to make and detonate a bomb in a major city. According to the International Atomic Energy Agency (IAEA), between 1993 and 2011, there were more than 2,000 cases of illegal trafficking, theft or loss of nuclear and radiological materials around the world, of which only 40 percent has been recovered.[2]

In South Africa, there have been several cases of infiltration of the Pelindaba nuclear research facility outside Pretoria. The site, where the apartheid government conducted nuclear weapons research and production and which gave its name to Africa's nuclear-weapon-free zone in 1996, is believed to store enough weapon grade material for up to 25 nuclear bombs.[3] In 2005, a portable computer was stolen from there. In November 2007, two groups of armed men broke into it from different directions, deactivated several layers of security, penetrated the control room for 45 minutes and escaped, albeit without taking any nuclear material. In April 2012, a third violation of protective measures at the facility was described as an act of 'common' criminality. The national nuclear regulator spokesperson, Gino Moonsamy, was quoted as saying that thanks to 'adequate physical protection, no nuclear or radioactive material was accessed, lost or stolen'.[4] The hundreds of pounds of weapon grade highly enriched uranium being held there may be stored in 'locked down' secure conditions, but the number of breaches of the site has to be of concern.

Pakistan is often dubbed the most dangerous place on earth because of the lethal cocktail of an unstable military-dominated regime, Islamist groups bitterly hostile to the West, terrorists, and nuclear weapons. Serial attacks have done little to dispel international fears over 'the risk of terrorists breaching Pakistan's defenses'.[5] On 16 August 2012, several gunmen wearing military uniforms and suicide vests attacked the Minhas base of the Pakistan air force 65km northwest of Islamabad.[6] In September 2012, the Inter-Services Intelligence reportedly intercepted plans by the Tehreek-e-Taliban Pakistan to attack one of the country's largest nuclear facilities in Dera Ghazi Khan, described by a military officer as 'the first-ever serious security threat' from the terrorist group.[7]

Charles Ferguson, president of the Federation of American Scientists, claims that in the United States, 'a radioactive source is lost, stolen or missing about once a day',[8] albeit only a small proportion is of any security or public health concern. The United States is supposedly secure compared to Russia or Pakistan. In January 2008, in a hilarious, tongue-in-cheek press conference, Pakistan's military spokesman, Brigadier General Atta M. Iqhman, pointed to US command and control being lax relative to Pakistan, the history of US nuclear accidents, the record of US proliferation to allies Britain and France, a commander-in-chief who confessed to having been an alcoholic, and the fundamentalism and religious fervour of the American people and administration. The Pakistani general even offered technical advice and assistance to the United States to improve its nuclear weapons handling procedures, to which Pentagon officials responded stiffly that the US role was to give, not receive, advice on nuclear weapons safety and security issues.[9]

It is possible to interpret the illustrative catalogue of incidents in two ways. The first is to argue that it is unnecessarily alarmist and exaggerates the importance of the incidents, for none of them has actually led to anything consequential. Recalling them is equivalent to crying wolf, alerting the international community to a nonexistent danger. The alternative conclusion is that significant risks are inherent in this sphere. Authorities have to be vigilant and succeed in preventing theft and attacks every single time. True, so far all alarms have been detected in time and none has led to a major incident, let alone a catastrophe. Unfortunately, this is no guarantee of good luck holding always and forever: the boy who cried wolf did indeed get killed and eaten by a wolf.

The incidents show the urgent need to raise international nuclear security standards. The objective of nuclear security is to ensure that nuclear weapons and radioactive materials are secure from unauthorized access and theft, the facilities in which they are manufactured and stored are secure from sabotage, and terrorists and other criminals are prevented from acquiring, making and using nuclear explosive devices. Nuclear terrorism is a subset of nuclear security and falls into the low probability, high impact category of global threats. It remains difficult to accomplish, but the potential consequences are such that it must be taken seriously.

The basic knowledge and skill to make a crude nuclear explosive device is readily available and acquired. It is far more challenging to produce weapon grade fissile material – highly enriched uranium (HEU) or separated plutonium – on any substantial scale. Only states are likely to have the necessary level of infrastructure. But if their material, facilities and personnel have security vulnerabilities, then the nuclear material or even a nuclear bomb could be stolen. Those seeking it will raid not the facility or the country with the most nuclear material, but that which is the most vulnerable. Any country could be a target; all could feel the effects. This is why measures for the physical protection of all nuclear materials, facilities and activities are essential and critical components of international nuclear security. As well as guards, gates and fences at nuclear plants and facilities, this requires thorough background checks on personnel employed there and rigorous training after recruitment in order to inculcate a culture of nuclear security.

HEU is 'the most accessible fissile material for a terrorist nuclear device'.[10] It has a threefold attraction for terrorists: it can be used in the simple 'gun-type' fission weapon with no need for sophisticated detonation equipment; it is smuggler-friendly because it emits only faint radiation signals that make it hard to detect; and, being less radiotoxic than plutonium, it is safer to handle. The bulk of HEU in the world is used for military purposes, but significant amounts are also used in civilian programs. Almost 1,700 tonnes of weapon grade nuclear materials in the world – enough for 100,000 bombs, compared to the present stockpiles of under 18,000 – are stored in hundreds of sites in 32 countries.[11] This is in addition to an estimated 111 sites spread across 14 countries in which nuclear weapons are stored.[12] While some of the sites are well-secured, many are not, hence the risk of sabotage and theft by, or illicit sales to, terrorists or other criminals. Materials used in the nuclear fuel cycle can be lost, abandoned or removed from decommissioned and inactivated facilities without proper authorization. The risks are multiplied in conditions of fragile and failing states, of fragmented authority structures, of a pervasive culture of corruption among public officials, or when widespread unemployment and poverty can weaken resistance to inducements offered by various groups.

HEU stocks should be eliminated where feasible or minimized and consolidated into fewer sites. Over half the world total of weapon grade material is in Russia. There are no precise and reliable figures on how much HEU or separated plutonium is missing. The elements of a perfect nuclear security storm are the abundant supply of weapon-useable nuclear materials; the explosion of knowledge and technical expertise, much of it relatively easily accessed through the Internet; the determination of terrorists to get it; and the known ruthlessness of terrorists to use it.

In order to limit opportunities for theft and sabotage, states must restrict access to nuclear material and facilities only to authorized personnel and to the minimum number of personnel consistent with safe operational requirements; keep material that is not in use in secure vaults; and monitor all storage and access of materials. Physical protection systems should be subject to periodic inspection and testing. Accountability mechanisms include an appropriate legislative and regulatory framework, a competent and independent oversight authority or nuclear regulator and a clear assignment of responsibilities for nuclear security and safety.

Global governance architecture

Global governance consists of formal and informal arrangements that provide more order and stability than would occur otherwise. The *content* of global governance embraces the totality of laws, norms, policies and institutions that define, constitute and mediate relations between citizens, societies, markets and states in the international system – the wielders and objects of the exercise of international public power. The *architecture* of global governance is made up of formal international organizations, with the UN system as the core of the organized multilateral order; formal regional and subregional organizations; informal general purpose groupings, of which the most visible example in recent times is the G-20,[13] but which also include the G-7/8 and BRICS (Brazil, Russia, India, China, and South Africa);[14] informal and single problem institutions like the Proliferation Security Initiative and the NSS; and transnational civil society and market actors.

The mandated multilateral system

The main global components of the nuclear security regime centered on the UN system are:

1 The Convention on the Physical Protection of Nuclear Material (CPPNM).
2 The CPPNM Amendment.
3 The International Convention for the Suppression of Acts of Nuclear Terrorism (ICSANT).
4 UN Security Council Resolution 1540.
5 IAEA activities and documents.

The CPPNM, signed in 1980 and in force since 1987, establishes measures related to the physical protection of nuclear material during international transport and a general framework for cooperation among states in the protection, recovery and return of stolen nuclear material. The 2005 amendment extends obligations to the protection of nuclear facilities and material in peaceful domestic use, storage and transport, and also provides for expanded international cooperation on measures to locate and recover stolen and smuggled nuclear material, and to mitigate any radiological consequences of sabotage.

ICSANT, adopted in 2005 and in force since 2007, seeks to protect against attacks on nuclear targets, punish the perpetrators through domestic criminalization of acts of nuclear terrorism and promote international cooperation in the prevention and investigation of acts of nuclear terrorism and the prosecution and extradition of the alleged terrorists. To facilitate the 'prosecute or extradite' regime, these offenses are explicitly described as 'non-political' so that the defence of any of these acts being a political offence is not available to block extradition.

UN Security Council Resolution 1540 affirmed proliferation of weapons of mass destruction (WMD) as a threat to international peace and security and expressed concern over the threat of WMD terrorism and of illicit trafficking in WMD material, weapons and delivery systems. It obligates all states to criminalize getting, using and transferring WMD to nonstate actors, and to take and enforce effective domestic control, physical protection, accounting and border control measures to prevent proliferation to nonstate actors, and prohibit assisting or financing such proliferation. All states are expected to report on the progress of their implementation; 176 of 193 UN member states had submitted reports by December 2012.

The IAEA is the lead international organization for the safe, secure and peaceful use of nuclear energy, science and technology. It pursues a three-pronged strategy to combat nuclear risks: prevention of illicit and non-peaceful use of nuclear material; the timely detection of any such efforts; and swift and decisive recommendations to the UN Security Council when nuclear risks are apparent. Because nuclear security is a more recent concern than the three established legs of peaceful uses of nuclear energy, nonproliferation and disarmament, it has not been a priority item in the distribution of funding and agenda for the agency. Yet even in nuclear security, the IAEA has taken a lead role, if by default, because of its technical expertise, institutional credibility and legitimacy, and the lack of practical alternatives.

The IAEA offers advisory and peer review services on nuclear security to member states on request and has helped them to develop integrated plans for nuclear security improvements and assistance. Its International Physical Protection Advisory Service (IPPAS) missions offer one example of a peer review mechanism. Since the first one in 1996, 56 missions have been performed in 37 countries.[15] In its Nuclear Security Series, INFCIRC/225/Revision 5 (2011) – a set of non-legally binding guidelines – is the cornerstone of the international physical protection regime for nuclear materials and facilities; it has been incorporated in the domestic law of many states and also in many suppliers' bilateral agreements as a condition of peaceful nuclear cooperation. The US '123' (so-called because it is pursuant to Section 123 of the US Atomic Energy Act) civil nuclear cooperation agreement with the United Arab Emirates (UAE) is a good example of this. Australia, Canada and the European Atomic Energy Community (EURATOM) countries have similar bilateral agreements.

The IAEA's Code of Conduct on the Safety and Security of Radioactive Sources applies to the development and harmonization of policies, laws and regulations on the safety and security of radioactive sources from initial production to final disposal; that is, also to radioactive wastes not covered by the CPPNM. The IAEA has operated the Illicit Trafficking Database Programme since 1995 as an information system on incidents of illicit trafficking and other unauthorized activities and events involving radioactive material. Other IAEA activities include performing analyses of confiscated samples, assisting states with border controls, testing detection and monitoring equipment and conducting training courses.[16]

Nuclear forensic analysis is another key technical capability. Experts in the IAEA Office of Nuclear Security trace the 'signatures' of each of the production processes in the manufacture of nuclear material by analyzing the chemical constituents and physical properties to determine the geological features of the place from which the uranium ore might have been extracted, or the process by which it was concentrated into yellowcake, made into nuclear fuel pellets and burned in a reactor. By determining that the illicit material originates from a particular country, nuclear forensics can highlight the need to improve its nuclear security regime.

Extra-UN cooperative arrangements

Since the Cold War, the United States has implemented a series of programs and projects, much of it in the former Eastern bloc countries, to reduce the risk that nuclear and radioactive materials would escape from safe custody.[17] In 2004, a number of projects were consolidated into the Global Threat Reduction Initiative under the management of the Department of Energy and these have reduced and protected vulnerable nuclear and radiological material worldwide by a combination of reactor conversion, removal of material and physical protection. The Department of Defense managed the implementation of the Cooperative Threat Reduction (Nunn–Lugar) Program, begun in 1991–92, that was primarily intended to facilitate arms reductions in the framework of the Strategic Arms Reduction Treaty (START I) but included elements relevant to nuclear security. The projects helped Russia consolidate nuclear warheads and fissile material in military stocks in safe and secure facilities. The Global Partnership Against the Spread of Weapons and Materials of Mass Destruction, launched at the 2002 G-8 Summit in Kananaskis, Canada, and the Global Initiative to Combat Nuclear Terrorism, set up by Presidents George W. Bush and Vladimir Putin in St. Petersburg, Russia, on 15 July 2006, are other examples of cooperative efforts to enhance global nuclear security and strengthen protection against nuclear terrorism.

In July 2012, the US National Nuclear Security Administration (NNSA) announced that it had monitored the elimination of more than 450 tonnes of Russian HEU under the 1993 US–Russia HEU Purchase Agreement. This agreement is a leading example of the practice of 'down-blending' weapon grade HEU into low enriched uranium for commercial energy use. The Russian weapon grade HEU is fabricated into nuclear fuel and used in nuclear power plants to generate about 10 percent of US consumer electricity, or nearly half of all commercial nuclear energy produced in the United States. The 'megatons-to-megawatts' agreement is now 90 percent complete and on track for the conversion of the total of 500 tonnes of Russian nuclear weapons HEU to low enriched uranium by the end of 2013, when the NNSA will have monitored the elimination of HEU equivalent to about 20,000 nuclear weapons.[18] Progress has also been made in the global efforts to eliminate excess weapon grade plutonium, including under the US–Russia Plutonium Management and Disposition Agreement, which was signed in 2000, amended in 2010, went into force in 2011 and will commence disposing of surplus plutonium in 2018.

Nuclear security summits

Two nuclear security summits have been held, in April 2010 in Washington, DC and in March 2012 in Seoul. A third summit is planned for 2014 in the Netherlands. They were convened to strengthen, consolidate, elevate and energize the many existing national, multilateral and cooperative institutions and structures to strengthen nuclear security. They are important for having affirmed US presidential leadership and elevating the issue to the level of a global leaders' summit. The two summits to date reaffirmed the international treaties, instruments and institutions that backstop national efforts to strengthen nuclear security and prevent nuclear terrorism. But both summits took care to reaffirm the rights of states to develop and utilize nuclear energy for peaceful purposes.

In January 2012, the Nuclear Threat Initiative (NTI) published a benchmark study, *The Nuclear Materials Security Index*.[19] The analysis was based on five categories (quantities and sites, security and control measures, global norms, domestic commitments and capability, and societal factors like political stability and corruption), which were subdivided into 18 indicators that went beyond 'guns, guards and gates' and also beyond nuclear materials control and accountancy practices. The study concluded that although governments have become more aware of the threats, there is still no global consensus on the most important steps to achieve nuclear security; state accountability is problematic because of lack of transparency; stocks of weapon-useable materials continue to rise in some countries; almost a quarter of the states scored poorly on societal factors; and many lag on joining international agreements. The index was complemented by an assessment of national commitments that concluded that of the more than 60 national commitments made by 30 participants at the 2010 summit, 80 percent had been completed by the Seoul 2012 summit.[20] However, progress on some promises is impossible to measure because they are not quantifiable and are hedged with many qualifiers.

Global governance anomalies and disconnects

'Global governance', which became popular as a state of the art term only in the 1990s, is an unfinished journey owing in part to four significant disconnects: between global problems-cum-solutions and state sovereignty; between the robustness of global challenges and the speed with which they arise and the slow, hesitant and feeble institutional responses to them; between legitimacy and efficiency, and the differing balance between the two struck by countries of the global North and South; and between those with the formal authority to make decisions and the growing numbers, role and credibility of nonstate actors from civil society and the market.[21]

Problems without passports,[22] solutions subject to passports

Of the five analytical gaps whose narrowing and widening explain the advance and retreat of global governance,[23] compliance gaps (implementation, monitoring, enforcement) are the most problematic and result from the anomaly of the organizing principle being sovereign statehood when critical threats have long escaped border controls. International order rests on a system of global governance without world government. The most pressing problems are global in scope and require global solutions and the globalization of the process of policymaking. But the threats to peace and security lie within rather than between states and the policy authority and resources for tackling them remain vested in states that guard their sovereignty zealously.

Thus, the force of the two NSS outcome documents was weakened by the fact that they were vague, non-binding and full of escape clauses like 'as appropriate', 'where technically and economically feasible', 'taking into account the need for assured supplies of medical isotopes', and 'consistent with national security considerations and development objectives'. In July 2014, the CPPNM had 150 states parties, so around one-quarter of the world's countries still have not acceded to it;[24] the CPPNM Amendment had only 77 of the 99 required number of accessions to enter into force; while 94 nations had ratified ICSANT. This explains the contradiction between the high compliance rate of NSS-participating states, as recorded by the Arms Control Association, and the conclusion, 'Four years ago, President Barack Obama called preventing nuclear terrorism a top security priority, but the United States is only marginally safer from that threat today'.[25]

Several regimes have been refined and additional ones promulgated to treat nuclear security as a matter subject to both domestic and international law; to require states to use and, if necessary, strengthen domestic legal systems to fight nuclear terrorism; to use international law as a basis and the United Nations as a key forum for international collaboration and action to meet the threat of nuclear terrorism; and to encourage and facilitate interstate cooperation in meeting the challenge in other ways. However, the development and widespread adoption of international best practice in nuclear security culture is inhibited by concerns over national sovereignty if multilateral standards are

Table 13.1 Status of CPPNM, CPPNM amendment, and ICSANT (21 July 2014)

	Date adopted	Entry into Force	Parties	Signed but not Parties
CPPNM	26.10.1979	8.2.1987	150	
CPPNM Amendment	8.7.2005	–	77	N/A
ICSANT	13.4.2005	7.7.2007	94	21

Sources: http://www.iaea.org/Publications/Documents/Conventions/cppnm_status.pdf; http://www.iaea.org/Publications/Documents/Conventions/cppnm_amend_status.pdf; http://treaties.un.org/Pages/ViewDetailsIII.aspx?&src=TREATY&mtdsg_no=XVIII~15&chapter=18&Temp=mtdsg3&lang=en.h

made more stringent and international institutions are given expanded authority to enforce compliance.

Hinderstein, Newman, and Reistad have argued that the time has come to move from HEU minimization to elimination.[26] Although significant progress has been made on reducing the number of and securing fissile material storage sites, and in conversion of HEU to low enriched uranium, states have been reluctant to ban HEU use in civilian applications. It is difficult to see this happening in the foreseeable future with states fiercely protecting national sovereignty. States, led by the major powers, are even more jealous of their sovereignty with respect to military security. In the global stockpile of weapon-useable material, almost all HEU and about half of the plutonium remain outside civilian programs.[27]

Thus only a small fraction of the world's HEU and less than half of the world's separated plutonium is subject to international discipline with respect to nuclear material accountancy.[28] HEU fuel use for powering submarines and aircraft carriers in the navies of the world poses a further challenge. Some progress is evident in the removal of fissile material no longer required for military purposes from nuclear weapons programs and in the decommissioning and dismantling of weapon grade fissile material production plants. The challenge remains to devise systems and procedures that secure non-civilian nuclear material and facilities 'to international standards, guidelines, best practices, or mechanisms for international assurance'[29] without downgrading national security.

Non-civilian nuclear material under military protection is generally better protected than civilian material. But not all material and facilities under military protection can be assumed to be totally safe and not all nuclear material for non-civilian use is under military protection. Warhead components, warheads undergoing maintenance or awaiting dismantlement, and the large stockpiles of US legacy material, for example, are in the custody of the Department of Energy and under the protection of civilian contractors. On 28 July 2012, in what may have been 'the biggest security breach in the history of the nation's atomic complex',[30] three activists – including an 82-year-old nun – broke into a heavily guarded section of the Y-12 National Security Complex in Oak Ridge, Tennessee, that houses several hundred tonnes of weapon grade HEU and had been assumed to be secure against armed terrorists. This is a government but not a military facility.

The tension between state sovereignty and international peace, discussed mainly in the context of the Responsibility to Protect doctrine,[31] is relevant here also. Nuclear security is a sovereign responsibility. But a major nuclear security vulnerability or crisis anywhere would pose an unacceptable risk and threat everywhere and therefore all countries have an interest in the effectiveness of the global nuclear security regime. Individual state determination of adequate nuclear security standards and national implementation of the standards is not enough. Therefore, strengthened international standards and accountability are required on early detection; prevention of attacks, thefts and sabotage; and recovery of missing nuclear material. Securing the world's most dangerous materials is the universal responsibility of all states and a common responsibility to all humankind.

The protection agenda of the Responsibility to Protect principle-cum-norm is not relevant to nuclear security, as it is restricted to mass atrocities. But the sovereignty as responsibility doctrine is fully applicable: there is no reason at all to restrict its scope in principle just to atrocity crimes. Reframing sovereignty by relegating state prerogatives and emphasizing state duties instead implies that, in the social contract that imposes obligations on citizens to comply with authoritative state demands, states are responsible for providing all the public goods, including physical safety from threat within state borders and national security against foreign threats; responsible to citizens and the international community of states as a collective body for fulfilling the duties of statehood in domestic governance and international discourse; and they can be held responsible, that is accountable, by citizens domestically and by the international community globally. When national acts of omission and commission have global systemic consequences – whether with respect to financial disasters, atrocity crimes or nuclear issues of safety, security, safeguards, doctrine, use, proliferation and disarmament – determining the balance between state sovereignty and international responsibility is not solely a prerogative of states: the international community does have a voice and should have a vote, if not a veto.

Robust global challenges, slow and feeble institutional responses

The evolution of international institutions to facilitate cooperation and mute conflict lags behind the rise of collective action problems with cross-border dimensions. With the institutions that do exist, there is often a significant gap between demonstrated and supposedly agreed needs, norms and policies on the one hand, and the resources available to global problem solving institutions on the other hand. Thus there is a big gap between the exalted expectations of what the IAEA can accomplish and the modest resources given to it.

The NSS as a single issue institutional response to this specific problem had two unusual features: it was brought about with exceptional promptness and it engaged the heads of government directly at the very apex of public diplomacy. Unlike the G-20, which is the world's premier economic forum for leaders but which emerged primarily as a crisis response mechanism of global governance, the NSS is an example of a crisis prevention global governance mechanism.

Summits are made possible because of advances in transport and telecommunications, which also facilitate the active participation of civil society networks and their role as watchdogs of government performance.[32] Summits are necessary because of the growing interdependence among nations and interconnectedness among issues that cut across ministries and responsibilities and require collective management at the highest levels. Like international finance and trade, pandemics and terrorism, climate change and biodiversity, nuclear security too spills across national boundaries.

However, not all topics lend themselves equally well to summit diplomacy, not all summits are successful and not all successful summits or topics are suitable for ongoing institutionalization. Summits should make the most difference in those problem areas where leadership commitment is the critical variable (the discipline of 'the pay grade test'[33]), where the primary obstacle to identifying policy overlap and convergence and reaching consensus is the unavailability or inadequacy of an appropriate forum and where speedy resolution is essential. Conversely, if the chief impediment is a fundamental clash of interests and the issues in dispute are technical more than political, then a fresh institutional setting is not the answer to the lack of common interest that can override national or sectional differences.

Unlike cabinet ministers with single portfolio responsibilities, leaders must oversee the broad agenda and interrelationships across issues and domains, domestic and international, political and economic, governments and markets. Their engagement catalyzes officials to focus on and resolve interagency differences, jurisdictional turf battles and veto points before the summit. At the summit, their involvement makes it possible for states to bargain across issues in order to cut deals (that is, trade apples for oranges). Among leaders, summit agreements can result in diffuse reciprocity: not tit-for-tat bargaining but rather a general atmosphere where the interests of counterparts are carefully considered across a range of issues. After the summit, their commitment to the agenda invests it with legitimacy, prioritizes its implementation and can help to redirect resources even amid fiscally constrained budgetary environments.

In sum, with broad, overarching responsibilities, leaders – and only leaders – can best weigh priorities and seek to balance interests across competing goals, sectors, national and international objectives, and between the immediate, medium and long terms. According to former Canadian Prime Minister Paul Martin, an appropriately structured and adequately prepared summit 'should get political leaders doing what they alone can do – making tough choices among competing interests and priorities'.[34]

In powerful testimony to the value added by summit diplomacy, the extent of voluntary reporting by states at the Seoul NSS in 2012 of the compliance of their nuclear security systems with commitments made at the 2010 NSS was higher than under the legally binding international instruments.[35] The CPPNM was already adhered to quite widely (but not universally) before the first NSS. Since then, several more states have become parties to the CPPNM Amendment and acceded to ICSANT. Nevertheless, summits produce diminishing returns. The NSS was always envisaged as an ad hoc and temporary mechanism, not a permanent institution. Yet once established, summits can generate their own inertia. The NSS will be exceptional if after the third one in the Netherlands in 2014, it draws to a close. The summit communiqués and other documents already make the political commitment to nuclear security measures and it is neither practical nor desirable to keep bringing large numbers of world leaders together to announce minor incremental steps toward the already agreed goal.

As the summit process concludes, the 2014 summit should be animated by a three-part, high-level policy objective:

1   To have a high degree of confidence in the nuclear security standards, arrangements and practices.

2   To build a unified and cohesive nuclear security architecture that is robust, resilient and rugged; that prioritizes and emphasizes weapon-useable fissile material protection but also embraces radiological sources and security culture; and that nests nuclear security in the other nuclear regimes dealing with peaceful uses, nonproliferation and disarmament.
3   To structure incentives and disincentives in such a way as to shift the balance of standards, arrangements, understandings and practices towards threat elimination and risk minimization.

Will there be life for the nuclear security agenda after 2014? There is a serious issue of how to sustain the necessary commitment. One option would be for the IAEA – the only existing international organization with a (limited) nuclear security mandate – to leverage its institutional credibility, integrity and legitimacy, based on near-universal membership and technical expertise, to take over the NSS agenda.[36] Its work on nuclear security has been given greater prominence, visibility and importance since the 2010 summit. Its dedicated office on strengthening nuclear security provides global leadership as well as invaluable technical information, guidance, training and assistance. But it lacks authority to establish mandatory baseline standards for nuclear security and to monitor and enforce compliance with the standards. Regular, independent international review of safety, security and safeguards measures should be the international norm. As the world's premier nuclear regulator, the IAEA must be mandated to negotiate binding agreements that establish global nuclear security standards and given the authority and the responsibility to certify compliance with these standards by monitoring national implementation.

That said, it is difficult to visualize states agreeing to give the IAEA mandatory and intrusive authority and powers in the foreseeable future. Another possibility is the negotiation of a framework convention on nuclear security,[37] similar to the UN Framework Convention on Climate Change (UNFCCC), that would bring together the existing disparate and loosely defined nuclear security conventions, rules and standards. The Fissile Materials Working Group believes that a framework convention would solve the problem of the 'patchwork of voluntary, nonbinding, nontransparent national commitments, ad hoc bilateral and multilateral initiatives, and vague legally binding measures' without specific standards that currently exists.[38]

However, given the reputational damage to the Framework Convention on Climate Change at and since the Copenhagen climate conference, an explicit parallel may not be politically wise. A Nuclear Threat Initiative-sponsored global dialogue on nuclear security has concluded that while legally binding mechanisms may be desirable in the future, the search for it now, when no consensus for it exists, is likely to delay urgently needed security upgrades that are feasible within voluntary mechanisms.[39] Thus the negotiation of a new legal mechanism or convention does not appear to be an immediate priority. The IAEA could be made the convention's executive agent to monitor and assess national implementation of the international standards and requirements. As already indicated, the best solution is to empower and fully capacitate the IAEA instead of pursuing a framework convention.

The efficiency-legitimacy gap and the north–south divide

During the Cold War, the main axis around which world affairs rotated was East–West. Since the end of the Cold War, this has morphed into a North–South axis.[40] While the former often pushes for improved efficiency and justifies the more compact groupings like the G-7/8 on this basis, the latter insists on inclusiveness and representation as the price of international legitimacy. Over the past decade, this pathology has been cross-infected with a second development. There is a growing gulf between the distribution of authority in the artificially constructed world of international intergovernmental institutions and the international distribution of military and market power and political clout. The approaches of Asia in general,[41] and China in particular,[42] to managing and reforming the global governance architecture become especially important. In the emerging new architecture, the old global political imbalances need to be readjusted to the new global economic imbalances.

Most developing countries put higher priority on their own pressing concerns of poverty alleviation and economic development. Some countries fear that the nuclear security agenda is a trap by the industrialized countries to deny them scientific and technological advances. Others remain unconvinced of the urgency to remove or eliminate HEU stockpiles. Non-nuclear weapons states (NWS) provide confidential reporting on HEU stocks under IAEA safeguards agreements. But there is no binding transparency or public declarations regime of HEU holdings, military non-explosive stockpiles, inventories of material resulting from nuclear disarmament, in excess of defence needs, and in active and reserve stockpiles for military and naval propulsion.

Many developing countries are similarly suspicious of calls to strengthen the IAEA mandate, authority and powers. Some IAEA members are concerned that incorporating a nuclear security budget into the regular budget while simultaneously freezing the regular budget will displace activities that are more important to them, including technical assistance. If we take this in conjunction with the effort to develop the so-called state level approach to safeguards, it feeds into the wider debate: there a risk that the IAEA is being reconfigured as an instrument to implement Western priorities (nonproliferation, counter-terrorism) at the expense of global concerns (disarmament and development). Such complaints are not justified objectively: all the concerns that the IAEA is seeking to redress are genuinely global and should be shared by all members of the international community. To escape the trap of the sterile debate, David Santoro recommends the cultivation of 'national security champions', with in-depth understanding of the political, legal, economic and technological aspects of the subject, as an effective means of fostering a culture of nuclear security at the national level.[43]

The government–governance gap

There is an unsustainable mismatch between the numbers and types of actors playing ever-expanding roles in civil, political and economic affairs within and among nations, and the concentration of decision-making authority in intergovernmental institutions. Many grave threats are rooted in nonstate actors who are neither party nor subject to global regimes that are negotiated among governments. Like global governance in general, global nuclear governance is being increasingly shared among state, intergovernmental and nonstate actors through standards and best practices that play complementary and parallel roles in ensuring security. A standard defines objectives; the IAEA's Nuclear Security Recommendations on Physical Protection of Nuclear Material and Nuclear Facilities (INFCIRC/225/Revision 5) is the primary nuclear security standards document. A best practice is a method or technique that produces results consistently superior to those obtained with other means.

Founded in Vienna in 2008, the World Institute for Nuclear Security (WINS) facilitates the sharing of information and experience among security professionals in the nuclear industry, promotes training and best practices and develops peer review systems. In consultation with industry and government stakeholders, WINS has developed more than 30 best practice guides.[44] These cover topics from nuclear security culture to threat assessment and effective security regulation and implementation. WINS offers a peer review mechanism for security management on a voluntary basis on request and is creating training programs for professional managers and operators of nuclear facilities and is thus creating 'a community of practice' in nuclear security.[45]

In the nuclear industry, there exists significant public-private cross-ownership, not just partnership. As commercial, nonproliferation and nuclear security interests can overlap or collide between industry and government stakeholders, accountabilities in managing nuclear risks have to be shared between parliaments and boardrooms. Just as nuclear security events will add to the financial and commercial costs of the nuclear industry, so industry can help governments to reduce risks. Yet, at the Seoul National Security Summit, industry was given only a side event, even though Australia's Prime Minister Julia Gillard did say that 'we should find mechanisms to foster co-operation between governments and the private sector'.[46] This should be taken up, for nuclear security will remain fragile without the full and active involvement of the private sector nuclear industry.

Conclusion

The nuclear security regime of agreements, regulations, resolutions and guidelines either existed or were close to being finalized before 2010. It has made further progress in national implementation since being elevated to a leaders' level summit in 2010. National ratification of treaties and several projects were accelerated so they could be announced at the summits. But it still lags well behind the other nuclear regimes for safety, safeguards and arms control. If a robust nuclear security culture is to be created, some issues will have to be addressed, including lack of universality, binding standards, transparency and accountability mechanisms, compulsory IAEA oversight and broadened scope to include nuclear weapons and other non-civilian dimensions of the problem. The current regime relies almost entirely on national protection and control systems in those countries that possess nuclear and radiological materials. It needs to be more comprehensive instead of incremental, covering all materials and all facilities at all times; integrated rather than disparate and piecemeal; and backed by global mechanisms in order to make the regime both robust and resilient. The key to strengthening and improving the nuclear security regime is 'balancing the principles of national sovereignty with international responsibility'.[47]

Following from that, this analysis offers key recommendations for solving each of the four global governance disconnects. The global problems–sovereignty gap can be filled by reframing sovereignty from sacrosanct state privilege to shared responsibility for assuring nuclear security along with other dimensions of collective and common security. The institutional gap can be addressed by empowering and adequately resourcing the IAEA. The efficiency–legitimacy disconnect can be rectified by brokering agreements, after the 2014 Netherlands Nuclear Security Summit, in other appropriate groupings like the G-8, BRICS and, especially, the G-20, and then having these deals validated by the UN system as the mandated multilateral system. And the restrictive decision-making ambit of the mandated multilateral system in turn can be compensated by bringing national champions and civil society and private sector actors into the consult-and-cooperate model of global governance rather than the command-and-control-by-government-fiat model.

Epilogue

The third NSS was held at The Hague in the Netherlands in March 2014 with 58 world leaders in attendance; the fourth and presumably last will be held back in Chicago in 2016. In the three year period from the first to the third NSS, '12 countries have completely eliminated their HEU stockpiles, 15 have reduced theirs, and the number of countries that possess enough nuclear material to build a nuclear weapon has fallen from 39 to 25'.[48] The Hague summit advanced the global agenda on nuclear security on two fronts. Some countries promised to begin reducing their stockpile of plutonium as well as HEU. Japan, for example, pledged to return 330kg of plutonium and 170kg of uranium to the US and UK respectively from whence they had come. More importantly for the central organizing theme of this chapter, 35 countries, led by the three summit hosts, announced a new Strengthening Nuclear Security Implementation Initiative to implement the IAEA-recommended nuclear security standards.[49] And most importantly for the central organizing theme of this book, as Paul Meyer notes, a group of prominent mostly nonaligned states highlighted the narrow interpretation and remit of the NSS in concentrating on the small and miniscule civilian holdings in non-NWS, when 98 percent of HEU and 86 percent of separated plutonium stockpiles in the world are possessed by the NWS. The greatest threat to humanity, Brazil told the summit, is posed not by civilian nuclear facilities but by nuclear bombs.[50]

But let us end this chapter on a positive note. The former Soviet Union carried out a total of 456 nuclear tests in Semipalatinsk (116 atmospheric and 340 underground), Kazakhstan. When Russian scientists and military personnel withdrew after the collapse of the Soviet Union, they left behind abandoned equipment, tunnels and bore holes filled with plutonium residue that, if recovered, could be used to make dozens of nuclear bombs. Indeed scavengers looking for abandoned Soviet-era valuable metal and equipment came within metres of the unguarded fissile material between 1991 and 2012. Over 17 years from 1996 to 2012, scientists from Kazakhstan, Russia and the US worked together in a $150mn operation to secure the material in the tunnels of Degelen Mountain and surrounding bore holes by filling them with special concrete, 'greatly reducing one of the largest nuclear security threats since the collapse of the Soviet Union'. In October 2012 they unveiled a three-sided stone monument with the simple sentence in all three languages etched on it: 'The world has become safer'.[51]

Notes

* Originally published as *Policy Analysis Brief* (Muscatine, Iowa: Stanley Foundation, March 2013). Reprinted by permission of the Stanley Foundation.
1 'Remarks by President Barack Obama, Hradcany Square, Prague, April 5, 2009', (Washington, DC: White House, Office of the Press Secretary, 2009).
2 Kim Joong Keun, South Korean ambassador to India, writing on the eve of the Seoul Nuclear Security Summit, 'Beyond security, towards peace', *Times of India*, 26 March 2012.
3 Peter Goodspeed, 'Ongoing nuclear threat looms over Seoul Summit', *Toronto National Post*, 24 March 2012.
4 'Another infiltration reported at South African atomic site', *Global Security Newswire*, 13 July 2012, http://www.nti.org/gsn/article/new-infiltration-reported-south-african-atomic-plant/.
5 Banyan, 'Nuclear Profusion', *Economist*, 25 August 2012.
6 'Gunmen storm military air base in Pakistan', *BBC News*, 16 August 2012, http://www.bbc.com/news/world-asia-19278302.
7 Abdul Manan, 'Taliban threat: nuclear site in DG Khan cordoned off', *Express Tribune*, 6 September 2012, http://tribune.com.pk/story/432295/taliban-threat-nuclear-site-in-dg-khan-cordoned-off/.
8 Quoted in Goodspeed, 'Ongoing nuclear threat'.
9 Hugh Gusterson, 'A Pakistani view of U.S. nuclear weapons', *Bulletin of the Atomic Scientists*, 4 February 2008, http://thebulletin.org/pakistani-view-us-nuclear-weapons.
10 Fissile Materials Working Group (FMWG), *Preventing Nuclear Terror in the 21st Century: Policy Recommendations* (Washington, DC: January 2012), 6.
11 International Panel on Fissile Materials (IPFM), http://www.fissilematerials.org.
12 Belfer Center for Science and International Affairs, *Nuclear Terrorism Fact Sheet* (Cambridge, MA: Harvard University, 2010), http://belfercenter.ksg.harvard.edu/files/Nuclear-Security-Fact-Sheet.pdf.
13 See Andrew F. Cooper and Ramesh Thakur, *The Group of Twenty (G20)* (London: Routledge, 2013).
14 See Andrew F. Cooper and Ramesh Thakur, 'The BRICS in the New Global Economic Geography', in Thomas G. Weiss and Rorden Wilkinson, eds., *International Organization and Global Governance* (London: Routledge, 2014): 265–78.
15 Khammar Mrabit, 'International Physical Protection Advisory Services (IPPAS), paper delivered at the conference on U.S. Nuclear Regulatory Commission's International Regulators Conference on Nuclear Security, 4–6 December 2012, Washington D.C.; http://www.nrcsecurityconference.org/slides/Dec5/IPPAS.pdf.
16 The IAEA maintains a good website where all this information is available up to date: http://www.iaea.org.

17 See Amy F. Woolf, *Nonproliferation and Threat Reduction Assistance: U.S. Programs in the Former Soviet Union* (Washington, DC: Congressional Research Service, RL31957, 6 March 2012).
18 'NNSA announces elimination of 450 metric tons of Russian weapons highly enriched uranium', 9 July 2012, http://www.nnsa.energy.gov/print/mediaroom/pressreleases/450tons070912. The final shipment was completed in November 2013: Andrew E. Kramer, 'Last shipment of nuclear fuel from Russian bombs heads to U.S.', *New York Times*, 14 November 2013.
19 *NTI Nuclear Materials Security Index: Building a Framework for Assurance, Accountability, and Action* (Washington, DC: Nuclear Threat Initiative, January 2012).
20 Michelle Cann, Kelsey Davenport and Margaret Balza, *The Nuclear Security Summit: Assessment of National Commitments* (Washington, DC: Arms Control Association, March 2012).
21. Thomas G. Weiss and Ramesh Thakur, *Global Governance and the UN: An Unfinished Journey* (Bloomington: Indiana University Press, 2010).
22 Kofi Annan, 'Problems without Passports', *Foreign Policy* 132 (September–October 2002), 30–31.
23 Weiss and Thakur, *Global Governance and the UN*; the five gaps are knowledge, normative, policy, institutional and compliance.
24 South Africa, where three incidents are known to have occurred at its Pelindaba nuclear facility, has not yet signed the amendment.
25 Kenneth C. Brill and Kenneth N. Luongo, 'Obama's modest gains in nuclear security vision', *Politico*, 18 January 2013, http://www.politico.com/story/2013/01/obamas-modest-gains-in-nuclear-security-vision-86414.html.
26 Corey Hinderstein, Andrew Newman, and Ole Reistad, 'From HEU minimization to elimination: time to change the vocabulary', *Bulletin of the Atomic Scientists* 68:4 (2012): 83–95.
27 IPFM, http://www.fissilematerials.org.
28 In June 2014, Japan acknowledged that it had failed to include 640kg of unused plutonium in its annual reports to the IAEA in 2012 and 2013, enough to make about 80 nuclear bombs; Kyodo, 'Japan failed to report 640kg of nuclear fuel to IAEA', *Japan Times*, 7 June 2014. Pavel Podvig notes 'the troubling fact that we know very little about the amounts of fissile material that are circulating around the globe'. The voluntary INFIRC/549 civilian plutonium reports to the IAEA 'are a useful transparency tool, but they are not nearly sufficient to establish a good record of the global civilian plutonium stock'. Data collection and reporting standards vary from one country to another, for example with respect to whether excess military plutonium is included or not. Pavel Podvig, 'How fissile material falls through the cracks', *Bulletin of the Atomic Scientists*, 7 July 2014, http://thebulletin.org/how-fissile-material-falls-through-cracks7296.
29 'Options for Strengthening the Global Nuclear Security System', *Global Dialogue on Nuclear Security Priorities* (Washington, DC: Nuclear Threat Initiative, 2 October 2012), 9.
30 William J. Broad, 'The nun who broke into the nuclear sanctum', *New York Times*, 10 August 2012.
31 See Ramesh Thakur, *The Responsibility to Protect: Norms, Laws and the Use of Force in International Politics* (London: Routledge, 2011).
32 This subsection draws in particular on Cooper and Thakur, *The Group of Twenty*, and Richard Feinberg, 'Institutionalized Summitry', in Andrew F. Cooper, Jorge Heine and Ramesh Thakur, eds., *The Oxford Handbook of Modern Diplomacy* (Oxford: Oxford University Press, 2013): 303–18.
33 David Shorr, 'Making the G-20 a Reservoir of Global Leadership – A Maximalist Argument', *Policy Analysis Brief* (Muscatine, IA: Stanley Foundation, April 2011), 5.
34 Paul Martin, 'A Global Answer to Global Problems: The Case for a New Leaders' Forum', *Foreign Affairs* 84: 6 (2005), 6.

35 Nuclear Security Governance Experts Group (NSGEG), *Improving Nuclear Security Regime Cohesion: Summary Report and Initial Policy Recommendations* (Muscatine, IA: Stanley Foundation, September 2012), 6.
36 Since this Policy Brief was published, Trevor Findlay too has argued that 'both logic and economy' suggest that the IAEA should 'fold the best of the summit processes into its existing nuclear diplomacy role'. Trevor Findlay, 'Beyond Nuclear Summitry: The Role of the IAEA in Nuclear Security Diplomacy after 2016', (Cambridge MA: Project on Managing the Atom, Belfer Center for Science and International Affairs, Harvard University, March 2014), 29.
37 Kenneth C. Brill and Kenneth N. Luongo, 'A security system commensurate with the risk of nuclear terrorism', *Bulletin of the Atomic Scientists*, 16 April 2012.
38 FMWG, *Preventing Nuclear Terror*, p. 8.
39 'Options for Strengthening the Global Nuclear Security System', pp. 1–2.
40 Ramesh Thakur, *Towards a Less Imperfect State of the World: The Gulf between North and South* (Berlin: Friedrich Ebert Stiftung, Dialogue on Globalization Briefing Paper no. 4, April 2008).
41 Amitav Acharya, 'Can Asia Lead? Power Ambitions and Global Governance in the Twenty-first Century', *International Affairs* 87:4 (2011): 851–69.
42 See Gregory Chin and Ramesh Thakur, 'Will China Change the Rules of Global Order?' *Washington Quarterly* 33:4 (2010): 119–38.
43 David Santoro, 'Championing Nuclear Security', Carnegie Endowment for International Peace, 10 September 2012, http://carnegieendowment.org/2012/09/10/championing-nuclear-security/dsz2.
44 NSGEG, *Improving Nuclear Security Regime Cohesion*, 6.
45 'Options for Strengthening the Global Nuclear Security System', 4.
46 Quoted in Martine Letts, 'Nuclear Security: Partner with Industry', *Interpreter* (Sydney: Lowy Institute, March 28, 2012), http://www.lowyinterpreter.org/post/2012/03/28/Nuclear-security-The-case-for-a-PPP.aspx.
47 NSGEG, *Improving Nuclear Security Regime Cohesion*, 2.
48 Tanya Ogilvie-White, 'Hard-won progress at the Nuclear Security Summits', *Australian Outlook*, 4 April 2014, http://www.internationalaffairs.org.au/australian_outlook/hard-won-progress-at-the-nuclear-security-summits/.
49 'The Hague Nuclear Security Summit Communiqué', 25 March 2014, http://www.consilium.europa.eu/uedocs/cms_data/docs/pressdata/en/ec/141885.pdf; and 'Strengthening Nuclear Security Implementation', 25 March 2014, https://www.nss2014.com/sites/default/files/downloads/strengthening_nuclear_security_implementation.pdf.
50 Paul Meyer, 'The fissure at the Nuclear Security Summit', OpenCanada.org, 27 March 2014, http://opencanada.org/features/the-think-tank/comments/the-fissure-at-the-nuclear-security-summit/.
51 Eben Harrell and David E. Hoffman, 'Plutonium mountain: Inside the 17-year mission to secure a dangerous legacy of Soviet nuclear testing', (Cambridge MA.: The Project on Managing the Atom, Belfer Center for Science and International Affairs, Harvard University, August 2013), http://belfercenter.ksg.harvard.edu/files/Plutonium%20Mountain-Web.pdf.

14 The problem of nuclear weapons and what to do about it

The world faces two existential threats: climate change and nuclear Armageddon. Those who reject the first are derided as denialists; those dismissive of the second are praised as realists. Nuclear weapons may or may not have kept the peace among various groups of rival states; they could be catastrophic for the world if ever used by both sides in a war between nuclear-armed rivals; and the prospects for their use have grown since the end of the Cold War. Even a limited regional nuclear war in which India and Pakistan used 50 Hiroshima-size (15kt) bombs each could lead to a famine that kills up to a billion people.[1] Having learnt to live with nuclear weapons for 70 years (1945–2015), we have become desensitized to the gravity and immediacy of the threat. The tyranny of complacency could yet exact a fearful price with nuclear Armageddon.

The nuclear peace has held so far owing as much to good luck as sound stewardship. Deterrence stability depends on rational decision-makers being always in office on all sides: a dubious and not very reassuring precondition. It depends equally critically on there being no rogue launch, human error or system malfunction: an impossibly high bar. For nuclear peace to hold, deterrence and fail-safe mechanisms must work every single time. For nuclear Armageddon, deterrence or fail-safe mechanisms need to break down only once. This is not a comforting equation. It also explains why, unlike most situations where risk can be mitigated after disaster strikes, with nuclear weapons all risks must be mitigated before any disaster.[2] As more states acquire nuclear weapons, the risks multiply exponentially with the requirements for rationality in all decision-makers; robust command-and-control systems in all states; 100 percent reliable fail-safe mechanisms and procedures against accidental and unauthorized launch of nuclear weapons; and totally unbreachable security measures against terrorists acquiring nuclear weapons by being able to penetrate one or more of the growing nuclear facilities or access some of the wider spread of nuclear material and technology. It is far from clear that the old, Cold War parameters of classical deterrence will prove adequate to the new contingencies and risks. It really is long past time to lift the shroud of the mushroom cloud from the international body politic.

Five paradoxes set the context for this final concluding chapter. First, the central paradox of nuclear deterrence may be bluntly stated: nuclear weapons are useful only if the threat to use them is credible, but they must never be used. Second, they are useful for some but must be stopped from spreading to anyone else. Third, the most substantial progress so far on dismantlement and destruction of nuclear weapons has occurred as a result of bilateral US and Soviet/Russian treaties, agreements and measures, most recently a new Strategic Arms Reduction Treaty (New START). But a nuclear-weapon-free world will have to rest on a legally binding multilateral international instrument such as a nuclear weapons convention (NWC). Fourth, although nuclear weapons play a lesser role in shaping US–Russia relations today than during the Cold War, the prospects of their use by others in some tense, conflict-prone regions have grown. Fifth, the existing treaty-based regimes have collectively anchored international security and can be credited with many major successes and significant accomplishments. But their accumulating anomalies, shortcomings and flaws suggest that they, or at least some of them, may have reached the limits of their success. The critical challenge, therefore, becomes how to manage the transition to their replacement for the post-nuclear order without undermining their achievements and jeopardizing the security of the existing nuclear orders.

On the edge of the cliff

Forty-five years after the NPT came into force in 1970, the world is still perilously close to the edge of the nuclear cliff. The cliff is perhaps not quite as steep as it was in the 1980s, but going over it would be fatal for planet Earth. Authoritative roadmaps exist to walk us back to the relative safety of a denuclearized world, but a perverse mixture of hubris and arrogance on the part of the nuclear-armed states exposes us to the risk of sleepwalking into a nuclear disaster. The point to remember about sleepwalking is that people doing it are unaware of it.

The number of times that we have come frighteningly close to nuclear holocaust is simply staggering. According to one study by a US nuclear weapon laboratory in 1970 (obtained through the Freedom of Information Act), more than 1,200 nuclear weapons were involved in accidents (most trivial, but some significant) between 1950 and 1968 because of security breaches, lost weapons, failed safety mechanisms or accidents resulting from weapons being dropped or crushed in lifts, etc.[3] For example, a B-52 bomber loaded with 12 hydrogen bombs and nuclear warheads caught fire in Grand Forks, North Dakota, in September 1980. In the same month, a dropped socket punctured the fuel tank of a Titan II ICBM mounted with 'the most powerful nuclear warhead ever built by the US' until then at a missile silo near Damascus, Texas. One man was killed in the resulting explosion and the warhead was thrown several hundred feet from its basing silo.[4]

It has now been confirmed that on 21 January 1961, a four-megatonne bomb (that is, 260 times more powerful than Hiroshima) was just one ordinary switch away from detonating over North Carolina whose effects would have covered Washington, Baltimore, Philadelphia and even New York City. Just days after President John F. Kennedy's inauguration, a B-52 bomber on a routine flight went into an uncontrolled spin. Two four-megatonne hydrogen bombs fell loose over Goldsboro, North Carolina, and one, assuming that it had been deliberately released over an enemy target, began the detonation process. Three of the four fail safe-mechanisms failed and only the final, a simple dynamo technology low-voltage switch, averted what would have been the greatest disaster in US history with millions of lives at risk.[5] In the 1962 Cuban missile crisis, the US strategy was based on the best available intelligence which indicated that there were no nuclear warheads in Cuba. In fact, there were 162 warheads already stationed there, including 90 tactical warheads, and the local Soviet commander had taken them out of storage to deployed positions for use against an American invasion.[6] Recently declassified British cabinet documents show that there was another near miss in November 1983. In response to NATO war games exercise Able Archer, which Moscow mistook to be real, the Soviets came close to launching a full-scale nuclear attack against the West under the misapprehension that a NATO nuclear attack was imminent. And the West was blissfully unaware of this at the time.[7]

In January 1995, mistaking a Norwegian weather rocket for a US SLBM, Russia's senior military officials reportedly advised President Boris Yeltsin – the first leader in Moscow to have the 'nuclear suitcase' opened for him – to launch Russian missiles. He demurred.[8] In 2007, a weapons crew at the US Air Force (USAF) base in Minot, North Dakota, mistakenly loaded a B-52 bomber with six nuclear-armed cruse missiles. The plane flew across the country to the USAF base in Barksdale, Louisiana, where the bombs were left unsecured for 36 hours. When eventually personnel there realised that the bombs were nuclear, not conventional, they informed their counterparts back in Minot – who had not detected the missing bombs until then.[9]

In a closely argued article, Gareth Evans systematically demonstrates the fallacy or extraordinary weakness of the deterrence-based arguments.[10] Nuclear weapons have failed to stop wars between nuclear and non-nuclear rivals (Korea, Afghanistan, Falklands, Vietnam, the 1990–91 Gulf War). Their deterrent utility is severely qualified by the belief among potential target regimes that they are essentially unusable because of the powerful normative taboo. The utility of nuclear deterrence is questionable in shaping relations between: a) major nuclear rivals, b) asymmetric middle-power nuclear rivals, and c) small–major power nuclear pairs of countries. On the first, the role of nuclear weapons in having preserved the peace during the Cold War is debatable. How do we assess the relative weight and potency of nuclear weapons, West European integration and West European democratization as explanatory variables in that long peace? Nor has there been any evidence produced to show that either side had the intention to attack the other at any time during the Cold War but was deterred from doing so because of nuclear weapons held by the other side.[11] Conversely, the Soviet Union's territorial expansion across Eastern and Central Europe behind Red Army lines took place in the years of US atomic monopoly, 1945–49, and it imploded after, although not because of, gaining strategic parity.

With asymmetric middle-power nuclear rivals too national security strategists face a fundamental and unresolvable paradox. In order to deter a conventional attack by a more powerful nuclear adversary, each nuclear-armed state must convince its stronger opponent of the ability and will to use nuclear weapons if attacked. But if the attack does occur, escalating to nuclear weapons will worsen the scale of military devastation even for the side initiating nuclear strikes. Because the stronger party believes this, the existence of nuclear weapons may add an extra element of caution but does not guarantee complete and indefinite immunity for the weaker party. Are those who profess faith in the essential logic of nuclear deterrence prepared, following Waltz,[12] to support the acquisition of nuclear weapons by Iran in order to contribute to the peace and stability of the Middle East which at present has only one nuclear-armed state?

It is equally contestable that nuclear weapons buy immunity for small states against attack by the powerful. North Korea is often held up as an example of this, especially against the backdrop of the invasion of Iraq in 2003 and the 2011 fate of Muammar Gaddafi after Libya's 2003 abandonment of clandestine nuclear weapons pursuit.[13] However, the biggest caution in attacking North Korea in response to its serial provocations lies in uncertainty about how China would respond, followed by worries about the DPRK's conventional capacity to devastate Seoul and other parts of South Korea. Pyongyang's puny present and prospective arsenal of nuclear weapons and the rudimentary capacity to deploy and use them credibly is a distant third factor in the deterrence calculus.

Nuclear weapons status comes with a significant economic cost. They have not permitted any of the nine states that have them to buy defence on the cheap. There is the added risk of proliferation to extremist elements through leakage, theft, state collapse and state capture. There are political costs and risks of creating a national security state with a premium on increased secretiveness and reduced public accountability.

The NPT has passed its use-by date, but . . .

As previous chapters have shown, on the one hand, the NPT has achieved many significant successes with respect to two of its three legs, namely limiting the spread of nuclear weapons to states beyond the N5 (the five NPT-defined NWS: China, France, Russia, UK and US) and facilitating the expansion of programs of peaceful uses of nuclear energy with minimum risk of misuse and diversion of the material and facilities for military purposes. The near universal NPT has kept the nuclear nightmare at bay for over four decades. The number of countries with nuclear weapons is still – if only just – in single figures. On the other hand, the NPT has been an overall failure on the agenda of nuclear disarmament. The nuclear arsenals of the N5 expanded enormously after the NPT was in force, peaked in the mid-1980s and have been falling since.[14] The NPT has been buttressed and reinforced over the decades with supplementary agreements and mechanisms like the Comprehensive Nuclear Test Ban Treaty (CTBT), Nuclear Suppliers Group (NSG), the safeguards Additional Protocol of the IAEA, the Nuclear Security Summits (NSS) and various UN Security Council resolutions like Resolution 1540. The original 1968 treaty plus the cluster of supplementary instruments together make up the broad NPT regime.

In retrospect, 1996 was the zenith of progress on arms control and disarmament. The NPT was indefinitely extended in 1995, the International Court of Justice (ICJ) affirmed the NPT's disarmament obligations in July 1996 and the CTBT was approved in September. Unfortunately, it proved a false dawn as over the next decade we saw but a few faint glimmers of hope amidst a blinding glare of disappointments. Nonproliferation took a seismic jolt with the India–Pakistan nuclear tests of 1998, followed by North Korea's withdrawal from the NPT and tests this century. Its politics worsened with the war against Serbia and the invasion of Iraq. Suddenly, many countries wanted to re-examine the merits of the bomb for deterring attacks by a moral majority disdainful of international law that guaranteed the territorial integrity of sovereign states. New nuclear weapons, for example 'mini-nukes' and bunker busters, were developed and used to threaten non-nuclear states. The disarmament benchmarks of the 2000 NPT Review Conference were quietly abandoned and the 2005 NPT Review Conference was a total failure. Scandalously, the 2005 UN summit's outcome document failed to include even one sentence on the nuclear challenge. It took the advent of the Obama administration to rescue the NPT regime from the brink of collapse, including a remarkable eight days in 2010 during which a new Nuclear Posture Review (6 April) reduced the role of nuclear weapons in US security policy, a New START agreement (8 April) between Russia and the United States cut their deployed strategic nuclear warheads by one-third, and the inaugural NSS in Washington (12–13 April) – the largest and most senior-level conference on nuclear policy until then – affirmed the world's determination to secure nuclear weapons, materials and facilities. This was followed by a modestly successful NPT Review Conference in May. As Joseph Cirincione generously puts it:

> Obama seemed to hit the nuclear policy sweet spot: inspiring idealists with his vision and winning pragmatists with his practical programs. Each of the changes introduced by the Obama administration was relatively modest. . . . Cumulatively, however, the changes marked a significant change of direction. . . . The arc of U.S. policy now bent toward deeper reductions in nuclear arsenals with reduced roles for these weapons in the U.S. national security strategy, a greater emphasis on collective diplomatic action to stop proliferators, and strong cooperative efforts to block nuclear terrorism.[15]

But the record of implementation of these various conferences and summit decisions is modest rather than spectacular.[16] This leads to two broad conclusions. First, the NPT may have reached or be very close to the limit of its potential and its frailties expose us to grave risks and dangers. The stalled nuclear disarmament agenda puts at risk the substantial achievements on nonproliferation and peaceful applications. The existence of more than 16,000 warheads, with 2,000 on high operational alert, and the stocks of fissile material held by various countries contain inherent risks of deliberate or unintended use by state or non-state actors, unauthorized or accidental launch caused by rogue commanders or misinformation, cyber error or system malfunction. Hence the need to invest with urgency in the search for an alternative security order that transcends and is more robust and less flawed than the NPT: the good (the NPT regime) must not be permitted to be the enemy of the best (an NWC). But because the accomplishments are very real and they underpin the existing international security order, the transition to a post-NPT world has to be managed with great care and delicacy, else the best really would become the enemy of the good.

The inseparable logics of nuclear nonproliferation and disarmament

Nuclear weapons were invented to pre-empt and cope with Germany, used to defeat Japan and deployed most extensively against the Soviet Union. As their primary strategic rationale disappeared with the end of the Cold War, Washington's evolving nuclear policies acquired greater regional specificity. In East Asia, for example, continued US attachment to nuclear weapons and doctrines was seen as proof of a shift in stance – from deterrence to compellence and coercion – and provoked more assertive Chinese nuclear policies and nuclear brinksmanship by North Korea, which in turn produced self-vindication in Washington.[17] Conversely, even a cursory probing of the sources of instability that impel countries towards nuclear acquisition confirms the link between the denuclearization of individual states, the regions in which they are located and universal disarmament. For example, as we saw in Chapter 10, Iran's national security strategy cannot be delinked from regional and global dynamics.

At the heart of the NPT lie three bargains involving nuclear energy, nonproliferation and disarmament:

1   The non-nuclear countries established a bargain among themselves never to acquire nuclear weapons.
2   They entered into a deal with the NWS whereby, in return for intrusive end-use control over nuclear and nuclear-related technology and materials, they were granted access to these on a most favoured nation basis.
3   They struck a second deal with the NWS that in return for the non-NWS forever forswearing the bomb, the NWS would pursue good faith negotiations for complete nuclear disarmament.

All three bargains are under strain. The problem was that there was a marked imbalance of obligations between the different bargains. The non-nuclear weapons status was immediate, legally binding and internationally verifiable and enforceable. But there were no intrusive safeguards for the NWS in their roles as suppliers of critical technology and components. More importantly, their commitment to disarm was neither timetabled, precise nor binding. By relying on the promise of signatories to use nuclear materials, facilities and technology for peaceful purposes only, it empowered them to operate dangerously close to a nuclear weapons capability, as the world has discovered with respect to Iran. It is impossible to deal with non-NPT nuclear-armed states from within the treaty. Israel, even though it is not an NPT signatory, will not openly admit to its nuclear weapons stockpiles. India and Pakistan have been accepted, more or less, as de facto nuclear weapons powers. The odd result is that the five NPT-licit NWS have a legal obligation to eliminate their nuclear weapons under Article 6, but India, Israel and Pakistan have no such obligation. It also means that the non-NPT nuclear-armed states cannot be asked to join the nuclear-weapon-free zone (NWFZ) protocols, even if they are regionally relevant.

The NWS policy on nuclear disarmament recalls St. Augustine's possibly apocryphal lament: 'O Lord, make me chaste – but not just yet'. Some years ago, a group of people in UNESCO were trying to have peace inscribed as a human right. The American representative at the discussion objected on the grounds that if peace was declared to be a human right, it would be much more difficult to start new wars. If nuclear weapons were abolished, nuclear war too would be very much more difficult to start. There is a gathering sense around the world that nuclear threats are intensifying and multiplying. There is a matching, growing conviction that existing policies have failed to mute the threats. In the meantime, scientific and technological advancements since the NPT was signed in 1968 have greatly expanded our technical toolkit for monitoring and verifying weapons reduction and elimination. It is time to supplement and then supplant the sword-and-shield nuclear diplomacy of the United States with the pen diplomacy of a multilaterally negotiated, non-discriminatory and universal NWC. The emergence of new leaders in a range of nuclear policy-relevant countries, not the least the United States, brings into power a post-Cold War generation less burdened by the rigid analytical and policy framework of the second half of the twentieth century.

The highly influential series of articles by four Cold War-era heavyweights from the US strategic policy community in the *Wall Street Journal* (2007–13)[18] gave 'street credibility' to the goal of nuclear disarmament within the US political process and political legitimacy to it worldwide. The nuclear agenda was re-energized with the Prague promise of President Obama in April 2009 to aim for the peace and security of a world without nuclear weapons. The Washington NSS looked closely at the safety and security requirements of nuclear programs and materials. The 2010 NPT Review Conference was a modest success. Commissions like the International Commission on Nuclear Non-Proliferation and Disarmament (ICNND) and campaigns like Global Zero helped to mobilize key constituencies. Russia and the United States negotiated, signed, ratified and have brought into force New START to cut back their deployed (but not total) nuclear arsenals by one-third.

The Ukraine hiccup

Yet there is a palpable and growing sense that New START might mark the end of nuclear accomplishments instead of being the first step on the road to abolition – and the mood of pessimism can only deepen after the 2014 crisis in the Crimea and Ukraine. In the wake of political instability and volatility in Ukraine in early 2014, Russia organized a hastily conducted sham referendum in Crimea and reincorporated it into Russia based on its outcome. Some commentators were quick to pronounce that if only Kiev had kept the substantial stockpile of nuclear weapons it inherited from the collapsed Soviet Union, instead of relinquishing them in 1994, it would not have lost Crimea.[19] The nuclear arsenal would have effectively deterred any Russian invasion. This is simplistic to the point of being simple-minded, for four reasons. All that a Ukrainian bomb would have done is to add yet another layer of extreme hazard to an already very volatile crisis.

First, the bombs were not in fact Ukrainian, any more than NATO nuclear weapons stored on West European soil or US bombs that used to be kept in South Korea belonged to the countries on whose territory they were located. They were always Russian bombs that happened to be based in Ukraine. Moscow retained complete command and control and Kiev never had access to the authorization codes necessary to launch them.

Second, Ukrainian scientists and engineers would probably have had the knowledge and skills to overcome the technical difficulties and acquired operational control over the weapons in due course. They would still have faced substantial legal and political difficulties. The NPT recognizes only five legitimate NWS. Legally, therefore, even as a successor state to the former Soviet Union, it is hard to see how Ukraine could have been accepted as a NWS within the treaty. Russia would not easily and willingly have surrendered its stockpile of nuclear weapons to a suddenly independent Ukraine. And their resistance would have been backed by the West, which certainly would have been in no mood to countenance the emergence of another nuclear weapons power with a stockpile of 1,900 strategic and 2,500 tactical nuclear weapons; bigger by several factor-fold than those of Britain, China and France combined. In effect Ukraine would have struggled to survive as an international pariah state and the whole history of the region would have been so different that the deterrent claim for the events of 2014 simply cannot be constructed as a credible counterfactual narrative.

Third, if Ukraine had emerged as a nuclear-armed state, the likelihood is that Moscow would have kept a tighter reign to ensure it stayed pro-Russian. In which case, it is more probable that Washington and its European allies would have exercised far more caution and not interfered in nuclear-armed Ukraine's internal affairs to overthrow the elected pro-Russian president through street mobs to install a pro-West government instead.

Fourth, even if Ukraine had the bomb and the same sequence of events happened, Russia could still have invaded the Crimea as an existential threat in its core security zone. The pull of history and geopolitics can trump the push of nuclear caution.[20] Would Kiev really have risked its own existence and escalated to a nuclear war in response? Not only does this not make any strategic, political or even common sense. We also have the example of Kargil in 1999, when the known fact of nuclear weapons on both sides of the border did not deter Pakistan from clandestinely capturing Kargil nor India from launching a massive and successful conventional assault to retake it. To go even further back in time, despite knowing that Britain had the bomb, non-nuclear Argentina was not deterred from invading the Falkland Islands in 1982.

The Ukraine crisis is likely to damage the already enfeebled efforts to promote the eventual elimination of nuclear weapons.[21] Russia has clearly broken the

Budapest Memorandum of 1994 pledging to respect the territorial integrity and existing borders of Ukraine in return for the latter giving up the nuclear weapons. This will not reassure the 184 countries that have signed the NPT as non-NWS on their security concerns. Yet paradoxically, Russia is so weak today that if the United States and West had led the campaign for a denuclearized world and succeeded, they would have been in a commanding position to use conventional military superiority to compel Russia to withdraw or face defeat in a costly war. Moreover, the presence of US tactical nuclear weapons (B-61 gravity bombs) in Europe failed to deter Russian annexation of Crimea and, after that, failed to reassure other former Soviet republics of NATO credibility and reliability. To reassure them NATO emplaced *conventional* troops and planes in the Baltic states, thereby confirming the uselessness of its 'nuclear umbrella' for the purpose either of deterrence of enemies or reassurance of allies.[22]

There is little evidence of significant domestic political constituencies in the nuclear-armed states to get disarmament back on track. Tellingly, not one country that had the bomb in 1968 when the NPT was signed has given them up 47 years on. Indeed, judging by their stockpiles, modernization/upgrade plans and programs, deployment practices and doctrines, all nuclear-armed states are determined to retain their weapons status indefinitely and are contemplating expanded use of these weapons for several decades ahead. Not one of them is prepared to make the total verified elimination of nuclear weapons the central organizing principle of its nuclear policy. To would-be proliferators, the lesson is clear: nuclear weapons are indispensable in today's world and for dealing with tomorrow's threats. Reflecting the technical state of 1968 when the NPT was signed, Iran insists on its right to pursue the use of nuclear energy for peaceful purposes to the point where it would be a screwdriver away from the bomb. The world is at a loss on how to stop Iran from crossing the nuclear weapons threshold and how to persuade, coax or coerce North Korea to step back into the NPT as a denuclearized member in good standing.

The progress to date in nuclear arms control and disarmament is more in the nature of correcting the excesses of the Cold War – an end to nuclear testing and the nuclear arms race and the dismantlement of the superfluous nuclear stockpiles.[23] Agenda and attention need to refocus on future challenges: the universalization of the ban on intermediate range nuclear forces; the incorporation of all nuclear-armed states into the strategic arms reduction negotiations and treaties; the extension of the nuclear arms control normative architecture to non-state actors; and a critical debate on nuclear doctrines and postures. Three specific examples are to take nuclear weapons off high-alert status, universalize no first use policy and emphasize the humanitarian dimensions of the nuclear debate.

Launch alert status

A good example of a Cold War nuclear legacy posture is weapons held on high alert. Historically, alert levels of US and Soviet/Russian nuclear weapons systems have varied with changes in the overall security environment, the deployment patterns of the adversary, fiscal elasticity and political pressures. At present, Russia and the United States keep about 1,000 warheads each on high alert, with the posture dictated by the approximately 30-minute flight time of a putative enemy missile.[24] In a conversation on 29 March 2012, Zbiegniew Brzezinski noted that as National Security Adviser to President Jimmy Carter (1977–81), he had indeed once been woken up by a call at the now proverbial time of 3.00 a.m. from his military assistant, a general, telling him that the United States was 'under nuclear attack,' with 200 Soviet missiles having been fired '30 seconds ago' that would hit the United States in a little over 30 minutes. He had three minutes in which to notify the president, who would have had four minutes in which to decide how to respond. With two minutes left, the alarm was shown to be false and Brzezinski did not have to notify the president but informed him of the incident the next morning.[25] What if the confirmation had come: a) after the initial three minutes, b) after seven minutes and the president had ordered the launch of US missiles, or c) after 30 minutes as the US missiles were about to hit Soviet targets?

US officials contest the view that current launch status is 'dangerously high', arguing that a prudent balance has been struck between the survivability of nuclear forces and the capacity to implement a legal order from the proper command authority. The United States has combined a launch posture that safeguards against unauthorized launch of ICBMs with procedures that allow for rapid re-targeting and launch of strategic forces after a valid order is received from the national command authority. But taking nuclear warheads and weapons systems off high alert can deepen the stability of nuclear deterrence so that nuclear-armed rivals will not attack each other regardless of any rise in tension between them. Like nuclear terrorism, the launch of nuclear weapons on high alert by mistake, miscalculation or through a malfunction is low probability but high impact. In the tense environment of nuclear decision-making, high-alert weapons carry a four-fold risk of unnecessary nuclear war:

- Accidental launch (technical failure caused by malfunction);
- Authority to launch being usurped by a subordinate official or by terrorists (custody failure leading to rogue launch). Although the least likely, the risk of unauthorized use increases in the middle of a crisis dispersion of nuclear weapons and in the case of countries like Pakistan, whose organizational and technical safeguards may be brittle rather than robust;[26]
- Misinterpretation of incoming warning data (information failure leading to miscalculation);
- Premature and ill-judged response to an actual attack (miscalculation caused by decision-making failure in a crisis).

Conversely, anything that lengthens the decision-making fuse such that there is a significant extension of the timeline – from the first report of an incoming threat, to a decision to use a nuclear weapon, then the actual launch of the weapon – can only add to the existing tight margins of security from nuclear weapons. By moving to retaliatory strike postures, de-alerting is a strategic step in downgrading the military role of nuclear weapons.[27] It is also a necessary step in transforming relations between nuclear adversaries from one of strategic confrontation to strategic collaboration. It confirms the now generally assumed status of nuclear weapons as weapons of last resort. There is also a moral hazard argument. Indefinite reliance on nuclear weapons on short notice alert can legitimize the nuclear ambitions of others. There is thus a nonproliferation as well as a disarmament and crisis stability argument for de-alerting. And reducing alert status is a confidence-building measure not just among NWS but also between them and non-NWS.

No first use

In Chapter 8 we saw how the nuclear stability/instability paradox has permitted Pakistan to engage in greater conventional adventurism through military incursions and terrorist proxies than would not have been possible without the subcontinent's nuclearization. An analogous paradox concerns the intent to be the first to use nuclear weapons. If the adversary is a non-NWS, the use of nuclear weapons would exact too heavy a moral and political price for the threat to be credible. This explains why Argentina invaded the Falkland Islands in 1982 despite the British nuclear deterrent: it was confident that the United Kingdom would not escalate to the use of nuclear weapons. If the adversary is nuclear armed and has credible second-strike retaliatory capability, then too a first-use posture is not credible, as its execution would inflict unacceptable damage on the initiator of nuclear hostilities; a military defeat is always preferable to national annihilation. It would also put the full weight of world moral opprobrium on the side using nuclear weapons first.

The only rational strategy is to threaten but not actually to use nuclear weapons first. But if carrying out the threat would be national suicide, then the threat cannot be credible. And a non-credible threat cannot deter. Thus what is important is not a first-use policy but credible second-strike capability. Once that is attained, a no first use policy, backed by appropriate nuclear force posture and deployment patterns, is a critical step back from nuclear brinksmanship while shifting the onus of nuclear escalation on the adversary. Furthermore, a no first use policy avoids the need for forward deployment, launch on warning postures and pre-delegation of authority to battlefield commanders, thereby significantly dampening the prospects of accidental and unauthorized use. A no first use policy also counteracts crisis instability in that it reduces the pressure on decision-makers to 'use or lose' their nuclear arsenal. The incentive and temptation to use nuclear weapons pre-emptively are lessened. It is simplistic, therefore, to dismiss no first use as merely declaratory, easily ignored in wartime. A universal no first use policy by all the nuclear armed states would have considerable practical import with flow-on requirements for nuclear force posture and deployment, for example, de-alerting, de-mating and de-targeting. In turn this would reduce trust deficits and promote confidence building while strengthening the norm of non-use of nuclear weapons

Humanitarian dimensions

The most productive way forward for committed states and nongovernmental organizations (NGOs) to generate political momentum for the nuclear disarmament cause may be to emphasize the catastrophic humanitarian consequences of any use of nuclear weapons. The Ottawa convention banned antipersonnel landmines as a result of a coalition of NGOs and like-minded civic governments highlighting its humanitarian consequences over its military utility.[28] The almost indescribable horror associated with any such use informed the very first resolution of the UN General Assembly in 1946 and has been a recurring campaign theme ever since. It was the primary motivation for the challenge to the legality of nuclear weapons mounted in the ICJ by the UN General Assembly on the initiative of the World Health Organization, which resulted in the 1996 Advisory Opinion concluding that their use was indefensible except, possibly, in self-defence when a state's very survival was at stake.[29]

Recently, the humanitarian dimension has resumed prominence in high-level state discourse. In the 2012 NPT PrepCom, sixteen countries issued a joint statement arguing that 'it is essential that the humanitarian consequences of nuclear weapons are thoroughly addressed'.[30] A key message from the inaugural humanitarian consequences conference held in Oslo in March 2013 was that no country or international body has the capacity to address the immediate humanitarian emergency caused by a nuclear weapon detonation or provide adequate assistance to victims. The second conference was held in Nayarit, Mexico, on 13–14 February 2014 with 127 states represented, and Austria is scheduled to host the third in late 2014. India and Pakistan attended the Nayarit conference from among the nuclear-armed states. But all five NWS boycotted both the first and second, with Washington being more progressive in its own views on the matter but unwilling to break P5 solidarity.[31] Many allies sheltering under extended nuclear deterrence have attended but pressed for engagement with the NWS and dilution of the humanitarian impact statements. The NWS allies are far more forceful and robust in protesting the risks of nuclear nonproliferation and markedly more timid in demanding concrete disarmament from their protectors. Building on a cohesive and growing partnership between civil society organizations and like-minded states, the momentum building up behind the humanitarian impact movement is proving to be embarrassing to them and a diplomatic irritant to the NWS.

Restarting the stalled nuclear disarmament agenda

All parties need to accept the interrelationship between the different NPT pillars. A lack of progress on disarmament makes it more challenging to hold the line on nonproliferation, while any additional or suspected instance of proliferation makes progress on disarmament more difficult. The NPT has been shown to have congenital defects, built-in flaws, ripening contradictions and increasing fragility. The broader NPT regime also remains incomplete, for example with respect to the formal entry into force of the CTBT and the negotiation of a fissile materials cut-off treaty (FMCT). The net result is that the NPT may no longer be fit for the purpose of achieving global denuclearization, and a failure to promote nuclear disarmament could jeopardize its accomplishments on nuclear nonproliferation and peaceful uses of nuclear energy.

Nuclear weapons are the common enemy of humanity. Like chemical and biological weapons of mass destruction, nuclear weapons too cannot be disinvented. But like them, nuclear weapons too can be controlled, regulated, restricted and outlawed under an international regime that ensures strict compliance through effective and credible inspection and verification. Japan is the *emotional* touchstone in the discourse as the world's only victim of the bomb. The *circuit breaker* in the countervailing nuclear weapons capability spiral is the United States. It has a special responsibility to light the way to nuclear abolition as the only country to have used them and as the world's biggest military power. If its case to retain the bomb is persuasive, then by all objective analysis it should be even more persuasive for those countries that live in insecure neighbourhoods and lack the panoply of conventional military tools, underpinned by technological primacy, available to Washington. By destroying its nuclear stockpile, Washington would prove that national security and foreign policy autonomy can be safeguarded without nuclear weapons capability.

New START permits the United States and Russia to deploy up to 1,550 strategic nuclear warheads aboard 700 or fewer launchers, distributed between land, sea and air platforms. Consistent with these limits, the two countries' planned deployment of strategic warheads in 2020 are shown in Table 14.1. These numbers are far surplus to requirements. In 2010, Col. B. Chance Saltzman, chief of Strategic Plan and Policy Division at USAF headquarters and colleagues – who do *not* believe in nuclear elimination – came to the dramatic conclusion that the United States can meet all its national security and extended deterrence requirements with just 311 nuclear weapons: 192 single warheads, hard to detect and highly survivable and accurate SLBMs aboard 12 Ohio class submarines, each of which can hold 24 missiles; 100 single-warhead ICBMs; and 19 air-launched cruise missiles aboard stealth B-2 bombers.[32] Whether Russia followed suit or not is irrelevant. Even a substantial numerical superiority is of no military-operational consequence, although it could have political-psychological effects.

Conversely, the spread of nuclear weapons to other countries would erode the United State's primacy as the world's dominant power and multiply the number of potential trouble spots where it might be required to intervene. A zero option

Table 14.1 Planned nuclear warhead deployments in 2020

	Russia	*United States*
ICBMs	542	420
SLBMs	640	1090
Bombers	76	40

Source: Joseph Cirincione, *Nuclear Nightmares: Securing the World before It Is Too Late* (New York: Columbia University Press, 2013), 115.

that destroyed the infrastructure of the nuclear weapons industry would be far easier to police even against non-state groups. The best way to keep nasty weapons out of the hands of nasty groups is to keep them out of the hands of governments, including good governments. What we need is a multi-phased roadmap to abolition that prioritizes concrete immediate steps in the first few years, like introducing more robust firewalls to separate possession from use of nuclear weapons; further significant cuts in existing nuclear arsenals and a freeze on production of fissile materials in the medium term; further constraints on the deployment of their nuclear weapons on the territories of other states, for example by means of regional NWFZs; and an NWC that requires total and verified destruction of all nuclear stockpiles within our lifetime.

Implementing Article 6 instead of dusting it off occasionally as a rhetorical concession would dramatically transform the NPT from a nonproliferation into a prohibition regime. That is both its attraction and its fatal flaw. Because the NPT has become a de facto nonproliferation regime, the time has come to look beyond it to a cleaner alternative that gathers all the meritorious elements into one workable package in a universal, non-discriminatory, verifiable and enforceable NWC that bans the possession, acquisition, deployment, testing, transfer and use of nuclear weapons by everyone, backed by a criminalization of these activities in domestic law. This will not self-materialize merely because we wish it so. Nuclear abolition is both desirable and feasible. But there are many technical (with respect to verification), legal and political challenges to be overcome. However, nor will it ever eventuate if we always push it to a distant future. Serious preparatory work on it needs to be started now, with conviction and commitment.

Those who worship the most devoutly at the altar of nuclear weapons issue the fiercest fatwas against others rushing to join them. The most powerful stimulus to nuclear proliferation by others is the continuing possession of the bomb by some. Supporters argue 'that it's just like a home-insurance policy – your house will probably never burn down, but would you rather not have the policy?'[33] Except that *everyone* should have a house insurance policy and governments advise citizens to that effect. It is difficult to convince others of the *futility* of nuclear weapons when all who have them prove their continuing *utility* by insisting on keeping them. The threat to use nuclear weapons, whether to deter their use by others or to prevent proliferation, legitimizes their possession, deployment and use. That which is legitimate cannot be stopped from proliferating. Hence the axiom of nonproliferation: as long as any one has them, others, including terrorists, will try their best (and worst) to get them. Strengthening the original NPT nonproliferation–disarmament linkage, and implementing both with equal commitment, would be a win-win outcome for national and international security.

Those who dismiss this as naive – a utopian dream – must confront a stark reality. In the real world, the only choice is between nuclear abolition or cascading proliferation with several countries acquiring nuclear weapons. The notion, that a self-selecting group of five countries can keep an indefinite monopoly on the most destructive class of weapons ever invented, defies logic, common sense and all human history. Critics of the zero option want to keep their bombs but deny them to others. They lack the intellectual honesty and courage to show how nonproliferation can be enforced without disarmament, to acknowledge that the price of keeping nuclear arsenals is uncontrolled proliferation and to argue why a world of uncontrolled proliferation is better for national and international security than abolition. They refuse to openly acknowledge their preference for a world of uncontrolled proliferation over total elimination for fear of well-deserved opprobrium for such a counsel of despair.

The NPT's anomalies and flaws mean we need to look beyond and perhaps outside the treaty to realize the goal of nuclear elimination. But its very real, substantial and continuing contributions to international security mean we must not jeopardize it until we are ready to replace it with a better regime. In the journey to a post-NPT world in which all nuclear weapons have been eliminated and their associated infrastructure has been destroyed under a universal and verifiable NWC, we have to guard against two critical risks in particular. First, at present a significant number of countries (such as NATO members, as well as Australia, Japan, South Korea and others) shelter under the US nuclear umbrella to meet their perceived national security needs. With any hasty or premature dismantlement of the US nuclear stockpile, one or more of them could be tempted to break out and acquire an independent nuclear weapons capability. Second, in moving towards a world without nuclear weapons, we have to make sure that we do not tip back into a world that is safe once again for major power conventional wars like the First and Second World Wars.

As part of a forward-looking agenda, the **United States and Russia** could initiate negotiations for a new treaty to reduce stockpile numbers for all classes of weapons, significantly cut back on their 2,000 warheads held in high-alert status, embrace the principle of 'no first use' in their nuclear doctrines, and perhaps resurrect their draft treaty from the late 1970s to prohibit the development, production, stockpiling and use of radiological weapons ('dirty bombs').[34] **Washington** could also address Chinese and Russian concerns about ballistic missile defence and prompt global strike capabilities. The **United States, China, India and Pakistan** could move to rapid ratification of the CTBT, with the last three not holding their ratification conditional to the United States. **China, India and Pakistan** could freeze their nuclear capabilities at present levels and Pakistan could helpfully lift its veto on negotiations for an FMCT. **India and Pakistan** should avoid destabilizing steps like the development of battlefield tactical nuclear weapons and missile defences. **North Korea** could freeze its nuclear arsenal; not conduct any more tests; refrain from quality upgrades in the sophistication of its bombs; and not export nuclear or missile material, components or technology. Finally, **US allies** could accept a significantly reduced role for nuclear weapons in their security protection, in particular by accepting and clearly stating support for the United States declaring that so long as nuclear weapons exist, the 'sole purpose' of its nuclear weapons is to deter their use by others. None of these steps would jeopardize the national security of the country concerned; each would make the world a little bit safer for all of us; all together collectively would make the whole world much safer for everyone.

Conclusion

This book has demonstrated the essentially irrational instrumentality of nuclear weapons in numerous ways. The case for nuclear abolition is simple, elegant and eloquent. Without strengthening national security, nuclear weapons diminish our common humanity and impoverish our soul. Their very destructiveness robs them of military utility against other nuclear powers and of political utility against non-nuclear countries. As long as any country has any, others will want some. As long as they exist, they will be used one day again by design, accident or miscalculation. We must make the transition from a world in which the role of nuclear weapons is seen as central to maintaining national and international security, to one where they become progressively marginal and eventually unnecessary.

The barriers against the acquisition, spread and use of nuclear weapons include legal conventions, norms and the fact of their non-use for 70 years. But the focus on nonproliferation to the neglect of disarmament ensures that we get neither. The problem is not nuclear proliferation, but nuclear weapons. They could not proliferate if they did not exist. Because they do, they will. The very fact of their existence in the arsenals of nine countries is *sufficient guarantee* of their proliferation to others and, some day again, use. Conversely, nuclear disarmament is *a necessary condition* of nuclear nonproliferation. The policy implication of this logic is that the best guarantee of nuclear nonproliferation is nuclear disarmament. If we want nonproliferation, we must prepare for disarmament.

Confronted with a world we cannot change, reasonable men and women adapt their behaviour to the real world. But the turning points in history have come from the efforts of those visionaries who set themselves to change the world instead, from Gautam Buddha to Jesus Christ, Mahatma Gandhi and Nelson Mandela. The walk to freedom from fear of nuclear weapons may prove to be very long indeed, but we must neither step off the path nor stop short of the destination. Within our lifetime, either we aim for controlled nuclear reduction and abolition or we learn to live with slow but certain nuclear proliferation and die with the use of nuclear weapons.

Notes

1 Ira Helfand, *Nuclear Famine: A Billion People at Risk – Global Impacts of Limited Nuclear War on Agriculture, Food Supplies, and Human Nutrition* (Somerville, MA: International Physicians for the Prevention of Nuclear War, April 2012), http://www.ippnw.org/nuclear-famine.html.
2 See Martin E. Hellman, 'How risky is nuclear optimism?' *Bulletin of the Atomic Scientists* 67:2 (2011): 47–56.
3 Eric Schlosser, *Command and Control* (London: Allen Lane, 2013), 327. See also Patricia Lewis, Heather Williams, Benoit Pelopidas and Sasan Aghlani, *Too Close for Comfort* (London: Chatham House, 2013), http://www.sre.gob.mx/en/images/stories/cih/chathamhouse.pdf.
4 Eric Schlosser, 'Nuclear weapons: an accident waiting to happen', *Guardian*, 14 September 2013.
5 Ed Pilkington, 'US nearly detonated atomic bomb over North Carolina – secret document', *Guardian*, 21 September 2013.

232 *The nuclear regime*

6. Robert McNamara, 'The Conference on Disarmament should focus on steps to move toward a "Nuclear Free World"', *Disarmament Diplomacy* 4 (April 1996), http://www.acronym.org.uk/dd/dd04/index.htm#T-0023.
7. Nate Jones, 'Countdown to declassification: Finding answers to a 1983 nuclear war scare', *Bulletin of the Atomic Scientists* 69:6 (2013), 47–57; 'How Nato war games took the world to the brink of nuclear holocaust in 1983', *Mail on Sunday*, 3 November 2013.
8. Joseph Cirincione, *Nuclear Nightmares: Securing the World before It Is Too Late* (New York: Columbia University Press, 2013), 53.
9. Ibid., 55.
10. Gareth Evans, 'Nuclear Deterrence in Asia and the Pacific', *Asia & the Pacific Policy Studies* 1:1 (2014): 91–111.
11. Ward Wilson, *Five Myths about Nuclear Weapons* (New York: Houghton Mifflin Harcourt, 2013); James E. Doyle, 'Why Eliminate Nuclear Weapons?' *Survival* 55:1 (2013): 7–34. The last article has an interesting sequel. Doyle was working as a political scientist at the Los Alamos National Laboratory at the time he published the article, the thrust of which is to embrace President Obama's vision of a nuclear-weapon-free future. He was fired on 8 July 2014, ostensibly for having revealed classified information, even though the article had been pre-cleared for publication by the laboratory authorities. There is reason to believe he was dismissed for questioning the laboratory's central mission of continued development and production of nuclear arms at an annual cost of almost $2 billion. That is, in effect he was fired for supporting the president's policy. See Douglas Birch, 'Fired from Los Alamos for pushing Obama's nuclear agenda', *Daily Beast*, 31 July 2014, http://www.thedailybeast.com/articles/2014/07/31/fired-from-los-alamos-for-pushing-obama-s-nuclear-agenda.html.
12. Kenneth N. Waltz, *The Spread of Nuclear Weapons: More May Be Better* (London: International Institute for Strategic Studies, Adelphi Paper 171, 1981), and 'Why Iran Should Get the Bomb', *Foreign Affairs* 91:4 (2012): 2–5.
13. See the reference to Gaddafi's fate by Ayatollah Ali Khamenei in Chapter 10.
14. The two parts of the story are told well in Richard Rhodes, *Arsenals of Folly: The Making of the Nuclear Arms Race* (New York: Knopf, 2007) and Jonathan Schell, *The Seventh Decade: The New Shape of Nuclear Danger* (New York: Metropolitan, 2007).
15. Cirincione, *Nuclear Nightmares*, 40.
16. See in particular Ramesh Thakur and Gareth Evans, eds., *Nuclear Weapons: The State of Play* (Canberra: Centre for Nuclear Non-Proliferation and Disarmament, 2013).
17. See Wade L. Huntley, 'Nuclear Threat Reliance in East Asia', in Waheguru Pal Singh Sidhu and Ramesh Thakur, eds, *Arms Control After Iraq: Normative and Operational Challenges* (Tokyo: United Nations University Press, 2006): 181–99.
18. George P. Shultz, William J. Perry, Henry Kissinger, and Sam Nunn: 'A world free of nuclear weapons', 4 January 2007; 'Toward a nuclear free world', 15 January 2008; 'How to Protect Our Nuclear Deterrent', 19 January 2010; 'Deterrence in the age of nuclear proliferation', 7 March 2011; and 'Next steps in reducing nuclear risks', 5 March 2013.
19. Elisabeth Braw, 'After Ukraine, countries that border Russia start thinking about nuclear deterrents', *Newsweek*, 15 April 2014, http://www.newsweek.com/2014/04/25/after-ukraine-countries-border-russia-start-thinking-about-nuclear-deterrents-248133.html; Walter Russel Mead, 'Putin invades Crimea: Obama hardest hit?', *The American Interest*, 3 March 2014, http://www.the-american-interest.com/wrm/2014/03/03/putin-invades-crimea-obama-hardest-hit/. Many recalled a two-decade old article: John J. Mearsheimer, 'The Case for a Ukrainian Nuclear Deterrent', *Foreign Affairs* 72:3 (1993): 50–66.
20. See Ramesh Thakur, 'Why Crimea is vital to Russia', *Tribune* (Chandigarh), 12 March 2014, and 'Geopolitics through the Ukrainian looking glass', *Tehelka Magazine* (Delhi), 11:19 (10 May 2014): 38–41.
21. In August 2014, one of the most expansive collaborations ever envisaged between US and Russian scientists, including reciprocal visits to one another's nuclear sites, was

aborted just eleven months after the accord was signed. David E. Sanger and William J. Broad, 'U.S.–Russia nuclear deal stalls as tensions over Ukraine rise', *New York Times*, 2 August 2014, http://www.nytimes.com/2014/08/03/world/europe/us-nuclear-deal-with-russia-fails-as-tensions-rise.html?_r=0.

22 See Tom Sauer, 'Ukraine shows uselessness of NATO nukes in Europe', *Bulletin of the Atomic Scientists*, 23 June 2014, http://thebulletin.org/ukraine-shows-uselessness-nato-nukes-europe7257.

23 Camille Grand, 'The Current Deadlock in Nuclear Arms Control: A Difficult Mutation to a New Era?' *Disarmament Diplomacy* 34 (February 1999), 10.

24 James Cartwright et al., *Modernizing U.S. Nuclear Strategy, Force Structure and Posture*. Global Zero US Nuclear Policy Commission Report (Washington, DC: Global Zero, 2012), 5; http://www.nytimes.com/2014/08/03/world/europe/us-nuclear-deal-with-russia-fails; http://www.globalzero.org/en/us-nuclear-policy-commission-report.

25 Council on Foreign Relations, transcript, 'A Conversation with Zbigniew Brzezinski', http://www.cfr.org/us-strategy-and-politics/conversation-zbigniew-brzezinski/p27829.

26 Cartwright et al., *Modernizing U.S. Nuclear Strategy, Force Structure and Posture*, 5.

27 Department of Foreign Affairs, Switzerland, East–West Institute, and Ministry of Foreign Affairs, New Zealand, *Re-framing Nuclear De-Alert: Decreasing the Operational Readiness of U.S. and Russian Arsenals* (New York: East–West Institute, 2009), 15.

28 See Ramesh Thakur and William Maley, 'The Ottawa Convention on Landmines: A Landmark Humanitarian Treaty in Arms Control?' *Global Governance* 5:3 (1999): 273–302.

29 In April 2014, the tiny Republic of the Marshall Islands, site of 67 nuclear tests from 1946–58, lodged nine separate lawsuits in the ICJ against all nuclear-armed states, claiming their failure to eliminate their nuclear arsenals was in material breach of the NPT in the case of the five NWS and customary international law in the case of the four non-NPT nuclear-armed states; http://www.icj-cij.org/presscom/files/0/18300.pdf. Regardless of eventual success or failure, the 'lawsuit accentuates the rise of a new kind of politics of nuclear disarmament, a politics that ties nuclear disarmament to humanitarian issues'; Avner Cohen and Lily Vaccaro, 'The import of the Marshall Islands nuclear lawsuit', *Bulletin of the Atomic Scientists*, 6 May 2014, http://thebulletin.org/import-marshall-islands-nuclear-lawsuit7143.

30 'Joint Statement on the humanitarian dimension of nuclear disarmament' (New York: 22 October 2012), available at: http://www.psr.org/resources/joint-statement-on-the.html.

31 See William C. Potter and Benjamin Pack, 'Advancing nuclear disarmament: The US role', APLN/CNND *Policy Brief* No. 10 (Canberra: Asia Pacific Leadership Network and Centre for Nuclear Non-Proliferation and Disarmament, March 2014), 5–6.

32 James Wood Forsyth, B. Chance Saltzman, and Gary Schaub, 'Remembrance of things past: The enduring value of nuclear weapons', *Strategic Studies Quarterly* 1 (Spring 2010): 74–89, at 82–83.

33 Michael Bilton, 'Dive bombers (Britain's Trident nuclear submarines)', *Sunday Times*, 20 January 2008.

34 Potter and Pack, 'Advancing nuclear disarmament: The US role', 8.

Index

Able Archer exercise 218
Acronym Institute 30
Advani, Lal Krishna 96
Afghanistan 152, 156, 218; and Soviet Union 28, 43, 49, 87, 94, 111; and US 94, 99, 148, 150
African Commission on Nuclear Energy (AFCONE) 171–2
Agency for the Prohibition of Nuclear Weapons in Latin America and the Caribbean (OPANAL) 171
Ahmadinejad, Mahmoud 156
Alamagordo Air Base, New Mexico 4
Albright, Madeleine 196
alert status 224–6
Algeria 65
All India Congress Committee 79
Amano, Yukiya 147–8, 150
Amnesty International 75
Andaman and Nicobar Islands 174
Angola 49
Annan, Kofi xx, 183, 192–3
Antarctic Treaty (1959) 5, 83, 164
Anti-Ballistic Missile Treaty (ABM) 4
Argentina 87, 127, 173–4, 223, 226
arms control 52, 220; arms race 46–9, 81, 120; Carter administration policies 49–50; confidence building measure 47, 178–9; disarmament 83–4, 134–5, 186–8, 194, 224; India 91, 110, 125; NPT 78, 183, 191, 211; nuclear technology 47, 48; NWFZ 166–7, 170, 174; publications 30; Reagan administration policies 49; reverses 54–5; UN 32
Arms Control Association 205
Arms Control Today 30
ASEAN Regional Forum (ARF) 31–2, 61, 102
Asia Society 99

Asplund, John 26
Association of Southeast Asian Nations (ASEAN) 31, 72, 102, 130, 167
Atomic Energy Commission (AEC) 4, 93, 103, 105
Auschwitz xxi
Australia 125–38, 171; ASEAN 72; Australian Labor Party (ALP) 125–6, 128, 133; China 126–7, 130–2, 137; CTBT 70; Department of Foreign Affairs and Trade 31; French nuclear testing 71–3; Green Party; India 124, 130–2; Indonesia 72–3, 130; Japan 130, 132; National Consultative Committee on Peace and Disarmament 32; New Zealand 130; Papua New Guinea 130; South Korea 211; SPNFZ 171; uranium policy 124, 126–8, 132–7; US 127
Australia–Indonesia Timor Gap Treaty 73
Australia, New Zealand, United States Security Treaty (ANZUS) 71
Australian National University 23, 31
Australian Strategic Policy Institute (ASPI) 23

Bajpai, Kanti 82
ballistic missile submarine (SSBN) 5, 7, 11, 228
Bangkok, Treaty of 164–5, 168, 171–2, 174
Bangladesh War 117
Baruch Plan 4
Beg, Mirza Aslam 80
Begin, Menachem 8
Belarus 87, 185
Bell, Robert 68, 70
Bhagvad Gita 109
Bharatiya Janata Party (BJP) 83, 86, 93–5
Bhutto, Benazir 96

Index

Bhutto, Zulfikar Ali 93
Biological Weapons Convention (BWC) 47
Blix, Hans 150
Bolger, Jim 73
Bonn International Center for Conversion (BICC) 27
Bosnia 129
Brazil 87, 108n45, 177, 183, 212
Brent Spar 74
BRICS (Brazil, Russia, India, China, South Africa) 112, 201, 212
Brzezinski, Zbigniew 49, 225
Buchenwald xxi
Budapest Memorandum (1994) 224
Buddha, Gautam 51, 231
Bulletin of Atomic Scientists 30
Bush, George H. W. 191
Bush, George W. 5, 94, 117, 134, 141, 154, 186, 189–91, 203
Butfoy, Andy 130

Canada Deuterium Uranium (CANDU) 80
Canberra Commission on the Elimination of Nuclear Weapons 28, 98
Carle, Christophe 32
Carlucci, Frank 196
Carnegie Endowment for International Peace 188
Carnegie–Tsinghua Center for Global Policy 145
Carr, Bob 128
Carter, Jimmy 49, 225
Cartwright, James 14
Catholic Bishops of America 36–7
Central America 49
Central Intelligence Agency (CIA) 97
Centre for Strategic and International Studies, Jakarta 31
Chagos Archipelago 173
Chander, Avinash 120
Chari, P. R. 116
Chechnya 55
Chellaney, Brahma 89
Chemical Weapons Convention (CWC) 31–2, 91
Cheonan 143
Chernobyl 12
Chidambaram, Rajagopala 103, 105
Chile 74
China 5–6; CTBT 70; ICBM 5; India 93, 96–100, 105, 111–3, 115–16, 119–20; Japan 58, 145–6; Kosovo 57; MIRV 5; no first use 6; North Korea 145–6; NWFZ Protocols 165, 169, 175; Pakistan 94, 96–7, 99, 115, 135; Second Artillery Force 5; South China Sea 128; South Korea 145–6; US 49
China–UN arms control conference (2002) 32
Chirac, Jacques 65, 68–9, 71–3
Christ, Jesus 51, 231
Christopher, Warren 196
Churchill, Winston 61
Cirincione, Joseph 193, 220
Clapper, James 149
climate change 126, 207
Clinton, Hillary R. 186
Clinton, William J. 53, 58, 70, 96, 111, 141
Cohen, Stephen 32
Cold Start 114, 119
command, control, communications and intelligence (C3I) 100–1
Commission for Southeast Asian NWFZ 171
Commonwealth Games 118
Commonwealth Heads of Government Meeting (CHOGM) 73
compellence 111
Comprehensive Nuclear Test Ban Treaty (CTBT) 29, 56, 59, 69–73, 170, 172, 182–3, 219–20; arms race, end to 5; entry into force 192, 227, 230; France 69, 75; India 7, 52, 56, 76, 78–9, 82–7, 95–6, 103–5, 110, 131; Preparatory Commission for the CTBT Organization (CTBTO) 29; US 12, 51, 56, 193
Conference on Disarmament (CD) 29, 55, 70–1, 84–5, 182, 184
Convention on the Physical Protection of Nuclear Material (CPPNM) 201–2, 205, 208
Cote-Harper, Giselle 28
credible minimum deterrence 7, 9–10, 56, 112, 115–17
Crimea 222–4
Cuba 49, 78, 170, 175, 218
Cuban Missile Crisis 47, 170, 175, 218

Daalder, Ivo 2
Danilenko, Vyacheslav 151
de Klerk, F. W. 87, 106
d'Estaing, Valery Giscard 69
Degelen Mountain 213
Democratic People's Republic of Korea (DPRK) *see* North Korea
Deng, Francis 26

Dera Ghazi Khan 199
detente 22, 48–9
deterrence 112–16
Dhammapada xxi
Dhanapala, Jayantha 28, 166
Diego Garcia 173–4
diplomacy, modes of 31
Disarmament Diplomacy 30
disarmament dividend approach 39
Disarmament Forum 30
Donowaki, Mitsuro 81
Downer, Alexander 85
Doyle, James E. 232
Doyle, Michael 26

Egypt 69, 83, 108n45, 196
Eisenhower, Dwight D. 187
ElBaradei, Mohamed 13, 147–50
empirical information on armaments 27
Eshkol, Levi 8
Ethiopia 49, 102
European Atomic Energy Community (EURATOM) 172, 202
Evans, Gareth 71, 130, 218

Falk, Richard 28
Falkland Islands 173, 223, 226
Fangataufa 65
Federated States of Micronesia (FSM) 168
Federation of American Scientists 199
Financial Times 30
Findlay, Trevor 32, 215
Ferguson, Charles 199
Ferguson, Martin 128
fissile material cut-off treaty (FMCT) 5, 29, 135, 182, 184, 192, 228, 230
Fissile Materials Working Group (FMWG) 209
Foreign Affairs 30
Foreign Policy 30
France 6, 65–75; Algeria 65; CTBT 69–71, 75; Greenpeace 74–5; nuclear testing 65–9; NWFZ Protocols 76n1, 165; *Rainbow Warrior* 69; White Paper (2008) 6
Frankfurt Peace Research Institute 32
Fraser, Malcolm 126, 130, 136
Fukushima 13, 137

G-8 96, 203, 212
G-20 118, 201, 207, 212
G-77 74
Gaddafi, Muammar 144, 148, 219
Gandhi, Indira 79, 95, 116

Gandhi, M. K. (Mahatma) 51, 231
Gandhi, Rajiv 95, 120–1
Gates, Robert M. 106n7
Germany 23, 31, 56, 72, 89–90, 117, 153, 193, 221
Ghose, Arundhati 122
Gillard, Julia 125, 128–30, 133, 211
Gingrich, Newt 107n29
Global Gender Gap Index 118
Global Initiative to Combat Nuclear Terrorism 203
Global Partnership Against the Spread of Weapons and Materials of Mass Destruction 203
Global Slavery Index 118
Global Zero 13–4, 222
Gorbachev, Mikhail 4, 191
Greenpeace 74–5
Gregory, Shaun 115
Grenada 49
Group of Scientific Experts 29
Guantánamo 175
Gujral, I. K. 95
Gujral doctrine 91

Hagel, Chuck 14
Hague Peace Conference (1899) 4
Hamre, John J. 196n30
Hanson, Marianne 130
Harvard Nuclear Study Group 43–4
Hersh, Seymour 94, 149
hibakusha xx–xxii
highly enriched uranium (HEU) 7, 142, 155, 200, 203, 206, 210, 212
Hinderstein, Corey 206
Hiroshima xx–xxii, 4, 25, 37, 40–1, 69, 217
Hoffmann, Wolfgang 84
Holum, John D. 70
Howard, John 126–7, 129, 190
humanitarian impacts of nuclear war 227
human security 24, 99
Hyun Hak-bong 195n14

Ignatieff, Michael 26, 28
India 6–7, 78–91, 93–106, 109–21; Archaeological Survey of India 118; arguments for weaponization 112, 113; *Arihant* 110; Australia 126–7, 130; Canada 80; *Chakra* 110; chemical weapons 91; China 93, 96–100, 105, 111–13, 115–16, 119–20; Cold Start doctrine 114, 119; costs of weaponization 81–2; credible minimum

deterrent 115–17; CTBT 7, 52, 56, 76, 78–9, 82–7, 95–6, 103–5, 110, 131; Defence Research and Development Organization (DRDO) 105, 117; Department of Atomic Energy 117; disarmament 83–4; fissile material production 7; HEU 7, 89; IAEA 127; India–US civil nuclear cooperation deal 2, 112, 117, 127, 136, 185, 190; international isolation 117, 118, 119; Japan 81, 102; National Crime Records Bureau 118; National Security Advisory Board 7; NPT 52, 82–3; nuclear ambiguity 88–9, 98; Nuclear Command Authority (NCA) 116; nuclear tests 95, 109; Operation Brass Tacks 94; Pakistan 93–101, 112–7; peaceful nuclear explosion 6, 80; Russia 112; Security Council permanent membership 83, 90, 98; Security Council Resolution 1172 105–6; status 117–19; US 80; *Vikrant* 110; warheads 3, 7, 145

intercontinental ballistic missiles (ICBMs) 4, 5, 9, 11–12, 47, 110, 217, 225, 228

Intergovernmental Panel on Climate Change (IPCC) 29

Intermediate Range Nuclear Forces Treaty (INF) 4, 78

International Atomic Energy Agency (IAEA) 4, 27, 93, 110, 134, 142, 144, 168, 171–3, 175, 207; Additional Protocol 66, 126, 187, 192, 219; Board of Governors 187; Code of Conduct on the Safety and Security of Radioactive Sources 202; INFCIRC/66 136; INFCIRC/153 136–7; INFCIRC/225/Revision 5 202, 211; INFCIRC/549, 214; Illicit Trafficking Database Programme 202; International Physical Protection Advisory Service (IPPAS) 202; Iran 147–56; nuclear fuel cycle 29, 171, 193, 200; nuclear security 198–201; Nuclear Security Recommendations on Physical Protection of Nuclear Material and Nuclear Facilities 211; Nuclear Security Series 202; Nuclear Technology Review 12; Office of Nuclear Security 203; politicization 150

International Campaign to Abolish Nuclear Weapons (ICAN) 136

International Commission on Nuclear Non-Proliferation and Disarmament (ICNND) 13–14, 28, 222

International Convention for the Suppression of Acts of Nuclear terrorism (ICSANT) 201, 205, 208

International Convention on Intervention and State Sovereignty (ICISS) 28

International Court of Justice (ICJ) 73–4, 105, 172, 220, 227

International Criminal Court (ICC) 59

International Herald Tribune 30

International Institute for Strategic Studies (IISS) 22, 27

International Monetary Fund (IMF) 82, 102

International Monitoring System 29

International Organization 30

International Peace Academy 32

International Physicians for the Prevention of Nuclear War (IPPNW) 29

International Security 30

International Studies Association 33

International Studies Quarterly 30

Iqhman, Atta M. 199

Iran 146–56; Geneva agreement 156; IAEA report (2011) 147–8; North Korea 142; nuclear weapons production 149; regional security complex 146; terrorism 152; threat perceptions 147–8; uranium enrichment 155; western response 150–3

Iraq 8, 149

Ireland 108n45

Israel 1–3, 7–8, 21, 27, 60, 69, 78, 134, 136, 147, 149; Iran 147, 151–2; Middle East NWFZ 169–70, 176, 180; nuclear ambiguity/opacity 7; Palestine 150; Samson Option 8

Italy 102, 194

Iyengar, P. K. 116

Japan: China 58, 145–6; emotional touchstone 56, 228; France 72–3; India 81, 102; non-nuclear principles 145; North Korea 142–3, 145; surge capacity 58; US xxi, 40, 58, 147

Jha, C. S. 92

Jinnah Institute 121

John Paul II, Pope 37

Kalam, Abdul 105, 116

Kargil war (1999) 119

Kashmir 24, 51, 53, 80, 84, 87, 95–6, 98–101, 108n32, 112–13

Kazakhstan 87, 127, 185, 212–13

Keating, Paul 74

Kelley, Robert 157n18
Kelly, Paul 128
Kennedy, John F. 1, 44, 45
Khamenei, Ayatollah Ali 148, 152
Khan, Abdul Qadeer 13, 27, 94
Khobragade, Devyani 118
Kim Il-sung 170
Kim Jong-il 143
Kim Jong-un 144
Kim Joong Keun 213
Kissinger, Henry 26, 190
Korean War 145
Kosovo 28, 55, 57, 129
Krasner, Stephen 26
Krauthammer, Charles 196
Krugman, Paul 30
Kuehne, Winrich 31

Laird, Melvin 196
Lakshadweep Islands 174
Lam, Willy Wo-lap 62
launch on warning 39, 46, 114, 116, 192, 226
League of Nations 4
Le Monde 75
Lewis, Patricia 32
Li Bin 6
Libya 27, 100, 148, 184, 188, 195n13, 219
Lodal, Jan 2
Los Alamos National Laboratory 232

McNamara, Robert 44–5
McNamara, Thomas E. 195
Mahmud of Ghazni 107n19
Malaysia 12
Mandela, Nelson 231
Manhattan Project 109
Marashi, Reza 150
Marschall, Peter 84
Marshall Islands 68, 168, 233
Martin, Paul 208
Mauritius 173
Medcalf, Rory 130
megatons-to-megawatts agreement 203
Menon, Raja 114
Mexico 69, 108n45
Meyer, Paul 212
Milosevic, Slobodan 57, 129
Mishra, Brajesh 116
missiles: Agni V 110; Agni VI 119; Brahmos 114; cruise 45, 47, 112, 183, 228; Ghauri 97; Nasr/Hatf-9 114; Pershing II 45, 49; SS-20 48; Titan II 217; Trident 10

Mitterrand, Francois 68
Mohan, C. Raja 123–4
Mongolia 127, 164, 179
Monterey Institute of International Studies 30, 32
Moon Agreement 164
Moonsamy, Gino 199
Morgenthau, Hans 129
Moruroa 65–8, 74–5
Mousavian, Hossein 154
Mueller, Harald 32
Muhhamad of Ghur 107
Murayama, Tomiichi 72
Musharraf, Pervez 188

N5 2, 53–6, 59, 148, 14–5, 187–8, 191, 193, 219
Nagasaki xviii, xx–xxi, 4, 25, 37, 40, 69
Nalanda 107n19
Namibia 127
Nayar, Kuldip 94
negative security assurances 92, 164–5, 175, 192
Nehru, Jawaharlal 4, 83, 95
Netanyahu, Binyamin 170
New START 9, 11, 217, 220, 222, 228
New York Times 30, 150
New Zealand 32, 65–6, 69–71, 108n45, 171
Newman, Andrew 206
Nicaragua 43, 49
Nishimura, Shingo 58
Nixon, Richard 180
no first use 116, 226; China 6; India 7, 105, 121, 135; Pakistan 113; Russia 183
Non-Aligned Movement (NAM) 80, 102–3, 150
Nonproliferation Review 30
North Atlantic Treaty Organization (NATO) 2, 45–6, 49, 191
North Korea 8, 15, 141–6; Agreed Framework (1994) 142; China 145–6; HEU 142; Iran 142; motivations 143–4; NPT 141–2; nuclear program and status 141–3; nuclear tests 15; Panel of Experts 142; Security Council Resolution 1718 142; Security Council Resolution 1874 142; Six Party Talks 29, 142, 184; solutions 144–5; Syria 142; Yongbyon reactor 142–3
nuclear abolition 58–60
nuclear first strike 42, 47, 100, 116
nuclear forensics 203
nuclear hedging 151–2

nuclear morality 36–40
Nuclear Nonproliferation Treaty (NPT) 1–2, 182–94, 219–21; Article 1 186–7; Article 2 186–7; Article 3 136–7, 187; Article 4 126, 136, 187; Article 6 104, 185–6, 229; Article 7 166; Australia 126–7; India 78–9, 82–3, 93, 110, 120; North Korea 141–2; Prepcom 57, 179, 227; regime change 182–94; Review Conference (1990) 81, 113; Review Conference (1995) 5, 31, 51, 53, 193; Review Conference (2000) 5, 57, 193, 220; Review Conference (2005) 141, 192, 220; Review Conference (2010) 2, 32, 179, 222
nuclear security 198–215; global governance architecture 201–4; Nuclear Security Summits 3, 12, 204, 212, 219
Nuclear Suppliers Group (NSG) 28, 117, 127; China 135; India 110, 127, 134, 137
Nuclear Threat Initiative (NTI) 204, 209
Nuclear Utilization Theories or Nuclear Utilization Target Selection (NUTS) 43–6
nuclear-weapon-free zones (NWFZ) 163–81; CBMs, as 177–8; Central Asian 58, 179; Central Europe 163; definition 163; geographic scope 173–4; limitations 175–8; membership 168–9; Middle East 148, 153, 156, 164, 167, 170, 176, 179–80; nature and goals 165–7; Northeast Asian 169; Protocols 164–6, 172–5, 179; regional initiatives 167–8; South Asian 164, 167–70, 174–6; South Pacific 164; Southeast Asian 171; treaty 168; verification 171–2
nuclear weapons convention (NWC) 105, 120, 135, 186, 217, 222, 229
Nunn–Lugar Soviet Nuclear Threat Reduction Act 4, 203

Obama, Barack 1, 5, 12, 151, 153, 198
Oppenheimer, Robert J. 109
opportunity costs 81, 101
Organization for the Prohibition of Chemical Weapons (OPCW) 27
Organization of African Unity (OAU) 167, 172
Organization of American States (OAS) 167, 172
Organization of Petroleum Exporting Countries (OPEC) 48
Osama bin Laden 9
Oslo accords 170

Oslo Conference (1997) 30
Oslo Conference on Nuclear Disarmament (2008) 34
Ottawa Convention on Landmines 59, 227
Outer Space Treaty 47, 164
Ozawa, Ichiro 185

P5+1 153
Pakistan 8–9; China 94, 96–7, 99, 115, 135; credible minimum deterrence 9, 112; India–Pakistan CBMs 112; ISI 199; managed instability 113; Minhas air force base 199; missiles 97, 114; nuclear doctrine 9; nuclear reactors 135; nuclear security 114; nuclear tests 8; Pakistan's People Party 96; US 199; warheads 3, 8–9
Palmerston, Lord 128, 134
Papua New Guinea 130
paradiplomacy 31
Park Geun-hye 157n14
Parsi, Trita 154
Parthasarathi, Ashok 116
Parthasarathy, G. 139n34
Partial Test Ban Treaty (PTBT) 5, 47, 183
Peace Research 22–5
Peace Research Centre, Canberra 28, 31
Peace Research Institute of Oslo (PRIO) 22
Pelindaba, Treaty of 87, 164–6, 168, 171, 173–4
Pelindaba nuclear research facility 198–9
Perkovich, George 88, 155
Permissive Action Link (PAL) 45
Perry, William 190
Pfaff, William 57
Philippines 74
Podvig, Pavel 214n28
Poland 163
Porter, Gareth 151, 154, 157n16
Portugal 73
positive security guarantees 79, 96
Powell, Colin 196
Proliferation Security Initiative (PSI) 28–9, 201
Public Advisory Committee on Disarmament and Arms Control (PACDAC) 32
Pugwash Conference 29
Putin, Vladimir 10

Rainbow Warrior 69
Raja Rao Ram Bux Singh fort 118
Rajaraman, R. 114

Rao, P. V. Narasimha 95
Rapacki, Adam 163–4
Rarotonga, Treaty of 58, 136–7, 164–6, 168, 172
Rasgotra, M. K. 80
Reagan, Ronald 4, 44, 46, 49
Reistad, Ole 206
Responsibility to Protect 206–7
Reynolds, P. A. 129
Rhodesia 102
Rice, Condoleezza 26
Robertson, Kalman A. 136–7
Rocard, Michel 72
Rothwell, Don 136
Rouhani, Hassan 153–4
Rudd, Kevin 127, 132
Ruggie, John 26
Rumsfeld, Donald 192
Russia 9–10; CTBT 71; Kosovo 55; New START 9, 11, 217, 220, 222, 228; NWFZ Protocols 165, 175; robust nuclear deterrent 10; warheads 3

Sachs, Jeffrey 26
Saddam Hussein 27, 129, 141, 144, 148–9, 187
Saltzman, Colonel B. Chance 228
Samson Option 8
sanctions 26, 53, 59, 71, 96, 98–9, 102–3, 109, 142, 144, 149, 153–5
Santhanam, K. 116
Santoro, David 210
Saran, Shyam 114, 124n66
Sarkar, Shobhan 118
Sarkozy, Nicolas 6
Sasaki, Sadako xxi
Saudi Arabia 154, 183
Scientific Research Institute of Technical Physics 151
Scindia, Madhavrao 79
Sea Bed Treaty 47, 164
Semipalatinsk 212
Sen, Amartya 26
Serbia 220
Shaker, Mohamed I. 196n29
Sharif, Nawaz 83, 96, 121
Sharma, Sheel Kant 124n66
Shell 74
Shultz, George 190
Singh, Jasjit 104
Singh, Jaswant 98
Singh, Manmohan 116, 118, 121, 127
Slaughter, Anne-Marie 26
Slovenia 108n45

Smith, Ian 102
Somnath 107n19
South Africa 87, 108n45
South Asian Association for Regional Cooperation (SAARC) 167
South Korea 117, 127, 142–6, 183
South Pacific Forum 72, 167–8
South Pacific Nuclear Free Zone (SPNFZ) 66, 72, 76, 136–7, 164–5, 169, 171–3, 175
Southeast Asian Nuclear Weapon Free Zone (SEANWFZ) 171–3, 175
Soviet Union (USSR) 1, 4, 12, 42–4, 48–9, 66, 94, 170, 185, 212–13, 218
Sreenivasan, T. P. 110
St. Augustine 222
Stedman, Stephen 28
Stiftung Wissenschaft und Politik, Munich 31
Stockholm Peace Research Institute (SIPRI) 3, 22, 27
Strategic and Defence Studies Centre, ANU 23
Strategic Arms Limitation Treaty (SALT I) 46–7
Strategic Arms Limitations Treaty (SALT II) 44, 47
Strategic Arms Reduction Treaty (START I) 4, 203
Strategic Arms Reduction Treaty (START II) 4
Strategic Arms Reduction Treaty (New START) 9, 11, 217, 220, 222, 228
Strategic Defence and Security Review 10
Strategic Studies 22–5
Strengthening Nuclear Security Implementation Initiative 212
Subrahmanyam, K. 86
Sundarji, K. 86, 94
sustainable disarmament 52–3
Sweden 23, 108n45

Taiwan 168, 178
Talbott, Strobe 107n25
Tange, Kenzo xx
Tashkent Collective Security Treaty 165
Tehreek-e-Taliban Pakistan 199
terrorism, nuclear 200–5
Tewari, Manish 138n16
Thailand 12
theatre missile defence (TMD) 58
Three Mile Island 12
threshold NWS 78, 88, 176, 185
Threshold Test Ban Treaty 5, 183

Thucydides 135
Tlatelolco, Treaty of 47, 87, 164–6, 168, 171–5, 177
Tokyo Forum for Nuclear Non-Proliferation and Disarmament 28
Törnudd, Klaus 180
Transparency International 118
Trudeau, Pierre 26

Ukraine 12, 87, 92, 109, 153, 158, 185, 222–4
United Arab Emirates (UAE) 12, 202
United Kingdom: nuclear modernization 14, 15; Argentina 226; NWFZ Protocols 76n1, 165, 174; Strategic Defence and Security Review (2010) 10; submarines 5–7, 10, 43, 228
United Nations: 2005 world summit 193; arms control 2–4, 32–3; General Assembly 51, 61–2, 65, 72–4, 85, 102, 153, 166, 227; High-level Panel on Threats, Challenges and Change 18n63, 28; Human Rights Commission 91; Panel of Experts 142; Security Council Resolution 1172 105–6; Security Council Resolution 1540 201–2, 219; Security Council Resolution 1718 142; Security Council Resolution 1874 142; Security Council Resolution 1887 5
United Nations Convention on the Law of the Seas (UNCLOS) 173
United Nations Conventional Arms Register 27
United Nations Development Programme (UNDP) 118
United Nations Educational, Scientific and United Nations Organisation (UNESCO) xxi, 25, 222
United Nations Framework Convention on Climate Change (UNFCCC) 209
United Nations Institute for Disarmament Research (UNIDIR) 30, 32
United Nations University (UNU) xx, 32
United States: 2005 NPT Review Conference 192–3; Afghanistan 43, 49, 87, 94, 99, 148, 150; Air Force (USAF) 218, 228; Arms Control and Disarmament Agency (ACDA) 46, 70; Atomic Energy Act 202; circuit-breaker, as 228; Cooperative Threat Reduction (Nunn–Lugar) Program 203; CTBT 12, 51, 56, 193, 230; Department of Defense 11, 70, 203; Department of Energy 203, 206; flexible response 44–5; Glenn–Symington Act 102; Japan 58, 145, 170; massive retaliation 44; Middle East 49, 147, 154, 156, 170, 179; National Intelligence Council 132; National Military Strategy 11; National Nuclear Security Administration (NNSA) 203; National Security Council 150; nuclear employment strategy 1, 11; Nuclear Posture Review (NPR) (2010) 11; NWFZ Protocols 76n1, 165, 175; Senate 46, 48, 51, 55, 56, 97, 107n29, 149, 154; Senate Foreign Relations Committee 11; Vietnam 43, 48, 49, 87, 111, 128; warheads 3, 10–11; Y-12 National Security Complex 206
US–Russia HEU Purchase Agreement 203
US–Russia Plutonium Management and Disposition Agreement 204
US–Soviet Nuclear Accidents Agreement 47
USS Enterprise 117

Vajpayee, Atal Behari 99, 111
Varghese, Peter 131
Versailles, Treaty of 23
Vietnam 12, 28, 43, 48, 49, 87, 111, 128, 218

Wall Street Journal 2, 158, 222
Waltz, Kenneth 80, 219
Wanandi, Jusuf 31
Warsaw Pact 163
Washington Quarterly 30
Weapons of Mass Destruction (Blix) Commission 18n63, 28
weapons of mass destruction (WMD) 4–5, 31–2, 101, 176, 187, 202, 228
Weiss, Thomas G. 28
WikiLeaks 147, 158n29
Williams, Rob 114
World Bank 82, 102, 118
World Court. *See* International Court of Justice
World Economic Forum 118
World Health Organization (WHO) 39, 227
World Institute for Nuclear Security (WINS) 211

Yamaguchi, Tsutomu xx
Yeltsin, Boris 55, 218
Yeonpyeong Island 143

Zarif, Mohammad Javad 153